The Impact of Religion

Michael Welker | John Witte | Stephen Pickard (Eds.)

The Impact of Religion

On Character Formation, Ethical Education, and the Communication of Values in Late Modern Pluralistic Societies

EVANGELISCHE VERLAGSANSTALT
Leipzig

The project and the publication were supported by
the Alonzo McDonald Agape Foundation and
the University of Heidelberg.

Bibliographic information published by the Deutsche Nationalbibliothek
The Deutsche Nationalbibliothek lists this publication in the Deutsche Nationalbibliographie;
detailed bibliographic data are available on the Internet at http://dnb.dnb.de.

Cover: Kai-Michael Gustmann, Leipzig
Cover picture: © persephone3d / www.fotosearch.com
Typesetting: 3w+p, Rimpar
Printing and Binding: Hubert & Co., Göttingen

ISBN 978-3-374-06410-6 // eISBN (PDF) 978-3-374-06411-3
www.eva-leipzig.de

Inhalt

Part One
Christian Religion and Character Formation: Potentials and Risks

Part Two
Character Formation in Other Religious Traditions and General Morals

Part Three
Interdisciplinary and Ethical Perspectives on Societal Impacts of Religion

Contributors

Carnley, Peter Frederick, Rt. Rev'd. Dr. Dr. h.c. mult.
Former Archbishop of Perth and Primate of the Anglican Church of Australia

Etzelmüller, Gregor, Prof. Dr., Osnabrück University
Professor of Systematic Theology

Eurich, Johannes, Prof. Dr., University of Heidelberg
Director of the Institute for the Study of Christian Social Services (DWI)

Herdt, Jennifer A., Prof. Dr., Yale University Divinity School
Professor of Christian Ethics, Senior Associate Dean of Academic Affairs

Kosman, Admiel, Prof. Dr., University of Potsdam
Professor for Talmud and Rabbinic Literature at the School for Jewish Theology

Lai-Fan Ip, Renee, Prof. Dr., Chinese University of Hong Kong
Assistant Professor

Naudé, Piet, Prof. Dr., University of Stellenbosch
Dean of Stellenbosch Business School

Ng, Wai Hang, Dr., Hong Kong Baptist University
Assistant Professor at the Department of Religion and Philosophy

Nüssel, Friederike, Prof. Dr., University of Heidelberg
Professor of Systematic Theology and Ecumenical Theology

Oberdorfer, Bernd, Prof. Dr., University of Augsburg
Professor of Systematic Theology and Ecumenical Theology

Percy, Martyn, Prof. Dr., Christ Church, Oxford
Dean of Christ Church, Oxford, and Professor of Theological Education at King's College, London

Pickard, Stephen, Rt. Rev'd. Prof. Dr., Charles Sturt University, Canberra
Assistant Bishop of the Diocese of Canberra and Goulburn, Executive Director of Australian Centre for Christianity and Culture (ACC&C)

Sakrani, Raja, Dr. jur., University of Bonn
Research Coordinator at the Käte Hamburger Center for Advanced Study in the Humanities "Law as Culture"

Schweiker, William, Prof. Dr. Dr. h.c., University of Chicago Divinity School
Professor of Theological Ethics

Stoellger, Philipp, Prof. Dr., University of Heidelberg
Professor of Systematic Theology (Dogmatics and Philosophy of Religion)

Wai-Yiu Wan, Milton, Prof. Dr. Dr., Chinese University of Hong Kong
Professor in the Department of Management

Welker, Michael, Prof. Dr. Dr. Dres. h.c. University of Heidelberg
Senior Professor of Systematic Theology and Director of the FIIT–Research Center for International and Interdisciplinary Theology, Heidelberg

Witte Jr., John, Prof. Dr. Dr. h.c., Emory University School of Law
Professor of Law, and Director of the Center for Study of Law and Religion

Acknowledgments

In this book scholars from five continents and from different academic fields and religious traditions explore the impact of religion on character formation, ethical education, and the communication of values in late modern pluralistic societies. The fact that we focus on late modern pluralistic societies implies that special attention has to be given to Christian religious traditions in general and to Protestant traditions in particular.

This project started with a consultation in Heidelberg in the spring of 2018. Although the initial group had a broad international and interdisciplinary profile, we were aware of its limits and thus are most grateful that colleagues from Asia and from Jewish and Muslim traditions kindly agreed to participate. In several ways, this volume marks just a beginning. Volumes on the impact of the market, the impact of kaw and the impact of academic research on character formation, ethical education, and the communication of values in late modern pluralistic societies are in the making. Six more consultations are in the planning phase.

The Heidelberg consultation and this publication were made possible by a generous grant by the Alonzo McDonald Agape Foundation and the University of Heidelberg. We thank the late Ambassador Dr. Alonzo McDonald for his initial support and also his son Peter McDonald, now president of the foundation, who kindly participated in the Heidelberg consultation. Thanks go to the Internationales Wissenschaftsforum Heidelberg (IWH) and its staff for hosting the consultations. David Reissmann, Christine Böckmann, Hans-Joachim Kenkel, Viola von Boehn, and Daniel Stil helped us organize the consultations and prepare this publication. Dr. Gary Hauk, of Emory University, kindly agreed to support the editorial process. Finally, we are grateful to the publisher EVA, Leipzig, and Dr. Annette Weidhas for their cooperation in this ambitious project.

Heidelberg, Atlanta, Canberra, February 2020

M. W., J.W., S.P.

Preface to the Series

Character Formation and Moral Education in Late Modern Pluralistic Societies: *An Interdisciplinary and International Research Project*

Five hundred years ago, Protestant reformer Martin Luther argued that "three estates" (*drei Stände*) lie at the foundation of a just and orderly society—marital families, religious communities, and political authorities. Parents in the home; pastors in the church; magistrates in the state—these, said Luther, are the three authorities whom God appointed to represent divine justice and mercy in the world, to protect peace and liberty in earthly life. Household, church, and state —these are the three institutional pillars on which to build social systems of education and schooling, charity and social welfare, economy and architecture, art and publication. Family, faith, and freedom—these are the three things that people will die for.

In the half millennium since Luther, historians have uncovered various classical and Christian antecedents to these early Protestant views. And numerous later theorists have propounded all manner of variations and applications of this three-estates theory, many increasingly abstracted from Luther's overtly Christian worldview. Early modern covenant theologians, both Christian and Jewish, described the marital, confessional, and political covenants that God calls human beings to form, each directed to interrelated personal and public ends. Social-contract theorists differentiated the three contracts that humans enter as they move from the state of nature to an organized society protective of their natural rights— the marital contract of husband and wife; the government contract of rulers and citizens; and, for some, the religious contracts of preachers and parishioners. Early anthropologists posited three stages of development of civilization—from family-based tribes and clans, to priest-run theocracies, to fully organized states that embraced all three institutions. Sociologists distinguished three main forms of authority in an organized community: "traditional" authority that begins in the home, "charismatic" authority that is exemplified in the church, and "legal" authority that is rooted in the state. Legal historians outlined three stages of development of legal norms—from the habits and rules of the family, to the customs and canons of religion, to the statutes and codes of the state.

Already a century ago, however, scholars in different fields began to flatten out this hierarchical theory of social institutions and to emphasize the foundational role of other social institutions alongside the family, church, and state in shaping private and public life and character. Sociologists like Max Weber and Talcott Parsons emphasized the shaping powers of "technical rationality" exemplified especially in new industry, scientific education, and market economies. Legal scholars like Otto von Gierke and F.W. Maitland emphasized the critical roles of non-state legal associations (*Genossenschaften*) in maintaining a just social, political, and legal order historically and today. Catholic subsidiarity theories of Popes Leo XIII and Pius XI emphasized the essential task of mediating social units between the individual and the state to cater the full range of needs, interests, rights, and duties of individuals. Protestant theories of sphere sovereignty, inspired by Abraham Kuyper, argued that not only churches, states, and families but also the social spheres of art, labor, education, economics, agriculture, recreation, and more should enjoy a level of independence from others, especially an overreaching church or state. Various theories of social or structural pluralism, civil society, voluntary associations, the independent sector, multiculturalism, multinormativity, and other such labels have now come to the fore in the ensuing decades—both liberal and conservative, religious and secular, and featuring all manner of methods and logics.

Pluralism of all sorts is now a commonplace of late modern societies. At minimum, this means a multitude of free and equal individuals and a multitude of groups and institutions, each with very different political, moral, religious, and professional interests and orientations. It includes the sundry associations, interest groups, parties, lobbies, and social movements that often rapidly flourish and fade around a common cause, especially when aided by modern technology and various social media. Some see in this texture of plurality an enormous potential for colorful and creative development and a robust expression of human and cultural freedom. Others see a chaotic individualism and radical relativism, which endangers normative education, moral character formation, and effective cultivation of enduring values or virtues.

Pluralism viewed as vague plurality, however, focuses on only one aspect of late modern societies—the equality of individuals, and their almost unlimited freedom to participate peaceably at any time as a respected voice in the moral reasoning and civil interactions of a society. But this view does not adequately recognize that, beneath the shifting cacophony of social forms and norms that constitute modernity, pluralistic societies have heavy normative codes that shape their individual and collective values and morals, preferences and prejudices.

The sources of much of this normative coding and moral education in late modern pluralistic societies are the deep and powerful social systems that are the pillars of every advanced culture. The most powerful and pervasive of these are the social systems of law, religion, politics, science/academy, market, media, family, education, medicine, and national defense. The actual empirical forms of each of these powerful social systems can and do vary greatly, even in the relatively homogeneous societies of the late modern West. But these deeper social systems in one form or another are structurally essential and often normatively decisive in individual and communal lives.

Every advanced society has a comprehensive legal system of justice and order, religious systems of ritual and doctrine, a family system of procreation and love, an economic system of trade and value, a media system of communication and dissemination of news and information, and an educational system of preservation, application, and creation of knowledge and scientific advance. Many advanced societies also have massive systems of science, technology, health care, and national defense with vast influence over and through all of these other social systems. These pervasive social systems lie at the foundation of modern advanced societies, and they anchor the vast pluralities of associations and social interactions that might happen to exist at any given time.

Each of these social systems has internal value systems, institutionalized rationalities, and normative expectations that together help to shape each individual's morality and character. Each of these social spheres, moreover, has its own professionals and experts who shape and implement its internal structures and processes. The normative network created by these social spheres is often harder to grasp today, since late modern pluralistic societies usually do not bring these different value systems to light under the dominance of just one organization, institution, and power. And this normative network has also become more shifting and fragile, especially since traditional social systems like religion and the family have eroded in their durability and power, and other social systems like science, the market, healthcare, defense, and the media have become more powerful.

The aim of this project on "Character Formation and Moral Education in Late Modern Pluralistic Societies" is to identify the realities and potentials of these core social systems to provide moral orientation and character formation in our day. What can and should these social spheres, separately and together, do in shaping the moral character of late modern individuals who, by nature, culture, and constitutional norms, are free and equal in dignity and rights? What are and should be the core educational functions and moral responsibilities of each of these social spheres? How can we better understand and better influence the complex interactions among individualism, the normative binding powers of these social systems, and the creativity of civil groups and institutions? How can we map and measure the different hierarchies of values that govern each of these social systems, and that are also interwoven and interconnected in various ways in shaping late modern understandings of the common good? How do we negotiate the boundaries and conflicts between and among these social systems when one encroaches on the other, or imposes its values and rationalities on individuals at the cost of the other social spheres or of the common good? What and where are the intrinsic strengths of each social sphere that should be made more overt in character formation, public education, and the shaping of minds and mentalities?

These are some of the guiding questions at work in this project and in this volume. Our project aims to provide a systematic account of the role of these powerful normative codes operating in the social spheres of law, religion, the family, the market, the media, science and technology, the academy, health care, and defense in the late modern liberal West. Our focus is on selected examples and case studies drawn from Western Europe, North America, South Africa, and Australia, which together provide just enough diversity to test out broader theories of character formation and moral education. Our scholars are drawn from across the academy, with representative voices from the humanities, social sciences, and natural sciences as well as the professions of theology, law, business, medicine, and more. While most of our scholars come from the Protestant and Catholic worlds, our endeavor is to offer comparative insights that will help scholars from any profession or confession. While our laboratory is principally Western liberal societies, the modern forces of globalization will soon make these issues of moral character formation a concern for every culture and region of the world—given the power of global social media, entertainment, and sports; the pervasiveness of global finance, business, trade, and law; and the perennial global worries over food, health care, environmental degradation, and natural disasters.

In this volume, we focus in on the role of religion in shaping character development, ethical education, and the communication of values in late modern pluralistic societies.

Michael Welker, University of Heidelberg
John Witte, Jr., Emory University
Stephen Pickard, Charles Sturt University

Introduction to the Present Volume

Michael Welker

This book investigates the impact of religion on the formation of character and the communication of values in late modern pluralistic societies. Scholars from five continents and many different academic fields are involved. Since the focus lies on the impact of *religion in pluralistic societies*, the concentration on Christian traditions in the West is predominant. We are all the more grateful to the colleagues with Jewish, Muslim, and Chinese backgrounds for their willingness to participate in this challenging enterprise.

The book offers a rich variety of thematic concentrations as well as academic, ethical, and religious perspectives. Some of the contributions welcome and embrace the rich polyphonic individualism, the wealth of lively civil societies, and the healthy multisystemic configuration of normativities in late modern societies in the West. They associate these configurations not only with personal, moral, and political freedom but also with a religious and theological appreciation of the creativity of the multimodal divine spirit. Other contributions are more concerned with models of integration and synthesis, models that aim at providing clear orientation in complex social and cultural environments. We trust that both approaches with their diverging and yet partly complementary perspectives will prove to be helpful for our readers.

Part one deals with "potentials and risks" in the character-shaping impact of Christian religion. *Michael Welker* ("Comfort, Freedom, Justice, and Truth: Christian Religion, The Formation of Character, and the Communication of Values") launches the conversation with critical comments on widespread forms of an empty liberal piety and theology in the West, a piety and theology that abstract from the divine spirit and God's supporting, saving, judging, elevating, and ennobling powers and activities. These empty religious forms produce and defend what could be called cheap devotion in connection with mostly appellative moral communication. The longstanding fixation on a merely intellectual understanding of the human spirit, as valuable as it was and still is for many developments, could not do justice to the emotional, ethical, aesthetic, and religious powers of the divine and the human spirit. Investigations in early childhood development clarify the strengths and weaknesses of such reductionistic understanding and show the false dualism of spirit and body, even the ignorance of bipolar thinking in general. A deeper look at the breadth of human existence opens the eyes not only to its cognitive, emotional, volitional, and communicative powers but also to the potential influence and effects of the divine spirit. The divine spirit bestows energy and hope in persons who are oppressed by feelings of futility and impotence. This spirit provides orientation and strength with respect to the values of justice, freedom, truth, peace, and love.

The extremely rich understanding of "comfort" in the Heidelberg Catechism integrates many dimensions of the character-shaping powers of the divine spirit: "comfort" conveys the notions of security, confidence, trust, courage in life, and hope. It is equated with enduring reliability, help, support, and counsel; with saving, reassurance, and repose; with strength, backing, shielding, and protection; but also with sympathy, empathy, and encouragement. Welker's contribution unfolds this richness with respect to an understanding of "the love of neighbor" and human benevolence which are not confined to individual and person-to-person experiences, and which can draw on a multitude of inspirations provided by Christian and other religious spiritual sources.

Gregor Etzelmüller's contribution ("Anthropology and Religious Formation") expands these insights by reflecting on the "shift from natural evolution to cultural development" in general and by reflecting on the fascinating lessons about child development through processes of imitation and overimitation, even among toddlers. An abundance of cultural resources is created and addressed by these processes and the cultural and historical variability they generate. The enormous human plasticity gains orientation not only by cognitive training and ethical communication but also by religious education.

Religious education can "turn out to be a training ground of pro-social orientations, which see their task in advocacy on behalf of the weak and which support the culture of benevolence" (Sigrid Roßteutscher). Etzelmüller demonstrates that biblical law traditions—which connect justice and mercy with worship on one hand and table fellowship on the other—develop powerful combinations of religious ethos, family ethos, and neighborhood ethos, with huge impacts on character formation and ethical education in the communication of life-furthering values.

Under the title "'Values of the Gospel': The Formative Role of Christian Values for Social Cohesion in Modern Societies," *Friedrike Nüssel* examines reflections and discourses on values in the nineteenth and twentieth centuries. She shows that only recently have ecclesial and ecumenical bodies reconciled with the discourse of secular value, even speaking of "values of the gospel" or "values of the kingdom" with a strong focus on justice, peace, and the protection of the environment. Subtle differences between Protestant and Roman Catholic public statements do not negate agreement that there are "basic values" "rooted in the Christian spiritual heritage," such as "peace, justice, freedom, tolerance, participation, and solidarity."

Nüssel shows the fruitful coinciding of, on one hand, impulses in the churches to contribute to the European unification and, on the other hand, subtle reflections on the potential of "canon law to give ecumenism a legally legitimized space and framework" in important processes of political and moral transformations. She also argues for a not only ecumenical but also multidisciplinary cooperation in the discovery that "narrativity" is essential for the "formation of perception and emotion" in the processes of shaping ethical development and the communication of religiously inspired values.

A voice of warning comes in the contribution of *Peter Carnley* on "The Fallacy of 'Individual Autonomy' and Moral Value in the Community of Christ." He uses hero images from the first part of the twentieth century to illuminate the cultural rise of a strong individualism, supported not only by Enlightenment philosophy but also by the growing influence of electronic media. His concern is ignited by the growing support of the legalization of "assisted suicide" based on an ambivalent defense of the exercise of "individual autonomy," in particular by recent political developments in the State of Western Australia but also elsewhere. Carnley asks: "Who would agree with the contention, for example, that we could justifiably act upon a request for assistance in injecting a person with heroin on the ground that he or she wished to exercise his or her 'individual autonomy'"? He respects the concern to alleviate anticipated protracted pain and suffering. But he argues that we should not confuse a "quality-of-life argument" with an unqualified recourse to individual autonomy.

He sees the responsibility of religious education and practice to nurture the communication of values "defined by the human virtues for living well in community with others." He asks for visions of moral growth from "less self-concerned and more caring, less prone to racism and more accepting and respectful of human diversity, not just awkwardly tolerant of difference, but positively embracing it as an enrichment to community life, that is not defensive and self-justifying of their own behavior and more open and forgiving of others." Deeper notions of freedom have to be communicated than the concept of individual autonomy can provide.

William Schweiker ("Should Religion Shape Character?") challenges the naïve view that religion and moral communication are intrinsically good. He discerns different sources, traditions, and perspectives in religious and theological attempts to shape human ethics. He proposes to use the orienting power of "theological humanism" in order to offer resistance against "manipulation by time, place, and language." He challenges theology and theological ethics to engage "critically and imaginatively [with] . . . religious interpretations of reality." In these interpretations of reality, the concept of virtue has played a dominant role. Schweiker shows that this concept drew together other concepts important in ethical reflection, especially "reason, desire, conduct, and valuing." He also opens the eyes to the importance of goods as motivations for actions—"bodily, social, reflective, local, and above all moral goods."

Substantial reflections on the polyphony of virtue ethics allow a nuanced understanding of "character," namely "the moral and mental qualities that distinguish an individual self." This understanding allows Schweiker to test theological and anthropological "sources of normativity." In his view it is crucial to place all these considerations in a realistic awareness of the normative picture of pluralistic environments which do not offer a "'master discourse' or a 'master narrative,' orchestrating the reflexive interrelations that constitute a (late modern) society." In its aim to contribute to character formation and ethical education, religion should not dream of a totalitarian orientation. It should not try to resituate ancient ideas of "an isomorphism between the character or soul of the individual and that of the social community." Schweiker argues for a differentiated defense of individual human dignity and the social common good against all sorts of "system-paternalism" (*Habermas*), and this requires a self-critical stance of religion over against its own normative powers.

Jennifer Herdt develops a different line of argumentation in her chapter on "The Dialectic of Religious Formation." In contrast to the positions and voices presented in the "Foreword" and in the other contributions of Part one, she argues that "there are negative lessons to learn from Weber's understanding of the differentiation of social spheres," and "positive lessons to take from the longstanding Christian doctrine of the orders of creation, with its roots in natural law discourse." While she regards Weber as "exaggerat(ing) the autonomy of the various social spheres," she finds a "fluidity" in the conception of the orders of creation, dismissed by its critics.

I am grateful for her gracious attempt to integrate positions held by Oliver O'Donovan and myself, as "contemporary critics of natural law discourse," into a broader scheme that might reconcile our views. At the heart of our differences, I see different concepts of God. In her understanding, God is the final good, whereas I grasp God as living and (not predominantly natural) life-giving spirit. This different approach generates partly differing and partly overlapping perspectives on "Cultivating the Virtues in Late Modernity." We can easily agree that "human beings do not live well on a diet of thin abstractions." But we will also compete in our differing evaluations of the meaning of "thin abstractions" or helpful orienting insights. Jennifer Herdt's contribution offers a bridge to many concerns raised in the second part of this book.

Part two ("Character Formation in Other Religious Traditions and General Morals") presents alternatives and fruitful challenges to religious, theological, and other academic attempts to affirm and constructively deal with late modern pluralistic public textures. The contributions explore the powers of personalistic "I-Thou thinking," intergenerational learning, inspirations by classic religious and secular literature, and the combination of theological, moral, neurological, and practiced leadership perspectives.

Admiel Kosman ("Buber vs. Weber: Future Sociological Research According to Buber's Proposal—The I-Thou Relationship in Scholarly Research") joins Herdt's reservation against a Weberian spirit. He argues with Buber that all perceptions and insights have to "pass through the researcher's unique personality." In order to reach truth-bound insight and valid ethical orientation, however, the individual has "to be connected to the nature of these everyday encounters within the flow of life" in all personal, societal, and political spheres. This can be reached only in an encounter with "the spirit of the 'Eternal Thou.'"

Buber demands a "loving science," a "true philosophy as a loving philosophy," which opens the researcher "to the unconditional mystery which we encounter in every sphere of our life." In this attempt, every person can become a "vessel for the resting of the spirit," every person can become enabled to encounter the "Absolute" and to hear the voice of truth. A loving attentiveness to "the Thou" in all cognitive and ethical orientation is the key to "discern the enigmatic countenance of the universe."

Raja Sakrani ("Elements of Religious Socialization in Islamic Cultures: How to be a 'Good' Muslim in Europe?") analyzes the complex processes in which Muslim communities in Europe experience "religious socialization . . . as an indispensable avenue for transmitting values to future generations." She describes the "players" and institutional locations of these intergenerational activities and their impacts on communicative and collective memory. She explains difficulties in preserving "ethnocultural belonging," in communicating the experiences, the traumas, and the ritual practices of the parents, and in overcoming all sorts of prejudices in the cultural and political environments.

With respect to very different significant foci of attention (the active participation of women in public life; the role of circumcision; conversion; and the problem of prisons) she highlights important transformations, continuities, and partly ambivalent attractions of Muslim religious socialization. "Islam is a powerful attractor given its current position in the world and its status as a subculture. It gives dignity to those who feel oppressed . . . and it mobilizes the values of the strong in the sense of virility." Many tensions within the will to belong to "a common shared culture"—tensions between the traditional and the contemporary as well as between family history and the dominant European environment—have to be dealt with. The educational challenges on all sides are enormous.

"Chinese Family Education and Spiritual Intervention: Voluntary and Involuntary Moral Actions from Neurological and Theological Perspectives"—under this topic *Milton Wai-Yiu Wan* and *Renee Lai-Fan Ip* deal with moral education in late modern pluralistic societies in interdisciplinary reflections. They address the important relation of the human will to "moral desire," a mobilizing and motivating power. And they deal with neurological roots that stimulate and balance involuntary and voluntary actions, the mechanisms of "habit functioning and habit formation." A crucial question is how to change and to build new "habit loops." They see strong resources to support these transformations in Chinese family education, a tradition now more than two thousand years old.

Two paths have to be discerned, namely "the development of moral character and virtue" and "the successful social adjustment and the building of interpersonal relations . . . , interdependence, cooperation, collaboration." Pious and respectful relations to parents and elders are crucial, as are the careful choice of friends and the cultivation of trustworthy, understanding, and discreet behavior. Family education aims at a "self-cultivation" with a "strong sense of self-demand, of self-discipline with training of willpower." This self-cultivation is correlated with impulses from the Christian ascetic tradition. The goal is a "spiritual victory" over the "powerlessness weakened by the sinful nature." Neurologically induced habit loops, traditional family education, and impulses from Christian spirituality interact in the gradual transformation of the "old self" into a new person with a good moral character.

Waihang Ng ("Literary Form, Paideia, and Religion: Comparing Case Studies from the Ancient Greek, Traditional Chinese, and Early Christian Contexts") intends to contribute orientation from ancient moral and religious traditions to "the platform for competition among values and beliefs" in modern pluralistic societies. For this purpose, he investigates key ideas in Homer's *Iliad*, Luo Guanzhong's *Three Kingdoms*, and the Gospels from the New Testament. He is particularly interested in the connection between aesthetics and ethical education (cf. Auerbach, *Mimesis*).

In the *Iliad*, Ng sees central topics in the role of anger, the defense of honor, and an ineluctable human fate, all of which condition processes of education, paideia. *Three Kingdoms*, "one of the four classical novels in Chinese literature," centers on three political and military power blocs, and in this context on cases for and against revenge, heavenly providence, the higher duties of righteousness, and selfless friendship over against an orientation toward prudence and success. Ng contrasts these models of paideia with the discussion of anger and "holy anger" (of Jesus) in the Gospels. He concludes from his investigation that it is important to control and overcome anger and to develop a democratized "aristocratic ethic" (Gerd Theissen), empowering every single individual life. In the three texts he examines, Ng sees examples of "religious underpinnings of literary works from different traditions" that can stimulate the "communication and negotiation of value differences" in pluralistic societies.

Martyn Percy ("Humility, Humiliation, and Hope: An Extended Homily on the Crucible for Authentic Character in Leadership"), in a "homiletic tone," explores character qualities in human political and economic leadership. Quoting Jim Collins, Percy observes "a paradoxical mixture of personal humility and professional will" in successful leaders. He looks for analogous constellations in biblical traditions and influential literature (Charles Dickens, Arthur Miller) and finally refers to personal experiences in his own career.

For Christians, God's revelation in Jesus Christ opens the eyes to the transformation of "notions of omnipotence and omniscience . . . by kenosis"—"a term that generally refers to the 'self-emptying' of Christ, . . . an aspect of the doctrine of the Incarnation." In religious, social, and professional praxis, the exercise of humility results, according to Percy, in "kindness"—and a "culture of kindness . . . can have a positive energizing effect, creating improved interpersonal relations and increasing commitment. Moreover, it is infectious." An invitation to practice kindness is a sum of reflections on character formation, ethical education, and the communication of values—not only in late modern pluralistic societies.

Part three ("Interdisciplinary and Ethical Perspectives on Societal Impacts of Religion") begins with South African perspectives. *Piet Naudé* ("The Impact of Religion on Shaping Values in Pluralistic Societies: A Case of Opposing Interpretations and Unintended Consequences?") offers two case studies. First, he reviews the misuse and use of Karl Barth's theology, first in the co-opting of that leading Protestant theologian to defend the apartheid system, and later in his reception as a "modern and critical social voice" even under apartheid and beyond its rule. Naudé uses this example to demonstrate the massive political, moral, and educational impact of readings and their interpretations of influential theological texts.

The second case study starts with the "advent of a cluster of liberation theologies" in general and Gustavo Gutierrez's publications on "the option for the poor" in particular, based on humanitarian and biblical-ethical insights and spreading from Latin American Catholicism into ecumenical discourse. Naudé impressively shows that the book *A Theory of Justice*, by the political philosopher John Rawls, is based on similar ethical principles. These are further developed by the economist and Nobel Prize–recipient Joseph Stiglitz in his works on globalization and "fair trade for the poor" and the defense of "so-called noneconomic values such as social justice, the environment, cultural diversity, universal access to health care, and consumer protection."

Like Naudé, the Australian *Stephen Pickard* ("Optimal Environments for the Formation of Character: Challenges and Prospects for Religion") argues that the evident "capacity of religion to remain a source and power for the shaping of character, moral vision, and values both for individuals and societies" requires the self-critical examination of these potentials. It also requires a careful analysis of what he calls "the corrosive powers of host cultures." With John Fitzmaurice, Alasdaire MacIntyre, and others he critiques the infectious "growth mantra of the market economy."

Pickard sees a correlation between decline in many churches in the West and the deep influence "by the modern competitive market economy with an emphasis on material and corporate success and growth." The complexity of late modern pluralistic societies—with their competing hierarchies of values but above all with spiritual resources such as the presence of Christ in the power of his spirit and the present and coming reign of God—offers orientations both demanding and inspiring. "Long-distance runners know how critical it is to pace themselves in order that they will have sufficient energy and stamina to finish and can respond to unforeseen contingencies on the way (Hebrews 12:1–2)." Pickard asks for a theologically circumspect and wise pacing in ecclesial cultural orientation.

Bernd Oberdorfer offers a German perspective following the great nineteenth-century theologian Friedrich Schleiermacher ("*With* Religion, not *from* Religion': Christian Antimoralist Moralism and Its Impact on Moral Formation"). He shows that Schleiermacher counters the widespread identification of Christianity with a more or less rigid moralism—whether moralism affirmed or critiqued. Oberdorfer offers a nuanced approach to this position. On one hand, "something like a Christian ethos . . . does actually *include* moral norms." On the other hand, this ethos "develops sensitivities for the destructive consequences of enforcing norms" in forms of moralism, and it "entails specific forms of dealing with deviance." Already the biblical law traditions emphasize "the crucial relevance of mercy and forgiveness."

Oberdorfer speaks of "second-order values," which cannot be enforced but are crucial when legal and first-order moral communication reaches its limits and even becomes impotent. Character formation, ethical education, and the communication of values on this second-order level are operative in various religious forms. Oberdorfer names forms of liturgical life, exemplary authentic experiences of reconciliation, the work of diaconia (cf. the contribution of *Johannes Eurich*), and public advocacy (cf. the examples presented by *Piet Naudé*).

An even stronger critique of a moral theology with normative claims is offered by *Philipp Stoellger* ("Formation as Figuration: The Impact of Religion—Framed by Media Anthropology"). He cautiously suggests that "the normative interest of theology can appear as an outdated model." He proposes a "metaethical" approach that tries to "order things in the name of the extraordinary," an ethos of "*passions* and *fruitful passivities.*" He sees a strong Christological and pneumatological position supported by the insight that "Christ is the epitome of prenormativity . . . , the embodiment of a singular passion for the neighbor—not just a value maker."

The claim of a prenormativity, of course, should not be one of the many familiar religious strategies to bring religion into a comfortable, all-overmastering attitude. Stoellger argues that religion is a "medium of communication," a symbolic, deictic, and medial power in *framing* communication. It derives its framing powers from "God in Christ by the Spirit." Godself is the decisive medium and reveals this power as a "soft power in all communication." This media power is the "decisive presupposition for formation (of character, education, sociality, etc.)." In Protestantism, he argues, those soft media powers come in the forms of *speech, living images* (potentially a prenormative root for image critique) and "specific modes of *institutionalizing*, that is, *orders*" in the light of the "extraordinary." A passion for the "crucial difference between salvation and morality" inspires Stoellger's strong stance over against "outdated" models of theological and moral communication.

The final contributions on the areas of diaconia and law deal with problems and sources rooted in extremely long religious and ethical traditions (documented by witnesses already more than four thousand years ago). These traditions had and still have strong normative impacts on Protestant religion and its surrounding political, legal, and medical environments. They are loaded with dimensions of the extraordinary and with all sorts of passion. Yet by no means could they be termed "old" in the sense of "outdated."

Johannes Eurich ("Learning to Care for the Whole Person: The Significance of Body and Soul for Diaconal Work") starts with historical examples of organized diaconal care for the poor, the marginalized, and the sick in nineteenth-century Europe. He illuminates the struggles to improve organized physical help and at the same time to search for a deeper understanding between physical illness and spiritual needs—on the side of the care receivers and the caregivers. He then turns to contemporary intensified concentration on "corporeality as a mode of existence." He also deals with new investigations of the biblical witnesses that stress the high importance of bodily existence and do not support its downplaying and downgrading.

He addresses processes of theological and diaconal learning that intensify the awareness of the "vulnerability and fragility of the body," including deeper reflections on physical dimensions of human dignity, human suffering, and death. He concludes with reflections on phenomena in contemporary cultures such as "body cult and body oblivion," the body as "primary medium of self-presentation," body styling, and marketing of the body. In Eurich's view, new explorations in these areas are necessary, as are "rediscoveries of the spiritual dimension of the physical." Multidisciplinary investigations and developments of innovative practices of comprehensive care should reenforce each other.

The book concludes with *John Witte's* contribution, "The Uses of Law for the Formation of Character: A Classic Protestant Doctrine for Late Modern Liberal Societies?" He sets out with the observation that "religion is also present in all kinds of spaces and specialties that would seem to be hermetically and hermeneutically closed to religion." His contribution explores a set of "distinct repositories of tradition, wisdom, and perspective"—what is known as the teaching of the "threefold use of the law of God," also called the "uses of the moral law." The teaching of the uses of the law has roots in the biblical traditions and in patristic and scholastic thought, but it comes to a culmination in the Protestant Reformation. The doctrine differentiates the morally and legally active *civil or political use of the law;* the *theological use of the law* in revealing human sin and lostness and driving towards intensive search for God's saving grace; and the *educational use of the law*, "enhancing the spiritual developments of believers."

Witte shows that the theological doctrine of the three uses of the law did not die with the great reformers. It was maintained and further developed in the following centuries, up through leading theological positions in the twentieth century. Its continued radiating creativity and its unquestionable role in "character formation, ethical education, and the communication of values" in contemporary societies and cultures can be demonstrated with respect to "the legal doctrine of the purposes of criminal law and punishment." The criminal law has a *deterrent function, a retributive function, and a rehabilitative function*. Although it would be "too strong to say that the Protestant theological doctrine . . . was the source of the modern legal doctrine," one could observe "ample doctrinal cross-fertilization" between them. Witte concludes with the observation that the United States Federal Sentencing Act can be seen in these traditions, and he illustrates that the "criminal law of the state is directly involved in character formation, moral education, and the communication of values in late modern societies." The hard normative stipulations are accompanied and expanded by softer strategies of "nudging and legal channeling" which—beyond the impulses of law and religion—need the support and interplay of the other social systems of pluralistic societies, such as family, education, academic research, media, politics, and health care—social systems which will also be addressed in this series of investigations.

Part One

Christian Religion and Character Formation:
Potentials and Risks

Comfort, Freedom, Justice, and Truth

Christian Religion, the Formation of Character, and the Communication of Values

Michael Welker

Part one of this chapter discusses two widespread forms of liberal theology and religiosity in the West that I believe are not really capable of influencing in any meaningful way the formation of character and the ethical communication of values.

Part two addresses the notion of human character, which in classical conceptions is generally viewed as in some way the bearer of distinct individuality or as distinguished by ethical constancy or stability. Here I will pay particular attention to human emotionality and the human spirit, especially as the latter is itself shaped by body-based emotions, the intellect, and an exchange with its social surroundings.

Part three illuminates, on one hand, the breadth and expanse of human existence and, on the other, the power of both the human spirit and the divine Spirit. Both divine Spirit and human spirit constitute the foundations of the charisma and vibrancy of any substantive theology and religiosity.

Part four considers the theological and religious elements that are constitutive for the formation of character and for the ethical communication of values, namely, comfort (or consolation and peace), freedom, justice, and truth.

Forms of the Western Christian Religion Incapable of Influencing Character

Certain dominant forms of Christian theology and religiosity in the West, rather than promote, sooner *block* or *thwart* the potential for religion to influence the formation of character, the shaping of ethical disposition, and the communication of values. Such theologies and theologically emptied forms of religiosity, by masking or concealing the unique *content* of religion, thereby also systematically blur or screen God and the divine powers. They generally declare God to be "wholly other" or to be somehow equated with transcendence or the numinous, and then develop conceptual models in which God's living quality, God's revelation, God's supporting, saving, judging, elevating, and redemptive activity either have no place at all or at least no possibility for further elaboration. Examples of such theologies include rigorously apophatic theologies, negative theologies, many metaphysical theologies of the absolute or of the *deus simplex* and the "ultimate point of reference," (Gordon Kaufman and others) as well as multiple variations of mystical theology.

The propagation of such theologies—some of which, of course, have traversed a lengthy and sometimes complex history—can probably be attributed to a twofold set of intentions. On one hand, religion itself is to be situated with as low a threshold as possible to render it easily or, indeed, even arbitrarily accessible. Inconveniently static or stipulated content would merely constitute a hindrance. The goal is instead what one might call "cheap devotion." On the other hand, however, this tactic is quite capable of relieving religion of many potential critical objections, that is, objections and doubts invariably provoked by the complexity and copious fields of tension inherent in much of religion's content. The familiar but uncomfortable question of theodicy is one such inconvenience that these theologies especially single out for such "sedation." Wolfgang Huber and I maintain that such theologies conceal within themselves a religious trap that for us evokes the notion of a "self-secularization" of religion, which in its own turn is generally accompanied by "self-banalization" as soon as this emptied religiosity, unable to bear its own emptiness, seeks relief by sucking up all sorts of ostensibly entertaining and distracting content and objects, including every conceivable "personal story," then also candles, rocks, flowers, scarves, light, water—truly, such symbolic kitsch knows no boundaries. Unfortunately, such "religion lite" offers nothing of substance for the formation of character, for the shaping of a person's ethical disposition, or for any serious communication of values.

At least to a certain extent, a second common worldview veils the full wretchedness of such emptied and banal religiosity that sinks below the level of common sense. This particular form is found in the alliance of theology and religiosity with philosophical (ultimately Aristotelian) metaphysics and morality. Let us duly acknowledge that such metaphysics and morality do indeed promote at least to a limited extent the formation of character, the shaping of ethical disposition, and the communication of a spectrum of values, albeit only within the parameters of a kind of rational piety concerned primarily, if not exclusively, with a cultivation of the intellect and an increase or enhancement of knowledge.

Aristotle—quite ingeniously, by the way, and with particular trenchancy in book 12 of his *Metaphysics*—situated the unity of reason and spirit within human thought itself. Whenever the activity of human thinking relates to objects, surroundings, and situations, it is also always relating to *itself*; the result, not surprisingly, is a mutual enhancement or augmentation of cognition, self-knowledge, and the corresponding disclosure of world. That is, thinking unfolds precisely in its cognitive disclosure of the objects and world around it, and the enhanced elaboration of self in this sense similarly enhances its disclosure of reality. The vanishing point of this perpetually advancing or higher development is allegedly nothing less than the divine itself.[1] Theology and religion that are content with an intellectualized and rationalized concept of the spirit are certainly capable, within these parameters, of allying themselves effectively enough with simple educational programs, lending a quasi-religious aura to the previously mentioned striving for a maximization of cognitive self-knowledge, knowledge of world, and their concomitant developmental hopes.

Over against blockades of the sort posed by emptied and intellectualized religious forms, how, in late modern, pluralistic societies, is one then to assess the potential significance of religion for the formation of character, the shaping of ethical disposition, and the communication of values? For these societies are characterized not only by the cultivation of a bewildering multiplicity of individual points of view and value hierarchies, but also by a resolute defense of their individual import and dignity. Late modern pluralistic societies, moreover, also require that a limited majority of value hierarchies be respected that are to a high degree viewed as normative. We encounter these hierarchies in the social systems and larger organizational forms that are indispensable for the health and growth of these societies, namely, in economics, politics, the media, education, science, legal systems, medical systems, and military and defense systems. Does religion today have more to offer than merely catalytic contributions to questions concerning personal intellectual development and—sharing a certain natural interest in such development—families, or more than perhaps occasional contributions with respect to politics, law, science, and media?

Character, Emotionality, and Spirit

Among the various considerations used to determine or assess character throughout history and up into the present, attention has consistently been paid both to value-neutral perspectives on "the uniquely individual mode of experience and behavior"[2] as well as to evaluative interpretations of "qualities such as strength of will, reliability, and steadfastness with respect of principles."[3] These considerations respect, on one hand, the absolute uniqueness of every individual human existence (that is, every person is to develop his or her own unique character!)

---

[1]   Aristotle, *Metaphysik XII*, Klostermann Texte: Philosophie, ed. H.-G. Gadamer, 4th ed. (Frankfurt: Klostermann, 1984), esp. 31–35; Michael Welker, *God the Spirit*, trans. John F. Hoffmayer (Minneapolis: Fortress Press, 1994; reprint Eugene, OR: Wipf & Stock, 2013), section 5.1.

[2]   *Historisches Wörterbuch der Philosophie*, Vol. 1 (Basel: Schwabe, 1976), 991.

[3]   Ibid. See also William Schweiker's contribution in this volume, chapter 5.

and, on the other, the sort of ethical constancy and stability that separate a person's character from mere "individuality" or from a more or less utterly idiosyncratic personality. Religion, too, should neglect neither of these two guiding perspectives in addressing its concerns with respect to the formation of character.

Many contemporary societies protect and promote the development of a person's "uniquely individual mode of experience and behavior" through the politically and legally guaranteed freedom of opinion (the right to freedom of expression), of the media, of the arts, and of science. By contrast, the development of ethical constancy cannot be addressed merely individually and is instead dependent on a culture of reciprocity. That is, it presupposes the development of a moral (and legal-political) continuum in which all individuals are accorded participation in the communication of mutual respect. This moral continuum is tied to an ethos of equality and to the notion of serving the common good. This arrangement ascribes to all participants a sense of responsibility, on one hand, and unconditional personal dignity on the other. What, however, is left for religion to contribute above and beyond these admittedly valuable and impressive attainments with respect to the formation of character, the shaping of ethical disposition, and the communication of values? One contribution from religion whose value should by no means be underestimated is of a catalytic nature and consists in the tenacious or even dogged commitment to the freedom of religion and in the emphatic support of the other broad social institutions that defend the freedom and equality of all human beings.

Within this same context, and moving one step further, it is important to see that religion, with its enormous wealth of formative and educational possibilities, of concepts, ideas, imagery, texts, memorable personalities and events recounted in countless stories, dialogues, liturgies, and rituals, similarly also in the celebration of rites of passage and through the structuring of the year itself, and all this together with the shared remembrance of significant events across the centuries—that with all these things, religion cultivates not only our thinking and ethical judgment but also, and to an extraordinarily high degree, our emotions.

Indeed, religion addresses not merely our understanding but above all our hearts and spirits. In the "profundity of its being," the heart combines cognitive, emotional, and volitional forces, and the human spirit in its own turn provides the power to activate—or commit to latency—a whole ocean of memories, expectations, and imagination, and is, moreover, a communicative force across immense spatial and temporal expanses.[4]

Influential theologians such as Friedrich Schleiermacher explicitly emphasized the connection between religion and feeling. Unfortunately, religious feel-

---

4   Michael Welker, "Flesh–Body–Heart–Soul–Spirit: Paul's Anthropology as an Interdisciplinary Bridge-Theory," in *The Depth of the Human Person: A Multidisciplinary Approach*, ed. Welker (Grand Rapids, MI: Eerdmans, 2014), 45–57.

ing was then often abstractly juxtaposed to thinking and related to pure "subjectivity" and/or to some vaguely conceived "totality" (Schleiermacher writes that "religion is sense and taste for the infinite," an "intuition of the universe," etc.). Picking up and expanding on the findings of more recent discussions of "embodied cognition,"[5] we are better able to assess the various interdependencies between thinking and feeling within the human spirit, and thus also the human spirit itself. The human spirit is significantly richer and more complex than the customary, largely bipolar notion of thinking in relation to object and self, something that comes to vivid expression in a consideration of the seemingly simplest deictic operations of early childhood.

In the ninth or tenth month of life, infants begin using deictic gestures, among which one might single out the gesture of pointing with an outstretched arm and index finger. What is happening here? An incidence of concentrated perception, that is, a selection from out of the plethora of optical stimuli, is but one of the many processes that must be adduced and connected. This optical selection and concentration are joined here by a differentiated, partial control of the body in the form of the raised, extended arm and the hand with the outstretched index finger. A repetition of this operation is, as a rule, accompanied by bodily movement within natural space (for example, the child runs back or at least turns its head and body to point yet again). This repetition is likely also accompanied by powerful operations that anticipate the representation itself and recollect previously successful engagements of such gesturing. One might certainly also anticipate some precise vocalization associated with acoustic self-perception—nota bene *preceding* any more clearly differentiated linguistic articulation: "There!"

Optical, acoustic, and tactile operations must be coordinated. In our hypothetical deictic "There!" the optical, acoustic, and haptic perception is, as it were, thrown into relief against the weave of other sense perceptions (for example, gustatory and olfactory), which in other contexts may be precisely the ones that do indeed acquire relevancy. Even at this early stage, however, we should acknowledge such preliminary forms of mental operations. The orchestra of sense perception demands that the operations of both association *and* differentiation continually come to bear. Prodigious processes of abstraction and psychosomatic synthesis must be engaged before even allegedly "primitive" deictic operations can be successfully performed.

If we now trace further the personal development of the child through its acquisition of language and its construction of a linguistic world, its participation in social interaction and the shaping of the social sphere of even quite small children, its assumption of differentiated perspectives and roles, its elaboration of additional spaces of individual and shared memory and of imagination and planning—if we survey this entire array of developmental stages, we become vividly

---

[5]   Cf. the contribution of Gregor Etzelmüller in this volume, chapter 2.

aware of the extraordinary power of the individual and social spirit, and we are called to assess the (in many senses) breathtaking *multimodal power of the spirit in organizing what we call the "person" (and its social spheres).* And although cognitive processes and rationality doubtless play a considerable role here, they are nonetheless permeated, spurred on, and also checked by an enormous wealth of emotional impulses and affective psychosomatic interdependencies.[6]

Whereas many classical forms of philosophy and theology reduce the spirit (and, broadly, "mind," German *Geist*) to mental operations and intellect, it is not merely in the admiration of graceful beauty (so Friedrich Schiller) that culture at large has discovered the fascinating power of a body shaped or influenced by spirit or mind. Today electronically mediated competitive sports and electronically mediated musical entertainment attain almost religious-like resonance. Here the singularity or uniqueness of individual psychosomatic existence couples with universal charisma and potential for identification. As is the case in intellectualism, however, here, too, the formation of character and ethical disposition (self-discipline, the will to achieve, in part also team spirit) along with the communication of values is restricted to an often extremely narrow spectrum. What can religion offer above and beyond this? What in the way of specific contributions between intellectualism and the spirit of Olympic achievement might one expect from religion that might address the formation of character and the shaping of ethical disposition?

The Breadth of Human Existence and the Power of the Spirit

A religion that would once again contribute in a way worthy of consideration to the formation of character, the shaping of ethical disposition, and the communication of values in our societies must acknowledge and take measure of the entire scope of human existence, and at the same time rediscover and facilitate the discovery of the dynamism and attractiveness of the human spirit and the divine Spirit.

The remarkable breadth and expanse of human existence for which theology and religion raise our awareness come to vivid expression in passages in the biblical Psalter. On one hand (NRSV), "For he knows how we were made; he remembers that we are dust" (Ps. 103:14). "When you take away their breath, they die and return to their dust" (Ps. 104:29; see also Eccl. 3:20; Sirach 10:9; 17:32, et passim). Human existence is an existence from dust to dust. On the other hand:

---

[6]   I elaborate this in Michael Welker, *In God's Image: A Spirit-Anthropology*, The Edinburgh Gifford Lectures, 2019/20 (Grand Rapids, MI: Eerdmans, 2021), second lecture; (= *Zu Gottes Bild: Eine Anthropologie des Geistes*, Leipzig EVA, 2021).

"Yet you have made them a little lower than God, and crowned them with glory and honor." "You have given them dominion over the works of your hands; you have put all things under their feet" (Ps. 8:5.6–7; cf. Gen. 1:26–28; Heb. 2:6–8; 1 Cor. 15:27; Eph. 1:22): here, of course, the human being is understood as the very image of God, as *imago Dei.*

Even the dust from which we human beings are made and to which we return, however, is quite an affair, for the natural sciences have taught us that according to present calculations, it took 13.8 billion years of cosmic existence for galaxies to come into being, which, however, had to disintegrate into the cosmic dust of which all life on earth consists. "Every atom of carbon in every living being was once inside a star, from whose dead ashes we have all arisen."[7] Certainly no less impressive, however, are the formative forces of nature and culture that have flowed into the grand ocean of the–individual and sociocultural–human spirit with all its power of memory, representation, and orientation and its astonishing communicative and formative potential.

Religion focuses on the formative powers of the divine Spirit and the human spirit and on the vast, expansive scope of the individual human person–from a person's individual finiteness, mortality, and the accompanying feelings of fragility and misfortune, to the definition of the human being as the image of God, to the attendant promises, powers of blessing, and lofty expectations. One rather gloomy contemporary theology, addressing this powerful arc of human existence from dust to the image of God, speaks about a "consciousness of ambivalence" that must be borne and collectively endured,[8] a position that begs the question whether its advocates are not, on one hand, concealing both religion's commission and charge to contribute to the shaping of character and ethical disposition, and the value systems received and cultivated by religion, and, on the other hand, shying away from the labor and effort required for critical and self-critical assessment of this commission and its implications. The careless imprecision of references to such "consciousness of ambivalence" that human beings are somehow to "endure" becomes oppressively clear in light of the numerous perils attaching to any resigned, fatalistic, cynical, or simply obscurantist mode of dealing with human misery and suffering, and the illusory, irresponsible forms of dealing with human greatness.

---

[7] John Polkinghorne, *The Faith of a Physicist: Reflections of a Bottom-Up Thinker,* The Gifford Lectures for 1993/94 (Princeton: Princeton University Press, 1994), 72.

[8] Michael Klessmann, *Ambivalenz und Glaube. Warum sich in der Gegenwart Glaubensgewissheit zur Glaubensambivalenz wandeln muss* (Stuttgart: Kohlhammer, 2018); Anja Kramer and Freimut Schirrmacher, eds., *Ambivalenzen der Seelsorge. Festschrift für Michael Klessmann zum 65. Geburtstag* (Neukirchen-Vluyn: Neukirchener Verlag, 2009); Walter Dietrich, Kurt Lüscher, and Christoph Müller, eds., *Ambivalenzen erkennen, aushalten und gestalten* (Zürich: TVZ, 2009).

The foundations of human character development, the self-elaboration of human freedom, and the equality of all human beings within the context of ethical constancy are constantly being threatened and even self-threatened. Such threats are countered, however, by the unconditionally good divine Spirit with its myriad gifts and powers, which strengthen and refresh the human spirit through its cognitive, emotional, volitional, and communicative powers. Indeed, the influence and effects of the divine Spirit extend into the innermost depths of the human personality, bestowing energy and hope when a person is oppressed by feelings of futility and impotence, and providing orientation ever anew with respect to the values of freedom, justice, and truth.

Comfort, Freedom, Justice, and Truth

The Heidelberg Catechism, one of the most famous and globally widespread expressions of faith from the Reformation period, begins with the question, "What is your only comfort in life and death?"[9] The German word *Trost* (comfort, consolation)—the word translated as "comfort" in the passage from the catechism—exhibits an astonishing semantic spectrum, and certainly not just in German, variously conveying the notions of security, confidence, trust, courage (in life), and hope. It is equated with enduring reliability, help, support, counsel, saving, reassurance and repose, strength, backing, shielding, and protection, though also with sympathy, empathy, and encouragement. The most comprehensive dictionary of the German language since the sixteenth century, *Das Deutsche Wörterbuch* by Jacob and Wilhelm Grimm, remarks that the German word *Trost* had in more recent times increasingly come to refer to the "steadfastness or firmness given or received as spiritual reinforcement through reassurance and encouragement."[10]

Within this development, the semantic background related to religion, family, friendship, and general psychological considerations has come to predominate over that associated with military protection, defense, and other contexts. The notion of comfort or consolation has come to be associated with a source or resource from which one can draw certain types of succor, for example, a source such as light, peace, joy, or even salvation and redemption. In Christian contexts, references to the comfort provided by God, God's word, Jesus Christ, the cross, and the Holy Scriptures are almost always associated with positive, affirming reassurance, even without references to specific applications in daily life, which is also

---

[9]   Cf. Michael Welker, "What Profit is the Reign of Christ to Us? The Heidelberg Catechism and its Potential for the Future," in *Remembering the Heidelberg Catechism in Southern Africa Today: Essays on the Occasion of the 450th Anniversary of a Reformed Confession, Acta Theologica*, Suppl. 20 (2014): 280–92.

[10]   Vol. 22, col. 903.

why references to comfort and consolation emerge so naturally and plausibly in connection with the love associated with parents, children, life partners, and good friends.

The Heidelberg Catechism maintains that we human beings cannot through our own power give ourselves the inner steadfastness that comfort bestows "in life and death," regardless of how hard we try. This catechism understands human life to be profoundly threatened from both within and without. We are finite, and we must die. Deliberately or not, and with or without our own actions, we are constantly at risk, in danger, and ensnared in tangles of guilt and fate from which, somehow, we must be freed.

The grand purpose of comfort—its function, if you will—is liberation from the powers of evil and from the myriad open and often concealed feelings of impotence and even aggression that this power sets in motion. God provides such comfort to us through his Spirit and, according to the conviction of Christian faith, in Jesus Christ, in whose life and ministry this Spirit acquires content, clarity, and definition. This comfort enables people to live liberated lives by providing security, confidence, trust, courage (in life), and hope, even in the most difficult life situations, and does so by disclosing forces of dependability, succor, support and counsel, stability and protection. God's activity on our behalf, however, comes about not in some abstract fashion, but rather always also through our fellow human beings, who are either consciously or unconsciously moved and filled by God's word and Spirit. And God bestows these powers precisely that we ourselves might become persons who provide comfort to others. Thus, while God does provide reassurance and repose, God also prompts sympathy and empathy, so that we ourselves, in our love of neighbor and in humanitarian benevolence, can dispense comfort round about us.

Love of neighbor, which does no harm to our fellow human beings and wishes them only good, strengthens their own freedom. Such love lives and flourishes in liberating freedom by restricting its own self-assertion in life and by embracing a free and creative self-withdrawal on behalf of one's fellow human beings. In Christian perspectives and convictions, the profoundly charitable existence of Jesus Christ reflects these liberating forces of the Spirit through the forgiveness of sins, healing, table fellowship, and liberating education. Love of neighbor thus embraces a concomitant striving for justice, which in its own turn prompts resolute engagement on behalf of the protection of the weak. Justice, mercy, and love of neighbor are the bearers of freedom and the basis for a dynamic ethos of equal rights for all human beings.

Love of neighbor, however, also actively embraces a search for truth that cannot be reduced to certainty and consensus, correctness, coherency, and rationality. Although all these elements are doubtless essential for any search for truth, the engagement on behalf of truth of which we are here speaking emerges only, on one hand, through mutual stirring up and enhancement of certainty and consensus and, on the other, through contextual correctness, coherency, and rationality. Engagements on behalf of freedom, justice, and truth are necessarily set in contexts of mutual strengthening and consolidation and are indispensable for the formation of character and ethical communication of values. And as gifts of the divine Spirit, they consistently prevail against myriad obstacles and interference.

Human beings, however, yearn not only for consolation and liberation in earthly life, along with personal and social support structures and the energy to assert oneself against threats from both within and without; they also yearn for blessed and eternal life, for firmness and stability that also provide comfort, reassurance, and support in death and beyond transient life. In this respect as well, an element of what one might call joyous pneumatological discovery must be developed. Such joy can be elicited within the context of a sensitive yet realistic assessment of the spiritual wealth that is, on one hand, inherent in all human beings and, on the other—in Christian contexts—resident in and received from the divine Spirit as mediated by Jesus Christ and shaped by his person and ministry.

Religion not only promotes the development of character that, over the entire breadth of its varied individual complexity, yet remains steadfast, grateful, responsible, and quick to become engaged; religion also elicits trust in the power of the divine Spirit, which with the hunger for truth and wisdom, justice and mercy, freedom and peace does not merely bestow the powers necessary for successful earthly life along with comfort and consolation in times of distress and affliction. Even more, it is through the sort of love of neighbor and God so eloquently attested to by this striving for freedom, justice, and truth that the creative Spirit also mediates the powers of eternal life.

But this Spirit that inspires and fills human beings is not even remotely to be understood as infinity or the Absolute or the Numinous or some similar metaphysical monstrosity. Biblical texts refer to the remarkable wealth of its gifts and blessings with the image of the "outpouring of the Spirit." Indeed, in the twentieth century, the largest faith movement in human history—namely, the Pentecostal churches and charismatic movements with half a billion members—has located the very center of its faith in this outpouring of the Spirit or baptism in the Spirit.[11]

Nourished by the Enlightenment, on one hand, and by an envisioned reactivation of biblical and spiritual training on the other, a Christian religion that seeks to apply itself to the shaping of character and ethical disposition, and to the communication of values, should concentrate on the divine and human powers of the Spirit. In this connection, orientational help can be found in the fields of Christology, anthropology, and the theology of law, the latter of which, of course, is crucial in the quest for justice.[12] We are currently investigating many promising

---

[11] Frank Macchia, *Baptized in the Spirit: A Global Pentecostal Theology* (New York: Zondervan, Harper Collins, 2009).

[12] Cf. John Witte's contribution in this volume, chapter 17.

alliances with scholarly and scientific disciplines both inside and outside theology that can offer critical and constructive support to religion in fulfilling this task. We are anticipating fresh insights and considerable help in this context from the multisystem investigation of value hierarchies in our late modern societies of precisely the sort we are envisioning and striving to actualize within our own shared research project.

Anthropology and Religious Formation

Gregor Etzelmüller

Anthropology—in the German sense of the term—means an interdisciplinary research project. Anthropology answers the question: how can we understand humanity if no longer through the lens of classical metaphysics? A crucial insight of twentieth and twenty-first century research has been that humans are by nature predetermined to learn through culture how to live. In this sense, humans by nature require education and formation to develop human opportunities. Humans not only come into the world "unfinished" and therefore dependent on culture as a kind of second nature. Humans also learn in a specific way: everyone builds on the experiences of their ancestors, so that each individual does not have to repeat those experiences. Not everyone has to reinvent the wheel. Anthropological research in the last few decades has shown that this human ability to learn culture from others is distinctive.

In the following, I first present anthropological research from the last few decades that supports this thesis. We will come to see in what sense we can say that humans by nature require education and formation, how human learning takes place, and how humanity's approach to culture leads to a plurality of cultures. Whoever claims that humans are by nature oriented towards culture is claiming at the same time that human nature cannot be described in an essentialist way.

In the second part of this chapter, I ask what religious education contributes to general human learning. My thesis is that religious education has to do with orientational knowledge, which shows human beings their true vocation (*Bestimmung*). Nature does not teach us what the ultimate purpose of human life is. Religious education and formation attempt to do so. Thereby, religious formation raises our awareness that humanity always falls short of its vocation.

The Shift from Natural Evolution to Cultural Development

In the history of humanity, natural evolution reaches a tipping point when it begins to shift and becomes a cultural process. As a consequence, the dynamics of change accelerate dramatically.[1] A simple consideration illustrates that the rise of modern humanity cannot be described in biological terms only:

The fact is, there simply has not been enough time for processes of biological evolution involving genetic variation and natural selection to have created, one by one, each of the cognitive skills necessary for modern humans to invent and maintain complex tool-use industries and technologies, complex forms of symbolic communication and representation, and complex social organizations and institutions.[2]

As a result, we need to ask when and how natural evolution shifts to cultural development in such a way that the dynamics of change accelerate rapidly. In this endeavor, we first need to keep in mind that the origins of human culture are already prefigured in the evolution of living organisms. Every living organism not only adapts to the environment but also contributes to the shape of the environment—thus, in a sense, creating it. However, we also cannot ignore the extraordinary character of human culture and its genesis. Human culture must be described in terms of both continuity and discontinuity with the behavior of other living organisms in general.

According to Charles Darwin, the decisive difference is located at the level of the cognitive, even if this is only a gradual process. While human cognitive capabilities are the result of a long evolutionary process, what distinguishes humans from other living organisms—primates especially—seems to be the capability for cultural learning. Humans "can learn not just *from* the other but *through* the other."[3] For this reason, humans can build on what has been learned in previous generations. This unique procedure of "cultural transmission" creates a "ratchet effect"[4] that speeds up cultural developments immensely. In this way, cultural development is decoupled from natural processes.

To learn "*through* the other" means, in an elementary sense, to learn by imitating the other's physical behavior. In humans, this form of imitation appears especially pervasive, as the phenomenon of so-called overimitation

---

[1]   Cf. Gregor Etzelmüller, "The Lived Body as the Tipping Point Between an Evolutionary and a Historical Anthropology," in *Embodiment in Evolution and Culture*, ed. Gregor Etzelmüller and Christian Tewes (Tübingen: Mohr Siebeck 2016), 205–25.

[2]   Michael Tomasello, *The Cultural Origins of Human Cognition* (Cambridge, MA: Harvard University Press, 1999), 2.

[3]   Ibid., 6.

[4]   Ibid., 4.

demonstrates.[5] It has been observed only in human children but occurs in all cultures.[6] Starting at about age three, toddlers tend to imitate another's action "overly precisely."[7] In contrast to chimpanzees, for example, toddlers imitate even those aspects that are obviously causally irrelevant for reaching the goal. An experiment by Horner and Whiten often referred to in this context demonstrates this with great force.

> Young wild-born chimpanzees from an African sanctuary and 3- to 4-year-old children observed a human demonstrator use a tool to retrieve a reward from a puzzle-box. The demonstration involved both causally relevant and irrelevant actions, and the box was presented in each of two conditions: opaque and clear. In the opaque condition, causal information about the effect of the tool inside the box was not available, and hence it was impossible to differentiate between the relevant and irrelevant parts of the demonstration. However, in the clear condition causal information was available, and subjects could potentially determine which actions were necessary. When chimpanzees were presented with the opaque box, they reproduced both the relevant and irrelevant actions, thus imitating the overall structure of the task. When the box was presented in the clear condition they instead ignored the irrelevant actions in favour of a more efficient, emulative technique. . . . In contrast to the chimpanzees, children employed imitation to solve the task in both conditions, at the expense of efficiency.[8]

Children imitate the action that is obviously causally irrelevant, even if they assume that they are not observed or if they are encouraged to reach the goal in such a way as makes sense to them. Lyons and colleagues demonstrated that in many cases, children imitate an action with high precision, even if this constitutes a disadvantage in a competitive situation: "children will continue to overimitate even when doing so imposes motivationally salient costs."[9]

---

5   I am grateful to Stefanie Höhl (University of Vienna) for the literature referenced in the following.

6   Tom Froese and David A. Leavens, "The Direct Perception Hypothesis: Perceiving the Intention of Another's Actions Hinders its Precise Imitation," *Frontiers in Psychology* 18 (2014): 2.

7   Stefanie Hoehl [Höhl], et al., "The Role of Social Interactions and Pedagogical Cues for Eliciting and Reducing Overimitation in Preschoolers," *Journal of Experimental Child Psychology* (2014): 122–33, at 122.

8   Victoria Horner and Andrew Whiten, "Causal Knowledge and Imitation/Emulation Switching in Chimpanzees (Pan troglodytes) and Children (Homo sapiens)," *Animal Cognition* 8/3 (2005): 164–81, at 164.

9   D.E. Lyons, et al., "The Scope and Limits of Overimitation in the Transmission of Artefact Culture," *Philosophical Transactions of the Royal Society London B: Biological Sciences* 366 (2011): 1158–67, at 1163.

In addition, toddlers imitate even actions not demonstrated intentionally—that is, in a pedagogic context or by trusted care givers:

> Interestingly, and in contrast to our prediction, children initially reenacted the irrelevant actions no matter whether these actions were demonstrated by a pedagogical experimenter or by an unfamiliar and non-communicative experimenter. This was true even though the no-contact experimenter never interacted with children and avoided any contact before or during the experiment.[10]

Human children seem to assume that an action performed by a parent or a care giver, or by any adult person in general, is meaningful, even if they do not see or understand its point. The child imitates these actions as exactly as possible precisely because it does not see the point.

> On this view, and in direct contrast to the traditional view of imitation, understanding the other's goals and intentions does not facilitate imitation, but actually hinders it because such direct insight obscures the precise means. Imitation requires individuals to change attention from *what* the other's goals are to *how* the other's actions are precisely realized, while emulation is possible without this extra effort.[11]

Accordingly, it is not the recognition of the other as an intentional actor[12] that is foundational for the specifically human mode of learning by imitation, but the assumption of there being a point to imitation, in the sense of a leap of faith. Humans assume that others' actions are meaningful even if their actions do not seem so at first glance.

That this assumption of meaning amounts to a leap of faith is demonstrated by experiments in which toddlers are confronted with a conflict. They are presented with two different courses of action and then need to decide which strategy to pursue.

> After being shown two strategies, they chose to maintain the strategy or switch to the strategy employed by the pedagogical experimenter (pedagogical-then-no-contact and no-contact-then-pedagogical conditions), with whom they presumably shared a stronger bond (i.e., social affiliation) and whose normative behavior they may have been

---

Hoehl, et al., "The Role of Social Interactions," 131.

Froese and Leavens, "The Direct Perception Hypothesis," 5.

Tomasello has revised his previous thesis according to which only humans can understand conspecifics as intentional agents. Recent research has shown that "nonhuman great apes not only are intentional agents themselves but also understand others as intentional agents": Michael Tomasello, *A Natural History of Human Thinking* (Cambridge, MA: Harvard University Press, 2014), 20; see also ix–x.

more motivated to copy. In the pedagogical-then-pedagogical condition, both experimenters were equally familiar and pedagogical. Here, it seems that children's behavior was flexible and they performed the strategy they had seen last.[13]

The capability of toddlers to imitate the actions of others precisely shapes even their neuronal system. The difference between human children and apes is even reflected in their mirror system. While mirror neurons in apes seem to react only to goal-directed action, "the human mirror system . . . codes both transitive and intransitive motor acts, it is able to code both the goal of the motor act and the movement of which the act is composed."[14]

The significance of so-called overimitation in a typically human mode of life is revealed only once the difference between the contexts of one's lifeworld and the experimental setup in developmental psychology is taken into account. The experiments just mentioned prompt children to imitate a pointless action—and the reason they are set up this way is that researchers are aware of the significance of overimitation for children. Thus, in the lab, overimitation seems pointless, requiring a time commitment and incurring a competitive disadvantage. But what seems odd in the lab does indeed serve a purpose in one's lifeworld. In this latter context, children imitate the actions of their adult caregivers as well, yet these actions are typically goal directed. Evolution and history have optimized a multitude of types of action. Even noninstrumental actions such as greeting rituals, for example, often fulfill a precise purpose in the lifeworld.

In learning by imitation, human children explore not only the world that has already opened up for them through cognition but also an entire world of pragmatic options, even if the meaning of the options is not plain to them. We can observe this every day. For example, toddlers learn to close the fridge long before their parents have explained, linguistically, the result of an open fridge—melting ice, spoiling groceries, and a higher electricity bill. The fridge must be closed, and if an adult leaves it open too long, a child may well close it spontaneously. In mimetic learning, children grasp the difference between the necessity of closing the fridge and the possibility of leaving other doors, or windows, open. The same holds for noninstrumental actions. When attending a church service, children imitate their parents in taking a moment to stand for meditation or a silent prayer before taking a seat in the pew. This way they learn to enact, in an embodied way, the difference that distinguishes liturgical communication from communication in the everyday world—long before they are able to grasp this difference intellectually—and this will then enable them to adopt an autonomous stance toward these different modes of communication.

---

[13] Hoehl, et al., "The Role of Social Interactions," 131.

[14] Giacomo Rizzolatti and Corrado Sinigaglia, *Mirrors in the Brain: How our Minds Share Actions and Emotions* (Oxford: Oxford University Press, 2008), 124.

The specific way humans learn culturally, their ability to learn not only from but also through others, is manifest on an elementary level in the child's imitation of another. Thus, there is no point at which this kind of learning has taken place in a nonembodied form. Humans begin to learn culturally when one person imitates another, or even overimitates that person, to borrow the terminology of developmental psychology. Embodied imitation is the tipping point at which natural evolution shifts to cultural development. Evolution has brought forth a life form that tends to imitate others by nature—and which is thus shaped culturally from the outset.

Evolutionary Anthropology Advocating for a Plurality of Culture

Human beings are cultural beings by nature. To a large extent they shape their own behavior by learning and imitating other humans physically, rather than following natural instincts. The development of the human person is clearly shaped by cultural environment, and at different times and in different contexts, the person will develop differently. Based on this mutual interdependence of natural and cultural processes, we can conclude that humans do not live in a particular culture by nature. This has also been pointed out by the Jewish philosopher Michael Landmann (1913–84), who wrote that "what is prefigured already in nature is the mere fact of culture, but not its particular shape."[15] There is no type of culture that *necessarily* derives from human nature. He writes: "For that reason it is not correct either to conceive of culture in the singular as a human creation. Humans do not create culture in the singular, but particular people create their own culture. Humanity creates cultures."[16] Yet, since humans not only create diverse cultures but are themselves shaped by their respective cultures, there is no definite human essence. As both creators and creatures of culture, we always encounter human nature in the plural.

> The human person is just as diverse . . . as the cultures that shape the person. It is not that the human person brings forth different cultures while remaining the same, passing through them untouched as a constant entity. In creating cultures, humans finish creating themselves, and in each culture they provide themselves with a different form and direction.[17]

---

15   Michael Landmann, *Der Mensch als Schöpfer und Geschöpf der Kultur: Geschichts- und Sozialanthropologie* (Munich/Basel: Reinhardt, 1961), 60.

16   Ibid., 26.

17   Ibid., 61.

Due to the shape of each culture created by humans, human nature itself changes throughout history. "Historical variability is the radical human fate."[18] The notion of an unchanging human core thus turns out to be a fiction. "If we wish to speak of a core, this would be nothing but open plasticity."[19]

This philosophical realization is correlated with the biological fact of the enormous human plasticity in the process of ontogenesis. The elementary formation of the human baby during the first year is characterized by exchange with others, which amounts to cultural formation.

> Thus already during the first year, the life of the human child takes place in the realm of the "historic," in a time during which the human neonate—if it were a mammal in every respect—would still have to gain shape under the most pure conditions of natural law, i.e., in the darkness of the womb.[20]

But even processes that are seemingly purely somatic, "such as gaining an upright gait, the formation of the spine and the pelvis,"[21] take place in relationship to the social environment, in one's "own activity of striving, learning, and imitation."[22] This is even clearer for the "development of truly human opportunities,"[23] as in the varied uses of the hand, which can learn to write in an "elegant hand," to play the piano brilliantly, to touch gently. The "slow speed" of human somatic development allows for social and psychic shaping, thus bringing forth the human being as an entity characterized by an irreducible mutual interdependence of nature and culture, body and psyche.[24]

What the biologist Adolf Portmann described with respect to development and behavior corresponds to current thinking about the plasticity of the human brain. "The human brain is not only the most complex, but also the most adaptable organ that we know of. As the neurosciences show, all our experiences, perceptions, and interactions with the environment modify the neuronal structures throughout our lives."[25] Notably, the long maturation period of the human brain is hugely significant, since at birth it amounts "only to a little more than 25 percent of an adult's brain volume," appearing not to be fully mature even at the age

---

18   Ibid., 26.
19   Ibid., 62, see 27.
20   Adolf Portmann, *Biologische Fragmente: Zu einer Lehre vom Menschen* (Basel: Schwabe, 1944), 70, see 81.
21   Ibid., 125.
22   Ibid., 70.
23   Ibid., 101.
24   Ibid.
25   Thomas Fuchs, *Das Gehirn—ein Beziehungsorgan: Eine phänomenologische-ökologische Konzeption*, 4th ed. (Stuttgart: Kohlhammer, 2013), 156.

of ten.[26] Evolution has thus brought forth an organ that for its development depends on an environment conducive to life, only attaining its complex and detailed structure through interaction with the environment. The influence of the environment extends even into precise neuronal structures. Thus, brain research confirms an insight that Portmann, as a biologist, had attained in the 1940 s: "We see the biological characteristics of the human precisely in how inherited factors irreducibly grow together with the various social effects—in ways that are final and unique from the point of view of the individual."[27] The extent to which the human person is open to social influences can also be seen in human sexuality: "even that part of human behavior that is most instinctual, sexuality, is open for a far-reaching freedom of personal decision"[28]—and thus for cultural shaping.

Human Plasticity and the Creature's Freedom to Make Itself

The fact that human beings are by nature pure plasticity, that they can form and change their nature, demonstrates the great freedom which, theologically speaking, the Creator awards the creature.

If we understand human beings as pure plasticity, it is also clear that by nature they receive no determination about how to behave. Humans must discover their own vocation (*Bestimmung*). This fact corresponds precisely to the biblical description of humankind. In view of the Old Testament, Hans-Walter Wolff asserted: "In his dialogue with God above all, the human sees himself as called into question, searched out and thus much less established for what he is than called to new things."[29] In accordance with this, the New Testament also sees humanity as characterized by an open future. The First Epistle of John puts it paradigmatically: "what we will be has not yet been revealed" (1 John 3:2). This biblical insight goes well together with an evolutionary anthropology which does not aim to describe the essence of humanity, but rather to understand better those natural processes that allow humans to create and establish something new again and again.

---

[26]   Gisela Gruppe, et al., *Anthropologie. Einführendes Lesebuch*, 2nd ed. (Berlin/Heidelberg: Springer, 2012), 67 f.

[27]   Portmann, *Biologische Fragmente*, 127.

[28]   Ibid., 59.

[29]   Hans Walter Wolff, *Anthropology of the Old Testament*, trans. Margaret Kohl, reprint (London: SCM/Minneapolis: Augsburg Fortress, 1975), 3. Translation revised.

Religious Formation

Religious education gives people a sense of orientation. Theologically, one could say that the Creator not only gives humans freedom to explore their own possibilities but also accompanies them in this process, by showing them their calling (*Bestimmung*). Biblically speaking, this is expressed by the fact that creation ultimately aims at the law. The Creator of the world is conceived in the Bible as the God of Israel, who gives God's people the law and the commandments. Here we come across the proximity of religion and law, which characterizes all monotheistic religions.

All legal corpora of the Old Testament have a comparable structure: they comprise regulations which deal with the legal regulation of conflicts and aim at justice; they contain regulations "that aim at the routine protection of the weak and the systematic safeguarding of their interests" (mercy), and they contain sections regulating the cultic life of Israel.[30] The law aims therefore at justice, mercy, and the knowledge of God. Humanity should use its freedom in order to embody justice, mercy, and the knowledge of God in this world; in this sense, humanity is called to be the image of God.

The significance of religious education and formation can also be demonstrated in a secular age. Religious education encourages an orientation toward justice and mercy. In this respect, civil society benefits from active and dynamic religious communities. Studies in the social sciences have demonstrated that such communities are very important for a lively and dynamic civil society. First of all, religious communities generate a large amount of volunteer work. In Germany, we may safely assume that more than four million persons involved with the two major churches are active as volunteers. Moreover, religious education foster attitudes from which civil society profits. Social scientist Sigrid Roßteutscher, from Frankfurt University, states, "Thus, religious institutions turn out indeed to be a training ground of pro-social orientation, which see their task in advocacy on behalf of the weak and which support a culture of 'benevolence.'"[31] Even the area of divine worship, so awkward for a secular society, is of social importance. Secularly speaking, the cultic aspect of religion expressed in worship aims to create and shape common memories and common expectations. Such memories and ex-

---

30 Michael Welker, "Justice – Mercy – Worship. The 'Weighty Matters' of Biblical Law," in *Concepts of Law in the Sciences, Legal Studies, and Theology*, ed. Michael Welker and Gregor Etzelmüller, Religion in Philosophy and Theology 72 (Tübingen: Mohr Siebeck, 2013), 205–24, at 206.

31 Sigrid Roßteutscher, *Religion, Zivilgesellschaft, Demokratie. Eine international vergleichende Studie zur Natur religiöser Märkte und der demokratischen Rolle religiöser Zivilgesellschaften*, Studien zur Wahl- und Einstellungsforschung 12 (Baden-Baden: Nomos, 2009), 423.

pectations shape our societies and our daily lives. What we remember and what we expect make a difference in how we live our lives.

Let me explain this with reference to the Old Testament, specifically the Old Testament's mercy code. It lays out the routines of mercy which are required by the law and are based on the memory of the Exodus. The book of the covenant already seeks to justify the commandments to protect foreigners with a reminder that Israel was once a foreigner itself in Egypt (Ex. 22:20; 23:9). Even more comprehensive is the approach taken by Deuteronomy, which derives not just the rights of foreigners but those of widows, orphans, and slaves from a reminder of Israel's bondage in Egypt and the experience of being brought out of Egypt by YHWH (Deut. 15:15; 24:18, 22). The priestly literature also subscribes to this tradition. The commandments to protect foreigners (Lev. 19:34) and the impoverished Israelites (Lev. 25:35–43) are based on the reminder that Israel was enslaved and then delivered out of Egypt. This means that by keeping the memory of the liberation from Egypt alive through the worship of YHWH alone, the Old Testament cult reinforces the routines of mercy required by the law. The cultic memory of the liberation of Egypt shapes social legislation in Israel.

Like the elementary processes of human learning, religious education and formation are not purely cognitive but always embodied. In Deuteronomy, people learn the law not only by listening to it during the worship but also by celebrating a common meal:

> And you shall eat before the Lord your God, in the place where He chooses to make His name abide, the tithe of your grain and your new wine and your oil, of the firstborn of your herds and your flocks, that you may learn to fear the Lord your God always. (Deut. 14:23)

What is more, not just free landholders but slaves, foreigners, widows, and orphans are expected to share in this meal (cf. Deut. 16:11, 14). The existence of slaves is still assumed, although the presuppositions of a slaveholding society are already being transcended in the feast, at least for a time. The miserable social situation of the typical welfare case in the ancient world—foreigners, orphans, and widows—is no longer ignored in the context of the cult; what is more, it is temporarily overcome in the shared sacrificial meal. The feast suspends class differences and unites Israel into one large family. According to the book of Deuteronomy, in the Old Testament cult a new society is not only proclaimed but realized and embodied. This did not change society immediately. Slaveholding was accepted by the Deuteronomic law. But in worship one thing becomes clear: slaveholding is not what God has intended for God's people. What is more, this insight began to change ideas about how to deal with slaves. Some Old Testament scholars have argued that Deuteronomy transformed slaveholding into an early form of wage labor (*Lohnarbeit*) instead.[32]

As with the Old Testament cult, the Christian celebration of the Lord's Supper suspends differences between Christians and unites all into one body and one people: "They need one and the same sacrament and become one and the same people and at the same time a sacred sworn community; they become one body and one people."[33]

It had already been the historical experience of Old Testament Israel that the people had not lived up to the law. All in all, whoever recognizes that humanity is called to impart righteousness, mercy, and the knowledge of God in the world must also acknowledge that humanity fails to pursue its true calling, that humans are, theologically speaking, sinners. Religious education not only recalls and teaches humankind's ultimate vocation but also makes us aware of how humanity fails to live up to it.

In the Reformed tradition, worship always begins with the confession of sin. Remembering and confessing that we are all sinners, we acknowledge that we can also go astray, even when we are united and intend to pursue a good path of action. This insight is of great political importance in our current situation. It calls not only for more democracy but for a sophisticated system of checks and balances, for a robust republic. Even John Calvin has inferred from the "vices or defects of men" that "it is safer and more tolerable when several bear rule, that they may thus mutually assist, instruct, and admonish each other, and should anyone be disposed to go too far, the others are censors and masters to curb his excess."[34] The knowledge of the power of sin not only about the people but also about the holders of state power requires the control of their power.

For Christians, it is the crucifixion of Jesus Christ which reveals human sin. The cross of Jesus Christ reveals that even the good gifts of law, religion, education, and public opinion can also work against God's good and positive intentions for creation: Christ is executed in the name of both Roman and Jewish law.[35] So it is clear that even the law itself can come under the power of sin.

By simultaneously providing an underpinning for the law while raising awareness about the law's potential endangerment, a biblically shaped religious

---

[32] Cf. Frank Crüsemann, *Die Tora. Theologie und Sozialgeschichte des alttestamentlichen Gesetzes* (Munich: Kaiser, 1992), 272.

[33] Cf. Huldreich Zwingli, *Sämtliche Werke* VI, 5, 161, 2–5: "Qui enim unis eisdemque sacramentis utuntur, una eademque gens ac sancta quedam coniuratio fiunt in unum corpus, inque populum unum coeunty."

[34] John Calvin, *Institutes of the Christian Religion* (Grand Rapids, MI: Eerdmans, 1970), IV, 20, 8.

[35] Cf. Michael Welker, *God the Revealed: Christology* (Grand Rapids, MI: Eerdmans, 2014), ch. 3.

formation fosters a powerful connection between different traditions and serves to strengthen and unsettle the law in equal measure. Just as law and prophecy mutually challenge one another in the Old Testament, religious education can foster powerful relationships in modern societies between social systems (such as the economic, legal, and political systems) and the voluntary associations of civil society, which continually critique these systemic forms in order to transform them.

In this sense, we can argue that religious formation seeks to cultivate an attitude of awareness of the high calling of humanity while also confessing that humanity misses the mark, fails to live up to its calling. In view of the knowledge of our vocation, and of our transgressions, religious education, in its Protestant form, teaches the justification of the sinner by faith. God is not only the creator who has given freedom to creation to develop itself, and the lawgiver, who continually accompanies created beings with God's commandment. God is also a God who acknowledges human weakness yet does not abandon the creation, repeatedly offering help instead. Religious education, therefore, generates hope because it perceives not only humanity in its sin, but also the God who empowers humans to bring justice, mercy, and knowledge of God into the world. Because faith knows that it does not deserve this saving action of God, and that the believer does not have an advantage over the unbeliever, faith also hopes for saving actions of God even outside the churches and the monotheistic religions. In this sense, religious education generates hope for all people and for all times and for all regions of the world.

Humans are by nature called to education and formation, but they are not predestined for a specific culture. Religious education wants to give humans a clear sense of orientation: it teaches us about our human calling, raises awareness of how we fail to live out this vocation, and reveals God as one who helps humanity in this situation, thus giving humanity, giving us, hope.

"Values of the Gospel"

The Formative Role of Christian Values for Social Cohesion in Modern Societies

Friederike Nüssel

The Ever-Present Reality of Values in Public Discourse

In modern industrialized societies, particularly in Europe and even in North America, value language is always a form of expression in media and politics. One prominent example of the way in which values are addressed in Western European politics can be found in Angela Merkel's congratulatory message to Donald Trump on his election as president of the United States. Having been heavily critiqued during Trump's election campaign for her migration policies, Merkel offered congratulation with a carefully phrased message:[1]

> Germany and America are bound by common values—democracy, freedom, as well as respect for the rule of law and the dignity of each and every person, regardless of their origin, skin color, creed, gender, sexual orientation, or political views. It is based on these values that I wish to offer close cooperation, both with me personally and between our countries' governments.[2]

While democracy, freedom, and respect for the rule and dignity of human persons are ideals and goods which have been discovered and affirmed in long and difficult processes of democratization on both sides of the Atlantic, the "value" concept used today to qualify these ideals *as* values is a product of nineteenth-century philosophy.[3] In contrast to an economic understanding of value, Immanuel Kant argued that the price of something could mark only its relative value, while absolute value and dignity could be ascribed only to autonomous persons who exist

---

[1]   https://www.nytimes.com/2018/03/04/opinion/angela-merkel-leader-free-world.html.

[2]   https://www.washingtonpost.com/news/worldviews/wp/2016/11/09/angela-merkel-congratulates-donald-trump-kind-of/?noredirect=on&utm_term=.64a0d734f26a.

[3]   Cf. Wolfhart Henckmann, "Wert I. Philosophisch," in *Theologische Realenzyklopädie* 35 (Berlin: De Gruyter, 2003), 648–53, esp. 648; Anton Hügli, et al., "Wert," *Historisches Wörterbuch Philosophie* 12 (Darmstadt: Wissenschaftliche Buchgesellschaft, 2004), 556–83.

54   Friederike Nüssel

as an end in themselves.[4] The philosopher Rudolf Hermann Lotze (1817–81) is the first thinker to give the concept of value a central role in his philosophical system.[5] Friedrich Nietzsche's famous claim for the *Umwertung aller Werte* (revaluation of all values) and the neo-Kantian value philosophies of Wilhelm Windelband and Heinrich Rickert helped to further implement the concept of value in philosophy. In response to this philosophical development, leading Protestant theologians in the late nineteenth and early twentieth centuries—notably Albrecht Ritschl, Martin Kähler,[6] Ernst Troeltsch, and Adolf von Harnack—employed value philosophy to clarify the special status of theological propositions as referring to the realm of divine revelation and the world of the invisible in contrast to the *Sinnenwelt* (sensory world).

Under the influence of dialectic theology, however—especially that of Karl Barth's critique of natural theology—value philosophy lost traction, even disappearing from leading Protestant approaches. In the debates about fundamental values regarding new legislation on abortion in the 1970 s, some influential Protestant theologians, such as Eberhard Jüngel, critiqued the plea for values in ethical argumentation as philosophically inconsistent and as a subtle form of religious tyranny which undermined Christian freedom as constituted by divine revelation in the word of God.[7] Correspondingly, more recent philosophical commentaries on value philosophy critically examine the ontological status of values. According to the philosophers Herbert Schnädelbach[8] and Andreas Urs Sommer, none of the different approaches of value philosophy were successful in developing a sound argument for the existence of values as objective entities. Sommer, in

---

[4]   Cf. Immanuel Kant, *Grundlegung zur Metaphysik der Sitten* (1785), Akademie-Ausgabe (Berlin: Walter de Gruyter & Co., 1968), 434 f.

[5]   In his teleological idealism, Lotze considers the basic role of the desires of the soul distinguishing between the indifferent from the valuable. Absolute value refers to the idea of the good. Cf. Hermann Lotze, *Metaphysik* (Leipzig, 1841), 4 ff., 323 ff.; Hermann Lotze, *Mikrokosmus. Ideen zur Naturgeschichte und Geschichte der Menschheit*, vol. 2, 5th ed. (Leipzig: S. Hirzel, 1905), 308–42; vol. 3, 6th ed. (Leipzig: S. Hirzel, 1923), 605–15.

[6]   Cf. Friederike Nüssel, "The Value of the Bible: Martin Kähler's Theology of Scripture and its Ecumenical Impact," in *Multiple Reformations? The Many Faces and Legacies of the Reformation*, ed. Jan Stievermann and Randall C. Zachman (Tübingen: Mohr Siebeck, 2018), 359–74.

[7]   Carl Schmitt, Eberhard Jüngel, and Sepp Schelz, *Die Tyrannei der Werte* (Hamburg: Lutherisches Verlagshaus, 1979; cf. the article by Eberhard Jüngel, "Wertlose Wahrheit, 'Christliche Wahrheitserfahrung im Streit mit der Tyrannei der Werte,'" in ibid., 45–73.

[8]   Cf. Herbert Schnädelbach, *Philosophie in Deutschland 1833–1931* (Berlin: Suhrkamp Verlag, 1983), also in English: *German Philosophy 1831–1933* (Cambridge: Cambridge University Press, 1984); cf. Herbert Schnädelbach, *Analytische und postanalytische Philosophie* (Frankfurt am Main: Suhrkamp, 2004), 229–31.

his book with the catchy title *Werte. Warum man sie braucht, obwohl es sie nicht gibt* (Values: why we need them although they don't exist),[9] systematically deconstructs an ontological understanding of values. He also critiques the pragmatist approach of Hans Joas,[10] who describes moral values as experiences of self-commitment and self-transcendence to present a metaphysic of the self.[11]

Nevertheless, Sommer acknowledges that, in spite of the theoretical questions, value language has become a part of the ordinary vocabulary of modern civilized societies and is used in all kinds of discourses, whether in politics, education, or business. According to his analysis, values are attractive because, in contrast to rigid principles, they are dynamic and flexible as they transcend traditional binary codes such as good/bad, existence/nonexistence, and other either/or distinctions.[12] In contrast to an ontological understanding, Sommer suggests conceiving of values as "regulative fictions" which do not entail a claim of absoluteness. In this way, values are attractive sources of orientation for modern pluralistic societies. The popularity of the values concept, which derives in large part from the semantic use of the term "value," may also explain why Christian theologians and Christian churches rediscovered value language in ethical debates, and why churches in the global and regional ecumenical movement adopted value language to frame ecumenical goals in a way that would speak to secular societies. In the second and third sections of this essay, I present two prominent examples.

"Values of the Gospel" in the Global Ecumenism of the World Council of Churches

Value language was rarely used in discussions and statements of the global ecumenical movement in the 1960 s and 1970 s;[13] it only really became prevalent in the debates of the World Council of Churches (WCC) on the system of global economy in the 1980 s. The phrase "values of the Gospel" in the title of this essay is

---

[9]   Andreas Urs Sommer, *Werte. Warum wir sie brauchen, obwohl es sie nicht gibt* (Stuttgart: J.B. Metzler, 2016).

[10] Cf. Hans Joas, *Die Entstehung der Werte*, 3rd ed. (Frankfurt am Main: Suhrkamp Verlag, 2009).

[11] Sommer, *Werte*, 78.

[12] Ibid., 83 f.

[13] One of the rare examples can be found in the paper by Dr. Emmanual G. Mesthene titled "Religious Values in the Age of Technology," presented at the World Conference on Church and Society held in Geneva in 1966; cf. Ökumenischer Rat der Kirchen, *Appell an die Kirchen der Welt* (Berlin: Kreuz Verlag, 1967), 43–56. Mesthene was executive director of the Program on Technology and Society at Harvard University.

taken from the 2013 WCC Faith and Order document titled "The Church: Towards a Common Vision."[14] It is the first Faith and Order text that uses this phrase, and in this way it presents an important step in the reception of secular value discourse. While the phrase "values of the Gospel" appears only in the fourth and final chapter of the document, it is based on the course of ecclesiological argumentation in the first three chapters. The first chapter, "God's Mission and the Unity of the Church," explores the theme of ecclesiology, which has been defined as the central topic of multilateral conversation after the convergence declarations on "Baptism, Eucharist and Ministry" (adopted in 1982). The theological foundation of ecclesiology is elaborated in the second chapter, "The Church and the Triune God," in which the nature and mission of the church is grounded in a Trinitarian theology. While the third chapter, "The Church: Growing in Communion," pays particular attention to the challenges resulting from ecclesiological differences among the churches, the fourth chapter, "The Church: In and for the World," explores the role of the church as a "sign and agent of God's love."[15] Here the document transcends denominational perspectives and reflects on the role of the church as a sign and instrument of God's love in interreligious contexts,[16] specifically with regard to the relation between church and world and in response to human suffering. It is the final part of this chapter where we find the distinction between moral and societal values being addressed in the Gospel:

> The Church does not stand in isolation from the moral struggles of humankind as a whole. Together with the adherents of other religions as well as with all persons of good will, Christians must promote not only those individual moral values which are essential to the authentic realization of the human person but also the social values of justice, peace and the protection of the environment, since the message of the Gospel extends to both the personal and the communal aspects of human existence. [17]

Not surprisingly, the social values mentioned here converge with the goals of the global ecumenical movement that began in 1910 with a call for the churches to work jointly for justice and peace. In the 1980 s, this movement also launched the so-called conciliar process for the preservation of creation and the environment.

---

[14]   Cf. "The Church: Towards a Common Vision," Faith and Order Paper nr. 214 (Geneva: World Council of Churches Publications, 2013).

[15]   Ibid., preface, p. 2: "The fourth chapter develops several significant ways in which the Church relates to the world as a sign and agent of God's love, such as proclaiming Christ within an interreligious context, witnessing to the moral values of the Gospel and responding to human suffering and need."

[16]   Ibid., 60.

[17]   Ibid., 62.

In the final paragraph of the text, three goals are addressed as "values of the Kingdom."

To speak of justice, peace, and protection of the environment as values of the Gospel and values of the Kingdom is a new and interesting move in light of the fact that value terminology is not derived from biblical language. By adopting value language, the Faith and Order Commission attempted to respond to two ecumenical concerns. The first concern was to explain and translate the impact of the Gospel to both secular societies and other religions while fostering cooperation in the work for justice, peace, and protection of the environment beyond the boundaries of different religions and worldviews. A second intention of the document's ecclesiological approach is to renew the relationship and connection between churches in the WCC in response to disappointment regarding the lack of progress in the goals of the ecumenical movement. According to the constitution of the WCC, the primary purpose of the fellowship of churches in the WCC is:

> To call one another to visible unity in one faith and in one Eucharistic fellowship, expressed in worship and common life in Christ, through witness and service to the world, and to advance towards that unity in order that the world may believe.[18]

The Faith and Order document on ecclesiology is honest about the fact that visible unity in one Eucharistic fellowship is not to be achieved soon, if ever. As a matter of fact, the drafting period of the ecclesiological text, which was meant to formulate convergences on the nature and mission of the church, had taken three decades and was unsatisfactory for many involved. While the goal of visible unity remains a declared goal of the WCC, churches could agree only on a "common vision" of the church. It seems that "visible unity" has turned into a "regulative fiction," to use Sommers's term. As a common vision and goal, visible unity creates a kind of ecclesial cohesion among WCC member churches. Nevertheless, it is also evident that the visibility is found primarily in joint engagement for the social value of the Gospel in the pilgrimage for justice and peace that the WCC called for at the plenary assembly in Busan in 2013.

---

[18]   https://www.oikoumene.org/en/resources/documents/assembly/2013-busan/adopted-documents-statements/wcc-constitution-and-rules. "The statement in the constitution regarding the purpose of the WCC has developed from the 1948 formulation, 'to carry out the work of the world movements for Faith and Order and Life and Work,' to the much more specific language of Nairobi (1975), which speaks of calling 'the churches to the goal of visible unity in one faith and in one eucharistic fellowship expressed in worship and in the common life of Christ, and to advance towards that unity in order that the world may believe'; to the even more detailed formulation adopted by the Harare assembly (1998)."

In light of this development, a second experience in the WCC is even more challenging. Over the last three decades, churches increasingly began to disagree about family values and sexuality, particularly the question of same-sex partnership and marriage and about the ordination of homosexual ministers. While controversies over these issues are a challenge for the opportunity of ecumenical relationships among churches in the West and the East after 1989, they also reinforce the North-South divide that the WCC has attempted to overcome since the 1960 s. Given the challenges the WCC faced, it is interesting to see that the Faith and Order document "The Church: Towards a Common Mission" explicitly characterizes the social values of peace, justice, and protection of the environment as *values of the Gospel* and puts all the emphasis on the joint effort of working towards these values, while at the same time it neither emphasizes nor specifies the moral values "essential to the authentic realization of the human person."

Basic Values in European Ecumenism

While global ecumenism attempts to preserve and enhance ecclesial cohesion in line with the values of the Gospel, there is a different way to employ value language in European ecumenism. The central ecumenical institution at the European level is the Conference of European Churches (CEC), which was founded in 1959 as a fellowship of Protestant, Anglican, Old Catholic, and Orthodox churches in Europe. As such, it is the parallel institution to the WCC on the European level. Previously, its office was in Geneva, but in 2014 it moved to Brussels. The Roman Catholic counterpart to the CEC is the Council of the Bishops' Conferences (Consilium Conferentiarum Episcoporum Europae, or CCEE). CEC was especially important in facilitating exchange among the churches on both sides of the Iron Curtain until 1989. After 1989, it began to focus on ethical challenges and on the European unification process.

The most important project of the CEC after 1989 was the Charta Oecumenica (CO), published in 2001.[19] The Charta is a remarkable document, as it delineates and fosters ecumenism among churches in Europe not just for the sake of overcoming divisions among churches but to help European countries grow together and develop a European identity. While CO affirms the goal of visible unity in global ecumenism, it also emphasizes the idea of visible fellowship in the cooperation among churches. CO sees the main task of European churches as responding, from within the context of rapidly growing secularization, to a "widespread lack of corporate and individual orientation and falling away from Christian

---

[19]   The text can be found at https://www.ceceurope.org/wp-content/uploads/2015/07/ChartaOecumenica.pdf.

values."[20] This situation challenges Christians and churches "to testify to their faith" and respond to the "quest for meaning" (*Sinnsuche*) in European societies. In order to fulfill the "most important task" to proclaim the Gospel "in both word and deed, for the salvation of all,"[21] CO tells churches to intensify "Christian education . . . and pastoral care in local congregations, with a sharing of experiences in these fields."[22]

Unlike the Faith and Order text, CO does not speak of values of the Gospel, nor can the terminological distinction between moral and social values be found in the text. Instead, CO speaks of Christian values in general and employs the category of basic values in the final chapter, titled "Our Common Responsibility in Europe":

> The churches support an integration of the European continent. Without common values, unity cannot endure. We are convinced that the spiritual heritage of Christianity constitutes an empowering source of inspiration and enrichment for Europe. On the basis of our Christian faith, we work towards a humane, socially conscious Europe, in which human rights and the basic values of peace, justice, freedom, tolerance, participation and solidarity prevail. We likewise insist on the reverence for life, the value of marriage and the family, the preferential option for the poor, the readiness to forgive, and in all things compassion.[23]

Note the fine-tuned wording and implicit distinction between basic values and other orienting ideas. Marriage and family are referred to as a value, yet they are deliberately placed in the middle of a list of other important attitudes that affirm and support human life. The category of "basic values," however, is reserved for peace, justice, freedom, tolerance, participation, and solidarity. These values are considered essential for the integration of the European continent and for the democratic process. While CO does not declare these values to be distinctly Christian values, the document insinuates that they are rooted in the Christian spiritual heritage.

The basic values are promoted in two ways. One way consists in a confession that "Christians have failed to prevent suffering and destruction from being inflicted by Europeans, both within Europe and beyond."[24] CEC churches committed to "share . . . responsibility for this guilt and ask God and our fellow human beings for forgiveness."[25] The second way of enacting basic values, consists in a

---

[20] Charta Oecumenica, chapter 2, nr. 2.

[21] Ibid.

[22] Ibid.

[23] Ibid., chapter 3, nr. 7.

[24] Ibid.

[25] Ibid.

number of self-commitments to joint work on formation.[26] Each paragraph of CO ends with self-commitments. Essential self-commitments to carry into an ecumenical encounter are to recognize religious freedom, to avoid competition in evangelization, and to enter into agreements with other churches.[27] The letter of commitment to enter agreements is especially important for the formative character of CO in light of the fact that neither CEC nor the Council of the Bishops' Conferences has any jurisdictional authority in relation to member churches. In the case of the CEC, member churches are either autocephalous, like the Orthodox churches, or have a regional or global head (as, for instance, the Church of England belonging to the Anglican Communion). In the case of the Roman Catholic Church, jurisdictional authority belongs to the pope and the College of Bishops. While national bishops' conferences have limited jurisdictional authority, the European bishops' conference (CCEE) has no authority.

For this reason, CO can only ask churches to engage in self-commitments and to create legal frameworks on the local and regional level, which is precisely what occurred in Germany. CO was officially signed by the Evangelische Kirche in Deutschland (EKD) and the German Bishops' Conference at the First Ecumenical *Kirchentag* in Germany in 2003. The consequence of this official appropriation was that many ecumenical parish partnerships in Germany were negotiated. It was the specific initiative of the Catholic bishops in Germany, under the leadership of Cardinal Karl Lehmann, who fostered this process.

To the surprise of Protestants, Catholic canon law proved to be a promoting resource. Unlike Catholic dogma, which can be interpreted but not changed, canon law can and should be changed if circumstances necessitate the change. The law's purpose is to serve the church as a visible society by governing the church adequately, such that the governance corresponds to the conception of the church as a visible society. Some Catholic bishops, like Cardinal Lehmann, had a vision to use the ordering capacity of canon law to give ecumenism a legally legitimized space and framework in Germany. This movement within the Catholic Church is mentioned here because the entire endeavor is a consequent application of the basic values CO wants to promote, particularly the values of freedom, tolerance, participation, and solidarity. These values require implementation in a democratic process and constitutional framework, not only in political but also in ecclesial contexts.

---

[26]   Cf. Friederike Nüssel, "Ökumene der Werte. Der ökumenische und kirchenrechtliche Beitrag der Kirchen zum Zusammenwachsen Europas," in *Christentum und Europa. XVI. Europäischer Kongress für Theologie (10.-13. September 2017 in Wien)*, ed. Michael Meyer-Blanck (Leipzig: Evangelische Verlagsanstalt, 2019), 509–30.

[27]   Charta Oecumenica, chapter 2, nr. 2.

The Role of Christian Spiritual Heritage in Value Discourse

Admittedly, neither global ecumenism nor European ecumenism has achieved the visibility and formative power in the public sphere that one might wish to see in order to develop new enthusiasm about ecumenism. Nevertheless, the two examples from the WCC and the CEC demonstrate how ecumenical institutions employ and incorporate social moral values into their ecumenical agenda. The agendas of the WCC and the CEC differ because of their different contexts and concerns. The WCC speaks of values of the Gospel to assemble churches on ethical issues in line with the ecumenical movement and to reinforce ecclesial fellowship and cohesion. The CEC, through the CO, speaks of basic values to engage churches in the European project and to enable them to jointly and visibly contribute to developing a European identity over and against growing secularization and continued marginalization of churches. While both approaches take values as a given entity of societal communication on questions of moral orientation, they neither define "values" nor give an explanation as to why it is theologically possible, legitimate, or fruitful to engage in value discourse. In the final paragraphs, I would like to add some reflections on this question in order to strengthen the argument in CO about the role of Christian spiritual heritage for societal cohesion in Europe and beyond.

For a general concept of moral values, I draw on a definition elaborated in discussions of social and political scientists. According to this definition, values are "conceptions of the desirable" [28] that engage moral consideration and serve as action patterns. Thus, when people use values as a resource, they want to share a vision or conception of what is desirable. However, the desirability of values such as human dignity, justice and peace, freedom and tolerance, participation and solidarity, are not articulated through these conceptions as such. Instead, the desirability of values is imbedded in a hermeneutic horizon shaped by certain traditions and experiences. Even though in modern value discourses the religious origins of values are ignored or deliberately dismissed for the sake of convergence and agreement beyond religious affiliations, the Jewish and Christian traditions are part of the hermeneutic horizon in which certain goals, principles, and attitudes are addressed as values.

To be more concrete, I would like to suggest that the Christian tradition, or the Christian spiritual heritage, supports basic values in modern societies (as mentioned in CO) in three ways: through its eschatological vision, through its narrative character, and through ecclesial life and ecumenical fellowship.

---

[28]   Jan W. Van Deth, "The Concept of Values," in *The Impact of Values*, ed. Jan W. Van Deth and Elinor Scarbrough (Oxford: Oxford University Press, 1998).

First, the Christian faith is directed to the future kingdom of God, in which justice and peace will be realized. This forward-looking aspect includes the vision of individual wholeness and freedom in a reconciled humanity and offers an eschatological framework for discerning what might be desirable for human flourishing and how to interpret basic values such as justice and peace, freedom and tolerance, participation and solidarity.

Second, several disciplines (for example, literary narratology, cognitive psychology, narrative ethics, and philosophical accounts of narrative identity) have discovered narrativity to be essential for the formation of perception and emotion and, in turn, for conceptions of the desirable (values) and their reception. Values are abstract concepts and do not resonate without a narrative. The Christian tradition shapes empathic perceptions and stimulates the desire of peace and justice in loving relationship, mutual respect, and responsibility since the tradition is based on a core narrative of divine salvation and reconciliation through Jesus Christ in the power of the Holy Spirit (cf. 2 Cor. 5:19) and proclaimed in a large variety of narratives.

Lastly, the history of Christianity is ambivalent. Serious discipleship exercised in proclamation through word and deed and charity work is counteracted by abuse of power, inquisition, exclusions, and divisions. In the ecumenical movement, churches have entered a process to overcome divisions and to work for visible unity. While this process is difficult, the approaches of the WCC and the CEC are two examples of ecumenical formation in light of the major contemporary challenges for churches and societies. They contribute to value discourse in three ways: (1) They point to the blind spot in secular value discourse as far as it dismisses the role of religion and religious narrative. (2) In the growing market of values, the two contributions emphasize and promote those values that really matter for societal cohesion and character formation. And (3) in prioritizing certain basic values such as freedom, solidarity, and participation over others, they offer models of how to moderate value conflict through adopting certain values as second-order values that help to preserve cohesion of groups, communities, and societies.

The Fallacy of "Individual Autonomy," and Moral Value in the Community of Christ

Peter Carnley

It is a truism that the modern pluralistic societies of the Western world are heavily committed to the fundamental ideal of individual autonomy. In the first instance, this ideal entails the freedom of the individual to decide for himself or herself in all matters relating to religious persuasion and personal morality, provided he or she does not encroach upon the freedom of others to do likewise. The same individualism also undergirds the political philosophy of all modern Western liberal democratic societies in which the church usually exists in separation from the state,[1] and the role of the state is to protect individual rights and freedoms by the rule of law. And this is not to mention the competitive individualism that is so important a feature of contemporary economic life, such as we saw pushed to extremes by Margaret Thatcher and Ronald Reagan.

The philosophical roots of this ideal of individual autonomy may be traced back to the thinking of such historically important figures as Immanuel Kant, in Germany, at the time of the European Enlightenment[2] and, somewhat later, very notably to John Stuart Mill, in England.[3] However, it is an ideal that today is most

---

[1]   There are some notable exceptions, such as Great Britain, where, nevertheless, individuals are not *obliged* to subscribe to the established religion.

[2]   Though it is pertinent to note that the Enlightenment contribution of Immanuel Kant has in fact become distorted by being transposed into a belief in the supremacy of the will of the individual in independence of the objectively shared moral order of the wider community. He famously said, for example, that suicide was always wrong; it was not just there for the taking or otherwise as a matter of individual autonomous decision. Unfortunately, subsequent history has taken a far more aggressively individualistic turn than Kant himself may have envisaged (cf. Immanuel Kant, *Critique of Practical Reason*, trans. and ed. Mary Gregor, introduction by Andrews Reath [Cambridge: Cambridge University Press, 1997]).

[3]   John Stuart Mill famously declared: "The only purpose for which power can rightly be exercised over any member of a civilized community, against his will, is to prevent harm to others. . . . Over himself, over his own body and mind, the individual is sovereign." John

often actually upheld and communicated, not so much through treatises and text-books as through its much more graphic representations in literature and the glossy print media, which these days are so effectively reenforced by constant replaying through the electronic forces that saturate our lives. As a consequence, this ideal of individual autonomy is not just a purely theoretical item floating free-ly in the miasma of abstract thought; rather, it is constantly drilled into our cor-porate subconscious.

The North American sociologist Robert Bellah has noted that we are bombard-ed in movies and via television with "mythic images" that express this kind of individualism.[4] Bellah points out, for example, that the paradigm of the individual hero in our culture, right through the second half of the twentieth century, was almost certainly the cowboy. In a cowboy movie, the stereotypical hero rides into a community and often does a good work on behalf of the community (for he is not selfish), but he never finds his own destiny within the community. Rather, he finds his destiny essentially as an individual—as in the case of the Lone Ranger, who rides off into the sunset, or goes off with his Indian companion, leaving the community the better off for his ridding it of crooks or cattle rustlers or whatever, but also leaving the local schoolteacher, standing behind her picket fence, looking wistfully after him as he goes. His human destiny is worked out as an individual, rather than as a belonging member of a community with others.

The more modern equivalent of the cowboy is the detective, often a male. We rarely see him in settled domestic arrangements or participating in normal com-munity life either. Sometimes he has a female colleague, but it is never quite clear if they are partners in a sexual sense; and whether they will marry and settle down is an entirely unanswered question. Indeed, in many cases their lives in relationship with others are problematic—think of Sweden's Kurt Wallander, or Agatha Christie's Hercule Poirot, or the young Endeavour Morse in Oxford, who systematically misses his chances for love. The same applies if the detective is a woman: Vera, in the British series that bears her name, and Miss Fisher, of the Australian murder mysteries, are paradigms. Their personal relationships are ambiguous; they work out their destiny essentially as separate individuals.

By contrast, the wider society in which the detective works tends to be por-trayed negatively. It is corrupt to the core. And that is why the detective cannot really belong to the community any more than the cowboy of the previous gen-eration. Moreover, these images of mythic individualism are reinforced daily in real-life news reports on television and in the press. One heroically survives in

---

Stuart Mill, *On Liberty and Other Essays*, ed. John Gray (Oxford: Oxford University Press, 1991), 14.

[4]   Cf. Robert Bellah, *Habits of the Heart: Individualism and Commitment in American Life* (New York: Harper and Row, 1985).

such a society essentially as an individual. Human destiny is rarely, if ever, presented as finding fulfillment within it.

The kind of individualism of modern Western liberal democratic societies to which I wish to draw attention inevitably finds expression in the moral pluralism of our age. Generally speaking, in such societies individuals are free to behave in ways they themselves choose, provided they do not encroach on the freedom of others to do likewise: "you do your thing and I will do mine." As John Stuart Mill put it: "The only freedom which deserves the name, is that of pursuing our own good in our own way, so long as we do not attempt to deprive others of theirs or impede their efforts to obtain it." [5] However, if the good is what one person happens freely to regard as good, while acknowledging that what another is free to regard as good may differ, then, inevitably, the concept of moral truth goes out the window, even before we start. Unfortunately, in this event, an insidious emotivism takes over, which holds that ethical statements "are neither true nor false but express emotions, desires or attitudes,"[6] with the result that society is condemned to get by on the basis of a kind of uneasy truce held together by appeal to the tolerance of an inevitable moral diversity. Understandably, in the wake of Kant and Mill, a kind of individualized voluntarism has come to prevail.[7]

The pity is that societies in which individual autonomy is so highly valued are, as a consequence, not very skilled when it comes to public moral discussion and debate. Instead, in such societies, resort to slogans and placards and street marches becomes a standard way of promoting a moral commitment.[8] Indeed, there is even a beguiling tendency to believe that appeal may legitimately be made to individual autonomy itself in order to resolve moral issues.

By way of concrete example, this may be illustrated from the current international debate about the possible legalization of assisted suicide,[9] specifically for those hospital patients in a terminal condition who face the prospect of an unwel-

---

5   Mill, *On Liberty*, 17.
6   "Emotivism is a theory of ethics in which, to affirm, for instance, that an action is morally right is to show a favourable attitude towards the action." Thomas Mautner, *Dictionary of Philosophy*, entry under "Emotivism" (London: Penguin, 1996).
7   Even if in Kant's case, at least, he may in fact originally have worked within a received moral framework.
8   As perceptibly observed by Alasdair MacIntyre in his enormously important book *After Virtue* (Notre Dame, IN: University of Notre Dame Press, 1981; 2nd ed., 1984).
9   Which proponents tend euphemistically to speak of as "voluntary assisted dying" (VAD). There is an obvious anomaly here: it is palliative care which is rightly described as assisted dying (by making dying as tranquil and pain-free as possible), whereas acting on the explicit intention to terminate life is, strictly speaking, assisted suicide. Clearly, we should be speaking with more honesty and candor about the legalization of assisted suicide.

come period of protracted suffering and perhaps intractable pain.[10] Those who support the legalization of assisted suicide tend to make a great deal out of the importance of the exercise of individual autonomy when life is judged to be "no longer worth living." This is the case, even in the face of the fact that professional medical associations[11] regularly do not support its legalization but prefer the current practice of palliative care of the kind now widely accessible across most Western liberal democratic societies. The current approach to palliative care of the dying involves reliance on the greatly improved advances in pain control of modern medicine, including the use of palliative sedation in cases of intractable pain.[12] In this way, medical professionals are able to sustain their historic commitment to the Hippocratic Oath by pledging to alleviate suffering and to save life rather than to terminate it. Despite this, supporters of assisted suicide regularly insist that doctors do not necessarily know best, and that it is a human right to exercise individual autonomy. In this way, appeal is made to the ideal of individual autonomy not just in matters relating to the living of life well but also in end-of-life situations, by freely exercising individual choice of the place and time of a patient's own death.

In Western Australia, a Joint Select Committee of the State Parliament that was appointed to look into this issue delivered its report in 2018. The report was titled *My Life, My Choice.*[13] In a sense, the title says it all: this report relies heavily on a fundamental commitment to the ideal of individual autonomy. The committee chair, in her foreword, makes this abundantly clear: the basic ideal of individ-

---

[10]   A challenging precedent for this development across Western liberal democratic societies generally has already been set in Europe (in the Netherlands, Belgium, and Luxembourg) and in the United States (in the states of Oregon and Washington), and in Australia (in the state of Victoria). In New Zealand and the state of Western Australia, governments are currently committed to considering legislation regarding assisted suicide.

[11]   For example, the BMA in Britain or the AMA in Australia.

[12]   The current medical practice of palliative sedation to deal with otherwise intractable pain in end-of-life situations is backed by the ethical principle of double effect (with its origin in Thomas Aquinas), which acknowledges that the administration of pain-killing drugs with the intention of alleviating pain can itself, as a secondary effect, hasten death. However, in this case there is no intention to terminate life. The distinction between *knowledge* and *intention* is important in this debate: the *knowledge* that a person in palliative care is going to die is what prevents medical practitioners from "officiously keeping a patient alive" by force feeding; this is entirely different from the *intention* to terminate life by actively assisting an individual's suicide.

[13]   Cf. Joint Select Committee of the State Parliament of Western Australia, Report: "My Life, My Choice" (Perth, 2018), https://www.parliament.wa.gov.au/Parliament/commit.nsf/ (Report+Lookup+by+Com+ID)/71C9AFECD0FAEE6E482582F200037B37/$file/Joint% 20Select%20Committe%20on%20the%20End%20of%20Life%20Choices%20-%20Report% 20for%20Website.pdf.

ual autonomy is said to ground the alleged right of an individual to determine his or her own time and manner of death. The chair argues that this is simply an extension of a "competent individual's absolute right" to refuse food, water, or medical treatment. These "absolute rights" are then taken to define a principle: "This principle means that competent patients are free to make their own medical treatment decisions." In end-of-life situations, this principle of absolute individual autonomy is then said to warrant the right of an individual to legalized assistance in terminating his or her own life.[14] On the assumption of the validity of this alleged basic right, the report concludes: "Individuals exercise independence and autonomy in their daily lives and want to be able to make autonomous choices when they are dying. One of those choices should be to manage the place and time of their own death, through voluntary assisted dying."

Now, though the principle of individual autonomy is often called on in this way to give some kind of ethical respectability to voluntary assisted dying, with its appeal to individual rights and freedoms, this principle is in fact irrelevant to this question. If anything, it actually has a noxious effect, insofar as it operates to camouflage and confuse the discussion of this important issue. In other words, appeal to individual autonomy is an ethical red herring.[15]

Despite being presented as a legitimate ethical argument, talk of the exercise of individual autonomy immediately becomes problematic when it is considered in other contexts: who would agree with the contention, for example, that we could justifiably act upon a request for assistance in injecting a person with heroin on the ground that he or she wished to exercise his or her individual autonomy? Freely deciding to become an addict hardly constitutes a compelling ethical argument. In this circumstance, we would surely be ethically right in refusing assistance.[16] Clearly, appeal to the exercise of individual autonomy is hardly sufficient reason to convince us of the rightness of offering assistance.

Similarly, the alleged right to assisted suicide actually has nothing to do with its alleged voluntariness. Despite the protestations of the Select Parliamentary Committee in Western Australia, it is clear from the case studies of the report itself that the real reason for supporting assisted suicide has to do *not* with an alleged principle of individual autonomy but with the alleviation of anticipated protracted pain and suffering. Assisted suicide is resorted to in preference to palliative care in circumstances where a patient anticipates experiencing diminished quality of life to the point where it is judged (by the patient himself or her-

---

14   In terms of the report's ethical argument, this alleged principle of absolute individual autonomy is sheeted back to Immanuel Kant and John Stuart Mill.

15   This is forcefully spelled out by David S. Oderberg, *Applied Ethics* (Oxford: Blackwell, 2000), chapter 2.

16   Even trial "safe injecting rooms" are designed to save life—in the hope of giving people time and opportunity to shake free of addiction and to live.

self and by others who, by legislation, must give assent) that his or her life is no longer worth living. In other words, this is actually a quality-of-life argument which is quite independent of talk of the exercise of individual autonomy.

The seriousness of this is that this very same quality-of-life reasoning may also be said to warrant involuntary or nonvoluntary assisted dying.[17] In other words, the judgment that life is no longer worth living could also be applied to babies born with spina bifida, perhaps to Down syndrome babies, in some places to baby girls (for example, not just in ancient Sparta but in modern China), to mentally retarded people, to the senile and the demented, the severely incapacitated, and those who are unable to enact the full range of behavior typical of healthy human beings, and on and on. Clearly, if a quality-of-life argument is brought to the justification of voluntary assisted dying or (to call a spade a spade) assisted suicide, it can also apply to nonvoluntary and even involuntary assisted dying.

I do not wish to be drawn into the scare tactics of slippery-slope arguments, but it is nevertheless very sobering to note some actual historical instances of this kind of extension of the quality-of-life argument by notorious twentieth-century political regimes, even to the point of including the unproductive and socially unwanted.[18] For the present, it is sufficient to note that talk of individual autonomy has a propensity to mask the real issues in this particular debate.

Apart from the illegitimate use of the alleged principle of individual autonomy to give an aura of apparent respectability to what is in fact a very spurious argument, this same principle tends also to shut down any concern even to consider, let alone to uphold and protect, communitarian values. In this same debate relating to the legalization of assisted suicide, the concentration on individual autonomy operates, for example, to inhibit any real consideration of the possible impact that the legalization of this practice could have over time on community attitudes to life and death generally. Not least, a lack of focus on wider communitarian concerns fails to take account of the influence that assisted suicide in end-of-life situations might unwittingly have on people contemplating suicide more generally in the community.[19]

---

[17]   "Involuntary" when it is contrary to a patient's conscious wishes; "nonvoluntary" when a patient is incapable of expressing any wish—e.g., a baby or a comatose patient.

[18]   In this regard, it is of some contemporary concern that the report of the Remmelink Committee that reviewed euthanasia in the Netherlands (between 1990 and 2005), noted that, when asked in 1990 and again in 1995, 50 percent of medical practitioners in the Netherlands said that they had gone ahead, or that they would be prepared to go ahead, with assisted dying even without a patient's explicit request.

[19]   There are reports of increased numbers of suicides both in the Netherlands and in the state of Oregon since the legalizing of assisted suicide. Noting these anecdotal reports, the Western Australian report then tends to pass over this issue: the Oregon reports are

Furthermore, it also deflects attention from the possibility that patients in end-of-life situations could be exposed to subtle psychological pressures once they are faced with the legalized possibility of assisted suicide. Patients may even be made (if ever so subtly) to feel that they are somehow obliged "to do the right thing" in order to please and help relatives, by releasing them from the burden of care. Indeed, there is the obvious danger of a patient's being actually manipulated into a course of action by relatives who might well be prone to act more out of their own self-interest than that of the patient.[20] It is instructive that none of these points relating to the possible negative impact on wider communitarian concerns even rates consideration in the report *My Life, My Choice* of the Western Australian Select Committee looking into voluntary assisted dying. Instead, the report is wholly absorbed with the alleged rights and freedoms of the autonomous individual.

Similarly, the almost exclusive reliance on the notion of absolute individual autonomy also means that nothing tends to be said about the impact over time on the community's shared perceptions of the medical profession and on the basic trust that the community normally places in medical practitioners—the trust in medical doctors *always* to try to save life and eliminate human suffering. Given this very serious communitarian concern, it is understandable that professional associations of medical practitioners are regularly very vocal in their opposition to assisted suicide. Their Hippocratic commitment to saving life rather than to terminating it, and to the rejection of death as an acceptable means of alleviating pain and suffering, is immediately put in jeopardy.

In addition, it seems a matter of simple logic that the legalized provision of the option of assisted suicide could immediately lessen the need for the universal provision of palliative care services. Assisted suicide would in fact be a cheaper option. In a similar way, once assisted suicide is embraced, it seems to follow that there would no longer really be a need to be too concerned about finding more refined and effective pain-killing drugs for use in end-of-life treatments and palliative care. Clearly, once we become hostage to the argument from individual autonomy, a whole range of communitarian considerations simply tends to slip from view as of no importance.

Now, this virtual lack of community concern which is so apparent in the context of discussions about the possibility of legalizing assisted suicide should alert us to a much more general ethical problem in modern Western liberal democratic societies. The overconcentration in such societies on the ideal of individual au-

---

said to be "disputed," and (somewhat irrelevantly) it is said that in Switzerland suicide rates have been falling. No further analysis or discussion of this issue is pursued.

[20]   Persistent anecdotal reports of elder abuse, including complaints about mistreatment at the hands of sons and daughters at rates exponentially higher than those reported in nursing homes, only increase our concern in relation to this possibility.

tonomy has a further noxious effect on community life, insofar as it leads to a corresponding lack of interest in teaching and promoting such other-regarding values as are commonly defined by the human virtues for living life well in community with others. Sadly, therefore, the alleged principle of individual autonomy, with its attendant ethic of individual rights and freedoms, thereby automatically leaves a huge deficit in terms of the formation and development of moral character.

Traditionally, the law of the secular state is understood to secure the minimal standard of behavior necessary for a society to hold together; the rule of law is designed to protect individual rights and freedoms and to secure a degree of peaceful coexistence, given the resulting moral pluralism of diverse and often logically competing individual viewpoints among its citizens. Understandably, the chief concern of secular states naturally comes to focus not on growth in the virtues and the development of moral character, but on securing and protecting the autonomous individual's rights and freedoms. Curiously, the possession (or not) of these democratic rights and freedoms is a very static matter: an individual either has them or does not—hence, the reliance on the operation of law to secure and protect them. But their possession or otherwise is not conducive to personal moral *growth and development* for the living of life well in community with others.

In this context, it is therefore the role of religion to call on human individuals to live by standards of behavior over and above those imposed by law. The state, for example, requires its citizens by law to pay income taxes for the provision of essential services. It is the role of religion to call on people to live by standards of behavior over and above what the law requires. Given the basic need to pay taxes required by the state, religion then exhorts its citizens to be financially generous and practically caring—that is to say, to actually forsake a concern for individual autonomy and to be not just self-regarding and self-concerned, but to pursue other-regarding virtues. Traditionally, it is the role of the church and other moral subcommunities (notably the family as the "domestic church") within the state, to uphold such other-regarding virtues as love of neighbor, respect for those of different races, concern for gender equality, neighborly care and forgiveness, and so on.

These other-regarding virtues, which call on people to live by standards over and above those required by law, are precisely those that invite people to personal moral *growth*, by calling on people to *move* in moral terms from where they happen to be to what they might become: less self-concerned and more caring, less prone to racism and more accepting and respectful of human diversity, not just awkwardly tolerant of difference but positively embracing it as an enrichment to community life, less defensive and self-justifying of their own behavior and more open and forgiving of others, and so on. In Western liberal democratic societies, it has primarily been the responsibility of the Christian church and other moral subcommunities to uphold and teach the virtues expressed in the values of the Gospel and exemplified in the actual life of Christ.

If the truth be known, modern Western liberal democratic societies probably have achieved the success that they have managed to secure to date only because of this largely unacknowledged reliance on religion. However, it is obvious enough that this traditional role of religion in character formation has come under siege in the context of the contemporary espousal of an aggressive secularism. As it transpires, this circumstance is ironically a direct casualty of the separation of church and state. For while such separation was originally designed to give autonomous individuals the freedom to make their own choices in matters of religion (including none), the separation of church and state tends to open itself to the tacit suggestion that the state can get along perfectly well without religion; indeed, sometimes the principle of the separation of the church from the state tends unwittingly to lead to the unfortunate tendency effectively to *exclude the church from the state*, as, for example, when church leaders are told by finger-wagging politicians that they should not be commenting on political matters. Instead, the pastoral care of their flocks is said to be their sole (state-approved) business.

It follows from the diminishing influence of religion in the context of a world of increasing secularization, therefore, that the individual tends to be left deprived of moral tutoring in the virtues. After all, if by appeal to the ideal of individual autonomy a person's destiny is found in separation from the community, what right does anybody have to teach others how to live their individualized lives? We may therefore feel justified in thinking that the weakening role of religion generally, in the increasingly secularized environment of contemporary competitive individualism, does not appear to augur well for the long-term future health of Western pluralistic societies.

Given the fallacy of individual autonomy and its readily apparent noxious influence—not just in relation to the moral debate of specific issues but as a contributing factor to the lack of real community concern characteristic of modern Western society—and given the consequent parlous quality of public moral discussion and debate generally in an emotivist environment, perhaps it is time for the pendulum to swing—back to the teaching of the human virtues and the fundamental importance of the corporate discernment of moral value by reasoned ethical argument in the community of Christ. A first step in this direction is to be aware that appealing to the ideal of individual autonomy is much more of a troublesome problem than might at first appear.

Should Religion Shape Character?

William Schweiker

The purpose of this chapter, like that of other contributions to this volume, is to explore the possible impact of religion on character formation. Many people believe that religion has character-shaping power—believed to be good—so that one must be religious in order to act morally and to have good character. Yet the twenty-first century, and actually every century of human history, is the empirical falsification of that common-sense idea. From religious terrorists to violent conflicts between religions (say, Buddhists against Muslims in Myanmar) and within a religion (think Irish Catholics and Protestants), good character and moral conduct are not obviously religious traits. The question then rightly shifts from a descriptive one of how religions do in fact shape character to a normative question: should religion shape character, and if so, how? That is the question the following pages seek briefly to answer, granting that any comprehensive answer is beyond the scope of this inquiry. Stated baldly, my answer will be yes and no. Yes, religion should shape character, but not as religion's exclusive function. No, religion *alone* should not shape character. My task in this essay is to explain that seemingly paradoxical answer.

A View from Somewhere

Before turning to the question at hand, a few introductory notes are needed to place my reflections within the context of current theological and ethical reflection. What follows is an argument from within theological ethics, and yet, other than noting a concern with matters ethical, this designation does not clarify the perspective in any detail. After all, some theologians interested in ethics deploy dogmatic claims like the theology of the cross, the *imago dei*, or the Trinity in order to help orient Christian life, while others draw on some creed or the life of a particular community, say, the Peace Church tradition, as the perspective from which to address moral questions. Others might appeal to natural law or scripture in order to orient their thought. The question of perspective is important, since any perspective both reveals and conceals something about what is going on. Insofar as we can only act in the world we see, as Iris Murdoch nicely put it, then human conduct and perspective are deeply interrelated.[1]

The perspective adopted in this essay is what I call *theological humanism*. That term means, first, admitting that we can only know in ways fit for our species as historical, social, and language-using beings. Even the Word of God must be understood in terms of our all-too-human ways of knowing marked by fallibility and fault. In distinction from what Thomas Nagel dubbed a "view from nowhere," human knowledge, and especially moral knowledge, is always situated.[2] But to speak of humanism also means that while we always know from "somewhere"—that is, from a particular historical, social, and linguistic context—we are not necessarily limited to that context. Humanists of various stripes have always insisted that nothing human is foreign to oneself. We have shared needs, goods, and experiences, each of which, I argue below, is morally relevant for how character ought to be formed. There is, then, from a humanist perspective, a form of objective judgment in ethics, given that some important features of our natural existence resist complete manipulation by time, place, and language.

Second, the perspective is "theological," an adjective that modifies the kind of humanism adopted. One of the basic premises of my argument is that religion, as a comprehensive interpretation of reality, is, at root, practical. That is, religion is about the interpretation and orientation of human life within the widest extent of relations that provide possibilities for and limitations on conduct, as well as within some symbolic-mythic interpretive framework. Theology is then an interpretation of a religious interpretation of life. Theology seeks to assess the meaning, truth, and goodness of religious interpretations for orienting human conduct. In this respect, theological ethics is a redundant idea, since theology qua theology must itself be practical and aimed at responsibly orienting life. Yet to see human existence within a religious outlook is to insist that what it means to be human is deeper and wider than many secular humanists and nonhumanists grant. It is to note possibilities and limitations too readily missed by philosophical perspectives.

The theological task, accordingly, is to think with classical texts, sources, and thinkers but likewise to think beyond them in order to address the questions, challenges, possibilities, and limits of our age. Theological thinking can and must open new horizons for human and nonhuman life rather than simply reiterating traditional claims, beliefs, and worldviews. On my account, theological ethics seeks, then, to articulate and to analyze the structures of lived reality in order to

---

[1] Iris Murdoch, *The Sovereignty of Good* (London/New York: Routledge, 2001).

[2] Thomas Nagel, *The View from Nowhere* (New York/Oxford: Oxford University Press, 1989).

responsibly orient life with others and before God. It does so by critically and imaginatively engaging religious interpretations of reality.

So defined, theological humanism could be seen as a form of natural theology. While not utterly mistaken, that definition would elide a facet of how I intend to practice this form of thinking. If to be human is always to be situated historically, socially, and linguistically, then it is important to note that the theological humanism at work here is drawn from Christian sources: it is a Christian theological humanism. Insofar as the object of reflection is human life and conduct from a Christian theological perspective, we can call this a type of Christian moral philosophy.[3] By the end of this inquiry, I hope to have at least established the importance of theological humanism for addressing the ways religion should and should not form character. In order to make my case, these reflections move on several planes of reflection: concepts, sources of normativity, character and social processes, and, finally, religion within the bounds of virtue.

Virtue and Basic Concepts

In order to reflect on how character ought to be formed by Christian faith and community, some basic concepts will help to clarify matters. An obvious one would seem to be "virtue," designated as the formation of character. Aristotle,[4] and later Aquinas,[5] thought of virtue as putting reason into the emotions. That is, if one assumes that the distinctive feature of human beings is the capacity to reason, then human excellence, seen practically, must be to guide life reasonably rather than to be motivated by desire and emotions alone.[6] Even Immanuel Kant, in his doctrine of virtue, insisted on duties to self and others that, again, meant orienting life rationally. In fact, ancient ideas about self-sovereignty, Kantian ideas of autonomy, and contemporary ideas of authenticity can be seen as the attempt to conduct life in distinctly human ways and so under the broad conceptual umbrella of "virtue."

---

[3] H. Richard Niebuhr, *The Responsible Self: An Essay in Christian Moral Philosophy* (Louisville, KY: Westminster John Knox Press, 1999).

[4] Aristotle, *Nicomachean Ethics*, ed. Roger Crisp (Cambridge: Cambridge University Press, 2000).

[5] Thomas Aquinas, *Summa Theologica*, trans. Fathers of the *English Dominican Province* (Westminster, MD: Christian Classics, 1981).

[6] It is not possible to discuss in this essay the extent to which other animals reason about their conduct, and given the current state of research, we should be careful not to circumscribe rationality to human beings alone. That said, this essay focuses on the formation of human character.

Clearly, ideas about virtue will always have a key place within ethical reflection, but they are not the whole of ethics. The same can be said of Christian ethics. Whether one speaks of love as the form of the virtues (St. Augustine), or supernatural virtues (Aquinas), or, as current thinkers do, the narrative formation of the virtues, human excellence and goodness have been tied by Christians to claims about God's redeeming and sanctifying work in the world.

When seen in this light, however, it is clear that the idea of virtue actually relies on other concepts for its intelligibility. In fact, virtue is a synthetic concept, insofar as it draws together and interrelates other concepts important in ethical reflection. Several ideas are particularly important, ethically and theologically, in order to analyze virtue as a discourse of character formation. First, insofar as one is interested in putting practical reason into desires and emotions that motivate action, then one is asking how human cares and interests (what is important or of value) provide motivation and are reasons for actions. Virtue discourse relies on a distinction but not a separation between human valuing (what we care about) and human reason. Some thinkers, like David Hume, insist that reason is and ought to be slave to the passions. Moral formation then draws on reason to help explain and invigorate social passions like benevolence. Others, like Kant, argue that reason itself can be practical, that is, a sufficient motive for action. Yet Kant too knew the struggle we experience between our desires and our moral duties. As imperfect creatures, we find that the moral life is about making ourselves worthy of happiness, which is an endless process. Put differently, human beings are mixed creatures often at odds with ourselves; without that insight, virtue discourse makes little sense. Virtue is about attaining some integration and excellence in life, finding some peace in balancing our reasoning, desires, and conduct.

The first observation about reason, desire, conduct, and valuing immediately unearths other ideas supportive of virtue discourse. What are the things that we desire and that move us to act? As Aristotle noted in the *Nicomachean Ethics*, human beings act for ends deemed good. Of course, those ends might not be genuinely good, and here too reason has a role to play in judgments about kinds of goods. Thinkers have therefore long debated the goods or ends of human life; there is no reason to rehearse the history of thought on this point. Suffice it to say that persons act with relation to five types of goods, with subtypes in each, subtypes we cannot explore here. People seek (1) *bodily* goods like health, sexuality, food, and shelter; (2) *social* goods of friendship, family, civic relations, meaningful work; (3) *reflective* goods, that is, goods of meaning and culture; and (4) *local* goods like a place to live, safe social communities, and a sustainable natural environment. Human beings, it appears, seek to integrate in their own ways the various goods of life, and how they do so is figured in their character. These goods and the human needs they signal are then ambiguous motivations for action; they can move a person to virtuous or vicious action. That is, one might pursue a specific value to an excessive extent, without good reason, or to the detriment of oneself or others.[7] Yet needs and goods remain reasons for action, that is, answers to the question, "why did you do that?"

People can also strive to integrate their lives in relation to the (5) *moral* good, that is, integration of one's own life while respecting and enhancing the integrity of others' lives as well. Indeed, we can formulate the imperative of virtuous character like this: respect and enhance the integrity of life in oneself as well as with and for others. Such a life is virtuous because it has put reason into our striving for what we value. It is a *moral* virtue because it includes respecting and enhancing other people's lives as a good in themselves.

What becomes clear, then, when reflecting on virtue discourse as a way to speak about the formation of character, is that, aside from the other concepts noted, virtue is a concept about giving form to something so that it might function excellently. Arising out of the Greek world, the idea of virtue has buried in it a Greek metaphysical framework: anything can be conceived in terms of form and substance. A virtuous shield, as Homer has it, has both a perfect form—that is, the idea used by the artisan to give the shield shape is an excellent one for the work of a shield—and excellent material of which it is made, given form by the idea. Of course, "substance" need not mean material stuff, as in a shield's wood and iron. The two concepts are interrelated: form is what gives shape; substance is what is shaped. So the morally virtuous person is one whose distinctive form—that is, reason—gives shape to the desires, appetites, emotions, and conduct that are the substance of moral virtues.[8] Interestingly, even an antimoralist like Friedrich Nietzsche speaks about the need to give form to life, and the long tradition of thinking about education in terms of *Bildung* (formation) makes the same point.

The idea of forming the substance of a person allows us to clarify the concept of "character" conjointly with virtue. By character is meant the moral and mental qualities that distinguish an individual self. This involves settled dispositions to live, feel, and act in certain ways—thus, the personality of the individual. In fact, virtues just are settled dispositions formed through habitual action. They are a species of habit and thus form the personality or character of the individual self. The fact that the idea of character is also associated with novels and dramas mere-

---

7   For an in-depth explanation, see David E. Klemm and William Schweiker, *Religion and the Human Future: An Essay on Theological Humanism* (Oxford: Blackwell, 2008).

8   One should recall that thinkers like Aristotle, Maimonides, Aquinas, and other classical virtue theorists distinguish between moral and intellectual virtues. Here I am discussing moral virtues: those that shape character and conduct rather than the virtues of the intellect. Of course, the two are related through practical wisdom, and, in any case, these distinctions are clumsy in thinking about human action, as is the metaphysical framework of form and substance. I deploy the concepts of moral and intellectual virtues here in connection with other concepts in order to provide what is hopefully a more robust and supple account of character formation.

ly indicates how a person's character manifests and shapes itself in conduct, often with respect to the roles we play in society and institutions as well as in the stories or narratives we adopt and tell about ourselves. In fact, one can speak about character in terms of narrative identity, which addresses certain questions about the coherence of the self through time.[9]

Granting the arcane metaphysical framework of form and substance, it nevertheless signals a profound insight about the formation of character. Who or what should rightly form our character? And if one understands that giving form to one's life is a kind of sovereignty or rulership, then the question is about who or what ought rightly to rule one's life.[10] Stated otherwise, the next concept one must explore in connection to virtue is that of normativity, its kinds and sources. Clarity on this point advances not only the conceptual task of this essay but also its overall argument, the yes and no. What do I mean?

Sources of Normativity

Historically, there have been four major sources and related kinds of normativity –that is, authoritative standards for how one's character "ought" to be formed. The first two of these are theological and anthropological. Within the Christian context, it is God's will and way manifested in Christ and present in the Spirit that should be the standard of virtue. Indeed, Christian ideas about sanctification indicate the working of God in the formation of people's character. Not every religion looks to God or gods as models of virtuous action (one thinks of the Greek gods, for instance), but the monotheistic traditions do so, and thus Christians speak of the *imitatio deo* or *imitatio Christi*. Aside from theological norms of virtuous character, thinkers have also sought to discern the norm for virtuous character in terms of the right functioning with respect to basic needs and goods. This anthropological perspective, found in Aquinas no less than in Aristotle, means that through an analysis of human capacities and needs, we can discern the perfection of our powers as the norm of virtue.

In addition to theological and anthropological perspectives on standards for forming virtuous character, there are also social and individual ones that can be briefly noted. Social ideals have long served as a source of normativity. From conceptions of heroes to Aristotle's claims about the "great man" of the polis, standards of virtuous behavior and character have often been exemplary moral persons. These persons embodied in their lives and conduct the authoritative standards of their communities and, as such, are not themselves the source of

---

9   On this see Paul Ricoeur, *Oneself as Another* (Chicago: University of Chicago Press, 1992).

10   Cf. Isaiah Berlin, *Two Concepts of Liberty: An Inaugural Lecture Delivered Before the University of Oxford On 31 October 1958* (Oxford: Clarendon Press, 1958).

normativity but, rather, exemplify the social source. In our time, these exemplary figures include the "shared saints" like M.L. King Jr., Gandhi, Dorothy Day, Harriet Tubman, Nelson Mandela, and others.

Finally, one can note individual sources of normativity, by which I mean the idea that the self can and ought to be sovereign over itself through either reason or will. Ancient Stoics, seeking to live according to nature, nevertheless sought self-sufficiency. Immanuel Kant argued that reason can legislate the norms for a person's conduct and, in doing so, make the individual autonomous, a law unto oneself. Friedrich Nietzsche asserted that one strengthens the will-to-power by giving form to one's own distinctive life. For him, one is to be the artist of one's own life with respect to values that affirm the worth of finite being. Current ideas about identity and personal authenticity continue this line of moral thought.

Thus far I have sought to unpack some of the concepts that help to explain the idea of virtue as a discourse for speaking about the formation of character. What has become clear, I believe, is at least twofold. First, the discourse relies on the metaphysical framework of form/substance that might need revision in our contemporary context, where substance is understood primarily in terms of matter. Second, we have isolated the normative challenge of thinking about whether or not religion should form character. Depending on how a religion is interpreted, it could elide or endorse other sources of normativity, that is, the social, individual, and anthropological kinds of normative standards for character. I want now to address these issues by turning to how contemporary social processes challenge or at least demand a revision of the form/substance framework of thought.

Character and Social Processes

Having unpacked the concept of virtue, we can say that in its traditional metaphysical form it denotes the reflexive relation between the human form and human substance, where "form" denotes rationality, and "substance" designates our various desires, appetites, and capacities. The relation is reflexive in that reason is put into the desires through conscious habituation, and those desires are then formed in such a way as to enable the person to act rightly: virtue denotes the interaction between form and substance. Since that is the case, we ought to be able to think about virtue within the interactions among the *rationalities* that give form and orientation to the social processes. That is to say, insofar as form and substance are formal and interrelated concepts, we can capture the insight of virtue theory about the formation of character without remaining in its metaphysical framework. The advantage of this point is that current human life is not formed—and deformed—in terms of one form of rationality alone, or even one primary political and social community, but through the interaction of diverse institutions, as we can call them, within social systems.

For the purposes of this inquiry, it is not necessary to review the ongoing debate about how to conceive, interpret, and even change social systems. Theologians like David Tracy, Max Stackhouse, Michael Welker, and myself, as well as social theorists such as Niklas Luhmann, Max Weber, Jürgen Habermas, and many others have noted, in various ways, that contemporary societies are not hierarchically ordered. Rather, they are structured through the interaction of various subinstitutions, each with its own norms, values, and codes of communication—that is, their own rationalities. Growing out of the estates designated by the Reformers (family, church, state), these subinstitutions range from media and law to economies and educational systems, with values as diverse as profitability and knowledge creation.[11] Human life nowadays is confronted with this bewildering complexity, the speed of which depends on different institutions. For example, the speed of media is different than that of the law, even as each also seeks to form life, say, through images on social media or police enforcement of the law. This makes the integration of personal and social life a mighty task, the more so because these institutions interact and adapt to each other even where there is no "master discourse," or "master narrative" orchestrating the reflexive interrelations that constitute a society. In this situation, it is hardly surprising that one finds attempts around the world to reduce complexity politically (populism and nationalism), economically (antiglobalization), religiously (fundamentalism), and even racially and ethnically (racism). Along with their conditions and outcomes, these developments must be seen as processes of character formation, even if those processes can lead to profound social conflict.

As noted above, virtue as a discourse about character formation relies on some conception of value or what is cared about. In differentiated societies there is no one master value, and even claims about the "Divine Good" as a comprehensive teleology for human life runs aground within the hurly-burly of contemporary social life.[12] Nevertheless, there do seem to be a few master values driving these societal dynamics that threaten the integrity of persons' and communities' lives insofar as they are fundamentally at odds: *speed* (already noted); *novelty* in terms of how a subinstitution seeks to adapt to its social environment and remains vital; and a drive to *hegemony* of one subinstitution (say, politics or economics) over others, such that its value and discourse are inscribed within those institutions. In this situation, a balance of power among institutions is also needed—

---

[11]   For a discussion to the historical background of contemporary differentiated societies in Reformation thought, see the essays by John Witte in this volume and the volume on law in this series. Of course, as readers know, this entire series of books is dedicated to this outlook on contemporary societies.

[12]   For an attempt to define such a position see Franklin I. Gamwell, *The Divine Good: Modern Moral Theory and the Necessity of God* (Dallas, TX: Southern Methodist University Press, 1996).

for example, strengthening education in order to combat the reduction of knowledge to price—as is a way to speak about the formation of character in order to live in such complex societies.

It is at this point that the ambiguity of my answer to the orienting question of these reflections can make some sense. Insofar as what endangers contemporary societies is the possible hegemony of any one social institution over every other, then the same must be said of religion. As seen too often in world history, theocratic societies and the attempt to form character within them by strict adherence to religious doctrine and practice demeans and destroys social flourishing and individual well-being. The same can be said for any hegemonic or totalitarian system. Because of this dangerous possibility, religion should form character in order to resist a tyranny of other social institutions, but it cannot do this alone because of its own impulses towards totality. Religious rationality alone cannot and ought not to form the "substance" of complex societies and the people whose lives are the moving force of those societies. To do so risks what Amartya Sen as helpfully called "the illusion of destiny," as if one religious, ethnic, racial, political, or other singular identity should alone form and motivate conduct.[13] The upshot of that illusion, other than being counterfactual, is ongoing conflict among groups sworn to live out their "identities." So, yes, religion should form character, but it should not do so alone. What does this mean in practice?

Religion within the Bounds of Virtue

Aside from isolating the various concepts drawn together by virtue discourse, we have also seen the deep connection between character formation and social life. Traditional virtue theories spoke about the *polis* in the Greek world, in philosophical schools like the Stoics, in the Roman Empire, and of course in the church. The same correlation of character and social world can be found in the virtue discourse of other traditions as well. A final point thus needs to be made in order to round out the "yes and no" answer I have been proposing to the orienting question of this essay.

In much ancient thought in the West and elsewhere, the claim was that there is and ought to be an isomorphism between the character or soul of the individual and that of the social community. Plato held that justice in the soul—its right ordering—depends on right order in the *polis*, and in each case, reason must rule. Here the idea of justice should form the substance of the soul and the city. St. Augustine argued that peace is the tranquility of order in the soul and also, albeit in different ways, in the earthly and heavenly cities. Love ought to be the ruling val-

---

[13]   Amartya Sen, *Identity and Violence: The Illusion of Destiny* (New York: W.W. Norton & Co., 2006).

ue, even if, in the earthly city, it is a disoriented love, a love of ruling rather than love of God and of others. I have also been fashioning a rough analogy between the multiple needs and goods that must be integrated in the formation of character and the challenge faced by highly differentiated contemporary societies.

However, every analogy entails a difference as well as a similarity between the analogues, and so too with the one I have been presenting. In order to clarify the point, I must pull together strands of the argument made thus far and also must note the different "yes and no" answer as to whether religion should shape character, depending on whether it is seen from the perspective of social institutions or that of the individual person. Making these points will conclude the inquiry.

The difference between character and social systems in this argument is the role which religion can and should rightly play in each one. I have argued that a hegemony of religion within society too easily leads to tyranny and, in doing so, threatens the flourishing of the social order, which requires the reflexive interaction of subinstitutions. Religion must, therefore, be seen as just one among many social institutions within the norm of a balance of powers. Let religious communities be as strong as they might, they cannot, for the sake of the greater good, be allowed to shape the social order alone. Insofar as a flourishing society requires a balance of powers, then yes, religion can and should help to shape the character of the common good. It does so, I contend, by insisting on the irreducible nature of human dignity and the common good to matters of price (economics), power (politics), communication (media), and even knowledge (the academy), because dignity and the common good are irreducible. They testify to a worth not equivalent to the sum total of social good or, the same thing, to general utility.

Individuals, on the other hand, can and must exercise their capacities to integrate their lives in ways that accord with their scheme of values. For some, this will mean the decisive formation of their character through their religious convictions, and freely so. For others, nonreligious values will orient the integration of their lives, relations, and conduct. In this way, on the personal plane of reflection, religion in some cases should shape character. However, the liberty to integrate a certain way of life and a specific character cannot be the warrant to deny that liberty to others. This is, we might say, the balance of power within interpersonal, social life. Freedom of conscience, or some such idea about persons, is inviolable, because, as most religious traditions grant, identity-conferring commitments cannot be coerced and still remain genuine. Apparently virtuous actions, if coerced, are not virtuous at all. In this respect, religion should not necessarily shape character. Call this, religion within the bounds of virtue.

One might designate the position just outlined as a kind of liberal naturalism, in that the good is defined with respect to the needs and goods required for individual and social flourishing. But how those goods are integrated into a person's character or a society is the labor of moral freedom.[14] Without elaborating that idea here, I hope one can see how this position is a theological humanist perspective on character formation. It affirms a religious source of human dignity and the common good, even as it places humanistic constraints on the right of religion and religion alone to shape personal character and social life. How, then, is this a specifically Christian theological humanism? In brief, because it makes its founding insight the reconciliation of life with life as enacted in Christ, and then draws from that source further insight into how religion can and should shape character. But exploring and articulating the meaning of this distinctly Christian claim for the conduct of life must await another inquiry.

---

[14]   Here the work of John Stuart Mill on liberty and Immanuel Kant's reflection on autonomy are important but set within a conception of the good as personal and social flourishing and the idea of the common good.

The Dialectic of Religious Formation

Jennifer A. Herdt

In order to think well about the impact of various social systems on character formation and ethical education in the context of late modern pluralistic societies, and to focus in particular on the impact of religion as one specific social system among others, we must hold fast to an agential stance rather than exchanging it wholesale for the spectatorial standpoint offered up by the social sciences. There are negative lessons to learn here from Max Weber's understanding of the differentiation of social spheres and from Michel Foucault's analyses of normalization and discipline, as well as positive lessons to take from the longstanding Christian doctrine of the orders of creation, with its roots in natural law discourse. Religion can fruitfully be regarded as one among other orders of creation, within which the Spirit is working to realize the divine intention for creation. This is not to sanctify the status quo of any religious institution, but rather to summon us to practical reason's ongoing task of discerning the work and direction of the Spirit. While our engagement with all social systems requires this sort of critical scrutiny of the practices and institutions that form our identities, this is especially so when it comes to religion, insofar as in religion we seek to be oriented to God, not just to the world in relation to God. I recommend, then, a "dialectic of religious formation," a kind of formation that is also an unsettling of formation, insofar as it is directed toward God as final end.

Social Formation and Practical Agency: Exorcising the Ghosts of Weber and Foucault

What is the impact of religion on character formation, ethical education, and the communication of values in late modern pluralistic societies? We might begin with the obvious—that religion seems to have increasingly little impact on character formation, ethical education, and the communication of values in this context. This is not to say that religion has no impact, or to deny that it has a highly significant impact on some. But it no longer offers an unquestioned set of background assumptions that do not even show up as assumptions and are therefore difficult to see, let alone question.[1]

We might of course question the extent to which this was ever really the case. Even remote tribes are aware of the existence of other tribes with other gods. And even Christians at the height of medieval Christendom were aware of Jews and pagans, and thus aware that Christian faith was not beyond question. But certainly, late modernity offers a social context of great religious plurality. Our most broadly shared, least questioned frameworks of meaning are not religious but rather those yielded by technology (even more than science, as the phenomenon of climate-change denial attests) and the market.

Even to begin to contrast the influence of religion with that of technology and the market is to think of late modern pluralistic society as being composed of an array of interwoven yet distinguishable social systems: family, law, politics, the market, religion, the academy, and so on. Today, when we function, as Charles Taylor writes, "within various spheres of activity—economic, political, cultural, educational, professional, recreational—the norms and principles we follow, the deliberations we engage in, generally don't refer us to God or to any religious beliefs; the considerations we act on are internal to the 'rationality' of each sphere."[2] This is a picture haunted by the ghost of Max Weber. Weber identified six social spheres, each governed by its own internal rationality and ultimate values. Among these are the economy, governed by maximization of profit; politics, governed by domination through coercive force; and religion, governed by salvation and the value of care for suffering.[3] To inhabit modernity is to inhabit a time when these social systems have become differentiated from one another. The blessing of modernity is seen all around us in the unleashed power of technical rationality. And the curse of modernity lies in the lack of any unifying value or ordered hierarchy of values.

To this Weberian frame we might bring a lens tinged, on one hand, by Foucault and, on the other, by the tradition of virtue ethics descended from the Greeks and transformed by Christianity. Insofar as Foucault, too, liked to cast his project of self-cultivation in terms of virtue and Greek paideia, the two traditions are con-

---

[1]   Charles Taylor, *A Secular Age* (Cambridge, MA: The Belknap Press of Harvard University Press, 2007), 3.

[2]   Ibid., 2.

[3]   Max Weber, "Religious Rejections of the World and their Directions," in *From Max Weber: Essays in Sociology*, ed. C. Wright Mills (New York: Oxford University Press, 1958). Weber's other three spheres are the aesthetic, the erotic, and intellectualism; see Guy Oakes, "Max Weber on Value Rationality and Value Spheres," *Journal of Classical Sociology* 3/1 (2003): 27–45, at https://pdfs.semanticscholar.org/f3fb/cb5a32c053fca297b7365 ce4292de99f0d23.pdf. See also Peter Berger, *The Sacred Canopy* (New York: Doubleday, 1969).

nected, even if also in creative tension with one another. The early Foucault was preoccupied with technologies of discipline and normalization, through which subjects are socially formed, and he could conceive of no resistance other than unmasking the various shapes of social control that successively present themselves as paths to freedom and enlightenment. Those who worry that social formation threatens freedom, creativity, individuality, or authenticity have no reason to rejoice at the decline of religion in the modern West, since we have not sloughed off social formation but have simply exchanged one sort of formation for another.

We may become distracted here by the temptation to adopt a spectatorial point of view that observes patterns of social formation and seeks to explain patterns of human behavior. Whatever these explanations give us, they do not give us reasons for acting one way rather than another. To employ the spectatorial stance *as agent* is precisely to give up one's agency, to exchange an internal for an external stance vis-à-vis oneself. The agent faces forward in freedom; in the context of deliberation, one's social formation, addictions, bad luck, etc.—the sorts of things that might predict or explain or excuse the behavior of another—become irrelevant.[4]

Having echoed and amplified the terrors of Weber's iron cage, Foucault groped finally for some sort of escape, finding it in a kind of aesthetic self-fashioning that he sought to articulate as, on one hand, irreducibly, idiosyncratically personal and, on the other hand, beautiful, and thus exemplifying a transcendent universal. He reached back to the Greeks to imagine a form of care of the self in which individuals turn themselves into subjects by freely submitting to some rule, form of life, or ascetic training of thought, desire, and action.[5] The coherence of this move, as of much of Foucault's thought, is contested. It is not finally clear that Foucault has at his disposal the conceptual resources necessary for resurrecting the freely self-fashioning subject.

Foucault does at least lead us back to the agential task that Christians inherited from the Greek ethical tradition, at which Weber merely threw up his hands. As Foucault began to realize, formation as such is not the problem, since we need to undergo some sort of formation in order to be fully human; to be human is to be naturally unfinished, to be *potentially*. For regardless of the ways in which our concepts and perceptions and judgments have been socially formed—and formed through our involvement in partially independent social systems—as agents we nonetheless find ourselves having to take responsibility for ourselves and our lives. Of course, formation can be malformation, and we are formed before we are

---

[4]   Oliver O'Donovan, *Finding and Seeking: Ethics as Theology*, Vol. 2 (Grand Rapids, MI: Wm. B. Eerdmans, 2014), 17.

[5]   Cf. Michel Foucault, "The Cultivation of the Self," in idem, *History of Sexuality*, Vol. 4, *Care of the Self* [1984] (London: Penguin, 1990).

able to recognize or assess our formation. This is not, though, the trap that it might appear to be; the critical reflection native to practical agency is always immanent critique, but it can be nonetheless transformative.

Even the late Foucault remained suspicious of the sorts of formation we associate with social systems. He yearned for something that could be uniquely personal; hence the attraction of an aesthetic image of forming oneself as a unique work of art.[6] But the aesthetic cannot so easily displace the ethical; beauty, truth, and goodness resist being detached from one another, and a work of art can be beautiful only insofar as it somehow honors that truth. We need not simply isolated spiritual exercises or skills that operate within limited domains, but virtues, skills that help to make their possessor *good*, because they help to constitute an excellently lived life. Foucault's care of the self, even if it draws from ancient sources, ends up with a striking affinity with liberal individualism. Care of the self is authentic when freely chosen by the individual. And there is something quite right about this yearning for subjective identification with one's character. And yet, what forms us to be capable of free choice, if a mere negative freedom from formation leaves us incapable of being a self and so incapable of owning our choices? One is made free not by not having been formed, but by being able to claim, to affirm, one's having been well-formed and so capable of living, in one's own wholly personal way, a worthy human life.

As agents, we cannot let our final answer be simply that we were tossed to and fro among the social spheres of economy, politics, religion, and so on, formed willy-nilly by whichever gained the upper hand, in a blind power struggle of competing social systems and rationalities. For we are nevertheless confronted with the task of moving forward as agents. And to become conscious of oneself as an agent is to awaken to oneself as a subject of action, responsible, globally, for the "successful or unsuccessful living of a life."[7] Moral reflection takes up the task of living a worthily *human* life.[8] The task of practical agency is precisely that of ordering all of the competing values and forms of rationality thrown up by various social spheres so as to hold together as a single agent, the subject of a life, which can be lived well—or not.

---

6   Ibid.

7   Oliver O'Donovan, *Self, World, and Time: Ethics as Theology*, Vol. 1 (Grand Rapids, MI: Eerdmans, 2013), 33.

8   Oliver O'Donovan, *Entering into Rest, Ethics as Theology*, Vol. 3 (Grand Rapids, MI: Eerdmans, 2017), 86.

Religion among the Orders of Creation

That said, Weber was not wrong to confront us with the differentiation of social spheres in the context of modernity, and he was right that it poses particular challenges for the task of practical agency. Where agricultural techniques and worship and artistic creativity are integrally interwoven in the dance that one performs to ensure the coming of the rains and a fruitful harvest, there is no competition between loyalty to one versus loyalty to the other. Further, the availability of the spectatorial standpoint, and all of the explanatory knowledge it yields, does burden practical agency with new layers of responsibility. Knowing, for instance, the particular sort of cognitive biases to which human beings are subject, from attentional bias to the fundamental attribution error, increases our responsibility to correct for these biases. The task of character formation is not an unchanging one.

If we do well to accept that Weber haunts any discussion of social spheres in modernity, that acknowledgement cedes too much ground if it does not go hand in hand with considering deeper historical debts that Weber himself inherited, notably to the Lutheran doctrine of the three orders of creation: household, state, and church. Today we are likely to be most familiar with this doctrine in the form that it took in the 1930 s by Werner Elert, Paul Althaus, Emil Brunner, and others, who sought to affirm the divinely sanctioned character of these core human social institutions.[9] It was this understanding of the orders of creation that elicited Karl Barth's sharp rebuke. Apart from God's revelation in Christ, Barth insisted, no orders, norms, or institutions had any validity. Barth regarded this radical Christocentrism as necessary in order to prevent human cultural creations from displacing the absolute priority of God's Word:

> at the root of [this] conception of "orders" there lies something akin to the familiar notion of a lex naturae which is immanent in reality and inscribed upon the heart of man, so that it is directly known to him. But does not this mean that there is not only a second (or first) revelation of God before and beside that of the Word of His grace, but also a second (or first) knowledge of God beside that of this Word of grace?[10]

---

[9]   Carl Braaten, "God in Public Life: Rehabilitating the 'Orders of Creation,'" *First Things* (1990): 33. We might think also of the American Christian sociologist Graham Taylor, who in the early years of the twentieth century sought to trace the realization of the kingdom of God within the five spheres of family, neighborhood, economics, politics, and religion. See Gary Dorrien, *Social Ethics in the Making: Interpreting an American Tradition* (Oxford: Wiley-Blackwell, 2011), 45.

[10]   Karl Barth, *Church Dogmatics* III/4 (Edinburgh: T&T Clark, 1961), 20.

In rejecting the orders of creation and, with them, natural law, Barth took himself to be recovering the authentic teaching of the Reformers. In fact, however, the first generation of Reformers simply took for granted an inherited understanding of natural law as God's intention for the ordering of human life, knowable by conscience and the light of nature and restated by way of revelation in the Decalogue.[11] Mapping this understanding of natural law onto the distinction between earthly and heavenly kingdoms, Lutheran and Reformed thinkers entrusted magistrates with plenary lawmaking responsibility.[12] This did not mean, however, that human lawmakers were regarded as free to legislate at whim. Rather, they were tasked with discerning the natural law in all bodies of inherited law, including Roman law and canon law, with reason, conscience, and scripture (particularly the Decalogue), all regarded as critical for this discernment process. Their responsibility was to legislate in harmony with natural law, refraining from imposing biblical laws that applied only to the Hebrew people, and instituting laws that applied natural law to particularities of their own circumstances. So understood, the doctrine of natural law provided a flexible conceptual resource for seeking to bring human laws and social institutions in line with God's will and intention while recognizing the particularities of time and place. In scholastic thought, natural law had served similarly not to preclude the development of human social institutions but to assess them according to God's purposes for creation. So, for instance, private property was judged to be in harmony with natural law, insofar as it served industriousness and security, even as property rights were limited by the needs of the poor.[13] That natural law served as a criterion for assessing human law meant that human lawgivers could be held responsible both by God and by their fellows; the tradition of Reformed resistance theories embodies this recognition.[14]

Luther's understanding of the orders of creation is quite fluid. Building on earlier medieval notions, and even on Aristotle's distinction between economics and politics, Luther speaks variously of three offices, hierarchies, orders, estates, and governments. In his commentary on Genesis 2:14, Luther invokes the "doctrine of the three," arguing that the church was established first, and the government of home and state established only later. He draws this conclusion from

---

[11]   For a survey of natural law in Reformation thought, see Jennifer A. Herdt, "Natural Law in Protestant Christianity," in *The Cambridge Companion to Natural Law Ethics*, ed. Tom Angier (Cambridge: Cambridge University Press, forthcoming).

[12]   Harold J. Berman, *Law and Revolution*, Vol. 1, *The Formation of the Western Legal Tradition* (Cambridge, MA: Harvard University Press, 2003), 4, 97; John Witte, *Law and Protestantism: The Legal Teachings of the Lutheran Reformation* (Cambridge: Cambridge University Press, 2002), 76.

[13]   Jean Porter, *Nature as Reason* (Grand Rapids, MI: Eerdmans, 2005), 21–25.

[14]   Berman, *Law and Revolution*, 85.

God's instruction to Adam in the garden, prior to Eve's creation. "Here," says Luther, "the Lord is preaching to Adam and setting the Word before him," giving Adam "Word, worship, and religion in its barest, purest, and simplest form."[15] The government of home is subsequently established with Eve's arrival and the instruction to marriage, while the state is introduced only after the Fall.

As Oswald Bayer has persuasively argued, Luther's orders of creation cannot thus be construed in a way that would reinforce a simple dualism between the secular (or temporal) on one hand and the spiritual on the other.[16] The church is instituted at creation, undermining the intelligibility of any independent "order of creation" to be neatly contrasted with an "order of grace." The church itself is thus to be regarded both as spiritual and as temporal; as Bayer argues, Luther thereby "makes it possible, and indeed necessary, to consider Christianity as a religion, as an institution and as a temporal phenomenon," albeit never only as this.[17] Luther found the doctrine of the three governments to be a useful tool for biblical exegesis, and cautioned of the importance of determining whether particular texts properly belonged to the government of household, state, or church.[18] Luther did, then, regard God's government of humankind as taking different forms, each with distinctive features. He did not, however, regard any of these as secular in the sense of being a space for autonomous human activity. Human creative activity in building and extending these social institutions was always to be measured in terms of its responsiveness to God's government.

There are four key conclusions to glean here for contemporary reflection on the role of religion among other social systems in late modern pluralistic societies. First, the notion of religion as one among an array of social spheres structuring human activity, each with its distinctive character and norms, is not itself modern or secular but is rather deeply rooted in Christian traditions of natural law reaching back even to antiquity. Second, there is nothing intrinsic to the conception of such social orders that requires that they be conceived of as walled off from one another and hence impermeable to mutual critique. That they are alike grounded in the divine intention for humankind and alike arenas for human responsiveness to God and loving responsibility to neighbor testifies to this. Third, if Weber's mistake was to exaggerate the autonomy of the various social spheres,

---

15   Martin Luther, WA 42, 79, 3-14, English translation of *Commentary on Genesis*, in Helmut Lehman, ed., *Luther's Works*, Vol. 1 (Philadelphia: Fortress Press, 1957), 104, 106.

16   Oswald Bayer, "Nature and Institution: Luther's Doctrine of the Three Orders," *Lutheran Quarterly* 12 (1998): 125-59, at 129. Translation of "Natur und Institution. Eine Besinnung auf Luthers Dreiständelehre," *Zeitschrift für Theologie und Kirche* 81 (1984): 352-82.

17   Ibid., 130.

18   Luther, WA 5, 218, 14-18, English translation in *Table Talk*, in *Luther's Works*, Vol. 54, 446.

essentially resigning the task of practical reason, the error of those Lutheran theologians, such as Elert and Althaus, who used the doctrine of the orders of creation to legitimate the Third Reich was to regard national law as the embodiment of natural law, and gospel as confined to inner intention and outward obedience to that law.[19] Fourth, not only Lutheran theologians who supported the Nazis but also Karl Barth, who offered his staunch "No!" to any gospel of accommodation, missed the core contribution made by Luther's fluid conception of the orders of creation: the way in which they provide, in all their unfolding variety, an arena both for human creativity and for ongoing responsiveness to the divine will and intention for creation.[20]

The Spirit and the Created Moral Order

Two important contemporary critics of natural law discourse, Oliver O'Donovan and Michael Welker, can nevertheless be viewed as furthering this tradition of reflection. Briefly considering how their rejections of natural law affirm the task of practical reason to critically elaborate received social spheres in response to God's intentions for creation will further prepare for a kind of reflection about the formative power of religion that is capable of deepening the insights of the long tradition of Christian thinking about natural law while avoiding its pitfalls.

O'Donovan rejects natural law as a doctrine of a created moral order that is universally epistemologically accessible.[21] This does not, however, mean a denial of created moral order as such. O'Donovan regards Christ's resurrection as God's vindication of the created order, a created order that we cannot properly know apart from the Christ event. In making this claim, O'Donovan is "concerned to overcome the confrontation between advocates of 'creation ethics' and of 'kingdom ethics.'"[22] He bemoans the fact that Barth failed in his critique of natural law to differentiate between ontological affirmation of a created moral order and epistemological affirmation of universal access: "in his pursuit of an uncompromised theological epistemology Barth allowed himself to repudiate certain aspects of the doctrine of creation (such as 'ordinances') which ought never to have fallen under

---

[19]   Hans Tiefel, "The German Lutheran Church and the Rise of National Socialism," *Church History* 41/3 (1972): 326–36, at 331–33.

[20]   Ryan Tafilowski has recently mounted a similar argument, albeit one focused on the challenges of global migration; see "A Reappraisal of the Orders of Creation," *Lutheran Quarterly* 31 (2017): 288–309.

[21]   Oliver O'Donovan, *Resurrection and Moral Order: An Outline for Evangelical Ethics*, 2nd ed. (Grand Rapids, MI: Eerdmans, 1994), 85–86.

[22]   Ibid., xv.

suspicion."[23] O'Donovan thus explicitly sides with Brunner against Barth on the question of created ordinances, without however embracing any created natural ethic independent of the gospel. The Holy Spirit is at work to enable us to participate in this renewed creation, that is, to participate "in the life of the one who reveals himself to us as Love."[24] There is thus an eschatological reference point to the created order, and thus a dynamism within it: "the order of love, the created moral order, does not have eternity in itself, but looks forward to a new creation to fulfill it and make it wholly intelligible."[25]

Michael Welker, like O'Donovan, has insisted on holding natural law discourse at arm's length, arguing that "the deficient systematic tenability of the association between nature, on the one hand, and law that takes its orientation from justice, on the other . . . enduringly deflates any hope that this instrument might take us further in the question of God's justice and righteousness."[26] And it is undoubtably the case that natural law must be rejected where it is invoked either to legitimize an unjust status quo as natural or to suggest that ethical norms may be read off of mere natural regularities or evolutionary processes. Yet Welker's own efforts to trace the formative workings of the Spirit of God in creation within unfolding human social institutions can be viewed as themselves an extension of medieval and Reformation reflection on natural law and the orders of creation, insofar as this reflection was directed toward the critical assessment and creative development of human social institutions in responsive to the divine vocation of humankind. So in the developing Biblical legal tradition, for instance, amid its various strands and layers, Welker discerns not a religious sanctioning of the powerful but rather a developing "sensitivity for the endangerment and fragility of all human life . . . which helps us to appreciate the co-evolution of religious, legal and mercy-moral aspects as we encounter them in the biblical law."[27] It is in reading nature and history with a view to discerning the activity of God's Spirit

---

23   Ibid., 87.

24   Ibid., 101, 246.

25   Ibid., 247.

26   Michael Welker, "God's Justice and Righteousness," in *Responsibility and the Enhancement of Life*, ed. Günther Thomas and Heike Springhart (Leipzig: Evangelische Verlagsanstalt, 2017), 179–90, at 185. See also: "The Human Spirit and the Spirit of God," in *The Spirit in Creation and New Creation: Science and Theology in Western and Orthodox Realms*, ed. Michael Welker (Grand Rapids, MI: Eerdmans, 2012), 134–42, at 134, and the introduction to Michael Welker and Gregor Etzelmüller, eds., *Concepts of Law in the Sciences, Legal Studies, and Theology* (Tübingen: Mohr Siebeck, 2013), 1.

27   Michael Welker, "Justice–Mercy–Worship: The 'Weighty Matters' of the Biblical Law," in Welker and Etzelmüller, *Concepts of Law*, 205–24, at 215.

that we are able, for instance, to discern "a developmental direction towards a 'just and humane law.'"[28]

Confronted by any existing social institution or system, the theological task, then, is always to ask whether and in what respects it can be viewed as part of the created moral order vindicated in the resurrection of Christ, and pointing to the eschatological fulfillment of creation—or whether instead it, or aspects of it, reflect a fallen creation that has departed from God's creative and loving intention. Recourse to the tradition of natural law and the orders of creation are not a way of turning from the gospel and the work of the Spirit, but rather a way of carrying forward a Christian commitment to unfailing critical scrutiny of the social forms in and through which our practical agency is formed.

The Forming that Unforms

We thus return to the task that faces practical agency, that of living worthily human lives, of orienting ourselves as unique nodes of responsible agency amid all of the competing systems of social formation that jostle around and within us. What gives the question of religion and formation a distinctive shape, alongside the question of formation in relation to other social spheres, is that religion is a social sphere that resists understanding itself as a mere social sphere. This surfaces even in Luther's discussion of religion alongside household and state in his commentary on Genesis. For "religion" here is God's instruction to Adam concerning what to eat and what not to eat, so as properly to honor God. It is, then, a divine rather than a human institution. Yet it is also one social institution alongside others, household and state, in some sense on a plane as social forms elaborated in many ways over the course of human history. Here, then, we are confronted by what I call the dialectic of religious formation. Religion is what aspires to integrate, to re-tie, *re-ligare* (to reach for the irresistibly illuminating etymology) all things together: the self with the collective, nature with culture, life with death, love with power, finite goods with goodness itself, creation with God. And insofar as religion aspires to this vision of wholeness, aspires to putting all things in their proper places, it is made precarious if it becomes merely one social sphere alongside others. Its guardians seek to take control of other spheres, or they retreat into sectarian isolation.

Of course, insofar as religion is a matter of human social institutions, of practices and commitments, of rituals and priests and doctrines, of course it is not the whole and cannot integrate the whole. It is a merely human enterprise alongside other merely human enterprises. Religion as a human enterprise forms well, we might say, when it points beyond itself, when it orients human activity to the final

---

[28]   Ibid., 213.

good, in Aristotelian terms, to that which allows all finite goods to assume an appropriate place in relation to one another.

Christian practices seek to worship the God made known in Jesus Christ and to form persons for the worship of God. To worship God is to know and love God, and all things in relation to God. It is to be formed for self-gifting friendship, for fellowship in the divine life. God is the final good toward which worshippers are directed insofar as other goods are each given their appropriate place in the worshipper's life. This end is not an alien imposition, not a constraint on freedom, but an enablement and empowerment of persons to become more fully what they in some not-yet-fulfilled sense are, that is, to become what they were created and called to be. The relation to God thus orders the relation to all other goods, which are therefore grasped as nonfinal. To relate to God as final good is to regard all finite goods, including our own dispositions, character, and actions, from an eschatological perspective. We anticipate how we and all that we are and do will appear in the light of God's fully revealed truth. O'Donovan suggests that "it is, indeed, this prospect of a world completed that allows us to think of our lives as a whole, and ourselves as continuous self-identical agents."[29] We are offered a perspective from which to assess our lives, our projects, both individual and collective. But, of course, we can only *anticipate* this perspective. It is not given to us in its fullness; it is properly God's. And so, while on one hand it allows us to think of our lives as wholes, and to order finite goods in relation to final good, on the other hand it *unsettles* the ways in which we have been formed, calling them into question. Alasdair MacIntyre has argued along similar lines that what we discover in discerning the final good or end (toward which we are directed insofar as other goods are given their proper place) is that a worthily lived life is one in which no particular finite good is treated as the final good necessary for living well. To grasp the finitude of all of the particular goods we encounter, in relation to the final good, is to grasp ourselves as directed beyond these finite goods. "We complete and perfect our lives by allowing them to remain incomplete."[30]

The sort of religious formation to which human beings should aspire, then, is one that remains necessarily incomplete, that unsettles, that questions the practices and institutions that shape us. Religion, so understood, can never simply shore up the status quo or hawk the opiates that stultify the masses. Marx regarded the criticism of religion as the prerequisite of all criticism. But here it is religion that itself funds critique.[31] It does so not simply by asking *cui bono*, whose interests are served by the status quo, necessary as that question is. It does so by ask-

---

[29] O'Donovan, *Entering into Rest*, Vol. 3, 43.

[30] Alasdair MacIntyre, *Ethics in the Conflicts of Modernity. An Essay on Desire, Practical Reasoning, and Narrative* (New York: Cambridge University Press, 2016), 231.

[31] Karl Marx, "A Contribution to the Critique of Hegel's Philosophy of Right" (1844), in *The Marx-Engels Reader*, ed. Robert C. Tucker (New York: W.W. Norton, 1978), 54.

ing always about the final good, the higher law, about that eschatological reality against which existing authorities, institutions, rules, norms are to be held up and assessed and remade. If the interests of some are being unduly privileged, then the interests of others are being given short shrift, and the common good, those social conditions that promote the flourishing of all persons in community with one another, is not being served. This is a critique that drives toward right relations among persons and goods, such that good and good are not set against one another.

Cultivating the Virtues in Late Modernity

The unsettling that flows from an eschatological orientation to God is of course not the whole story. Religious formation is dialectical, both a forming and an unforming. It is a particular sort of formation that sustains this sort of ongoing critique towards ever-higher justice and goodness. There are virtues needed to sustain this dialectic well, and social practices that assist in cultivating these virtues. Not all religious communities and practices, in fact not all Christian communities and practices, form persons in this way, by a sustained commitment to nurturing whatever forms of goodness and right relation have been recognized up to that point while remaining open to the need to revise and reconceive these, to transcend them in the pursuit of something more complete and perfect.[32]

What, then, are the religious practices that serve to sustain this dialectical formation? There is, of course, plenty of direct moral instruction that takes place in the context of religious communities and practices, lists of commandments, of deadly sins, of vices and virtues. These play less of a role in many religious communities today than they did in the past, when numbered lists were a critical memory aid for the nonliterate, as were proverbs and maxims. But in any case, these modes of didactic moral instruction do not on their own form character; to have a virtue is to have reliable dispositions, reasons, and motivations for acting, not just to know a set of instructions or even to have been behaviorally conditioned to adhere to them. One must have come to grasp particular ways of being and acting as good in themselves, as intrinsically worthwhile, not simply as things likely to elicit praise or condemnation, reward or punishment. Key pathways here involve empathy and admiration, with imagination playing a key role in both. Insofar as persons develop in nurturing contexts in which it is natural to grow to love what one's loved ones love, they learn to empathize with those af-

---

[32]   Cf. Jennifer A. Herdt, "The Virtue of the Liturgy," in *The Blackwell Companion to Christian Ethics*, ed. Stanley Hauerwas and Sam Wells, 2nd ed. (Malden, MA: Wiley-Blackwell, 2011); Jennifer a. Herdt, "Truthfulness and Continual Discomfort," in *The Difference Christ Makes*, ed. Charlie Collier (Eugene, OR: Cascade Books, 2015), 25–42.

fected by their own and others' actions and thereby develop resources for moral imagination.[33] And insofar as admiration naturally elicits a desire to emulate, and admiration is directed toward excellences of character, not simply toward inimitable strengths and talents, it, too, is centrally involved in moral development, as persons aspire to imitate not simply exemplars' external actions but also their reasons and motives for acting.[34]

Religious practices, including the reading of scriptures, hold up many exemplars and offer many opportunities for "wishfully picturing oneself" in the image of one's exemplars.[35] By way of this wishful picturing, one develops "as if" reasons for acting, "imaginative considerations" that "serve as narrative premises in light of which only some actions make sense as the continuation of his story."[36] Dialectical elements emerge as a matter of course as these processes unfold. If I rob Peter to pay Paul, imaginative identification with Paul will be pleasant, with Peter painful. I may admire exemplars who orient me in conflicting directions. Having been formed by my admiration of one exemplar, or by my imaginative inhabitation of one narrative, to privilege in-group members, and by another to reach out to out-group members, I shall have to work through these conflicts. Ethical formation is always a matter of identifying and working to resolve tensions of this sort, even if some communities name these dynamics more openly than others.

Most centrally, however, I want to point to the importance for the dialectic of religious formation of worship as such, insofar as worship is an orienting of oneself, together with a community of others, to God and God's purposes for the world. Whether in praise and adoration, in thanksgiving, in hearing the Word, in confession, supplication, being fed as the Body of Christ, or in being sent out into the world, worship decenters participants from their own understandings and projects and orients them to God. Worshippers assume a stance of receptivity; they take a step back from their own immediate daily contexts and activities and are invited to view these in relation to what God is doing in the world. It is worship that preserves religious communities from becoming mere clubs, mere lifestyle or political enclaves—even if this is something that they are always in danger of becoming.

---

[33]   Cf. Jennifer A. Herdt, *Religion and Faction in Hume's Moral Philosophy* (Cambridge: Cambridge University Press, 1997), 143–56.

[34]   Jennifer A. Herdt, "Enacting Integrity," in *Integrity, Honesty, and Truth-Seeking*, ed. Christian B. Miller and Ryan West (New York: Oxford University Press, 2020), 73–90; Linda Zagzebski, *Exemplarist Moral Theory* (Oxford: Oxford University Press, 2017), 33.

[35]   J. David Velleman, "Motivation by Ideal," *Philosophical Explorations* 5.2 (2002): 101. Zagzebski drew my attention to the work of Hallvard Fossheim and David Velleman; see her discussion in *Exemplarist Moral Theory*, 134–39.

[36]   Velleman, "Motivation by Ideal," 101.

Late modern pluralistic societies pose particular challenges and opportunities to inherited ways of cultivating the virtues. Today we are witnessing the pluralization and "fragilization" of religious identities and commitments, as persons in highly mobile, fragmented societies engage in newly individualized ways in the task of *religio*.[37] Not only are we aware of the immense variety of religious practices and beliefs that exist in the world, but more and more of us bump into that variety in the course of our everyday lives, in our local communities and neighborhoods. More and more of us marry persons from very different religious backgrounds, and more and more of us are raised within multiple religious traditions or none. Many have porous or multiple religious identities. Religious authority is contested in ways that science, technology, and the logic of the market are not.

Religion has not been privatized. For instance, some Western European nations retain their religious establishments and rely on them to operate basic social services. Arguably, Germans have come to regard their nation as Christian precisely as the population of Muslims has risen. In the United States, the separation of church and state has hindered the basic religious literacy of citizens. Yet tokens of Christianity are nevertheless pervasive: American presidents routinely invoke God's blessing on America; dollar bills proclaim "In God We Trust"; politicians invoke their faith. Western societies grapple with how sharia or Roman Catholic canon law is to be related to secular law. While religion has by no means retreated into a private sphere, the pluralism of late modern societies leaves a decisive mark in two particularly significant respects. First, religious adherence increasingly becomes a matter of conscious personal choice rather than of unquestioned background assumptions. Because observance is a conscious matter, it is accompanied by a heightened reflective awareness. One could have exited one's childhood religious community; one could have joined this congregation rather than that, adopted these practices rather than those. In some cases, adherence becomes dogmatic, as a community demonizes outsiders and thus shores up the plausibility structures that sustain absolute commitment in its members; fundamentalisms are a response to a perceived threat. In other instances, attachment remains somewhat ironic, detached, or multiperspectival; adherents slip in and out of varied perspectives and vocabularies, adopting different idioms for different contexts and audiences, comfortably fluent in each.

The challenges that this situation poses for the formation of character and the cultivation of the virtues are significant and quite obvious. For the virtues are identified and named as particular exemplars are celebrated, particular narratives of exemplary action are handed down. The moral worlds we inhabit are thick moral worlds, and our perceptions are theory-laden, informed by vocabularies in which these exemplars and narratives are sedimented. To participate, week-in and week-out, in the praise of a God who brings down the mighty and lifts up the

---

[37]   The term "fragilization" is Charles Taylor's coinage. See Taylor, *A Secular Age*, 556.

lowly, whose mercy endures forever, who sends his son to die on a cross, whose followers are told to pick up their cross and follow, decisively shapes moral perception. Christian imaginations are populated by good shepherds and good Samaritans and lambs of God, by wily serpents and reluctant prophets and irresponsible sons. Human beings do not live well on a diet of thin abstractions. Religious life weaves together bodily movement, story, and song, ritual reenactment and legal discourse, backward-facing remembrance and forward-facing imagination. But where this is not the reality in which one lives and moves and has one's being but merely a religious bubble one enters and exits, it offers not a final vocabulary but an occasional vocabulary; one reenters a world in which all goods are fungible commodities, nothing is sacred, and happiness is a mere feeling of subjective satisfaction: the world of the market.

It is a sobering situation. But I want also to suggest that there are positive aspects to this state of affairs, which assist in the task of precisely the sort of dialectical religious formation that I have argued, theologically, is appropriate to the pursuit of the final good in a worthily lived life. For the fluidity and fragilization of religious identities and loyalties is not simply a reality that undermines the formation of virtuous character. It also renders dialogical encounter a normal, everyday reality. And this can help keep us from idolizing finite goods. It can dispose us to question the adequacy of our current grasp on the good, true, and beautiful, the adequacy of our current naming of God. It can help to sustain what I have described as the dialectic of religious formation, that mode of forming that is also an unsettling of the ways in which we have heretofore been formed.

People today yearn to live worthily human lives, as they always have; as easily as we fall into compartmentalized forms of agency, we also find this compartmentalization profoundly unsatisfying. The dialectic of religious formation assists persons toward richer and more integrated forms of practical agency, and so contributes to the common good that sustains the flourishing of each and all, the extending of friendship to the stranger. Secular "nones"—those who prefer "none of the above" religions—draw on inherited religious traditions to the extent that they grasp these traditions as nonidolatrous, that is, as refusing to conflate finite goods with Infinite Good. One of the tasks that falls to religious insiders today is to display their traditions as nonidolatrous, and thus as capable of assisting in the task of ordering finite goods in relation to the final good. It is worship itself, I have argued, that lies at the heart of this undertaking, preserving religious communities from becoming mere lifestyle or political enclaves, refusing to allow religion to become merely one social system alongside others, insisting on viewing them all in relation to God's creative and redeeming intention. Christians will confess this "doing" as "receiving," as a participation in God's drawing all of creation to Godself in Christ.

Part Two
Character Formation in Other Religious Traditions and General Morals

Part Two

Buber vs. Weber

Future Sociological Research According to Buber's Proposal—The I-Thou Relationship in Scholarly Research

Admiel Kosman

I

This chapter seeks to clarify Martin Buber's critique of sociological methodology and to present his alternative method for examining human social life and for scientific methodology as a whole. I begin by setting forth Max Weber's unequivocal position regarding the work of the scientist. Weber thought that this demanded complete objectivity of the researcher, in the humanities as well as in the natural sciences and the social sciences. For him, this meant the complete neutralization of the researcher's spiritual world and values. Weber not only believed this to be possible but also maintained that such neutralization is a *precondition* for the proper development of research. In this spirit, he coined the term *Wertfreiheit*, or freedom from the world of values—freedom that is demanded of anyone devoted to scientific methodology.[1] In contrast, Martin Buber, despite the great esteem in which he held Weber as a researcher in his field,[2] did not accept this view. In various writings, Buber put forth an alternative position, one which we might call today (admittedly with several significant reservations; see below) "postmodern."[3]

---

[1]   See Richard Swedberg and Ola Agevall, *The Max Weber Dictionary: Key Words and Central Concepts* (Stanford, CA: Stanford University Press, 2016), 364–65. *Wertfreiheit* is translated into English as "value-freedom" or "value-neutrality." In this regard, mention should also be made of Weber's famous lecture on the work of the scientist that he delivered to students at the University of Munich in 1917; see Max Weber, "Science as a Vocation," in *The Vocation Lectures*, ed. David Owen and Tracy Strong, trans. Rodney Livingstone (Indianapolis, IN: Hackett, 2004), 1–31.

[2]   See Avraham Shapira, *Between Spirit and Reality. Dual Structures in the Thought of M. M. Buber* (Jerusalem: Mosa Byalik 1994), 146 [Hebrew].

[3]   On the affinity between postmodernism and Buber's stance, see Shmuel Noah Eisenstadt, "Martin Buber in the Postmodern Age," *Society* 34 (1997): 51–55; Eisenstadt explains that, despite this seeming closeness between Buber and postmodernism, there is also

According to Buber, as explained in detail below, although the scientist is to work with the greatest possible degree of objectivity, not only is the total neutralization of personality and world of values impossible (as Buber had already written in 1935: "I know that my interpreting, like everyone else's, is conditioned through my being"),[4] but the absolute striving for this, in the Weberian spirit, is *incorrect.* Buber viewed scientific work as the examination of an object in which, even though the initial intent of the inquiry must be based on an objective approach, to the greatest extent possible, in the course of the examination, it must nevertheless eventually pass through *the researcher's unique personality*–just as a work of art passes through the artist's singular character. Consequently, Buber also found it undesirable that *at the end* of the research, the researcher would strive to expunge the traces of personality left in the research.

To illustrate this, and to explain Buber's approach in this early stage of the essay in the simplest manner, I will summarize the conversation between the Israeli historian Ben-Zion Dinur and Buber in the early 1930 s. The conversation was documented by Dinur himself.[5] Dinur relates that when their conversation came to the use of quotations in the work of the historian, Buber objected to what he viewed as the excessive use by historians of quotations from the sources that they are investigating. He then added that someone (whom Buber described as "an educated person, with good literary taste"), referring to a certain book by Dinur, had told him that Dinur's numerous quotations "are a sort of barrier between the writer and the reader." He also told Dinur in the same conversation:

> Every historian . . . has his own view of the past, and this holistic personal view embodies his ability to cast the past in his image, in his likeness. This ability is both a great advantage for the historian, and an obligation incumbent upon him. And the de-

---

a disparity between Buber's position and that of the postmodern world. For the general discussion of the scientist's ability to attain objectivity in research at all, see (a somewhat current survey, until the late 1990 s): Michael Berube, "Objectivity," in *New Keywords. A Revised Vocabulary of Culture and Society*, ed. Tony Bennett (Malden, MA: Blackwell, 2005), 244–46. See there the discussion on the position of Rorty (e. g., Richard Rorty, *Philosophy and the Mirror of Nature* (Princeton: Princeton University Press, 1979), with which some scholars agree (not only as regards the social sciences and the humanities but also for the natural sciences!) quite straightforwardly (Berube, 248): "Some moral philosophers claim that Rorty's position on objectivity amounts to shallow relativism in which all value judgments are of equal standing."

[4]   Martin Buber, "Education and World-View," in *Pointing the Way: Collected Essays of Martin Buber*, ed. and trans. Maurice S. Friedman (New York: Harper, 1963), 98–105, at 100–01.

[5]   See Ben Zion Dinur, "Three Meetings with Buber," *Molad* 1 (1967): 234–35 [Hebrew].

sire to introduce the reader and the student to the world of the past, without presenting it in its entirety, as it is received by the historian['s authentic self], immediately
harms both the historian and the reader.[6]

I should note at the beginning that Buber himself completely consciously approached the objects of his inquiries with the I-Thou relation (which he saw as
the central value) functioning, at times openly and in other cases less noticeably,
as a hermeneutic tool through which he read the various texts which occupied
him during the course of his life: Hasidic works, the Bible, philosophical and sociological texts; and also when he sought to analyze contemporary issues.[7]

---

[6]   Ibid., 234.

[7]   See Steven Kepnes, *The Text as Thou: Martin Buber's Dialogical Hermeneutics and Narrative Theology* (Bloomington, IN: Indiana University Press, 1992), who emphasizes this
especially on 38–39. He argues, however, with a great degree of justification, in my opinion, that here we see where Buber failed: when he began his study of Hasidism, he already
was guided by his values, which caused him to somewhat lose the pure objectivity of the
historian and to ignore the elements of Hasidism that did not accord, from the outset, with
those values. See ibid., 35–40. Gershom Scholem's arguments against Buber's research
of Hasidism teach us of the need for balance between Buber's approach and Weber's demand for objectivity. On the other hand, even if Scholem's harsh criticism was justified,
this does not mean that Buber did not shine a spotlight on an element of Hasidism that,
without his unique methodology, would have remained forgotten and abandoned. Now,
many years after the echoes of this disagreement have faded away, Buber's work is increasingly appreciated by scholars of Hasidism. See Ron Margolin, *Inner Religion: The
Phenomenology of Inner Religious Life and Its Manifestation in Jewish Sources (From the
Bible to Hasidic Texts)* (Ramat Gan: Bar-Ilan University Press, 2011), 16–18; 27–33;
428–33 [Hebrew]. See also Tsippi Kaufmann, *In All Your Ways Know Him: The Concept
of God and Avodah be-Gashmiyut in the Early Stages of Hasidism* (Ramat Gan: Bar-Ilan University Press, 2009), especially 235–45 [Hebrew]. Moreover, some scholars even dare to
openly attack Scholem's objectivity and argue that his "screen of objectivity" actually
conceals "Oedipal" motives of rebelling against his teacher; see Israel Koren, *The Mystery
of the Earth: Mysticism and Hasidism in the Thought of Martin Buber*, trans. Jonathan Chipman (Leiden/Boston: Brill, 2010), 341–42, n. 6. If Koren's claims are correct, this teaches
of the great difficulty (if not impossibility, as Buber asserts) of implementing Weber's
demand. If so, then there might be some basis for the insistence by those postmodernist
scholars that the researcher not attempt to hide behind the mask of objectivity, and openly and sincerely set before the reader his or her personal world, from which the scholar—
presumably objectively—sets forth on research.
At any rate, Kepnes finds in Buber's Bible research the finest example that he gave the
scholarly world (*The Text as Thou*, 40; compare this, however, with Benyamin Uffenheim-
er, "Buber and Modern Biblical Scholarship," in *Martin Buber: A Centenary Volume*, ed.
Haim Gordan and Jochanan Bloch (New York: Ktav, 1984), 163–211, and especially Bub-

II

Now, before delving deeply into Buber's position, I wish to clarify in detail the fundamental nucleus that I identify as present in all of Buber's teachings, which obviously is relevant to the question of scientific methodology. I see this core as being at the heart of Buber's teachings, although this is not stated outright within the corpus of his writings, and, to the best of my knowledge, he did not devote a single orderly discussion to it in all his books and essays.[8] Nevertheless, this point is so cardinal for understanding his thought that it would not be an exaggeration to state that without it, we could not properly understand a single topic of the many which Buber addressed in his writings.

Unlike the Gnostics and adherents of the various dualistic conceptions that identify the element of evil in the world and in the flow of life as it is,[9] and following the Jewish sources that Buber found to be of prime importance for him (beginning with the time of the Bible to the teachings of the founder of Hasidism, the Baal Shem Tov, in the eighteenth century), Buber viewed the entire human reality in the world as the place of the potential for good—and nothing in the world lacks this potential. For him, the world (with no exception) is the place meant for the dialogical encounter between spirit and matter. Furthermore, Buber maintains, the world on its substantial level ("matter") is not only the place but also the goal of the real dialogue between man and God. He writes:

---

er's discovery—which is commonly accepted in literary research—of the "Leitworte" [key words] (Kepnes, *The Text as Thou*, 47-50).

[8]   Elliot Wolfson attempted to fill this void, which Buber himself expected to be reported in an orderly fashion. See Elliot Wolfson, "The Problem of Unity in the Thought of Martin Buber," *Journal of the History of Philosophy* 27 (1989): 423-44.

[9]   Without going into the details of this wide-ranging conception, it will be sufficient for our purposes to mention, purely as illustration, the amazing assertion of Plotinus, who identifies the source of evil in the desire to expand and flourish in the realm of the material reality— to the extent that, for him, even the principle of growth in plants belongs to the forces of evil (see Plotinus, *Plotinus in Seven Volumes*, trans. A. H. Armstrong [Cambridge, MA: Harvard University Press, 1984], vol. 5, Ennead 5, 2:1, 58-61). In contrast, compare what Buber states, in the name of Judaism, against this dualistic way of thinking: "nothing is evil in itself; what we call evil is only the undirected storming and rushing of the unredeemed sparks in their need for redemption": Martin Buber, "Spinoza, Sabbatai Zevi, and the Baalshem", in *Hasidism* (New York: Philosophical Library, 1948), 95-116, at 103.

God speaks to man in the things and beings which he sends him in life. Man answers through his dealings with these things and beings. All specific "divine service" is in itself only the ever-renewed preparation for and hallowing of this communion with God in the world.[10]

When the encounter between spirit and matter is done correctly, even in the most minor and the drabbest everyday meetings,[11] namely, the I-Thou dialogical encounter (as Buber called it),[12] it has a dimension of *tikkun olam*, the mending of

---

[10]   Buber, "Spinoza, Sabbatai Zevi, and the Baalshem," 98–99; see Koren, *Mystery of the Earth*, 223–24. See also Buber's recollection of the change he underwent: "Since 1900 I had first been under the influence of German mysticism from Meister Eckhart to Angelus Silesius, according to which the primal ground (*Urgrund*) of being, the nameless, impersonal godhead, comes to 'birth' in the human soul, then I had been under the influence of the later Kabbala and of Hasidism, according to which man has the power to unite the God who is over the world with his *shekhinah* dwelling in the world. In this way there arose in me the thought of a realization of God through man" (Martin Buber, "What Is Man?," in Buber, *Between Man and Man*, trans. Ronald Gregor-Smith (London/New York: Routledge, 2002), 140–244, at 219.
     We can gain a glimmering of just how difficult it was to understand this Buberian teaching from the insights of Michael Theunissen's studies on this question. He reached the (surprising, when one thinks about this) conclusion that the I-Thou realm of which Buber speaks does not exist in the material world, it rather *overcomes* the material and, in Theunissen's reading of Buber, is, as it were, "liberated from the world." See Michael Theunissen, *Der Andere. Studien zur Sozialontologie der Gegenwart* (Berlin: de Gruyter, 1965), 307–12; Michael Theunissen, *The Other: Studies in the Social Ontology of Husserl, Heidegger, Sartre, and Buber*, trans. Christopher Macann (Cambridge, MA: MIT Press, 1986), 321–29 (he writes [325] that the Thou "manifest[s] itself out of the present world"); see also the opposing view of Yochanan Bloch, "The Justification and the Futility of Dialogical Thinking," in Gordan and Bloch, *Martin Buber: A Centenary Volume*, 43–67, at 56–57. Bloch begins by declaring "I think we can put our finger on the exact spot where the logic of Theunissen's thinking becomes estranged from the essence of [Buberian] dialogism."

[11]   On *tikkun olam* (mending of the world) as a possibility on such occasions, according to Buber, in the mundane moments of daily life, in the office, the home, and the marketplace, see Admiel Kosman, "Introduction to Buber's Thinking," in Martin Buber, *I and Thou*, trans. To Hebrew (Jerusalem, 2013), 160–213, at 214–19 [Hebrew].

[12]   The theologically radical nature of this notion should be highlighted because of its consequent premise (which indeed is daring, and characteristic of Jewish theology throughout the generations; see Admiel Kosman, "Hesed II: Judaism," in *Encyclopedia of the Bible and Its Reception*, vol. 11 [Berlin/Boston: De Gruyter, 2015], 969–83): in the creation of man "God made no tools for himself, he needs none; he created for himself a partner in the dialogue of time and one who is capable of holding converse" (Martin Buber, "The Two

the world.[13] In Buber's conception of redemption, even though each individual in his or her place and cannot effect the final rectification, nonetheless, every such everyday encounter in which the dimension of "Thou" is present possesses some spark of correction that advances the entire reality with a small step of its own to the utopian future—which, one should emphasize, is cardinal in Buber's teachings.[14]

This enables us to understand why Buber found all ethical questions to be connected to the nature of these everyday encounters within the flow of life, in both the realm of the micro (in the personal sphere) and that of the macro (in society and state), as well as in the political activity between peoples. If such encounters are properly conducted, then the divine spirit, the spirit of the "Eternal Thou," in Buber's terminology,[15] rests on the activity of the material, and, thus,

---

Foci of the Jewish Soul," in Buber, *Israel and the World: Essays in a Time of Crisis* (Syracuse, NY: Syracuse University Press, 1976), 28–40, at 33); see David Barzilai, *Homo Dialogus: Martin Buber's System of Philosophical Anthropology* (Jerusalem, 2000), 255–57 [Hebrew]. Buber also explains (ibid.) why most people do not feel that such dialogue with God is a realistic option in their lives; for it to be tenable, a person must understand that God's speaking is always through total unity (what Buber calls "life"; he terms this understanding in its entirety as "the Jewish teaching of the wholeness [i. e., unity] of life" [Buber, "The Two Foci of the Jewish Soul," 33). He writes: "In this dialogue [between God and humanity] God speaks to every man through the life which he gives him again and again. Therefore man can only answer God with the whole of life—with the way in which he lives this given life" (ibid.).

[13] For Buber's "democratic" conception (that is, in his understanding, the task of *tikkun olam* mending the world is transferred from a single charismatic, messianic individual—as, for instance, in Christianity—to the efforts of each person, in his or her place and time) regarding the utopian, messianic correction that is the subject of biblical prophecies, see Buber, "Spinoza, Sabbatai Zevi, and the Baalshem," 112–14.

[14] See Eisenstadt, "Martin Buber in the Postmodern Age," who began his article by emphasizing the severity of the error made by those who do not realize the centrality in Buber's thought of the striving for utopia. See also the collection of essays on utopia in Buber's thought in Martin Buber, *Paths in Utopia* (Tel Aviv, 1983) [Hebrew] (translation of first section: Martin Buber, *Paths in Utopia* [Syracuse, NY: Syracuse University Press, 1996]); see also the essay on Buber's social utopianism appended to the Hebrew edition as an afterword: Avraham Shapira, *Social Groups in Formation and Tikkun Olam: The Social Utopianism of Martin Buber*, 276–314; see also Avraham Shapira, "Political Messianism and Its Place in Martin Buber's Conception of Redemption," in *In Memory of Martin Buber Twenty Years after His Death* (Jerusalem, 1987), 51–72 [Hebrew].

[15] See Kosman, "Introduction to Buber's Thinking," 208 n. 117, on the development of this concept in Buber's thought.

their ethical assessment will be positive[16] (and in the language of Judaism, they are actions of *mitzvah*–commanded). When, however, the spirit is divorced from the material world, alienation and evil come to dominate human existence (in the parlance of Judaism, human actions in this instance are transgressions).

To be precise, at this point in our discussion we seemingly can attempt to simplify this central Buberian principle, which, as noted, emerges either directly or obliquely from every article and book that Buber wrote during his life. We can argue that, for him, *egocentrism* (that is, concentrating a person's mental powers around the "I") is the greatest obstacle to ethical and spiritual life.[17] This is the basic trait of any average individual. We therefore can state that Buber's entire doctrine is based on the assumption that only when human actions are as free of egocentrism[18] as possible do persons naturally relate to the other as subject, as Thou, and then spirit rests upon human relations in the material world[19] (the

---

[16] A major principle for Buber is that someone whose relations in the world are Thou relations directly encounters also the correct ethical decisions that come from the divine sphere, which, in this context, he calls the Absolute. See Martin Buber, "Religion and Ethics," in Martin Buber, *Eclipse of God: Studies in the Relation between Religion and Philosophy* (Princeton: Princeton University Press, 2016), 83–89, at 84–85; see also 86–87, where he writes, concerning his ethical conception, of the erroneous claim that he was thereby defending a heteronomic position (held by those who accept the ancient methods of revelation transmitted to them by the religions, and act in accordance with them today, on the assumption that this is God's will now), just as it would be incorrect to argue that Buber was defending an autonomous approach (that is, of those who seek by their own means—such as Kant—to arrive at the truth). He argues there that his view is neither of these, but rather theonomic, meaning that humanity must hear directly from God today what is required. Buber believed that this is not only possible but demanded of each and every one of us. In this way, he writes: "In theonomy the divine law seeks for your own, and true revelation reveals to you yourself" (299). As regards ethical doctrines themselves, and also established religions (when they stand divorced from the Thou), he maintains: "there is nothing that can so hide the face of our fellow man as morality can, religion can hide from us as nothing else can the face of God" (Martin Buber, "Dialogue," in Martin Buber, *Between Man and Man*, trans. Ronald Gregor-Smith [London/New York: Routledge, 2002], 1–45, at 21).

[17] See Kosman, "Introduction to Buber's Thinking," 168–81; see also below, n. 25.

[18] Egocentrism is identified in human relations as the egocentric person relating to the other as It (that is, being blind to the other's existence as a subject) in Buber's terminology.

[19] As regards human egocentrism, Buber apparently believed, like the Buddha, that this element of human egocentrism is the one and only element that distances humankind from redemption. See Admiel Kosman, "Comments and Explanations to Buber's 'I and Thou,'" in *Judaism: Topics, Fragments, Faces, Identities: Jubilee Volume in Honor of Rivka*, ed. Haviva Pedaya and Ephraim Meir (Beersheva, 2007), 511–24, at 511–16 [Hebrew].

meeting can be with other human beings or with the natural world).[20] In my opinion, this latter formulation is not basically flawed, and in the past I proposed understanding the core of Buber's teachings in this manner.[21] Recently, however, in the course of my latest studies, I realized, in increasingly marked fashion, that Buber mainly refrained from using terms such as "ego" or "egocentrism," even when he was occupied with questions in which such terms presumably were necessary to advance his arguments.[22] When I realized this, I finally concluded that Buber's avoidance of these terms, which are common in the Buddhist literature,[23] was intentional. The reason for this omission, as I understand it now, is Buber's opinion that instead of the "egocentrism/lack of egocentrism" axis of opposites, he preferred using an axis of opposites that was more accurate for him, one taken from the Kabbalistic-Hasidic literature:[24] the "separated" individual in contrast with the "unified" one.[25]

---

[20]   Actually, in Buber's teaching there are three spheres (or four spheres; at times the scholarly literature refers to them as "realms," not "spheres," but this is purely a semantic matter), in which Buber claims that in the meeting, the presence of "the Eternal Thou" is possible (if people direct their hearts and are themselves open to this); see Kosman, "Introduction to Buber's Thinking," 171 n. 21.

[21]   See Kosman, "Comments and Explanations to Buber's 'I and Thou,'" 511–16.

[22]   It should be noted that even Emmanuel Levinas, who undoubtedly was greatly influenced by Buber, used these terms. On "egology" for Levinas (the original term is that of Edmund Husserl, but Levinas used it differently, to express his opposition to the centrality of the representation of the ego in Western philosophy), see Arnaud Josephus van der Ven, *The Shame of Reason in Organizational Change: A Levinassian Perspective* (Dordrecht: Springer, 2011), 74–75.

[23]   Despite Buber's closeness to Eastern teachings as a whole, and the great esteem in which he held those of Buddha (see Shapira, *Between Spirit and Reality*, 216–17; Kosman, "Introduction to Buber's Thinking," 210 n. 122), he had reservations concerning Buddhism. See Martin Buber, "The Spirit of the Orient and Judaism," in Martin Buber, *On Judaism*, ed. Nahum N. Glatzer (New York: Schocken Books, 1973), 56–78, at 69–70, where he expresses his objections to the teachings of the Buddha, which are meant to distance a person from the reality of actual life in the world. Buber also argues against Buddhism and similar religions in Buber, *I and Thou*, 125: "To this end [= contact with the "Thou"] one does not have to strip away the world of the senses as a world of appearance. There is no world of appearance, there is only the world—which, to be sure, appears twofold [i.e., both It and Thou] to us [in our inner world] in accordance with our twofold attitude. Only the spell of separation [i.e., the illusion of man's separation from the whole] needs to be broken." See also the essays included in Gordan and Bloch, *Martin Buber: A Centenary Volume*, in the "Buber and the Far East" section (325–64).

[24]   On the Kabbalistic term *alma de-peruda* (world of separation), see Zohar, Bamidbar 149b; R. Abraham Isaac Kook, *Lights of Return*, trans. Alter B. Z. Metzger (New York: Yeshiva University Press, 1978), chapter 12, section 5, 71, who explains the principle of separa-

What is the meaning of the "separation" of which Buber speaks? It means that, from two different aspects, the human being lives a bifurcated life: in the inner sphere and in the social, interpersonal one (which also includes encounters with the natural world).[26]

In the inner sphere: the separated individual feels that each of his mental and physical powers is split and is not organically united with other powers. A practical example of this (one of many) appears in Buber's own writings: Buber presents Claude-Henri de Rouvroy, comte de Saint-Simon (1760–1825)—considered to be the founder of French socialism—as one who advocated for social change based solely on rational understanding. Saint-Simon did not, however, realize that such change that is brought about only in the realm of rational understanding is insufficient, since, in Buber's opinion, true social change is one in which the spirit rests

---

tion and unity, which, in similar fashion, is prevalent in many Kabbalistic and Hasidic sources: "At the time that a man sins he is in 'the world of separation', and then every deed stands by itself, and evil is evil by itself, and it possesses evil and harmful value. When he repents out of love, there immediately shines upon him the existential light of the 'world of unity,' where all is interwoven into one form. In the general relationship there is no evil at all, for evil combines with virtue to facilitate and exalt even further the significant worth of goodness. Thereby are intentionally evil deeds transformed into veritable deeds of merit." On the conception of unity in Jewish sources, see also Benjamin Brown, "'The Two Types of Unity': Maharal, *Sfat Emet* and the Dualistic Turn in Late Hasidic Thought," in *Maharal: Overtures. Biography, Doctrine, Influence*, ed. Elchanan Reiner (Jerusalem, 2015), 411–48 [Hebrew]. It should be noted, however, that Brown gathered many sources from Jewish philosophy, most of which were not considered of value in Buberian thought, since they resulted from internal struggles between different groups in Judaism in the nineteenth and twentieth centuries on the question of the application of the concept of unity in religious society. It seems that the only source that Buber deemed of value was that which presented the conception of the Baal Shem Tov. See Brown, especially 444–45.

[25] Support for this position is provided by Wolfson, who argues that each of the three periods into which Buber's life and teachings are usually divided centered around the search for the dimension of unity of the self. Wolfson stresses that Buber's starting point is that the I is merely a collection of separated traits, which we forcibly keep in our mind and insist on calling the I; and all of Buber's inquiries, in all periods, were engaged in searching for the way to unify these separate powers. See Wolfson, "The Problem of Unity in the Thought of Martin Buber," 425, where he writes: "Echoing Hume's description of his everyday self, the I of perception (*Erkenntnis*) as 'nothing but a heap of collection of different perceptions,' Buber notes that one gives 'the bundle a subject and says "I" to it, but the subject is not a unity that is experienced.'"

[26] Actually, Buber's anthropological conception of humanity refers to one, or perhaps even two, additional spheres in which the encounter is possible in human life (see above, n. 20), but, for the time being, this suffices for our purposes.

on the material, both in humanity and in the larger world. And this, Buber explains, is possible only when human beings are unified in their inner world. Buber adds in this context: "the spirit of which I speak is not one of the potentialities or functions of man but his concentrated *totality*."[27] Avraham Shapira explains that Buber

> identifies "the spirit" with the comprehensive expression of a person's personality. The spirit is not "merely a piece of social [= natural] reality. Rather it is its partner," it rests above everyday life, as their source and authority. "Spirit is an event, something which happens to man," it is not an abstract idea but existence with a mission for life. . . . It exists in the one who is "ready . . . to make these decisions . . . and implement them without reserve and, to release them thereby as a working force in the world."[28]

In the interpersonal sphere and in relations with nature: individuals (again, because of the egocentric element) separate themselves from others. In this case, they do not allow the spirit to act within the context of their life in interactions with other people and with all that exists in nature[29] so that the dialogical unity will rest on the actions of the material included in these encounters.[30]

The difference between the bifurcated individual and the unified individual parallels, according to Buber, that between the I-It and the I-Thou relations. The former is occupied with collecting only objective information about the object of research, while the latter will absorb the existence of the object of inquiry as a subject—in a whole and unified manner.[31] Thus Buber says about the conception

---

27   Buber, *The Demand of the Spirit Versus Historical Reality* (Jerusalem: The University Press, 1938), 179.

28   Shapira, *Between Spirit and Reality*, 147. The quotations from Buber are from Buber, *Demand of the Spirit Versus Historical Reality*, 178, 187, 180, respectively.

29   On the dialogical encounter with all that exists in nature, see Kosman, "Introduction to Buber's Thinking," 171 n. 21 (we should also refer to Buber's response to his critics on this matter: see Martin Buber, "Replies to My Critics," in *The Philosophy of Martin Buber*, ed. Paul Arthur Schilpp and Maurice Friedman [La Salle, IL/London: Open Court, 1967], 689–744, at 707–08).

30   To exemplify the difference between the person who acts in a bifurcated manner and the one who acts in a unified way, see Admiel Kosman, "Obedience to the Law Versus Spontaneous Charismatic Action: Halakhah, Magic and Dialogue," *Bar-Ilan Law Studies* 18 (2002): 219–47, especially 235–36 [Hebrew]; Admiel Kosman, "Rereading the Story about Alexander and His Visit in Katzya in the Midrashic Tradition," *Sidra* 18 (2003): 73–102 [Hebrew].

31   For a more detailed depiction of this manner of absorption, see Shapira, *Between Spirit and Reality*, 130. In this instance, the objective rational cognition is combined with the intuition of the researcher who lovingly devotes himself to the object of his research: the text that "speaks to him." See also Kepnes, *The Text as Thou*, 21–32.

of the former, in an I-It relation: "For what they bring to him [= man] is only a world that consists of It and It and It, of He and He and She and She and It."[32] The Buber scholar Shalom Ratsabi explains:

> Man does not meet the world [through the It] directly, immediately, and with all his essence. To the contrary, he places what stands before him in a frame of time, place, and causation, and thereby collects "information" about it. Clearly, for this person the moment of his standing before his object is not a moment of an "I-Thou" encounter. After all, he does not approach things with all his being [i.e., in the way of unity], which alone can ensure a true meeting, he rather does so in the name of instinct or a certain value. Moreover, he is not interested in a thing for its own sake, but only when it is inserted in the contexts of time, place, and causality that he imposes on it. The things become known to him for the knowledge that he will generate from the encounter itself or for a scientific purpose beyond them. Consequently, the moment for him is an abstract point of time between the past, of his models and the knowledge derived from it, and the future, which is replete with information and the ability to fully utilize "Its."[33]

In contrast, Buber writes about the object of research of the latter type in the preceding quotation:

> [A] human being confronts a form that wants to become a work through him. Not a figment of his soul but something that appears to the soul and demands the soul's creative power. What is required is a deed that a man does with his whole being: if he commits it and speaks with his being the basic word [of the Thou] to the form that appears, then the creative power is released and the work comes into being . . . whoever commits himself may not hold back part of himself. . . . The form that confronts me I cannot experience nor describe; I can only actualize it. And yet I see it, radiant in the splendor of the confrontation, far more clearly than all clarity of the experienced world . . . but what can equal its presence? And it is an actual relation: it acts on me as I act on it.[34]

It is not surprising then that Buber could then speak about "loving science" (and that we, following Buber, can think of love as an epistemological force,[35] one that

---

32   Martin Buber, *I and Thou*, trans. Walter Kaufmann (Edinburgh: T. and T. Clark, 1970), 55.

33   Shalom Ratzabi (Ratsabi), "Zionism as a Theo-Political Doctrine and the Unnatural Character of the People of Israel," in Iyunim Bitkumat Israel, *Studies in Zionism, the Yishuv and the State of Israel* (2014), 97–129, at 107 [Hebrew].

34   Buber, *I and Thou*, 60–61. See Koren, *Mystery of the Earth*, 225–26.

35   This expression for the conception of Buber is that of Koren, *Mystery of the Earth*, 318. For the precise meaning of the term "love," which could also be understood in this context in

brings the researcher closer, in a Thou relation, to unity), and not about science as solely rational, as Weber thought:

> The loving man is one who grasps non-relatively each thing he grasps . . . at the moment of experience nothing else exists, nothing save this beloved thing, filling out the world and indistinguishably coinciding with it . . . the loving man's dream-powerful and primally-awake heart beholds the non-common. . . . What you extract and combine is always only the passivity of things. But their activity, their effective reality, reveals itself only to the loving man who knows them. And thus he knows the world. In the features of the beloved, whose self he realizes, he discerns the enigmatic conscience of the universe. True art is a loving art. . . . True science is a loving science. . . . True philosophy is a loving philosophy.[36] . . . Every true deed is a loving deed. All true deeds arise from contact with a beloved thing and flow into the universe. Any true deed brings, out of lived unity, unity into the world. Unity is not a property of the world but its task. To form unity out of the world is our never-ending work.[37]

Now, after the above discussion, we can allow ourselves to touch the nerve center of Buber's teaching. Without all the above prefaces, this nerve center would be totally incomprehensible for anyone not familiar with his thought. Buber was of the opinion that a "secret" is revealed to those present in every "loving contact" of an I-Thou relation. This secret is naturally connected to the resting of the spirit mentioned above. This survey of Buber's way of thinking will now enable us to properly understand his intent: Buber argues that this secret will *not* be revealed to the researcher who employs the conventional scientific methodology in the spi-

---

ways that Buber did not intend, see Kosman, "Introduction to Buber's Thinking," 177–78 and n. 62.

[36]   As least as regards philosophy, Buber's student and friend Samuel Hugo Bergman, following his teacher, viewed the situation of philosophy in his time as a methodology that had reached its end (because of what he called the "neutral nature of science"). Bergman accordingly awaited the day when professors would stand before their students and tell them the truth: "In your searches you have come to an iron wall. If you nevertheless wish to advance on the path of cognition, don't seek new solutions and new metaphysical suppositions, but rather change yourselves, conduct a moral revolution in your lives; keep away from any speck of falsehood; cease to be shaken from one end to the other by the vagaries of time. . . . teach yourselves to accept with equanimity everything that comes to you and is given to you; cease to be within the circles of your small 'I.' Aspire to this: identification with the great, comprehensive 'I'; inquire of the Lord, pray. . . . [T]his is the way to the understanding of the metaphysical questions that weigh heavy upon you" (Samuel Hugo Bergman, *Thinkers and Believers* [Tel Aviv, 1959], 29–30 [Hebrew]).

[37]   Martin Buber, "With a Monist," in *Pointing the Way: Collected Essays of Martin Buber*, ed. and trans. Maurice S. Friedman (New York: Harper & Row, 1963), 25–30, at 28–30.

rit of Weber's instruction;[38] this secret will be given over to research in loving science,[39] in which, according to Buber,

> the man who pursues such science is confronted by the secret life of things which has confronted none before him; this life places itself in his hands, and he experiences it [i. e., the secret life of a thing], and is filled with its happening to the rim of his existence. Then he interprets what he has experienced in simple and fruitful concepts.[40]

As regards this secret, Buber explains elsewhere that, as people living in the modern world, we should understand the consequent necessity for "holding ourselves open to the unconditional mystery which we encounter in every sphere of our life and which cannot be comprised in any formula. It means that, from the very roots of our being, we should always be prepared to live with this mystery as one being living with another."[41] Just because we live in a world with a plethora of distracting technological innovations, attention must be paid that the secret will not vanish from our lives. Buber then has to suggest to the scientist, or modern human being in general, to be closely attentive to the traditions of the world religions, based on the premise that they offer spiritually arousing tools for preserving the ability to uncover the secret:

> Real faith means the ability to endure life in the face of this mystery. The forms in which the mystery approaches us are nothing but our personal experiences. At times it is very difficult to live with the mystery, and to be constant to it in the midst of these ever new, unforeseen, surprising, precipitating and overpowering experiences. But there is something which can help us and there are helpers. There is the living transmission of those who have really lived with the mystery, and above all those who are of our kind and who had our tidings. They help us through the pure strength with which

---

[38] Buber, "Dialogue," 12–13 also speaks of reliance on science as a sort of "armor" that the modern human being wears so as *not* to hear the Thou speaking with him.

[39] In other places Buber defines this approach as "scientific intuition"; see Martin Buber, *The Prophetic Faith*, trans. Carlyle Witton-Davies (New York: Macmillan, 1949), 5–6; see Shapira, *Between Spirit and Reality*, 129–30, who emphasizes Buber's counsel to use science in two ways: in rational cognition, and with the intuition of the "lover"; neither alone is inconsistent with the other (see also Avraham Shapira, "The Sieve Approach and the Intuitive Approach" [in press], 14–19 [Hebrew]; I am grateful to Professor Shapira for sending me the text of his article).

[40] Buber, "With a Monist," 29. See Shapira, *Between Spirit and Reality*, 129–30. For more on Buber's conception of the secret, see Avi Sagi, "The Mystery of Being and the Creation of Hebrew Literature," *Iyyun. The Jerusalem Philosophical Quarterly* 59 (2010): 165–86, at 171–76 [Hebrew]. See also the sources brought by Admiel Kosman, *Gender and Dialogue in the Rabbinic Prism*, trans. Edward Levin (Berlin/Boston: De Gruyter, 2012), 26–27.

[41] Martin Buber, "The Prejudices of Youth," in *Israel and the World*, 41–52, at 49.

they experienced the mystery, faced it, and engaged their lives to it. For to believe means to engage oneself. I know only too well that all of this past reaches us in the rigid and often conventional form of mechanical religion. But it can be loosened up, and then the way will again open to the vital force of that which has been lived and transmitted to us, back to the life in our Bible. We too [now, each in his individual way] can hear the [divine] voice ring forth from the black letters.[42]

III

With this explanation in mind, we can now return to clarifying the foundation of Buber's position, which is the source of his refusal to accept Weber's view of the proper way to act in the context of scientific methodology. Buber's opposition to Weber on this point can be explained in two separate tracks, that eventually come together:

1. Buber maintains that the person of spirit is required—as was the prophet in the time of the Bible—to voice to the people the message of the spirit at that time and place, and not to become encloistered in the academic ivory tower, distant from actual life in the surrounding society.

2. In Buber's conception, the spirit can rest on every person—including the researcher—in a way unique to that person in encounters with the Thou; and the researcher must not stifle his or her singular voice, which emerges from the encounter, in a Thou relation, with the object of research.

For an explanation of these two tracks:

The first track is based on Buber's view of the role of the person of spirit (as explained above, whose world is not bifurcated but is oriented, to the greatest degree possible, to unity) as bringing the word of God to the people; and that in every contact of persons of spirit with the world, they must also be ready to voice the reproach that they receive as a sort of prophet to the people (even one who seems to be situated at the fringes of society, but who receives "hearing";[43] they, too, are required to the same degree, according to Buber, to transmit the word of the spirit to those who do not hear). Accordingly, it is inconceivable that a sociologist (or any other scientist) would work without speaking out when "hearing" in that inner voice the demand of the spirit for rectification by the society being

---

[42]   Buber, "The Prejudices of Youth," 49–50. See also Buber, "On National Education," in *Israel and the World*, 149–63, at 163: "Their [this generation's] ears and hearts must be opened to the voice of the mystery."

[43]   On "wanting to hear" and "not wanting to hear," see Martin Buber, "What Are We to Do about the Ten Commandments? Reply to a Circular Question," in *Israel and the World*, 85–88, at 86.

researched.[44] Against those who assert that academe is an intellectual ivory tower, distant and divorced from the tempestuous flows of life beyond it,[45] Buber declares that this seeming aloofness is actually a surrender to the social forces which the spirit demands must be opposed. He identifies those who follow Weber as being borne by a low spirit: "The demand for the 'value-freedom' of sociology has resulted in a resignation."[46]

Buber asserts, and thereby somewhat defends these academic circles who enclose themselves in the ivory tower by immersing themselves in the search solely for objective facts (albeit without agreeing with them), that their surrender ensues from the desire to preserve some niche that can remain unbuffeted by the stormy winds of the world outside:

> The spirit is still effective indeed, but only in so far as it places itself under the sway of powerful groups, under the dictates of what rules in history, that is, of power—we wish, therefore, to define its limits as a sphere where spirit is not to act but *only* to know, and within this sphere to guarantee still its independence.[47]

Now we can clarify the second track mentioned above. Buber is of the opinion that every person is potentially a sort of vessel for the resting of the spirit; and as an individual, each person is created as a vessel through which the divine spirit is expressed in his or her encounters with the material world—like an artist—in the manner singular to that person.[48] This path does not resemble the way in which

---

[44] I related at length elsewhere to the question of the ethical and sociological assessment of an entire society by the "objective" experts who are sent to study it (namely, anthropologists who fulfill this task in foreign societies) from the perspective of sociologists who have no knowledge of Buber's teaching. See Admiel Kosman, "The Cultural Crisis of Contemporary Israel: A Jewish Theological Perspective on Its Causes," *Israel Studies Review* 26 (2013): 28–53, especially 35–36. We should add to this the proposal by Peter Berger, *Invitation to Sociology: A Humanistic Perspective* (Hammondsworth, UK: Penguin, 1966), 37–67, especially 51–56, who perceives the work of the sociologist as "debunking" the society being investigated, since every society generally is inclined to aggrandize itself and ignore its faults.

[45] Buber sets forth similar opposition to the demand by Julien Benda in his famous essay, *La Trahison des Clercs* (*The Treason of the Intellectuals*), published in 1927; see the extensive discussion: Admiel Kosman and Yemima Hadad, "The Societal Role of the Man of Spirit according to Martin Buber," *Hebrew Union College Annual* (in press).

[46] Buber, "Demand of the Spirit," 182.

[47] Ibid.

[48] Some versions of the Kabbalistic-Hasidic conception add to this that each moment in a person's life is a unique and unparalleled one; see the sources brought by Admiel Kosman, "A Short Tractate on the Meaning of Life and the Source of Suffering in Forty-Six

this encounter happens in the world of another person.[49] In his best-known book, *I and Thou*, Buber calls this singular voice of each individual "organ" (that is, a brass instrument, the intent being to a trumpet, with the person then being a musical instrument, by means of which, through his one-time personality, the divine music distinctive to this personality is produced).[50] He writes on this:

Short Chapters," in *Search for Meaning*, ed. David Birnbaum and Martin S. Cohen (New York: New Paradigm, 2018), 55–75, at 74–75 n. 22.

[49]   Thereby giving expression to Buber's existentialist conception (see Martin I. Diamond, *Martin Buber: Jewish Existentialist* [New York: Oxford University Press, 1968]), which, in the spirit of Hasidism, encourages each individual person to realize the special "spark" within (see Rivka Horwitz, "Revelation and the Bible According to Twentieth-Century Jewish Philosophy," in *Jewish Spirituality: From the Sixteenth-Century Revival to the Present*, vol. 2, ed. Arthur Green [London: Routledge & Kegan Paul, 1987], 346–70, at 355–56). On existentialism in Hasidism, see Aviezer Cohen, "Self-Consciousness in Mei Ha-Shiloah as the Nexus between God and Man," PhD diss., Ben-Gurion University of the Negev, 2006, 52–56, 281–308 [Hebrew]—albeit, not as in other existentialisms, Buber does not view this realization as the bringing forth of something that exists within the person himself, which can be revealed through the individual's own monological self-discovery, as if it were a treasure concealed within. Rather, this is the discovery of one's authentic self that finds expression specifically during the encounter with the other. See Buber, "Distance and Relation," 71: "For the inmost growth of the self is not accomplished, as people like to suppose today, in man's relation to himself, but in the relation between the one and the other." Furthermore, in a letter to Hermann (Menahem) Gerson (Martin Buber, *Briefwechsel sieben Jahzehnten*, vol. 2: 1918–1938, [Heidelberg, 1973], 281, letter no. 240), he explains to Gerson in unequivocal language that we can never attain our authentic self, since it is not a "possession"; we can only encounter it, incidentally, when we direct our lives to the truth. Generally speaking, Buber believed that excessive and unilateral focus on the I is an expression of its contraction; while I-Thou relation enables the uncovering, expansion, and realization of one's authentic self (Koren, *Mystery of the Earth*, 278 n. 8). See also David A. Jopling, *Self-Knowledge and the Self* (New York: Routledge, 2000), 152–57. In the broader context of Buber's teachings, this discussion is connected to the tension between distance and relation. See Shapira, *Between Spirit and Reality*, 177–83. It should also be mentioned that this discovery of the individual authentic self also corresponds to a number of Hasidic Kabbalistic positions. On the existential orientations that emerged in the Hasidic movement, parallel to the existential thought of Kierkegaard, see Margolin, *Inner Religion*, 361.

[50]   For this notion's Kabbalistic and Hasidic sources, see Moshe Idel, *The Mystical Experience in Abraham Abulafia*, trans. Jonathan Chipman (Albany: State University of New York Press, 1988), 53–55. Idel adds that Philo and a Rabbinic midrash already hint of this metaphor of the human body as a lyre or lute on which God plays. See also Solomon Maimon, *An Autobiography*, trans. J. Clark Murray (Urbana/Chicago: University of Illinois Press, 2001), 165–67, on the exposition by the Maggid of Mezeritch.

[B]ut revelation does not pour into the world through its recipient as if he were a funnel: it confers itself upon him, it seizes his whole element in all of its suchness and fuses with it. Even the man who is "mouth" is precisely that and not a mouthpiece—not an instrument but an organ, an autonomous, sounding organ; and to sound means to modify sound.[51]

Since, as explained above, for Buber the world—the realistic world in which encounters between one person and another, and between a person and nature, are conducted all the time—is the place where the spirit rests on the material, the place where the human and the divine meet, it is understandable that in order for a person to become a vessel for the spirit, in encounters with others, the person must, to the greatest degree possible, make room for the spirit of Thou (that is, that encounters with others in life will be in the spirit of I-Thou relation—with openness to the other as subject).[52]

For Buber, there is no reason to claim that academic research work is exceptional. This labor is no different in principle from any other activity which a person has to do in the world. Thus, Buber believes (as transpired in the above conversation with Dinur) that the historian (as any other researcher) should refrain, at the end of research, from seeking to present it as completely objective and as lacking an authentic voice of its own.

Buber finely explained this in his opening lecture as a professor of sociology at the Hebrew University in Jerusalem in 1938:

None the less, all knowledge is an *ascetic* act. At the moment of knowledge the knower must bring something paradoxical to pass; certainly he must enter into the knowledge with his whole being, he must also bring unabridged into his knowing the experiences his social ties have presented him with. But he must free himself from the influence of these ties through the concentration of spiritual power. No one becomes a sociological thinker if his dreams and his passions have never mingled with the dream and passion of a human community; but in the moment of thinking itself, as far as it stands in his power, he must exist only as person, the person open to the subject of thought. If

---

51 Buber, *I and Thou*, 166.
52 The next point should be stressed: according to Buber, this is in no wise a call for any sort of religious-messianic calling clothed in garb representative of one of the religions. Buber rather posits the following: human beings are to maintain such a way of life of openness to the other as subject in the most banal everyday encounters, those in which they naturally finds themselves in daily life, in the course of their usual activities—completely in the world. Barzilai (*Homo Dialogus*, 256) writes: "But where is the encounter held? The arena of the encounter between God and man, for Buber, is the mundane reality, the concrete world in which I and you live. From here, according to Buber, we must go forth, in 'the creation which is entrusted to me,' Buber writes, 'in it the signs of address are given to us' [the quotation is from Buber, "Dialogue," 15]."

this relation is maintained, he need not unduly trouble himself with the question of how far his knowledge was determined against his will by his membership in a group. In the relationship of a man to the truth that he has discovered, freedom and obligation, vision and blindness, are always merged. Our concern is only this—to will with all the power of our spirit to achieve the free vision. On the basis of the knowledge thus won, the sociological thinker may value and decide, censure and demand, when the urgent question approaches, without violating the law of his science. Only so can the spirit preserve itself in the crisis that embraces it and historical reality together. The spirit asserts the demand that reality, the heart of sick reality, demands of it—of it as of its partner, not as its spokesman. The representative of the spirit speaks his word to a generation of the spirit that must be educated, and he speaks it to a world that must be changed.[53]

Additionally, Buber did not have an opinion only regarding the methodology itself, he also had what to say about the *contents* of research. Or perhaps, it would be preferable to say, the research contents before the Buberian researcher will frequently be different from those of conventional research—as a *result* of a shift in the perspective of the researcher. Shamir and Avnon, who discuss Buber's proffered approach to sociology, formulate the research goals that Buber presents as follows: the "Buberian sociologist" who examines interpersonal connection will not emphasize the fixed and the defined, but rather will highlight the constant flow that underlies the social structure. Buber as sociologist, they write, is interested in the possibilities that ensue from the form of social relationship in which the partners to the encounter relate to one another as concrete human entities (Thou relation), and not as imaginary entities as objects (It relation). As they understand Buber, he thinks that such social research is capable of yielding special qualities, ones which are still unknown to us, because researchers have yet to explore this innovative research direction.[54]

And further on the choice of research contents: we should add to the comments by Shamir and Avnon that Buber's personal experience (which has also been my own scholarly experience)[55] is that research open to the Thou of the researched object also is naturally inclined to be more selective. Although in principle any object can be studied, and this presumably with the same degree of dedication, for the researcher who is attentive to Thou, there often are texts from the past that more easily open themselves in order to broadcast the secret to us; while

53   Buber, "Demand of the Spirit," 181.
54   Ronen Shamir and Dan Avnon, "Martin Buber and Israeli Sociology," in *Fifty to Forty-Eight: Critical Moments in the History of the State of Israel*, ed. Adi Ophir (Tel Aviv, 1999), 47–56, at 49 [Hebrew].
55   See Admiel Kosman, *Women's Tractate: Wisdom, Love, Faithfulness, Passion, Beauty, Sex, Holiness* (Jerusalem, 2007), 231–34 [Hebrew].

for others, we sense their inherent difficulty. Thus, for example, Buber was attacked by Gershom Scholem and several of his students for giving premier standing in the study of Hasidism to the Hasidic storytelling genre, while overlooking the theoretical Hasidic literature. Buber responded to his critics by saying that when he was just starting out in his exploration of Hasidism–about the year 1910–he felt that "already at that time there grew in me the consciousness that my task by its nature was a selective one";[56] and that against his will "I have not made use of a filter. I became a filter."[57] That is, this selectivity had been forced on him during the choice of the objects of his research in Hasidism. (It should be added: just as in any other realm that occupied him.)[58] Buber further writes there that the goal of his research of Hasidism (again, as in any other object of his research) was the following:

> I have dealt with that in the life and teaching of Judaism which, according to my insight, is its proper truth and is decisive for its function in the previous and future history of the human spirit.[59]

Buber also emphasized in his response to his critics that the selective choice of the contents of his research was not arbitrary but was made according to objective criteria. It therefore could be explained, rationally, as he did in his answer to them. By doing so Buber vigorously stressed then that selectivity does not mean subjectivity at all.[60]

Now, to return to the question I posed in the beginning of this essay: I maintain that my clarifications of Buber's ideal academic methodology enable us to

---

[56]   Buber, *Replies to My Critics*, 731.

[57]   Ibid. See Shapira, "The Sieve Approach and the Intuitive Approach," 11.

[58]   Buber (partially) justifies his selective use of the Hasidic story-telling genre and his refraining from discussing Hasidic theoretical teachings in Buber, *The Prophetic Faith*, 5–6, where, writing about Biblical research, he explains: "Historical song and legend are to a large extent . . . the natural forms of the popular oral preservation of 'historical' events" from which "it is possible to separate off a content from the point of view of the history of the Spirit and especially the history of religion." To sum up, according to Buber's understanding, as formulated by Shapira: the popular traditions preserved the "soul of the people." Consequently, according to Buber, legend is better, since "legend transmits to us the effective reality, while the theoretical religious literature is secondary to it, and is merely interpretation." This is so, because "more important than the historical memory for the reliable transmission of historical facts . . . is its significance for the preservation of values of the spirit and belief" (Shapira, "The Sieve Approach and the Intuitive Approach," 11).

[59]   Buber, *Replies to My Critics*, 731.

[60]   See Shapira, "The Sieve Approach and the Intuitive Approach," 11.

understand why some found a certain closeness between Buber's view on this ideal methodology and the postmodernism prevalent today.[61] Despite this seeming affinity between them, especially in light of Buber's giving pride of place in research to the scientist's personal world, there nevertheless is a considerable, significant difference between them.

As regards Buber—not only did he not participate in the current deconstruction of the metanarrative of the belief in God, but his view that enables the various narratives of every researcher to be expressed in his or her scientific work ensues *specifically from the metanarrative* of belief in God to which he fully subscribed. For Buber, this metanarrative represented the "Absolute" that, he argued, reflects the objectivity of the truth. This already shows the vast distance between Buber and the relativistic postmodern worldview.

This God, from whom Buber identifies in his life experience the possibility of hearing the voice of the Absolute, does not demand that human beings set aside or totally abandon the unique core of their existence when they set out to explore the objects in the world (as Weber requires). All that is asked is this: that a person set aside *personal inclination* during this activity in the world (not only in the field of research, but in all activity of any sort). Nevertheless, from the moment that the researcher's personal inclination has been removed, and no longer "conceals" the object, then the investigation of the object becomes (in the methodology of loving science) attentiveness to the Thou. That is, deep attentiveness to what emerges from the object of research that comes to light following the profound attentiveness that the researcher devotes to it. Thus, it is transformed from an object, at the beginning of this path, to a subject, at its conclusion—to a subject that speaks to the researcher in its unique voice, received in the researcher's ear as the singular existence that whispers its secret. The product, as in art, is the researcher's masterpiece.

As we have seen, unlike Weber's position, and unlike what is accepted in academic research (at present, as in Buber's time), from Buber's perspective the researcher must commit to studying the objects of research with a Thou relation, which will enable a loving attitude to the object of research, and with sincere devotion and attentiveness to what is taught by the material placed before the researcher in the basic approach that Buber calls loving science. In this manner, the researcher learns: "In the features of the beloved, whose self he [the loving person] realizes, he discerns the enigmatic countenance of the universe."[62]

---

[61]   See above, note 3.

[62]   Buber, "With a Monist," 29.

Elements of Religious Socialization in Islamic Cultures

How to Be a "Good" Muslim in Europe?

Raja Sakrani

Introduction

> Can we ignore that today seven billion humans address Him [God] every day, feel His emotional closeness, fear His judgment and make appointments in magnificent places of prayer which we call churches, mosques, synagogues, and various temples? Could we not try to understand why this fundamental need so often drifts towards a totalitarian language that petrifies souls and, in the name of the loved one, sometimes turns into hatred of the Other?
>
> —Boris Cyrulnik[1]

Religions are necessary to socialize souls. While Boris Cyrulnik is fully engaged as a neuropsychiatrist in analyzing and exploring the best subject of the attachment theory—God—as illuminated in the introductory quotation, Ronald Dworkin demonstrates in *Religion Without God* that religion is deeper than God. A belief in a god is only one possible manifestation or consequence of a deeper worldview. Religious socialization gives meaning to human presence in the world: it provides benchmarks, a kind of grid for understanding why human life should have a purpose, and the universe order and values. Religion must then be understood in a very broad sociological sense, while its conceptual framework must also take account of nonbelievers. As the first influence on children's lives, the family transmits beliefs, values, and practices not only (and probably not primarily) through its explicit religious views and expectations but also through its own actions and guidelines. Thus, the family offers children the chance to build habits and to assume them as self-evident. It is this type of heritage that has characterized the cross-generational reproduction of religious affiliations and related practices as "sociological."[2]

---

[1] My own translation: Boris Cyrulnik, *Psychothérapie de Dieu* (Paris: Odile Jacob, 2017), 8 f.

[2] More generally on what is socially constructed, see John Searle, *The Construction of Social Reality* (London: Penguin Press, 1995).

Since the time of Émile Durkheim, Niklas Luhmann, Max Weber, and the other founders of sociology,[3] there has been general consensus to consider religious socialization acts as an indispensable avenue for transmitting values to future generations.[4]

> When it comes to the religious socialization of youth, we most often think of parents and peers. Studies repeatedly find parents to be the most important religious influence in the lives of youth. . . . And there is considerable research identifying the impact of peers on religious commitments. . . . Social institutions are also important . . . and [compare to] the importance of educational institutions and religious organizations for influencing religious commitments.[5]

However, it must be noted from the start that in Islamic cultures, such transmission has involved extremely complex and diverse coded processes. Indeed—and due to intertwined legal-religious, political, social, and moral spheres, which are also variable according to "Islams" or Islam in the plural[6]—religious socialization is the vector of normative orders par excellence. It is the fundamental place for moral and communal socialization, either in parallel to or independent of religious transmission. Moreover, the specificity of Islam is discernable in two regards. First, and strictly in institutional terms, there is no clergy in Islam. In other words, the personnel and mechanisms ensuring religious socialization and transmission are not subject to any institutionalized ecclesiastical framework. Second, an enormous gap exists between an enlightened Muslim elite—a significant part of which lives in Europe or North America—and a huge mass of frightened, worried, manipulable believers, who are "lost."[7]

---

[3]   Cf. Werner Gephart, *Gründer Väter. Soziologische Bilder* (Opladen: Leske & Budrich 1998).

[4]   For an overview on religious socialization, see Lisa D. Pearce, "Religion and Youth: Agents of Religious Socialization and Youth," in *International Encyclopedia of the Social & Behavioral Sciences*, 2nd ed. (Amsterdam: Elsevier, 2015); Vassilis Saroglou, "Personality and Religion: Personality Influences on Religiousness," in *International Encyclopedia of the Social & Behavioral Sciences*, 2nd ed., 2015.

[5]   Pearce, "Religion and Youth."

[6]   Raja Sakrani and Werner Gephart, "'Recht' und 'Geltungskultur'. Zur Präsenz islamischen Rechts in Deutschland und Frankreich," in *Rechtsanalyse als Kulturforschung* (Frankfurt: Vittorio Klostermann, 2012), 103–37.

[7]   This immense problem goes beyond the scope of this chapter. Reference is only made to previous work on the imbrication of normative orders in some Muslim societies, especially after decolonization, as well as to the question of the Muslim Other in Europe and its medieval roots. Cf. Raja Sakrani, "Des orders normatifs fragmentes à l'hybridité juridique: le cas du Maghreb colonial," in *Rechtsanalyse als Kulturforschung*, 231–65; cf. id.,

How, then, do Muslim communities in Europe experience religious socialization? How do they manage Islam's normative universe and the pressure of socialization through the image of family, neighbors, community, and religious leaders on one hand, and the creation of their own practices according to a plural globalized culture on the other? Beyond these questions, how can we identify the specificity of Islam as compared to other religions, especially in regard to belonging. Stated otherwise: how does one become a member of an Islamic (religious) community?

In examining this question, this chapter claims in no way to cover all the modes and processes of Islamic religious socialization, nor does it decode all immediate, distant, and shifting consequences both within Islamic cultures and in increasingly pluralistic European societies. Instead, it attempts to outline the mechanisms of religious socialization of Muslims in Europe in order to better understand the contours of the Islamic narrative identity in its three dimensions: personal, socioreligious, and cultural. In his new book *Identity: Contemporary Identity Politics and the Struggle of Recognition*, Francis Fukuyama revisits the concept of European nationalism and its counterparts in non-European colonized cultures as well as the emergence of identity problem in a pluralist Europe. In fact, modern Islamism "needed to be seen through a similar lens of modernization and identity."[8]

> Both nationalism and Islamism are rooted in modernization. The shift from *Gemeinschaft* to *Gesellschaft* has been occurring in the contemporary Middle East, as peasants or Bedouin have left the countryside for cities such as Cairo, Amman, and Algiers. Alternatively, millions of Muslims experienced modernization by migrating to Europe or other Western countries in search of better lives, settling in Marseille or Rotterdam or Bradford and confronting there alien culture. . . . The identity problem is particularly acute for young second-generation Muslims growing up in immigrant communities in Western Europe. They are living in largely secular societies with Christian roots that do not provide public support for their religious values or practices. . . . Like many children of immigrants, they are eager to distance themselves from their families' old-fashioned ways of life. But they are not easily integrated into their new European surroundings: rates of youth unemployment, particularly for Muslims, are upward of 30 percent, and in many European countries a link is still perceived between ethnicity and membership in the dominant cultural community. . . . Under these circumstances, confusion about identity becomes acute, just as it was for newly urban-

---

"The Law of the Other: An Unknown Islamic Chapter in the Legal History of Europe," *Rechtsgeschichte* 22 (2014): 90–118.

[8]   Francis Fukuyama, *Identity: Contemporary Identity Politics and the Struggle for Recognition* (London: Profile Books, 2018).

ized Europeans in the nineteenth century. For some Muslims today, the answer to this confusion has not been membership in a nation, but membership in a larger religious group–an *umma*, or community of believers.[9]

How to become a "good" Muslim in Europe is, therefore, at the heart of the facets and difficulties of religious socialization outlined in this modest essay.

Religious Socialization: Some General Considerations

If an individual wants to differentiate himself or herself by creating a "me and the others"[10] narrative, he or she is also motivated by identifying the group that shares the same values, religion, and culture, thereby creating a larger perception

---

[9]   Ibid., 67 f.

[10]   The differentiation between oneself and others inevitably raises the question of Other-ness in the European context. What about Islamic pasts in Europe? Is it a question of his-toriography or of Otherness? Cf. Sakrani, "The Law of the Other" (note 7), 91: "There is no doubt that historiography has to be selective for methodological reasons. That is one of Weber's legacies to legal history. But the direction of selectivity is steered, according to Weber, by interests and values. To this extent, the question is about the *Kulturbedeutung* of a nearly complete denial of an important part of European history. The category of the Other–in the philosophical sense–carries within it the self-deployment of thought. This goes beyond Hegel's perception, who regarded the Other as the motor of any dialectics. It is true, however, that within European culture, the Other has long been under the influ-ence of a universal developed from the unique experience of Europe. Today, questioning history, and legal history in particular, is not only an urgent task, but also one legitimated by the rarity of legal research when compared to anthropological studies that seek to move the world's center of gravity away from its Western focus. To imagine a cultural and legal Other is first and foremost to free the diversity of cultures from its dependence on European culture. However, such an act constitutes both a problem and a challenge for research into the history of law–in particular–as leaving Eurocentrism." On Otherness and its relationship to the problem of the European identity from a philosophical, psy-chological and historical point of view, by way of indication see Jörn Rüsen, *Das Andere denken. Herausforderungen der modernen Kulturwissenschaften* (Ulm: Humbold-Studien-zentrum der Universtät, 2000); cf. Tzvetan Todorov, *La conquête de l'Amérique. La ques-tion de l'autre* (Paris: Seuil, 1982); cf. id., *Nous et les autres. La réflexion francaise sur la divesité humaine* (Paris: Seuil, 1989); cf. Julia Kristeva, *Étrangers à nous-mêmes* (Paris: Fayard, 1988); cf. Emmanuel Levinas, *Altérité et transcendence* (Paris: Fata Morgana, 1995); id., *Totalité et infini. Essai sur l'extériorité* (Paris: Livre de poche, 1990); cf. Pierre Ouellet, ed., *Le soi et l'autre. L'énonciation de l'identité dans les contexts interculturels* (Que-bec: Les presses de l'Université Laval, 2002); cf. Seyla Benhabib, *The Rights of Others: Aliens, Residents, and Citizens* (London: Cambridge University Press, 2012).

of "us and them." However, while socialization involves a societal constraint on the subject, it also plays a key role in appropriating and subjectively interpreting the pressures of socialization. Even though the margin of individual choice is strongly at stake, it varies considerably with each religion. However, the specific focus here is the Islamic religion. We will revisit this facet of socialization later. In any case, the process of intergenerational religious transmission involves several players of socialization, including mainly the family, places of worship, religious schools, and peers.

In traditional societies, initiation rituals (circumcision, physical and psychological hardships, excision, dancing, etc.) mark children's and adolescents' entry into the adult world.[11] In modern societies, however, transmission has become profoundly different in nature since the mode of communication and the speed of change have heralded in a cultural imperative that causes what religious sociologists call a transmission crisis.[12] In pluralistic global societies, this crisis corresponds to the global modification of collective references, ruptures of memory, and reconsideration of values that question the very foundations of social cohesion and religious precepts. Thus, all religious socialization institutions (family, school, places of worship, associations, etc.) are confronted with this cultural discontinuity that forces them to define their mission. It remains to be seen whether the dynamics of this shifting transmission have also reached the transmitting actors of Islamic religion.

It is clear, however, that each religion activates collective memory through a universe of symbols, practices, and rituals.[13] In addition, one or more significant founding events give a collective meaning to religious transmission, such as the crucifixion and resurrection of Jesus for Christianity, the promise made to the chosen people for Judaism, the Quran and Muhammad's path for Islam, the enlightenment of the Buddha for Buddhism, and so on. Thus, rituals such as baptism or communion for Christians, as well as the *brit milah* (circumcision), Bar

---

[11] For the scientific breakthrough of my concept of "rites de passage," cf. Arnold van Gennep, *Les rites de passage* (Paris: Librairie Stock, 1924); cf. also: Victor W. Turner, *Le phénomène rituel: structure et contre-structure. Le rituel et le symbole: une clé pour comprendre la structure sociale et les phénomènes sociaux* (Paris: PUF, 1990); cf. id., *The Anthropology of Performance* (New York: PAJ Publications, 1986).

[12] Danièle Hervieu-Léger, *La religion en miettes ou la question des sectes* (Paris: Calmann-Lévy, 2001); cf. id., *Le Pèlerin et le Converti. La religion en mouvement* (Paris: Flammarion, 1999).

[13] Here by following the concept of religion as developed by Émile Durkheim; see *The Elementary Forms of Religious Life*, trans. Carol Cosman (London: Oxford World's Classics, 2008).

mitzvah,[14] and Shabbat for Jews, are essential to religious transmission. In Islam, apart from circumcision for boys, no obligatory rituals mark the entrance of girls and boys into the Islamic community. This "ritual poverty", however, accompanies a state of norms that determine what is allowed and forbidden in Islam. Skipping Ramadan, for example, does not mean that the subject is expelled from the Islamic community, but, as will be illustrated later,[15] this type of religious socialization plays a complex role, especially among young people and even Muslim children in Europe. Another decisive point of comparison is the future of religion in European societies. As these are subject to rapid change and innovation, opportunities arise for individuals to promote their own choices and conceptions of life and the world—often noncompliant with and thus detrimental to a transmitted religious legacy. One could say that the case of Islam is often reversed compared to the model described. The process of liberation also produces a certain destruction of the collective memory. This question intersects with the relationship of religion, society, and memory. Instead of a common reference to a shared socioreligious bond, religious socialization appears more as a kind of individual do-it-yourself project[16]—like feeling Christian while simultaneously deserting churches, or embarking on spiritual searches through the Internet, readings, or identification with non-European spiritualties.

Although this modest chapter is not dedicated to comparing processes of socialization among different religions, it should be stressed that the subjective form of individual religiosity[17] breaks—or at least hinders—forms of communalization and thus religious transmission. At the same time, this trend must be tempered insofar as this model does not determine the whole landscape of Christian religious socialization. In fact, it provokes an opposite mechanism of community gathering. As paradoxical as it may seem, individuals, despite their subjective tendency to their religion, also tend to validate their beliefs and values with the group that shares them.[18] Nevertheless, the particularity of this model is that it

---

[14] This ceremony, which takes place in a synagogue, marks the religious majority among Jews, which is thirteen years for men and twelve years for women. The young believer affirms that he or she accepts God's commandments and becomes a full member of the Jewish community, as young Christians do during confirmation.

[15] See below.

[16] This image of religion on the grocery market, where you put some sacred ingredients together—as some sociologists of religion have formulated for the Western world—does not apply to the Islamic case.

[17] The measurement of religiosity is a different task; see as a classical study in the field of religion Ursula Boos-Nünning, *Dimensionen der Religiosität. Zur Operationalisierung und Messung religiöser Einstellungen* (München/Mainz: Kaiser/Grünewald, 1972).

[18] Cf., e.g., Danièle Hervieu-Léger, "La transmission des Identités religieuses," *Identités* (2016): 154–69.

always reserves a considerable place for individual experiences to be exchanged and shared with other members of the group. This phenomenon, in turn, means that the confirmation of normative validity that churches and clerics provided for centuries has now gone elsewhere. The evangelists in England and the charismatic Catholic movements in France vividly illustrate this socioreligious normative displacement. In such instances, shared beliefs and worldviews can even prompt different group actions. Besides proselytizers such as Jehovah's Witnesses or Mormons, other religious groups prefer to rely on a community life outside the world, as is the case with followers of Krishna. But what about Islam?

Could it be said—given the absence of clergy in Islam and despite the major but sometimes problematic role of imams in Europe—that the tension between institutions and community processes constitutes a new source of a religious validity culture? Could we also say that the specificity here is that institutional staff (imams, muftis, community leaders, etc.) can play an active role at both institutional and community levels? While the answer to these questions must still be found, it is certain that this tension can lead to a split in the group of believers.[19] Those who think they alone hold the absolute and pure truth do not need institutional legitimacy anymore and start producing their own system of validity, which is best exemplified by the rise of fundamentalist groups over the past decades. This system is problematic, threatening Western values and norms, as its desire to impose a model of authentic religious socialization must distance itself from anything that could taint its purity, such as an Islam that is too "soft" or "tolerant."

Depending on the country and sociopolitical context, Islamic religious socialization in Europe allows for the cohabitation of the two models to varying degrees. Furthermore, the question about the real role of *fiqhu al-aqalliyāt*, minority jurisprudence, [20] is more than legitimate, since it involves complex legal conse-

---

[19] Classically analyzed by Max Weber as the tension between "virtuosi" and "laymen." Cf. "Sociology of Religion," in id., *Economy and Society: An Outline of Interpretive Sociology* (Berkley: University of California Press, 1978), 453–565.

[20] For the first time, Muslim communities constituted a minority outside the *dar al-islam* (House of Islam). What's more, this phenomenon is quite interesting from a normative perspective. This is demonstrated by new legal literature that started appearing from the 1990 s on—in both Arabic and English. In the United States, it was pioneered notably by Mohamed Jabir al-Alwani, and elsewhere by Cheikh Youssef Al-Qaradawi and many others. The literature is addressed to the Muslim minorities in the *dar al harb* (House of War). The Arabic name for this legal doctrine is *fiqh al-aqalliyat* (minority jurisprudence). I shall not further elaborate on this very complex legal phenomenon. Suffice it to say that it is still under development and will one day certainly form a part of the legal history in Europe. Cf. R. Sakrani, "Religion als Legitimation einer Geltungskultur? Islamische Rechtskulturen in Europa im Wandel," in *Religions-Politik 1. Zur historischen Semantik euro-*

quences regarding both the national judicial system and what is called "parallel justice" in Europe. Being developed in the United States and the Middle East, minority jurisprudence addresses, as an abundant legal literature since the 1990 s, Muslim minorities especially in Europe and North America.

The Muslim is an active actor within his or her individual culture. At the same time, the solidity among the community plays a major role not only in framing each individual, but especially in coding and fixing the group's identity and religious boundaries. Several forms of religious socialization will illustrate this dynamic: religious socialization of children, Ramadan, circumcision, religious education, and prisons.

Specificity of Islamic Religious Socialization

The religious claim of Islamic communities in Europe has grown significantly since the 1980 s. This growth has raised intense debates and unleashed passionate opinions, particularly in France when discussing whether veils could be worn at school.[21] Let us remember in passing that France is home to the two largest Jewish and Muslim communities in Europe.

---

päischer Legitimationsdiskurse, ed. Georg Pfleiderer and Alexander Heit (Zürich: Nomos, 2013), 406 f.

[21] France is passionate about what one could call "the phenomenon of the veil." At I write this essay, a new case broke out in France, provoking a social debate and even the intervention of the president of the Republic. The French Parliament wants to legislate again about the veil. Veiled mothers picking up their children from school risk being denied this right because they are veiled, even when they are outside educational institutions. The literature on this problem is immense; see, concerning France and only as example: *Droit § Société: Le voile en process. L'affaire du voile: regards croisés*, Paris, Vol. 68 (2008); Sakrani and Gephart, "'Recht' und "Geltungskultur" (note 6), 123–26; Thomas Deltombe, *L'islam imaginaire. La construction médiatique de l'islamophobie en France, 1975–2005* (Paris: Le Découverte, 2007), esp. 98–121 and 337–59. In the European context, see Bianca Brünig, "The Influence of Religious Socialization and Partnership Characteristics on the Religious Practice of Veiling," ISH-Arbeitspapier des Instituts für Soziologie der Leibniz Universtät Hannover, Jan. 2015, 1–19; Cees Maris, "*Laïcité* in Low Countries? On Headscarves in a Neutral State," New York University School of Law, European Union Jean Monnet Chair, 2007; Hugues Dumont and Xavier Delgrange, "Le principe de pluralism face À la question du voile islamique en Belgique," *Droit & Société* (note 21), 75–108; Schirin Amir-Moazami, "Production discursive et fabrication juridique: Le foulard de l'enseignante en Allemagne," in Ibid., 109–126; Maheila Malik, "Complex Equality: Muslim Women and the 'Headscarf (UK),'" Ibid., 127–52.

Beyond both the movement of "judicialization"[22] of Islamic normative orders in the wide sense[23] and the application of sharia by European judges or special councils,[24] there has been a growing interest of the humanities (and more recently legal studies) in what is felt and claimed by large Islamic communities in Europe in regard to the threat of identity loss. The inevitable question is, of course, whether this threat is due to what many researchers formulate in terms of confrontation, or even culture clashes,[25] or due to the fact that Islamic religious and cultural references are devalued or conflict with relations of domination and integration in host societies. Religious socialization would then play a specific role for millions of Muslim migrants and refugees, regarding the affirmation of oneself. Because of their dual enculturation, children and adolescents, for example, try–through religious socialization–to mobilize complex identity strategies that reflect their plural identities in European societies. In addition, several studies[26] have shown that the affirmation of oneself through Islam could be a response to social injustice and racism (unemployment, exclusion, stigmatization, etc.). Finally, it must be noted that the phenomenon of conversion[27]–increasingly widespread in Europe

---

[22]   Compare with the concept of "juridisme" used by Jacques Commaille in his book *À quoi nous sert le droit* (Paris: Callimard, 2015), 41 f.

[23]   The case of Lille concerning the annulment of marriage of a Muslim couple on the grounds that the bride was not a virgin and applying Article 180 § 2 of the French Civil Code is a prime example. See analysis and criticism in Sakrani and Gephart, "'Recht' und 'Geltungskultur'"(note 6), 118–21.

[24]   Cf. Sigrid Nökel and Levent Tezcan, eds, *Islam and the New Europe: Continuities, Changes, Confrontations* (Bielefeld: Transcript, 2005); Mathias Rohe, "The Formation of a European Sharīà," in *Muslims in Europe: From the Margin to the Centre*, ed. Jamal Malik (Münster: Lit, 2004), 161–84; Heiner Bielefeldt, "Political Secularism and European Islam: A Challenge to Muslims and Non-Muslims," in Malik. *Muslims in Europe*, 147–60; Katja Jansen Fredriksen, "Sharia in Norwegian Courtrooms?," *Society & the State* 20 (2007): 44–45.

[25]   Beyond the questionable concept used by Samuel P. Huntington in his book *The Clash of Civilizations and the Remaking of World Order* (London: Penguin, 2014), see Maurits Berger, "Islam in Europe: A Clash of Tolerances," in *Radicalization in Broader Perspective* (The Hague: NCTb/Clingendael, 2007), 1–7, at https://www.clingendael.org/sites/default/files/pdfs/20070500_cdsp_art_berger.pdf.

[26]   See among other studies: Thorsten Gerald Schneiders and Lamya Kaddor, eds., *Muslime in Rechtsstaat* (Münster: Lit, 2005). On the relationship of young Muslims to both religion and violence, see "Modalités et spécificités de la socialization des jeunes musulmans de France," *Revue francais de sociologie* 52 (2011): 311–52.

[27]   "Narrative of Conversion to Islam in Britain: Female Perspectives" was produced by the Centre of Islamic Studies (CIS) at the University of Cambridge in association with the New Muslims Project of Markfield in London. The conclusions are based on a series of forums and examines the experiences of nearly fifty British women who have converted to Islam: https://theconversation.com/converting-to-islam-not-for-the-faint-hearted-re

and often leading to religious radicalization or even violent militancy—questions not only the change of religion itself and its reasons, but above all the emotional and ideological potential of a particular conception of Islam that invites new converts. Indeed, those who convert often speak of "revelation," "new light," or "a huge journey," a "rebirth."[28] The conversion generally accompanies changing community dynamics and therefore a new worldview: new values, rituals, and practices. This change implies a new conceptualization of the world and an upheaval of the convert's social universe. It is a narrative reconstruction of a followed path.

Islamic identity and the religious sociability particularly of young people in the context of European acculturation is a very vast field, difficult to grasp in terms of empirical quantitative research, not to mention the political[29] or epistemological considerations that add more complications.[30] The definition of Islamic identity evokes a particular difficulty, that of reduction of belonging to Islam as a monolithic block. But in fact, there are "a thousand and one ways"[31] to establish a relation to it.

Transmission of Religion to the New Muslim Generations: Reinvented Culture?

Etymology is revealing. Among the Moroccan and Algerian diasporas in particular, there is an expression for host countries: *blād an-nasārā*, which literally means "land of Christians." At its core, this expression refers to two relationships of domination: that of the colonial period, and that of host societies. The intensification of the religious concern evident in the latter case actually characterizes the former. We should not forget that Morocco, for example, given its proximity to Spain, ceased to experience conquests and counterconquests between North Af-

---

port-says-14382. For a general understanding of women's conversion in France, see Virginia Riva, *Converties* (Paris: Éditions du Seuil, 2015).

[28]   Corinne Rostaing, Céline Béraud, and Claire de Galembert, "Religion, Reintegration, and Rehabilitation in French Prisons," *Archives ouvertes* (2018): 16.

[29]   The wide-ranging debate on Islam and Islamism is more pronounced in the intellectual and media world in Europe, particularly after the fall of the Berlin Wall in 1989—and especially after the fall of the World Trade Center in New York in 2001.

[30]   The concept of acculturation, for example, gives rise to variable criticisms, mainly sociodemographic and psychological: integration, insertion, assimilation, cohabitation, and marginalization.

[31]   An expression used by François Burgat in his writings.

rica and Europe from the conquest of the Iberian Peninsula[32] until French colonization in the nineteenth century. Beyond cult functions, religious socialization is a source of identification that has a mobilizing effect on Muslim migrants, especially in their relationship with the rest of society. Viewed from an ideological perspective, moreover, religious socialization allows the safeguarding of social order shaken by a host society or by global society. In other words, it activates preservation or defense. For many parents, religious socialization also serves as an intense control mechanism over their child's behavior—which they believe will protect specific cultural markers and solidify a sense of ethnocultural belonging. Thus, performing circumcision, celebrating Ramadan, forbidding the consumption of certain food and drink, prohibiting specific clothing, and barring entry to places such as bars and nightclubs are instrumental acts developing of one's self. Girls are often more affected by these limitations, which in turn influence their reaction to such socialization.[33]

Nevertheless, this observation must be nuanced and adapted to the Islamic diaspora in *each* European country. Some studies examining Maghreb communities in France and Belgium, for example, have shown that this more or less intense use of religious socialization regarding children plays a dual role, since it relates the originating society with the welcoming society. It is important to note that young people inherit the conditions, experiences, and traumata of their parents. Religious identity[34] appears crucial during confrontational or rivalrous situations with the welcome society. Young people live their parents' heritage as a kind of adversity. Certainly, the colonial past of the colonizer and colonized plays a major role, as decades of silence and amnesia cannot be erased from the collective memory of migrants. Besides, one should differentiate between religious practice and belief. The parents' ritual practices or religious knowledge is not automatically transmitted to children. There may even be religious ignorance that can easily be retrieved through a web of radicalization or other sources. In general, only male circumcision, followed by the consumption of halal products, particularly in relation to avoiding pork, are largely accepted, if not approved, by young people. The relationship between young people and religious practices like Ramadan, abstaining from alcoholic drinks, participating in prayer, and so on is

---

[32] For an overview on minorities' status in Muslim Spain, especially the legal status of *dhimmī* (Christians and Jews), see Raja Sakrani, "The *Dhimmī* as the Other of Multiple *Convivencias* in al-Andalus: Protection, Tolerance, and Domination in Islamic Law," *Rechtsgeschichte* 26 (2018): 95–138.

[33] See below.

[34] The fundamental relationship of "Religion und Identität" is discussed in Werner Gephart and Hans Waldenfels, eds., *Religion und Identität. Im Horizont des Pluralismus* (Frankfurt am Main: Suhrkamp, 1999).

flexible according to the context. It is important in this regard to insist on a major turning point in the religious socialization of young people.

On levels of argumentation and the legitimization of practices, young people distinguish themselves from their parents. Thus, and alongside the classic argument of cultural motivation and cultural identity under the family guise, the search to rationalize practices or seek an extrareligious argument attracts attention: Ramadan is practiced because fasting is good for one's health; circumcision is performed because it is hygienic. A very revealing psychosocial phenomenon is that of imaginary or postponed practice.[35] Prayer, for example, is likely to be a late-adopted, time-delayed practice among young people. This results in a kind of mimicry, or parent-child cycle, since the parents were in turn in their youth semipracticing or nonpracticing Muslims. Studies in France, in particular, have shown that the degree of practice among Muslims increases significantly with age. A French study on the practice of Ramadan by Muslim children has shown that they are embedded both in horizontal socialization processes (parents, families) and peer-to-peer socialization processes, that is, interchild exchanges. It is intriguing, for example, to see the strategies that children develop in the canteens of schools, when their parents and school regulations forbid them to fast during Ramadan. Schools' imperative (attending classes, eating in the canteen, participating in sports activities, etc.) takes the lead instead of the religious one. However, children adhere to the hierarchy in their own way, sometimes competing with one another to prove who is able to hold out the most and not "break" Ramadan. When the supervisors go to the canteen to see if the children eat, Muslim schoolchildren—girls and boys—pretend to eat, then spit out what was in their mouth to respect Ramadan. This parallelism of behavior, this self-reflexive attitude, of which fasting is the vector, serves as a marker of social distinction in inter-child socialization: it gives the child a certain superiority![36]

The main question therefore is the following: if Muslim identity[37] often references ethnic or ideological criteria and is considered a simple refuge, are young Muslims able to fulfill their desire to reconstitute their religious culture by going beyond the ethnic-segmentary relationship of Islam? Does this allow for a more universal socialization that is capable of reactivating this religion's rich spiritual reserve? No one can answer this question since the process is ongoing; no one can predict what the result will be.

---

[35] Cf. Guy Michelat and Michel Simon, *Classe, religion et comportement politique* (Paris: Presses de Sciences Po, 1977).

[36] Elza Zotian, "Expériences enfantines de rites et fêtes religieuses," *ethnographiques.org*, N. 25 (2012), 1–26.

[37] Cf. Jamal Malik, "Muslimische Identitäten zwischen Tradition und Moderne," in Gephart and Waldenfels, *Religion und Identität* (note 34), 206–29.

Reinvented Islamic Spiritual Culture?

Taking a critical look at the question of Islamic religious socialization leads us to an intriguing paradox: in European societies, Islam is represented or imagined as a monolithic, irrational, and rigid religion and set of laws. It is therefore hyper-mediatized and perceived as an archaic identity refuge for millions of migrants and refugees. However, this monotheistic religion itself, let alone its spiritual values, civilizations, and their place in universal heritage, is rarely studied. In several European societies—and this is a fact—the use of Islam as an identity refuge or the "Islamization" of many young people (especially in difficult neighborhoods and suburbs frequently marginalized and involved in petty and organized crime) marks a kind of subscription by default, or a forward flight from identity. However, focusing on Islam only as an ideology blinds us from other essential perspectives. Following Max Weber, Islamic *jihād* (not in the sense of war but in the sense of effort on oneself) becomes the task of surpassing oneself. Thus, practicing even the most demanding rituals, such as rigorous prayer and fasting, is an ascetical and certainly spiritual effort. At the same time, it is also "rationalized" to fight against the temptations of what Weber refers to as *orgiastische Trunkenheit* (orgiastic intoxication)[38] This crossroad in young people's lives is delicate and decisive: either conform to an excess of ignorant, rigid, and meaningless ritualization with the risk of societal rejection or even radicalization, or attempt to cultivate a habitus of salvation and social (re)integration. Complementing or combining Emile Durkheim with Weber, worship is not just an act of faith; it is the medium for inner peace, both with oneself and with others.[39] Faced with worrying spiritual poetry during prayer in mosques, for example, many young and old followers seek alternative paths to find less complementary forms of religious socialization. It should not be forgotten that European countries confront the problem of imams who come from other Muslim countries to varying degrees. Because they are socialized in a different environment, or within the framework of a mass radicalization project,[40] they are not able to assume an educational or leadership role.

---

[38]   Max Weber, *Economie et Société* (Paris: Librairie Plon, 1971), 550.

[39]   On the Durkheimien concept of "effervescence" in comparison with the concept of "acte d'institution" by Pierre Bourdieu, see W. Gephart, "Rituale der Ritualbeobachtung. Von Émile Durkheim 'effervescence' über Marcel Mauss' 'fait total' zu Pierre Bourdieus 'acte d'institution,'" in *Diskussionsbeiträge des SFB 619 "Ritualdynamik" der Ruprecht-Karls-Universität Heidelberg*, Nr 6, ed. Dietrich Harth and Axel Michaels, 2004, 1–27, at https://journals.ub.uni-heidelberg.de/index.php/ritualdynamik/article/view/347.

[40]   See for example the very pertinent analysis by Nicolas BEAU and Jacques-Marie BOURGET in their book *Le vilain petit Qatar. Cet ami qui nous veut du mal* (Paris: Fayard, 2013), denouncing—in the case of France—those responsible within French politics who, to escape the financial crisis, demand aid for a country that fosters a radical Islam, finances

Parallel to the construction of mosques, autonomous spaces are also created to offer alternative forms of religious and cultural socialization (associations, discussion rooms, interreligious dialogues, or recreational spaces, etc.). Is this a "culturalization" phenomenon of traditional religious socialization? Is this a more secular trend to deal with spiritual and cultural issues of the Islamic religion in a freer framework that often lacks in the homeland but is offered in Europe? While the scope of this chapter does not allow these immense questions to be answered fully, helpful elements can be identified. The gender dimension, for example, plays an important role. Despite the female's presence in this new kind of socialization, women are more attracted to education and continue to have a critical reaction to socialization in general. Indeed, girls who are more discriminated against and subjected to stricter family control since their early childhood,[41] particularly with regard to freedom and sexual relations, are more oriented to education and academic success. Girls look for socialization elsewhere. Here, it is important to note that cultural belonging, combined with Islamic religious socialization, is often seen as problematic—as if migratory communities and their descendants had to choose between two incompatible cultures, the Islamic and the Western; as if the mixture and hybridity[42] of two or more cultures is not reconcilable. Having said that, there is a clear desire among young Muslims to go beyond a vision of Islam based on ethnicity and identity and assume a dual culture: Islamic-European.

---

the satellite TV channel Al-Jazeera, and propagates hatred and radicalization throughout the world, a country that has snuffed out the embers of the Arab Spring to avoid a greater revolution, and, worst of all, offers billions to France to purchase the football club Paris Saint-Germain, invest in French real estate, acquire capital in companies, and finance, above all, plans to rescue the *banlieues* (suburbs). If the production of radicals (read terrorists) is part of the rescue plan, the mission has been quite successful. And with all this, France is no isolated case in Europe. Saudi Arabia plays a similar role in the region and globally. See in the same sense the excellent sociopolitical analysis by Mohamed-Ali ADRAOUI, *Du golfe aux banlieues. Le salafisme mondialisé*, with insightful introduction by Gilles Kepel (Paris: PUF, 2013).

[41]   A recent book published in Germany points out this discrepancy between girls and boys as well as the dominant male culture in many Muslim families: Ahmet Toprak, *Muslimisch Männlich Desintegriert. Was bei der Erziehung muslimischer Jungen schiefläuft* (Berlin: Econ, 2019).

[42]   Elisabeth Bronfen, Benjamin Marius, and Theresa Steffen, eds., *Hybride Kulturen. Beiträge zur anglo-amerikanischen Multikulturalismusdebatte* (Tübingen: Staufenburg Verlag, 1997).

Muslim Education and Religious Schools

The children of migrants and refugees—boys and girls alike—can often obtain European nationality. They have all been affected by the migratory disruption on their family history and communities, sometimes violent and traumatic.[43] They have been caught up in various periods by a great upheaval of Islam as a religion and as a civilization, with major historical events, often shortened and misunderstood, being particularly impactful: the Iranian Revolution and the oil crisis of 1979; the veil issue in France in 1989; the Gulf Wars in 1991 and 1994; terrorist attacks by Al-Qaida on September 11; violence by the Islamic State in Paris, Brussels, the United Kingdom, and Berlin; the relentless Israeli-Palestinian conflict; and the emergence of ISIS (Islamic State in Iraq and Syria) and the unbelievable crimes committed against "bad" Muslims, religious minorities in the Middle East, and even the human cultural heritage "from Mosul to Palmyra."[44]

A major issue at the crossroads of socialization and transmission strongly marked "generational consciousness"[45] at the turn of the millennium. In the 1980 s, there was a remarkable trend—albeit, different depending on the context of each country—of the emancipation of migrant status. The Beur March (march of the French Arabs) in France is a notable example. In the 1990 s, identity building was based on religious distinction (massive return of the veil, more religious practices and rituals, etc.). More recently, the fight has taken another turn: that of Islamic sociopolitical integration into European citizenship. Let us recall the flagship statement by the Archbishop of Canterbury, Rowan Williams, in 2008: "[A] form of Sharia Law [is] inevitable in the UK."[46] Or the statement by the German Chancellor Angela Merkel, in the midst of an influx of Syrian refugees in 2015,

---

[43]   The Algerian case is emblematic of French colonial history. This traumatic effect for post-colonial generations, children and grandchildren of migrants, is increasingly addressed through various artistic forms including literature. See, for example, the writings of Alice Zeniter, *L'art de perdre* (Paris: Flammarion, 2017); Jean-Luc Einaudi, *La bataille de Paris. Le 17 octobre 1961* (Paris: Seuil, 1991). See also the interdisciplinary approach in Pascal Blanchard, Nicolas Bancel, and Sandrine Lemaire, eds., *La fracture coloniale. La société française au prisme de l'héritage colonial* (Paris: La Découverte, 2006).

[44]   It is also partly the title ("Cités millénaires—Voyage virtuel: De Palmyre à Mossoul") of an impressive exhibition produced by l'Institut du Monde Arabe in Paris (October 2018–February 2019) which later travelled to Bonn, Germany, at the Bundeskunsthalle (von Mossul nach Palmyra) from August to November 2019.

[45]   Studies on this issue vary across disciplines and perspectives. One of the pioneers is Karl Mannheim, "Das Problem der Generationen," *Kölner Vierteljahrshefte für Soziologie* 7 (1928): 157-85, 309-30.

[46]   Ben Russel and Colin Brown, "Archbishop of Canterbury Warns Sharia Law in Britain Is Inevitable," *The Independent*, February 8, 2008.

that "Islam is a part of Germany" (*Der Islam gehört zu Deutschland*),[47] which was followed by a comment from Horst Seehofer, the leader of the Christian Social Union, in 2018 stating that "Islam is not a part of Germany."[48]

From a sociological point of view, methodological and epistemological critiques are necessary. Legal and social science research on Islamic religious socialization and age does not have extensive investigational resources compared to those dedicated to the study of European values over forty-plus years. Consequently, some sociological studies are conducted using "cohort reasoning, a concept based on an objective criterion, which makes it possible to combine individual and historical time, personal biography, and social dynamics."[49] Nevertheless, the problem is that not all cohorts necessarily transform into generations in the manner discussed. Stated more clearly, young Muslims are placed in socioreligious discontinuity due to the aforementioned traumatic events. Attitudes of rebellion and cultural innovation fall within a process of protest that challenges the identity and normative construction of which they are the object. However, generational consciousness requires more than rebellion or contestation. It is a question of at least two capacities: the conception and knowledge of identitarian belonging, and the production of reflective knowledge about the self and the other. The greatest difficulty lies in this hinge. How are young people—both as objects and social actors of religious socialization—capable not only of falling within religious transmission, but also reinventing it and therefore, reinventing a new normative order?

Thus, if religious transmission places young people in a collective "us" (which goes beyond the ethnic-religious connotations of the *umma* concept), they in turn reintegrate themselves into a pluralism of paths. Indeed, the family primarily ensures the transmission. Parents transmit the norms of beliefs and main practices like prayer, fasting, and the two main festivals in Islam, namely the end of Ramadan (*Eid al-Fitr*) and the feast of sacrifice.[50] The family also forges the personality and identity of children through the transmission of moral norms such as sexual prohibitions, food restrictions, gender relations, and so on. Other standards corroborate the transmission since it also depends on community belonging: an In-

---

[47]   "Der frühere Bundespräsident Wulff hat gesagt, der Islam gehört zu Deutschland. Das ist so. Dieser Meinung bin ich auch." Andreas Rinke, *Das Merkel-Lexikon: Die Kanzlerin von A-Z* (Lüneberg: zu Klampen, 2016), 191.

[48]   "Der Islam gehört nicht zu Deutschland." Bruno Heidlberger, *Wohin geht unsere offene Gesellschaft? 1968–Sein Erbe und seine Feinde* (Berlin: Logos Verlag, 2019), 289.

[49]   Point discussed, for example, in C. Saint-Blancat, "La transmission de l'islam auprès des nouvelles générations de la diaspora," *Social Compass* 51/2 (2004): 237.

[50]   Note that Islam is the only one of the three monotheistic religions that still celebrates the feast of the sacrifice of sheep, and that this celebration is linked to logistical and cultural complications in several countries in Europe.

dian Islam is not transmitted in the same way as a Turkish, Maghreb, or African Islam, let alone an Islam in the country of residence. In the end, this differentiation draws the group's boundary.

Certainly, the fact that transmission does not take place in a structured and institutional framework—because Quranic schools or mosques do not necessarily take the place of families or attract all parents or young people—gives young people's itinerary a varied or very individualized or unstable character. In this regard, Islamic schools and the integration of Islamic religious education in public schools in several European countries play a very significant role in the socialization of young people.[51] Simultaneously, the access to Islamic culture and law[52] not only for Muslims but also for non-Muslim Europeans allows a better mutual knowledge. In his excellent comparative study on the identity of young French and German Muslims, Nikola Tietze[53] rightly highlights the diversity of backgrounds and combines each individual biography with the cultural, emotional, communal, and ethical depths of religious affiliation.

A fairly new dynamic is happening in Europe. It is a process of redefinition, reframing, negotiation, reflection, and more interesting innovation.[54] A major intellectual and academic project is underway in Europe: the first female imams are there,[55] as are the institutes and universities of innovative Islamic theologies,[56] as

---

[51] Abdulkader Tayob, Inga Nichaus, and Wolfram Weisse, eds., *Muslim Schools and Education in Europe and South Africa* (Münster/New York: Waxmann, 2011). See therein especially Michael Kiefer and Irka-Christin Mohr, "The Pros and Cons of Islamic Religious Education in German Schools," 163–72.

[52] For the German context, legal empirical studies are crucial for understanding the evolution of Islamic law and its application, even in an extrajudicial frame. See for example, the recent study by Mahmoud Jaraba, "The Practice of *Khul'* in Germany: Pragmatism versus Conservatism," *Islamic Law and Society* 26 (2019): 83–110. *Khul'* is divorce initiated by the woman. See also Adel Theodor Khoury, Peter Heine, and Janbernd Pebbecke, eds., *Handbuch Recht und Kultur des Islams in der Deutschen Gesellschaft. Probleme in Alltag-Hintergründe Antworten* (Gütersloh: Gütersloher Verlagshaus, 2000); Hilmar Kruger, "The Study of Islamic Law in Germany: A Review of Recent Books on Islamic Law," *Journal of Law and Religion* 15 (2000–01): 303–30.

[53] Cf. Nikola Tietze, *Jeunes musulmans de France et d'Allemagne: Les constructions subjectives de l'identité* (Paris: L'Harmatta, 2002).

[54] This question covers an enormous field: families, schools, government, alternative spaces, private and public spaces, citizenship and rights, law and judicial apparatus. For further deepening, see Mark Sedgwick, ed., *Making European Muslims: Religious Socialization among Young Muslims in Scandinavia and Western Europe*, Routledge Studies in Religion (London: Routledge, 2015).

[55] The North American context shows significant differences from that of Europe. Indeed, feminist personalities such as Amina Wadud, for example, have been able to break into a very hermetic universe reserved for men—the imamat of prayer and the interpretation of

well as critiques of authoritarian Islam, gender hierarchy, and "cellars' Islam" (*l'i-slam des caves*).[57] The training of the young Muslim elite significantly shifts the debate on Islamic socialization and transmission. In addition, the active partici-pation of women in this process has in turn triggered a major debate on the re-appropriation of theological-legal knowledge by Muslim women, which is increas-ingly being used as a precursor to change. Women are often demanding the right to choose their studies and future husbands, and to play their own role in theo-logical-legal work of the historicity of the Quran, or at least its interpretation. In the same vein, the ambiguous and multifunctional use of the veil acts as a symbol

---

the Koran. One should remember that Wadud's research specialties include gender and Qur'anic studies. On Friday, March 18, 2005, she acted as imam for a congregation of about sixty women and forty men seated together with no gender separation, thus break-ing with Islamic laws, which allow only male imams to be prayer leaders. Female imams include Kahina Bahloul, Eva Janadin, and Anne-Sophie Monsinay. In recent years, the French Islamic community has been trying to catch up with its neighbors, a backward-ness that, according to Ghaleb Bencheikh, president of the Fondation de l'Islam de France, is due to the "global atmosphere polluted by violence and terrorism." In Germa-ny, England, and Denmark, women who lead prayer in mosques are no longer the excep-tion. On September 7, 2019, they organized a prayer: the first one led by women in France. The assembly was mixed, and some women did not wear a veil, as did the two imams, Janadin and Monsinay, who led the prayer in Arabic and French in a room rented for the occasion in Paris, which for Ludovic-Mohamed Zahed, a homosexual imam, marks the continuity of a "great movement." The purpose of this project is to offer "spaces for dia-logue free of any community and family pressure." According to Janadin and Monsinay, "there is a silent minority, perhaps not so much of a minority as that, of progressive Mus-lims, who no longer attend traditional mosques and find themselves practicing alone, and who are waiting for this project": https://www.journaldesfemmes.fr/societe/combats-de-femmes/2561874-islam-femmes-imam-france-priere/.

56   For the Nordic countries and Germany, these institutions are beginning to train a new generation of researchers in this field. Other European countries are still far from this new academic process. In the Arab-Muslim world ravaged by wars, the failure of postre-volutionary transitional justice, and disastrous socioeconomic conditions, the process of separation between Islamic theology on one hand and secular law on the other still strug-gles to take place in the academic landscape.

57   See the long report by Hakim El Karoui (more than six hundred pages–Institut Mon-taigne) to the French President Emmanuel Macron in September 2018: *La fabrique de l'islamisme*, especially part 3, "Comment l'islamisme se diffuse: des homes, des organi-zation, des medias," 265–316. See also the book by Gilles Keppel *Les banlieues de l'islam. Naissance d'une religion en France* (Paris: Seuil, 1991).

for the search of oneself and freedom. The latter aspect is not always as normative as stigmatization wants it to be, a sign of submission and domination by men.[58]

Paradoxically, this type of protest reappropriates religious transmission to question or even transgress it; becoming a female imam and not wearing the veil testifies to this. As does the feminine transmission of normative and religious knowledge, particularly in Northern Europe and Germany.[59] As does the hermeneutical and social work on the question of common values and citizenship rather than on the identity discourses of the Islamic *umma* within Europe. Stated differently, this is a European and noncommunity religious socialization. Facing the ever-real danger of orthodox and radical recovery of young people by preachers or transnational organizations, the academic structure of legal and theological studies is an emergency response.[60]

Circumcision

Circumcision is one of the most famous surgical procedures and can already be identified in Egyptian wall paintings dating back to 2300 BCE. In Judaism, baby

---

[58]　About this discussion, see Étienne Balibar, et al., *Le foulard islamique en questions* (Amsterdam: Editions Amsterdam, 2004); Régis Debry, *Ce que nous voile le voile. La République et le sacré* (Paris: Gallimard, 2004); Ismahane Chouder, Malika Latrèche, and Pierre Tevanian, eds., *Les filles voiles parlent* (Paris: La Fabrique Edition, 2008).

[59]　One could think of female scholars (Muslims and non-Muslims) such as Angelika Neuwirth in Germany and her researches on the Koran—for instance, *Der Koran als Text der Spätantike. Ein europäische Zugang* (Berlin: Verlag der Weltreligionen, 2010). At the level of female academics and imams at the same time, the list is getting longer in Europe. To name but a few: Seyran Ates, the Berlin lawyer of Turkish origin, lives under police protection and has had to interrupt her activities since she defended victims of so-called honor crimes. She studied Islamic theology and became the first female imam in Germany (June 16, 2017). All currents of Islam—Sunni, Shii, Alevi, but also homosexuals and transsexuals—are welcome in this progressive mosque, which intentionally bears the name of the German poet Goethe and the twelfth-century Arab Andalusian doctor and philosopher Ibn Rushd (Averroes). The American-Malaysian Ani Zonneveld is also one of the few female imams in the world. Sherin Khankan is the first imam of Denmark; a sociologist and psychologist by training, she is the founder of the Mariam Mosque in Copenhagen (February 2016), the first mosque reserved for women.

[60]　Significant differences exist among European countries. In the Nordic countries and Germany, there is a first generation of "Muslim elite" who train the next generations in institutes and universities of Islamic theologies and law. Great Britain is unique with sharia councils and imams, some of whom are beginning to combine theological knowledge with legal academic training to enable them to deal with normative heritage in a reflective and critical way. France and other countries are still far from this process.

boys are circumcised on the eighth day after birth. This operation is justified in the Torah by the covenant between Abraham and God (Genesis 17:10). Muslims are the largest religious group to practice circumcision, also called *tahāra* to indicate purification. Unlike Judaism, Islam does not establish an age for circumcision. Rather, it is done sometime between birth and puberty. Apart from religious reasons,[61] circumcision is also practiced for reasons of belonging[62] or as a rite of passage. In his famous book *Les rites de Passage*,[63] Arnold van Gennep describes various initiation rites in many circumcision rituals in Africa. They comprise three phases: the separation of children or adolescents from the rest of society, a phase of transformation (circumcision as well as sometimes extreme psychological and physical tests), and finally the reintegration into the group in a new social role—a role that can now be assumed, as the man is no longer a boy or "contaminated by a female element: the foreskin of the penis."

Circumcision is also widespread in Europe and the United States for different reasons. In the 1980 s, studies in the United States showed that mothers of circumcised babies cited hygiene as a first reason. The United Kingdom has known this tradition since the nineteenth century, and circumcision was rather practiced in high society. On a strictly legal level, it is necessary to know that there is a difference between the schools of Sunni Islam in classical Islamic law. *Shāfī* and *Hanbalī* schools consider circumcision compulsory, while the *Hanafī* school argues that it is no more than a recommendation. Lastly, the *Mālikī* school tends to recommend it unequivocally.

Despite these differences and despite *fatāwā* in Egypt (especially in the twentieth century), where circumcision is not considered compulsory,[64] circumcision is practiced almost 100 percent in Islamic communities. Basically, it is a Muslim practice and not a legal-religious norm of Islam. Above all, it serves to mark belonging to the group. Circumcision is seen as a religious ritual and as a normative and symbolic transmission mechanism—this is also true for Judaism.[65] What is then at stake is the collective memory, described by Maurice Halbwachs as "this current of thought, a continuity which has nothing artificial, since it retains from

---

[61]   One should remember that the Copts in Egypt and Orthodox Christians of Ethiopia practice circumcision, but other churches prohibit it worldwide.

[62]   This is the case for the Aztecs and Mayans in Latin America, the Australian Aborigines, and several Pacific islands, such as Polynesia, Fiji, and Indonesia.

[63]   Van Gennep, *Le rites de passage* (s. note 11).

[64]   *Fatāwā* of 1951 and 1958. Moussa Abou Ramadan, "Les débats sur la circoncision en droit musulman classique et contemporain," in *La circoncision rituelle* (Strasbourg: Presses universitaires de Strasbourg, 2015), 25–38.

[65]   See, e. g., "Die Beschneidungsdebatte—eine religionsrechtliche und religionspädagogische Herausforderung," *Theo-Web. Zeitschrift für Religionspädagogik* (2014), book 1, 1–75.

the past only what is still alive or capable of living in the consciousness of the group that holds it."[66] The rite is characterized in particular by the transmission function. Circumcision carries an affinity between religion and culture. It is a kind of identity marker written into the human body.[67] Circumcision is also the transmission of the paternal body and a diversion from or removal of the fear of loss. Symbolism therefore takes precedence over legalism from the legal-social dimension (debate on the sexual mutilation of children in light of criminal law, etc.). Thus, circumcision is doubly identity-based: it is both masculine (having the same *genitalia* as one's father and friends at school, for example) and religious. In Judaism, another issue is equally important: the imposition of paternal memory through the transmission of the masculine, thereby competing with maternal filiation (the standard of traditional Jewish law).

Conversion and the Problem of Prisons

The Islamic religion in European prisons has become a structuring norm on several levels. In all prisons, religion plays a variable role, depending on the context of each country and religious socialization. Prisoners generally use religion as a means of resistance or as an avenue to find meaning and seek new forms of socialization. Obviously, the relationship with religion varies according to the crimes committed, the severity of the sentence, the profile of the prisoner, and so on. These aspects prompt another investigation in its own right. In the context of this chapter, it is important to determine how the Islamic religion, as a normative reference, can be situated within prisons.

If religion in general can play multiple roles with individual religiosity, as well as in regard to connecting with family, for example, or other prisoners, Islam is unique in that its normative load and its great capacity of inclusion sometimes intervene in a problematic manner, especially when identity is shaken or narcissistic normative references appear. From this point on, a comprehensive and functionalist approach no longer applies. Instead, a radical shift in meaning—a rebirth of the individual and a radical change in his or her relation to the world—dominates. This last characteristic is particularly present among new Islamic converts in European prisons.

Religion could anchor another starting point that goes through the intensification of religious practice, lived in its ethical dimension. The Islamist prisoner declares his willingness to get by. Religion is part of a desire for another life. The

---

66 Maurice Halbwachs, *Les cadres sociaux de la mémoire–la mémoir collective* (Paris: PUF, 1950).

67 Cf. Pierre Bourdieu, *"Les rites comme actes d'institution,"* in *Actes de la recherche en sciences sociales, 1982.*

ritual practice of prison prayer thus becomes therapeutic. Two testimonies illustrate the psychological effect.

In the case of Nicolas, a Frenchman, the conversion to Islam came during his fourth incarceration. His testimony highlights the normative charge and adherence to rules that Islam offers: "It has changed a lot for me! My way of seeing life, my way of seeing my neighbor, . . . we are here for a purpose. There are rules to follow."[68]

The second witness is a Muslim who faces a heavy sentence, during which he "rediscovered" Islam in prison. The relationship to the Islamic transcendence of the priest has in his case had a "therapeutic," anxiolytic effect that has been facilitated through prayer: "It is stupid to say here, in the West, that they do not understand; but frankly if I feel anguished sometimes in prison, there are volcanoes that come. . . . I do my ablutions. I say two *rakats*,[69] and I get a feeling like I drank a bottle of whisky."[70]

For these detainees, be they lifelong Muslims or converts, the institutional framework that governs religious practices in prison varies from one country to another. In the French and Belgian contexts, which feature considerable Muslim prison populations, contentious situations can arise. This is fueled in part by the fact that in France there are significantly fewer chaplains available for Islam compared to Christianity or Judaism. Thus, when ethicized religion transcends the social—for example, when prisoners pray in public spaces—conflict breaks out. At the same time, this can be understood as a challenge to prison order and as an act to show that the divine law of Islam is superior to institutional regulations.

Another determining factor is forgiveness. Of course, all three monotheistic religions concern themselves with forgiveness; however, the sacrament of forgiveness does not exist in Islam. Only God has the power of forgiveness, without any human intermediary. The relatively recent arrival of Islam in Europe (although history claims otherwise)[71] has meant that the presence of chaplains has not been institutionalized for some time. France and its *laïcité* principal, unique in Europe, is the typical example. The presence of Muslim chaplains, few in number, is almost limited to the celebration of Friday prayer. There is also neither a clergy nor sacrament in Islam. Forgiveness therefore is not conveyed by an institution or by sacred personnel. The inmates' relationship to imams determines much, but these imams maintain close and lasting relationships with detainees without having an idea of the religious knowledge conveyed or their personal influence on convicts.

---

68   My translation. Rachel Sarg and Anne-Sophie Lamine, "La religion en prison," *Archives de sciences sociales des religions* 153 (2011): 90.

69   Bowing down. Twice in the text.

70   My translation; ibid., 91.

71   Raja Sakrani, "The Law of the Other" (note 7).

Islam is also characterized by its highly integrative capacity within the group. The group, or community, therefore, takes the lead over the individual. Group membership thus explains intriguing phenomena such as positioning in counter-power. Groups are more common in prisons where sentences are quite long. As found in a survey conducted in France, a group of Muslims encouraged new converts to refuse to see or shake hands with women (supervisors, inclusion advisors, social workers, etc.), or to claim a place for daily prayer by praying in groups in libraries or courtyards. Several prison staff say that having the protection of the group motivates most Muslim converts.[72] "Islam is a powerful attractor given its current position in the world and its status as a subculture. It gives dignity to those who feel oppressed."[73] While some researchers[74] have been interested in the role of Islam in the identity construction of troubled young people, others have focused on the polarization of the representation of the world. "[R]ejected by the wealthy, the religion of Allah fascinates those who are in conflict with social order. By marrying Islam, one opposes the society of the 'powerful' and the 'integrated' perceived as hostile."[75]

Islam thus becomes an attractive religion in detention because it mobilizes the values of the strong in the sense of virility: strong and virile men who are able to frighten society and the existing system. This gives it a high rank in the hierarchy of prison values. Unlike outside, the Muslim and the converted prisoner belong to the category of strong and virile men[76] in the social order of prisons. We should not only speak about wishful socialization processes and spaces: the prison is a "total institution," so much more interpretation of this *panopticon* (Foucault) may be desired. But so much more, as well, must we be aware of this ambiguous site of socialization.

Conclusion

This chapter intended to raise questions and give answers about the logic of socialization processes in the "Muslim personality" in an ideal typical way. How to transmit norms and values in a society that sometimes "refuses you by ignoring you, thus pushing you to the limits of the clandestine"[77]? How to transmit Islamic

---

[72] "La religion en prison" (note 68), 99.

[73] Ibid., 100.

[74] Tietz and others.

[75] Farhad Khosrokhavar, *L'islam dans les prisons* (Paris: Ballande, 2004), 38–39.

[76] We do not yet have systematic research on women and their conversion in European prisons.

[77] Abdalmalek Sayad, *La double absence. Des illusions de l'émigré aux souffrances de l'immigré*, preface by Pierre Bourdieu (Paris: Seuil, 1999).

religion if you are normatively constructed to the term of an "Islamic exception"?[78] How could young Muslims of Syrian, Turkish, Pakistani, North African, or Senegalese origin be able to rework and recompose the categories of belonging in the same way as their European Catholic or Protestant or Jewish peers, by mocking their cultural and religious specificities?

This essay has tried to demonstrate that the dynamics of Islamic religious socialization in Europe is negotiated across at least four central axes: transition in the religious transmission process through symbolism and rituals or practices; the problem of a new religious authority quest and creation of new theological and legal Islamic universities and institutes; the growing claim of gender identity for women through religion; and, finally, a new citizenship requirement. To the question how to be a good Muslim in European pluralistic societies today, the answer is certainly still to come, when the process of religious socialization reflects sociolegal contours more clearly. Furthermore, one has to be aware of the "integration paradox" (*das Integrationsparadox*), which reflects the complexity of Muslims' everyday life.[79] One thing is certain, at least among a large segment of the young Muslim generations in Europe: to be a good Muslim is to be a good citizen, free and autonomous. More uncertain is the identity of those who left that religion or remain part of an Islamic community mainly as a common, shared culture.

---

[78] This also the title of Hamadi Redissi's book, *L'exception islamique* (Paris: Cérès, 2004).

[79] See especially the work of Aladin El-Mafaalani, *Das Integrationsparadox: Warum gelungene Integration zu mehr Konflikten führt* (Cologne: Kiepenheuer & Witsch, 2018); (with Ahmet Toprak), *Muslimische Kinder und Jugendliche in Deutschland. Lebenswelten–Denkmuster–Herausforderungen* (Berlin: Konrad-Adenauer-Stiftung, 2017).

Chinese Family Education and Spiritual Intervention

Voluntary and Involuntary Moral Actions from Neurological and Theological Perspectives

Milton Wai-Yiu Wan and Renee Lai-Fan Ip

Introduction

Rapid advancements in technology have brought an unthinkable acceleration of changes in our global community, our means of communication, the raising of children, and human development generally. Core values that have long been accepted as absolute are being disputed, questioned, and altered. This disruption has created significant challenges to moral education, which focuses on cultivation of moral character and is rooted in an assumption of consensual sets of values and behavioral standards. Internalization of moral virtues and moral rules as the goal in moral education has been thoroughly criticized and refuted by contemporary philosophers for its ridding of one's ability to make adaptive decisions to respond to abrupt problematic social situations.[1] Different approaches and aims to moral education have been proposed. These attempts have deepened our understanding of morality and human nature.

In this chapter, to address some of the challenges in moral education, we intend to reexamine the considerations for moral education based on understandings from recent neurological findings, centuries-old family education in the Chinese culture, and Christian spirituality. Let us begin our journey with an analysis of moral action and its motivating dynamics.

---

[1]   See, e. g., M.H. Mitias, "Moral Development and Moral Education," in *Sustainable Human Development in the Twenty-First Century*, vol. 1, ed. I. Sirageldin (Oxford: EOLSS Publishers, 2009), 89–103.

The Dynamics Constituting Moral Action

Moral Action, Moral Motivation, and Moral Belief

All moral actions are intentional actions because they must be executed for a reason.[2] And all intentional actions must be caused by a certain belief-desire pair.[3] *Belief*, including moral belief, always presumes a process of value formation, and with it come corresponding moral judgments and consequential behaviors. In other words, like other kinds of beliefs, moral belief affects and shapes moral decision-making and moral actions. Moral belief does not occur contingently and is formed and developed through multiple means (for example, through experiences or the influence of others' thoughts and actions). Thus, there is always an involuntary aspect to the nature of moral belief and its formation.[4] Once a belief is developed, action will follow accordingly. With this involuntary characteristic of implementing belief, action or nonaction thus becomes inevitable.

Moral Desire and Moral Action

How does moral belief lead to moral action? To answer this, we need to discuss moral *desire*. Connie S. Rosati points out, "Belief is insufficient for motivation, which always requires, in addition to belief, the presence of a desire or conative state."[5] G. E. M. Anscombe also claims, "Whereas beliefs aim to fit the world, desires aim to change the world."[6] In other words, belief is knowledge and conceptualization of the world, whereas it is desire, the mobilizing power, that propels motivation.[7] However, desire and motivation are not endowed with a sense of direction for action. It is *will* that mediates motivation and the ultimate action through judgment.

---

[2] Rowland Stout, *Action* (Montreal/Kingston: McGill-Queen's University Press, 2005), 15–17.

[3] Cf. Simon Evnine, *Donald Davidson* (Stanford, CA: Stanford University Press, 1991).

[4] See Thomas E. Wren, "Externalist Moral Psychology," in idem, *Caring about Morality: Philosophical Perspectives* (Cambridge, MA: MIT Press, 1991).

[5] Connie S. Rosati, "Moral Motivation," in *Stanford Encyclopedia of Philosophy*, 2006, at http://plato.stanford.edu/contents.html#m.

[6] G. E. M. Anscombe, *Intention* (Cambridge, MA: Harvard University Press, 1957).

[7] See Valerie Tiberius, *Moral Psychology: A Contemporary Introduction* (New York: Routledge, 2015), 48, quoting Anscombe's *Intention* (1957) and the Humean theory of motivation.

Will and Willpower

Will, as a *voluntary* judgment, plays an essential role in the "belief-desire-motivation-action" schema in two places.[8] First of all, as an interface between motivation and action, will gives direction to desire and motivation. Secondly, moral decision-making itself is not a sufficient condition for moral action to be put into operation (for instance, when one believes and desires to save a person in danger but does not do it.). For desire and motivation to be actualized and moral action to be enacted, *willpower* is the inner strength needed to make a decision and subsequently take action, overcoming outer or inner resistances (as when we feel hungry and desire to eat but decide not to, for various reasons).[9] That is to say, willpower is not needed when will follows desire (wanting to eat and then just eating). However, will without power makes no impact (deciding not to eat but surrendering to the desire to eat out of a lack of willpower). Hence, willpower needs training to ensure persistent efforts until success and will-training produce *self-discipline.*

As we can see, then, the voluntary and involuntary factors in the belief-desire-motivation-action schema make determinant differences in these moral components and their dynamics when moral education is being considered. We will explore these two factors further in the following sections.

The Involuntary Reconsidered: Contributions from Neuroscience Understanding

Overview of Neurological Functioning for the Involuntary and the Voluntary

According to recent neuroscientific findings, morality-related components of human behavior are not merely abstract concepts but have neurological roots, especially when *goal-directed (voluntary)* actions and *habitual (involuntary)* actions are involved. First and foremost, it is well known in the field of neuroscience that the brain is inclined to save sequences of processing, or routines, as habits, in order to maximize its efficiency. Toward this end, everyday behaviors (e. g., brushing teeth or riding a bike) are chunked into sequences of actions, then converted into automatic routines and stored as habits, bypassing the thinking part of brain where decisions are made.[10] The basal ganglia region, situated in the center of the brain

---

8   Enoch Tan, "The Secret of Power," 2005, https://issuu.com/robertbayer/docs/secret-of-power-enoch-tan.

9   Remez Sasson, "Will Power and Self Discipline," 2003, www.SucessConsciousness.com.

10   Cf. Charles Duhigg, *The Power of Habit: Why We Do What We Do in Life and Business* (New York: Random House, 2014).

near the brain stem, controls *automatic behaviors* and is responsible for emotions, memory, and pattern recognition, and supports habit storage through internalization. Complex thinking takes place in the outer parts of the brain, and the orbitofrontal cortex (OFC) is a *decision-making* area. More recent neuroscience shows that the neurological circuits for both habitual and goal-directed actions occur in the OFC, while neurochemicals called endocannabinoids, in the neurons extending from the OFC to the dorsomedial striatum, enable the brain to *prioritize for habit,* inhibiting the circuit involved in goal-directed actions.[11] It is the balance between these two types of actions which allows us to carry out routine actions efficiently but break the habits when desired to give a different response based on new information.

The Habit Loop: Automatic Responses and Decisions

Since the brain favors habit, and habit is inseparable from decision-making in the brain processes, the mechanism of *habit functioning and habit formation* needs to be understood for purposes of moral education. Habit, like memory and reason, is said to be the root of our behavior. Many studies[12] have established that the habit loop of *cue→ routine→ reward* depicts the three steps of processing when the brain selects a response routine (e. g., waving and saying "Hi" to someone or ignoring them) to an external cue (e. g., someone waving to us) and receives a resultant reward (e. g., that person smiling back after our wave), which helps the brain decide to discard the memory or store it for future retrieval. Once the memory is stored repeatedly, this loop becomes automatic, a habit is formed, and these responses and decisions involved become automatic and effortless. Habits involve not only behavior but also thinking and emotion. In other words, we have habitual behavior, habitual thinking, and habitual feeling, which explain those automated actions, thoughts, and emotional responses to the same situations.

---

[11]   Cf. C.M. Gremel, et al., "Endocannabinoid Modulation of Orbitostriatal Circuits Gates Habit Formation," *Neuron* 90/6 (June 15, 2016): 1312–24.

[12]   Cf. A.D. Smith and J.P. Bolam, "The Neutral Network of the Basal Ganglia as Revealed by the Study of Synaptic Connections of Identified Neurons," *Trends in Neurosciences* 13 (1990): 259–65; J.G. McHaffle, et al., "Subcortical Loops through the Basal Ganglia," *Trends in Neurosciences* 28 (2005): 401–07; A.M. Graybiel, "Neurotransmitters and Neuromodulators in the Basal Ganglia," *Trends in Neurosciences* 13 (1990): 244–54; J. Thomson, *The Placebo Diet: Use Your Mind to Transform Your Body* (London: Hay House Inc., 2016).

Willpower and Voluntary Intention

For decisions made in the OFC, which include moral decision-making, the process involved is intentional or voluntary in nature and occurs when the brain alters the routine in response to an unfamiliar cue (like building a new habit) or selects a different routine for the same cue (like breaking an old habit). Willpower is warranted to follow through with decisions made in these situations, particularly for the latter situation, when a different response is required for a familiar cue. The automatic routine, the habit, would generate resistance and impede the new routine from being built into the loop. Nevertheless, as the new routine responds to a selected cue, which sets off the decision-making for the routine to follow in order to receive the reward, willpower can turn the new routine into a habit. This applies to both building a new loop and changing a habitual loop. Willpower is like a skill or muscle and becomes strengthened with repeated exercise. With practice, this willpower loop becomes automatic, and we continue to make the same decision to carry out the same routine in response to the same cue to receive the same reward, without deliberately thinking or making a decision. An old habit is then replaced by a new habit. Therefore, moral decision-making can change from voluntary to involuntary to "automated" without thinking through the intervention of willpower.

The Involuntary Revisited: From Neurological Findings to Family Education in the Chinese Heritage

The understanding of Chinese family teaching traditionally characterizes Chinese culture and Chinese education in a unique and paramount way. In fact, family teaching in the Chinese culture has evolved over the past two thousand years to become more than merely an enormous collection of sayings (*jia xun* [family teachings]) passed from generation to generation.[13] Family education (*jia jiao*) in

---

13 Historical development of family education in China, as A. Yan has indicated, began as early as the fifth century BCE. Family education had been widely implemented in the homes of educated intellectuals, as early Confucianists recognized the pervasive influences of family on children's character development and thus promoted family teaching through a variety of writings (e. g., *jia xun* [family teachings] or *jie zi shu* [advice for children]). See A. Yan, *Zhongguo gudai de jiajiao* [Family teachings in ancient China] (Beijing: Commercial Press, 1997). From the Tang Dynasty in the seventh century CE on, family education became so popular that a large number of standard texts was published for parents as reference. From then until now, prominent and popular standard texts have grown to number more than 120. See Z. Zhao, *Zhongguo jiaxun mingpian* [Famous Chinese writings on family teachings], (Hankou: Hubei Education Publishers, 1997). These

the Chinese culture is a specialized discipline and a kind of formalized, structured education in the home, with its own texts, aims, and principles. The most comparable concept in Western culture is parenting, yet Chinese family education distinguishes itself from parenting in its fundamental orientation as well as in sociological and pedagogical perception. To put it plainly, parenting does not have an equivalent concept in Chinese culture. It is not a Chinese concept. The concept of parenting in contemporary Western society, according to a review of literature, converges on the impact of parents' attitudes, values, and behaviors on the development of the individual child.[14] In other words, parenting has a child-focused orientation.

Moral Character Building towards Communal Adjustment

According to studies of the family teaching texts,[15] Chinese family education can be broadly categorized along two directions: one is development of moral character and virtue, and the other is the path to successful social adjustment and social achievement through the building of interpersonal relationship. These two paths contrast drastically with the contemporary prevailing Western parenting precept of "Make them happy." Comparison of research on parents' goals and expectations for their children also reveals cultural differences, which divide distinctly between modern Western culture on one hand and Asian and Latin American cultures on the other. The former highly values personal traits and qualities such as independence, self-reliance, and individual achievement for their children,[16] while the latter foster interdependence, cooperation, and collaboration.[17]

---

texts are to be followed by parents, reiterated by parents to children, and then eventually recited and memorized by children.

[14]   T.S. Berg-Nielsen, A. Vikan, and A. A. Dahl, "Parenting related to Child and Parental Psychopathology: A Descriptive Review of the Literature," *Clinical Child Psychology and Psychiatry* 7 (2002): 529–52.

[15]   See W. Wang and D. Wang, *Zhongguo jiaxun zhihui* [The wisdom of Chinese family teachings] (Hong Kong: Zhonghua Book House, 1994); Y. Zhang, ed., *Jiaxun jilan* [Anthology of family teachings] (Wuhan: Hubei Education Publishers, 1994); and Z. Zhao, *Zhongguo jiaxun mingpian.*

[16]   Cf. J. T. Spence, "Achievement American Style: The Rewards and Costs of Individualism," *American Psychologist* 40 (1985): 1285–95; H.C. Triandis, "The Self and Social Behavior in Differing Cultural Contexts," *Psychological Review* 96 (1995): 506–20; H.C, Triandis, et al., "Individualism and Collectivism: Cross Cultural Perspectives on Self-ingroup Relationships," *Journal of Personality and Social Psychology* 54 (1988): 323–38.

[17]   Cf. A. O. Harrison, et al., "Family Ecologies of Ethnic Minority Children," *Child Development* 61 (1990): 347–62.

With a child's development rooted in character building, Chinese family education aims far and high into the future for social adjustment and at outstanding social achievement through building of interpersonal relationships both within the family and outside of the family (that is, a communal orientation). Home is considered the ground for practice of discipline. At home, a child is to learn to be pious and respectful of parents and elders. With siblings, one has to strive to maintain a harmonious relationship. Outside the home, a child is taught to choose friends carefully, be humble and suppress one's desire, be trustworthy, be understanding without demanding, and be discreet in words and behavior.

Self-Discipline through Self-Cultivation and Training of Willpower

Chinese family education is a rigorous process, demanding self-discipline from parents themselves to follow this regime of setting aims and goals first, and then promoting development of the child's attitudes, values, and behaviors for social success in the future. Many of the popular family teaching texts provide suggestions for meticulous exercises for the development of various virtues. The way of such self-discipline in Chinese family education is a result of training of will and, as L. Stafford and C. L. Bayer point out, an extension of compliance and continuous, gradual development into moral development.[18]

---

[18]   See L. Stafford and C.L. Bayer, *Interaction between Parents and Children* (Newbury Park, CA: Sage, 1993). Stafford and Bayer examine parent-child interaction from three perspectives (unidirectional, bidirectional, and systemic) to help understand its influences on development of self-control, self-concept, and communication competency in the child. They identify three aspects of self-control: compliance, internalization, and moral conscience. Drawing from Lawrence Kohlberg's positions, they contend, "*Compliance, internalization, and moral development* appear to be integrally and (many contend) hierarchically related components of *self-control.* It has been proposed that obeying compliance requests promotes internalization, which is then predictive of the later development of a moral conscience" (37). This model finds growth in individual development in nature and parental influence cumulative in effect. One prerequisite to Chinese family education is the interaction of the child with parents, which, as indicated above, is a vital key for an individual to become a self-determining person through developing moral habit to moral conscience to self-control. In fact, within Lev S. Vygosky's Zone of Proximal Development (ZPD), R.G. Tharp and R. Gallimore have identified four stages of changes mediated by capable others (e.g., parents, teachers, or peers): the child's performance is initially assisted by more capable others (via their modelling or direction) with child being more imitative, then through others' scaffolding, thirdly through a structuring environment, and eventually the child increases responsibility by asking questions (33-36). When a child assumes the responsibility of asking questions, that is an indication of self-determining, a necessary component of moral decision-making, and moral thinking. See L.S.

The Significance of Chinese Family Education from a Neurological Perspective

The tradition of family education in Chinese culture aims to provide directive understanding for formation of moral character. Even though it instills moral values and prescribes behavioral expectations, which have long been questioned in modern Western education culture, analyses of the neurological bases of involuntary and voluntary noted above have given us a renewed understanding. In summary, there are two particular features:

a) According to the observation by R. A. LeVine,[19] parental goals and expectations have a broader, contextualized basis than those of the parents or of the child and are closely related to expectations of each society for individual adults of the communities. Chinese family education, with its emphasis on considerations of others when making a decision for an action, reinforces a community of interdependence and promotes an intention of cooperative and collaborative moral sense.

b) Family education, with its emphasis on self-cultivation, has a strong sense of self-demand, of self-discipline with training of willpower. From the neurological perspective, the reiteration of principles and modeling by parents and memorization of texts by children are cues to moral actions, which are positively reinforced by affirmation from others in the community. Over time, the moral habits, as involuntary actions, and the related neural pathways are formed.

One might debate whether moral habit and involuntary action, which are stagnant and fixed in nature, are detrimental to the development of a moral being's ability to respond to ever-changing interpersonal social problems in this volatile world. Moral judgment and moral thinking, which are voluntary in nature, are critical in this regard. Nevertheless, Chinese family education necessitates the context of parent-child interaction, which inarguably plays a paramount role in one's moral development, specifically in the areas of self-regulation and self-control for the implementation of voluntary moral decision-making and manifestation of moral motivation.

Vygosky, "Interaction between Learning and Development," in *Mind in Society: The Development of Higher Psychological Process* (Cambridge, MA: Harvard University Press, 1978), 79–91; and R.G. Tharp and R. Gallimore, *Rousing Minds to Life: Teaching, Learning, and Schooling in Social Context* (Cambridge: Cambridge University Press, 1988).

[19]   R. A. LeVine, "Human Parental Care: Universal Goals, Cultural Strategies, and Individual Behavior," in *New Directions for Child Development: Parental Behavior in Diverse Societies*, vol. 40, ed. W. Damon, R. A. LeVine, P. M. Miller, and M. M. West (San Francisco: Jossey-Bass, 1988), 3–11.

The Involuntary and Voluntary Complementarity: Family Education and Spiritual Intervention

In the preceding sections, examination of the neurological bases to the voluntary and involuntary processing involving decision-making in the belief-desire-motivation-action schema reveal that both processes are mutually enhanced through the habit loop and willpower. Chinese family education facilitates the generation of involuntary moral action through the habit loop to establish moral habit. It also builds self-discipline and self-regulation, which are critical for the actualization of moral intention. Not only that, this Chinese traditional practice also reinforces a community of interdependence and promotes an intention of cooperative and collaborative moral sense, thus strengthening the moral motivation for moral action in modern societies.

We thus come to the need to discuss the provisions of religious faith for our concerns, particularly in the areas of willpower and its training and spiritual intervention. In this essay, the particular religious faith concerned in the following considerations is the Christian religion.

Training of Willpower as Self-cultivation in Christian Ascetic Tradition

Since willpower is a cardinal element in moral action, it is not surprising that in the Christian spiritual tradition, training of the will has always been a main theme of spiritual exercise. Beginning with the Desert Fathers from the fourth century, mortification of will and the practice of self-renunciation have been regarded as a path to spiritual maturity and one's mystical union with God.[20] Pervading the history of Christian monasticism, practices of asceticism emphasized the training of will for monastics through poverty and hardship of life. For those who were required to let go of the worldly properties and even worldly enjoyment, it was not because the material world was regarded theologically as intrinsically evil, but because the practice of examining one's willpower, motivated by religious conviction, could restrain, resist, and stand against one's natural desires. Willpower has been valued as a very important virtue in Christian spirituality. On one hand, God's divine will and calling unavoidably clash with our human desires and thus naturally demand a strengthened willpower for voluntary submission. On the other hand, when one faces temptation, it is always our fleshly desire that resists

---

[20]   See e. g. Palladius, *Lausiac History* (Westminster, MD: Newman Press, 1965), §22; B. Ward, *The Sayings of the Desert Fathers: The Alphabetical Collection,* Rev. ed. (Kalamazoo, MI: Cistercian Publications, 1984), §1, 3, 7, 10, 16–18, 20–21, 32, 34, 41.

following God's command. In this instance, willpower is summoned to stand against temptation for spiritual victory and maturity.

Gratia Actualis: The Presence of the Holy Spirit and Spiritual Intervention

Spiritual intervention in Christian spirituality refers to the religious experience of our inner world and behavioral changes imputed to one's being by the Holy Spirit through one's reconciliation with God.[21] From our understanding in the preceding sections, we can say that when Paul states in Romans 6 that we should no longer be "slaves to sin" but "slaves to righteousness" in Christ (Rom. 6:6, 16,18), he exactly depicts the breaking of the habit loop by the power of spiritual intervention. Paul also announces in Romans 8:1–3 that "through Jesus Christ . . . the Spirit of life" is able to "set me free" in spite of my "powerlessness weakened by the sinful nature." The Bible does not delineate the exact dynamics behind this work of the Spirit. Nevertheless, drawing from our findings based on prior analyses and the cue-routine-reward loop, we may be able to conclude that being a slave to sin means that whenever the cue of temptation appears, the routine will involuntarily bring out consequent action to obtain the reward of satisfying one's carnal desire. The spiritual presence in this involuntary "temptation–sinful action" loop can intervene in two ways to break the habit loop.[22] One is that the Spirit could reveal and remind us of the negative consequence of the action ("reward"–e. g., our heart will be accused by guilt, or the behavior will hurt ourself or others), contrary to our original anticipation of desirable results. The second possible way of spiritual intervention is the disruption of the habitual loop, replacing the old routine with a new one (e. g., to determine to brake, or to go down a different path) thus leading to a desirable reward (e. g., peace at heart, harmonious relationship with others, and God's approval). Henceforth, we can contend that these processes and the dynamics of spiritual intervention in the halting of the involuntary compulsion to sin can be elucidated from the perspective of neuroscience.

---

21 See Lucien Cerfaux, *The Christian in the Theology of St. Paul* (London: Geoffrey Chapman, 1967), 295–311; Georg E. Ladd, *A Theology of the New Testament*, Rev. ed. by Donald Hagner (Grand Rapids, MI: Eerdmans, 1993), 530–31.

22 G.G. May, *Addiction and Grace* (San Francisco: HarperSanFrancisco, 1991).

Gratia Habitualis: Gradual Transformation in Christian Worldview

On the other hand, according to Erwin Staub,[23] the psychology of being good or evil comes from the constructive or negative gratification of seven basic human needs (including, for instance, the need for security, belonging, meaningful interpretation of suffering, and transcendent pursuits). One's good behavior comes from positive fulfillment or satisfaction of these needs, while evil behavior stems from distorted or negative fulfillment. In our case, when one is convinced by Christian belief and commits to it, one can become increasingly inclined to seek positive fulfillment (e. g., to look at one's sufferings from an eternal perspective, to build up self-esteem with God's unconditional love). As a result, a gradual transformation of life orientation occurs, leading to an aversion to the domination by the "old self," which impedes one's growing into a new person. Good moral conduct will then be manifested from corresponding moral decision-making. Consequently, that would mean the building of one's good moral character.

Conclusion

Moral education, its themes, and its ways of implementation have been in dispute in late modern pluralistic societies. This essay attempts to address the subject by exploring the voluntary and involuntary aspects of moral action and the motivation behind it. Our investigation covers three seemingly unrelated domains that have gone unnoticed by researchers. They include understandings from recent neurological findings, the practice of the traditional Chinese family education, and the place of spiritual intervention as a religious consideration. Our findings shed new light on the discussions of moral education.

---

[23] See Ervin Staub, *The Psychology of Good and Evil* (Cambridge: Cambridge University Press, 2003).

Literary Form, Paideia, and Religion

Comparing Case Studies from the Ancient Greek, Traditional Chinese, and Early Christian Contexts

Waihang Ng

Introduction

A modern pluralistic society can be understood as a platform for competition among values and beliefs. This competition is at times like the competition among commodities sold in the market. It might even arise in a radical form, manifesting itself as social unrest or even military conflict. Since many of the values held in a community are essentially bound up with religious beliefs, the competition among values can be considered as a form of "competition of deities." With the implementation of a democratic system, this kind of competition takes place in a more civilized and peaceful way, but not less insistently and pervasively. Such a political system can at best settle the conflict of values externally, but it is unable to address inner conflicts involving strife among different values. Nor is it very capable of affording genuine communication and mutual understanding when it comes to competing ways of seeing the world. In a modern pluralistic society, propagandistic approaches to moral values are ultimately of no avail. Therefore, in the long run, it is of great benefit to a society to promote a comprehensive ethical education and engage in genuine dialogue among religions.

To that end, the present chapter focuses on ancient Greek literature, classical Chinese literature, and literature from early Christianity, exploring how texts from these three traditions make use of literary writing to engage in ethical education. I first turn to the Greek concept of paideia and discuss how the Greeks conducted their ethical education through literary writing. Then I address the relationship between religious ideas and literary expression and see how the former can guide the latter. I argue that literature can take up a very strategic position when it comes to advancing ethical education and bringing religious ideas to light. To lay bare this dynamic relationship, I investigate how the moral teaching of "control your anger" is articulated in Homer's *Iliad*, Luo Guanzhong's *Three Kingdoms*, and the Gospels from the New Testament. The religious and moral characteristics of these three case studies will come into sharper focus via a comparison among them—a comparison that can, in turn, promote a genuine dialogue between literature and religion.

Paideia

In his three-volume study on Hellenism, *Paideia. Die Formung des Griechischen Menschen* (*Paideia: The Ideals of Greek Culture*), Werner Jaeger gives a thorough account of the development of ancient Greek thought in light of the Greek concept of paideia. The Greek word *paideia* originally "denotes the upbringing and handling of the child which is growing up to maturity and which thus needs direction, teaching, instruction and a certain measure of compulsion in the form of discipline or even chastisement."[1] Jaeger sees education as a natural—and indeed the paramount—function of any human society; this education has to do mainly with practical and moral issues. Whereas *techné* is an elementary and indispensable part of education, the transmission of values is even more crucial and profound. Education is thus, in principle, a general consciousness of the values that govern human life and "is the direct expression of its active awareness of a *standard.*"[2] This standard proves itself to be pervasive across different domains of a society, which exerts its shaping power over those who live and operate in these domains. In this regard, Jaeger finds that for the ancient Greeks, education was not confined to normal schooling but necessarily extended to include cultural education, that is, paideia.

In the Greek approach to paideia, human beings are the primary concern. As Jaeger puts it, "Other nations made gods, kings, spirits: the Greeks alone made men."[3] In Greek society, the poets and philosophers enjoy a special status in making human beings, by drawing on their creative artistry "to shape the living man as the potter moulds clay and the sculptor carves stone into preconceived form."[4] But measuring them against their degrees of success in accomplishing this task, Jaeger gives priority to poetry over philosophy: "The Greeks always felt that a poet was in the broadest and deepest sense the educator of his people."[5] Jaeger sees no separation between ethics and aesthetics in early Greek thought and thus resolutely refutes any attempt to use modern ideas like "art for art's sake" to study

---

[1]   Georg Bertram, παιδεύω, παιδεία, in *Theological Dictionary of the New Testament*, vol. 5, ed. Gerhard Kittel and Gerhard Friedrich, trans. Geoffrey W. Bromiley (Grand Rapids, MI: Eerdmans, 1967), 596.

[2]   Werner Jaeger, *Paideia: The Ideals of Greek Culture*, vol. 1, trans. Gilbert Highet (Oxford: Oxford University Press, 1973), xiv.

[3]   Jaeger, *Paideia* (note 2), xxiii.

[4]   Ibid.

[5]   Ibid., 35.

Greek poetry. Indeed, Greek poetry can succeed in the task of education only when it dexterously interweaves moral and aesthetic elements. The highest values acquire permanent significance and the force to stir the emotions thanks to the artistic expression of poets, giving poetry an advantage over philosophy in performing its educative function. Philosophy is by its nature too abstract to effectively perform the function of education, since it attains universal significance at the expense of the power of immediate appeal. In contrast, life has immediate appeal and is deficient in universal significance. Art in general and poetry in particular are of paramount significance in the Greek conception of paideia, because they enjoy both universal significance and immediate appeal.[6]

Literature and Religion

In his monumental work of literary criticism, *Mimesis. Dargestellte Wirklichkeit in der abendländischen Literatur* (*Mimesis: The Representation of Reality in Western Literature*), Erich Auerbach casts new light on the problem of the representation of reality in Western literature by stressing the enormous influence that religious ideas have wielded on forms of literary expression. In the first chapter of *Mimesis*, Auerbach compares the account of Odysseus's homecoming in Homer's epic *The Odyssey* with the account of Abraham's sacrifice of Isaac in Genesis 22, arguing that these two texts present their stories in diametrically opposed ways. Auerbach makes use of a pair of concepts—"foreground" and "background"—to describe these two different modes of literary presentation. In *The Odyssey*, nothing remains hidden or unspoken. The text represents phenomena as being connected together in a fully externalized form without lacunae, placing them in a perpetual foreground. As Auerbach puts it, "the Homeric style knows only a foreground, only a uniformly illuminated, uniformly objective present."[7] In sharp contrast, everything remains unexpressed or left in obscurity in the Elohistic text known as Genesis: "The personages speak in the Bible story too; but their speech does not serve, as does speech in Homer, to manifest, to externalize thoughts—on the con-

---

[6]   The traditional Chinese pedagogues likewise see no separation between ethics and aesthetics. In classical Chinese culture, there is, interestingly, a concept called *Shi Jiao*, which parallels the Greek notion of paideia. This concept, too, involves ethical education through poetry, as a pedagogical principle practiced by the Chinese for more than two thousand years. Although I do not go into further detail about the concept of *Shi Jiao* in the present essay, it is, in fact, closely cognate to the Greek notion of paideia that I draw on here.

[7]   Erich Auerbach, *Mimesis: The Representation of Reality in Western Literature*, trans. Willard R. Trask (Princeton: Princeton University Press, 2003), 7.

trary, it serves to indicate thoughts which remain unexpressed."[8] Auerbach sees the Elohistic style, emphasizing background, as occasioned by the peculiarly Jewish understanding of God and human beings. Since the Jewish God is "a wholly other" beyond human comprehension, any narration about God must include lacunae and be directed into a depth, where this unfathomable God is concealed.

Auerbach also finds that the human characters featured in Biblical stories, as compared with those in the Homeric epics, have greater depths of time, fate, and consciousness. Shaped by the hands of God in the course of time, the Old Testament figures are always what their pasts have made them. For instance, Abraham's actions are explained not so much by his character or what is happening to him in the present moment as by his encounter with God in the past. His soul is torn between what God has promised him and what remains to be accomplished, between acquiescence and disobedience. Jewish anthropology, in other words, is fundamentally multilayered. In contrast, the Homeric figures do not have any *historical* development in personality. Nor can time leave any marks on their souls. As Auerbach puts it, "So little are the Homeric heroes presented as developing or having developed, that most of them—Nestor, Agamemnon, Achilles—appear to be of an age fixed from the very first."[9] Whereas the Homeric poems are thus comparatively simple in their understandings of human beings, "the Jewish writers are able to express the simultaneous existence of various layers of consciousness and the conflict between them."[10] This example suggests how artistry in literature is shaped by the religious ideas with which a given text, or for that matter a larger literary tradition, is in dialogue.

Auerbach helps us be cognizant of the relationship between literary expression and religious ideas; the former is substantially shaped by the latter. Therefore, artistry is not arbitrary and purely personal; it is substantially guided by the writer's theological convictions. In addition, the Greek idea of paideia sees no separation between aesthetics and ethical education. The efficaciousness of value-oriented education, rather, hinges on how powerful a literary work aesthetically conveys its message. In a word, education about values can be effectively conducted only through paideia, which is in the end interconnected with the religious beliefs. With these premises in mind, I turn now to investigate how values are conveyed through an ancient Greek epic, a classical Chinese text, and the Gospels. I explore how texts from these traditions engage with the teaching of the idea of controlling one's anger, showing how religious understandings and moral teachings come together in each text in a distinctive way.

---

8   Ibid., 11.
9   Ibid., 17.
10   Ibid., 13.

Anger across Literary Traditions

The Iliad

The first lines of *The Iliad* summarize the theme of the whole epic.

> Anger be now your song, immortal one,
> Akhilleus' anger, doomed and ruinous,
> that caused the Akhaians loss on bitter loss
> and crowded brave souls into the undergloom,
> leaving so many dead men—carrion
> for dogs and birds; and the will of Zeus was done.
> Begin it when the two men first contending
> broke with one another—
> The Lord Marshal Agamémnon, Atreus' son, and Prince
> Akhilleus.
>
> (*Iliad* 1.1-10)[11]

The poem's first word in Greek is "anger" (*mênis*), an internal state of mind, which is generally considered the theme of the epic. Homer gradually proceeds from a character's inner condition to that character's external circumstances, as Achilles directs his anger not against his enemy but rather toward his own people. In these few lines, Homer delicately delineates various scenes related to Achilles's wrath, starting with the casualties in the Akhaian army, extending to a sorrowful view in the underworld, and finally seeing Zeus of Olympus as a prime mover. In this manner, the whole universe seems to be filled with Achilles's wrath. Then Homer comes to grips with Achilles's wild anger by turning to the present moment and the clash between Agamemnon and Achilles, which is followed by Agamemnon's demand for Briseis, Achilles's prize in a fair allotment.

As a culture, the Greeks had an insatiable thirst for honor and never hesitated to claim a reward as the honor worthy of a great deed that had been performed. Honor was the highest value of Homer and the aristocracy of his time, and thus fame after one's death was indicative of immortality. This sheds light on Achilles's well-known choice of gaining eternal personal fame over living a long but mediocre life unknown to the world. In this sense, Agamemnon's demand for Briseis does amount to a denial of Achilles's honor and an offense to him as a noble human being. Understanding that the denial of honor was for the ancient Greeks the greatest of human tragedies allows readers to situate Achilles's tempestuous fury in its proper context.

---

[11]   Homer, *The Iliad*, trans. Robert Fitzgerald (New York: Everyman's Library, 1974), 11.

As Achilles fights for his nobility and refuses to take any further part in the struggle with the Trojans, Agamemnon comes to be aware of his grave mistake. Though he makes some lavish offers to Achilles as an attempt at reconciliation, and though Odysseus, Ajax, and Phoenix—whose heroic actions give added weight to their eloquent speech—try to mediate the dispute, these efforts to placate Achilles prove futile. However, Achilles's single-minded defense of his honor later leads to the death of his beloved friend Patroclus. Subsequently, Achilles's anger becomes even wilder and knows no bounds. As he slays Hector in battle and barbarically abuses his corpse, Achilles also fully realizes that Hector's death is to be followed by his own; his ineluctable fate looms large.

Jaeger finds a principle of paideia at work in this episode. He interprets this episode as suggesting that "Against the vast irrational power of Até, the goddess Infatuation, every educational resource and every form of exhortation is vain."[12] As a divine power, Até comes to human beings despite their resistance, takes hold of them, deprives them of sanity, and has them commit terrible blunders. For Jaeger, "It is through a deep spiritual necessity that the Greeks, who considered man's highest self-expression to lie in heroic action, should have felt so strongly the daemonic power of infatuation, and seen that it lay in the eternal contradiction between man's will and his actions."[13] That both heroic noble human actions and a divine power of obsession come into play in the course of events is a distinctive feature of Homeric epic. Jaeger comes to the conviction that Homer keeps in view both divine and human perspectives as a way of reminding his audience about human limitations and about the short-sightedness of human actions. In contrast with the ancient Eastern belief that the gods are the chief actors in human affairs, the Homeric epics are characterized by an anthropocentric tendency. Homer does not treat human beings merely as the instrument of divine activity but rather places them and their fate in the foreground.[14] Achilles's anger is, from this perspective, suggestive of his lofty aspiration to be a noble human being, despite the triumph of his impregnable destiny.

Three Kingdoms

Three Kingdoms: A Historical Novel is a fourteenth-century work attributed to Luo Guanzhong and acclaimed as one of the four classical novels in Chinese literature. The story centers on three political and military power blocs—the states of Wei, Wu, and Shu—which compete with one another during the final years of the collapsing Han dynasty, in the second century CE. One of the blocs, Shu, is led by Liu

---

12   Jaeger, *Paideia* (note 2), 28.
13   Ibid., 48–49.
14   Ibid., 52–53.

Bei, a distant relative of the royal family, who takes the oath with Guan Yu and Zhang Fei as sworn brothers. They pledge their allegiance to the Han dynasty and devote themselves to reviving it. After having successfully invited the sage Zhuge Liang to his aid, Liu begins to consolidate the power of Shu by adopting a policy of alliance with Wu against the most powerful bloc, Wei. As long as Liu firmly adheres to this policy, he seems really to have a chance to succeed some days in accomplishing his mission. Unfortunately, Wu and Shu come into conflict over a strategically important province under the control of Guan, who is defeated, captured, and finally killed by Wu's army. As Liu learns about Guan's death, he is gripped by sorrow and wrath to such an extent that he becomes determined to avenge Guan, no matter what the cost. Liu's subordinates, including Zhuge, try to persuade him not to seek revenge, especially after Wu expresses willingness to make an abject apology. But their efforts are all in vain. The case against revenge is eloquently formulated by Liu's favorite general, Zhao Zilong: "War against the traitors to Han is a public responsibility. War for the sake of a brother is a personal matter. I urge Your Majesty to give priority to the empire."[15] However, this sensible argument goes nowhere, as Liu lets his anger dictate his state policy. Liu personally leads the military expedition but, in the end, suffers a crushing defeat in the battle with Wu. His forces are almost annihilated, and his hope for the renewal of the Han empire is thus dashed, with Liu's own death being marked by humiliation and remorse.

Luo drew on the materials of an official historical work, *Records of the Three Kingdoms*, composed by Chen Shou in the third century CE, and also on the oral traditions by which Chinese folk tales were passed down over thousands of years. However, he does not put these materials together randomly or in accordance with some arbitrary literary principles. Compared to Chen's work, Luo's novel displays a much more coherent and unitary account on this period of history in China; the novel is strictly guided by a specific historical philosophy, namely the philosophy organized around the providence of Tian (or Heaven). Luo describes this philosophy at the very beginning of the novel: "The empire, long divided, must unite; long united, must divide."[16] This historical philosophy repeatedly appears in the novel by way of various characters, both major and minor. For instance, in his last military deployment against Wei, Zhuge successfully dupes his most formidable opponent, Wei's commander, Sima Yi, who leads his troops into a valley where explosives have been planted. Zhuge's ingenious contrivance is on the verge of success; but no sooner do Zhuge's troops set a fire that will kill Sima, than torrents of rain gush down into the valley, extinguishing the flames. When Zhuge learns that Sima takes advantage of this marvelous chain of events to ach-

---

15   Luo Guanzhong, *Three Kingdoms: A Historical Novel*, trans. Moss Roberts (Los Angeles: University of California Press), 956.

16   Ibid., 5.

ieve a narrow escape, he can't help but heave a sigh: "Men devise, Heaven decides!"[17] He recognizes that the faint hope of uniting China under the rulership of Liu's house has now completely vanished. The providence of Tian always prevails, regardless of how assiduously human beings strive to control events.

The providence of Tian sometimes come to pass, too, through the failure of human beings. Charged with the mission of reviving the Han dynasty, Liu is expected to keep his emotions from causing him to make any unwise political decisions. Liu's inability to control his anger leads not only to his political downfall but also the final collapse of the once glorious Han dynasty. The critic Chih-tsing Hsia makes a highly perceptive comment in this connection, however, writing that "Liu [i. e., Bei] is seen in his last reckless act as a man of *i* (righteousness, selfless friendship) obeying a higher kind of duty than that enjoined by the ordinary dictates of prudence and success."[18] In the beginning of the novel, Liu takes an oath with his sworn brothers, vowing, "We dare not hope to be together always but hereby vow to die the selfsame day."[19] In the event, Liu does keep his word, staying true to his vow. As Hsia puts it, "although his death wish urges him to commit folly on an extravagant scale, yet his political failure spells his human success."[20] In Luo's narrative, in other words, the figure of Liu as a failed political leader unable to reverse the course of events is eclipsed by another image of Liu, in his guise as a manifestation of genuine *i*.

This *i* is a kind of virtue that has more to do with one's commitment to one's friends and never going back on one's words than with living up to certain political standards or values. Although Liu is powerless against the realization of the providence of Tian, his tragic commitment to Guan is nevertheless indicative of his freedom to choose this *i* and hence his own path of self-realization. The Chinese tradition places a stronger emphasis on the significance of the virtue *i* than on having the freedom to choose; in this respect, acting in accordance with *i* is considered less as a defiance of the will of Tian, as it might be in the Greek context, than as a way of adapting oneself to Heaven. Through Luo's literary re-creation, Liu's wrath does not merely denote his failure to live up to his public responsibilities; it also represents the realization of a private virtue that is situated even at a higher moral level. To this extent, Liu becomes a moral exemplar in the mode of paideia associated with Chinese tradition.

---

[17] Ibid., 1245.

[18] Chih Tsing Hsia, *The Classical Chinese Novel: A Critical Introduction* (Hong Kong: The Chinese University Press, 2015), 55–56.

[19] Luo, *Three Kingdoms* (note 15), 12.

[20] Hsia, *Chinese Novel* (note 18), 56.

The Gospels

When it comes to the discussion of anger discussed in the Gospels, the Sermon on the Mount readily comes to the mind.

> You have heard that it was said to those of ancient times, "You shall not murder"; and "whoever murders shall be liable to judgment." But I say to you that if you are angry with a brother or sister, you will be liable to judgment. (Matt. 5:21-22a, NRSV)

Since the act of killing is so often driven by the impulse of anger, the thesis and antithesis mentioned in Matthew 5:21-22 could be viewed as shifting focus from the act itself to the motivation behind the act, in order to come to grips with the root of the problem.

Interestingly, Matthew also includes a narrative about the cleansing of the temple, in which "Jesus drove out all who were selling and buying in the temple" as if he acted in a way of "holy anger" (Matt. 21:12-13). A radical ethic in the form of a logion and a realistic ethic in narrative form are put side by side in the Gospel, yielding, in Gerd Theissen's phrase, a contrast "between an ethic which is proclaimed and an ethic which is lived out."[21] Theissen, however, sees a deeper meaning in the juxtaposition of these two messages, namely the call to a higher righteousness and the preaching of divine grace. He notes that the prohibition against anger in the Gospel is expressed not in the form of a moral demand, as in the Decalogue—like "you shall not be angry"—but to the effect that "whoever is angry is guilty." The focus is thus less on moral persuasion than on admission of guilt. It follows from this admission that human beings are in dire need of the grace of forgiveness. As Theissen puts it, "The radicalized demand here potentially turns into a recognition of the inadequacy of all human beings—and this recognition is in turn the basis of a radicalized preaching of grace."[22]

In addition to drawing on traditional notions of ethics and grace, Theissen also sets the moral teaching of "control your anger" against its contemporary social background. He is aware of the close connection between killing and anger, not only in terms of causal relationships but also in terms of the political relationship of a ruler with the ruled. In this account, "Anyone who kills becomes lord over another's life. The key to coping ethically with this uncanny possibility lies within a person: in overcoming anger."[23] The less able one is to keep anger in check, the less competently one rules over others. As Theissen further notes, "such self-control is necessary above all where the rulers can give their emotions

---

[21] Gerd Theissen, *The Religion of the Earliest Churches*, trans. John Bowden (Minneapolis: Fortress Press, 1999), 30.

[22] Ibid., 30.

[23] Ibid., 89.

free rein without being damaged directly—but in the long term destabilize their rule."[24] This insight is completely consonant with the cases of Achilles and Liu. As Christians are asked to prevent themselves from giving their anger full rein, they are then expected to practice an aristocratic ethic. Theissen describes this distinctive Christian attempt to "[make] the values and norms of the upper class accessible to all"[25] as "a 'democratization' of an ancient aristocratic ethic of rule."[26] In engaging with the Gospels, ordinary people are exhorted to behave like the noble class and to adhere to the sorts of values once monopolized by aristocrats. In controlling their anger, common people, too, become the nobles, though in a very different kingdom.

Another form of democratization is at stake in Auerbach's analysis of the narrative about Peter's denial of Christ in the Gospel of Mark, parallel to Theissen's notion of "a democratization of an ancient aristocratic ethic of rule." Auerbach speaks of the rule of separation of styles (*die Stiltrennungsregel*) in classical literature, according to which only great and sublime events are considered worthy of being treated in tragedy. No serious literary treatment of daily events in the lives of ordinary people was allowed in antiquity, because the realistic portrayal of daily life was believed to be incompatible with the sublime. Such an event has a place only in comedy, at best. As Auerbach writes, "Everything commonly realistic, everything pertaining to everyday life, must not be treated on any level except the comic, which admits no problematic probing."[27]

This classical rule, however, undergoes a severe challenge in the Gospels. Peter's denial of Christ, as narrated in the Gospel of Mark, could be viewed as an insignificant event that, taking place in a remote corner of the Roman Empire and involving a fisherman from Galilee with a very humble background, falls short of classical criteria for tragedy. But Auerbach goes a step further and unearths the theological significance of this narrative. The authors of the Gospels see themselves obliged to portray "a historically active dynamism,"[28] that is, the awakening of a new spirit in those who have encountered Jesus's teaching and personality. As common people they witness a vital dynamic force unfolding itself in history—a force that engulfs them, completely transforms them, compels them to react to it in one way or another. Yet this dynamic force does not appear as a daemonic force like Até or an ineluctable destiny like the providence of Tian; instead, it animates ordinary lives—even those rife with guilt and wounds—and inspires them with a new spirit, enabling them to reset their course for the eschaton. This sort of animation should not be viewed as a tragic providence being visited on

---

24   Ibid., 88.

25   Ibid., 82.

26   Ibid., 82.

27   Auerbach, *Mimesis*, 31.

28   Ibid., 43.

human beings and sorrowfully determining their destiny, but rather as an inspiration for ordinary people to work out their own lives in their own distinctive ways. For Auerbach, that is the reason why the Gospels are replete with those stories of common people, "for it is not possible to bring to life such historical forces in their surging action except by reference to numerous random persons."[29] With the help of this dynamic historical force, every single individual is empowered to aristocratize their life.

Conclusion

The effectiveness of ethical education depends, at least in some contexts, on the literary form in which it is couched, and literary form is in turn deeply influenced by religious ideas. People receive many key ethical lessons by reading literary works, which impress them with the delicate creation of characters, complex patterns of imagery, memorable scenes, interesting plots, and alluring lines. We can also see in literature the shaping power of religious ideas in ethical education, given that each religion affords a distinctive way of seeing the world and understanding human beings. The more able a religion is to generate captivating and exquisite literary works, the more efficaciously it exerts its formative influence in ethical education, and the more powerfully it shapes society. Accordingly, if the competition of values can be understood as a sort of competition of deities in a pluralistic society, then literature can be viewed as a strategic battlefield where this competition takes place.

Comparative analyses like the one developed in the present essay can further sharpen understandings of the distinctive ways in which a particular religion guides the bringing together of the ethical and the aesthetic. Achilles's anger denotes his honorable endeavor to defend his noble dignity despite the triumph of an ineluctable destiny. Liu's wrath signifies his humiliating failure when it comes to his public responsibilities—a failure occasioned by his powerlessness in response to the irresistible providence of Tian. But his anger also leads to his admirable success in the domain of private virtue. Early Christian teaching concerning anger in the Gospels turns the classical world upside down by aristocratizing the mentality of ordinary people, who are incited by a dynamic power descending from the divine realm into history. More broadly, these case studies suggest how a genuine dialogue between religions, as well as effective communication and negotiation of value differences in a pluralistic society, can be facilitated by probing the religious underpinnings of literary works from different traditions. The ultimate aim of the present essay is to help further this dialogue and encourage mutual understanding among the members of different societies and cultures.

---

[29]   Ibid, 44.

Humility, Humiliation, and Hope
An Extended Homily on the Crucible for Authentic Character in Leadership

Martyn Percy

Some thirty years ago, I was preparing for ordination in the Church of England. As part of my training, I was dispatched on placement to a remote rural parish, where I found myself one day being assessed on my skills leading a Bible study. This is not something I have done much since, but I do recall a group of curious and engaged laity trying to grapple with the text I had set them and the discussion I was leading. They were at the same time grading me on my effort and expertise, while also trying to find the whole exercise vaguely educational and spiritually edifying.

What I especially remember about the Bible study was the passage I chose: John 13—Jesus washing the feet of his disciples, when he elects to serve them and so humbles himself. I asked individuals to talk about a time when they had humbled themselves. They told moving stories about service, costly sacrifice, and putting others before themselves. As we went around the room, we came to the vicar. But he had clearly missed the point of this exercise, and instead told a long story about a time when he had been humiliated. The room went silent, unable to process the vicar's story about his pride and self-worth somehow being devalued, and his perceived loss of status. Now, from this experience the difference between humility and humiliation appears obvious. It is one thing to humble yourself. It is another thing to be humiliated by others.

Humility is the quality of being humble. But in our person-centered and therapeutically attuned culture, we often conflate humility with humiliation. We assume low self-regard and unworthiness to be debasing. But in religion, humility is rooted in perspective and submission—and being "unselved," a liberation from consciousness of the self; a form of temperance that is neither having pride (or haughtiness) nor indulging in self-deprecation. True humility comes, ironically, from a deep inner self-confidence and attends to the needs of and the valuing of others. The humble person is not preoccupied with the self but, rather, occupied with the needs of others. Humiliation, in contrast, is imposed on us externally, and it frequently shames us.

One might suppose that true humility is almost unattainable, and real humiliation undesirable. Both terms are linked to the words "humus" and "hubris." Humus means being earthed, and the humble person is ultimately a *grounded* person —sure of their being, so not above themselves—and knows they are not above others, no matter what giftedness, rank, or status they hold. Hubris, in contrast, is self-inflated, puffed-up self-perception, and it lacks groundedness.

Research from the Harvard Business School—a famous study and essay from Jim Collins at the turn of the twenty-first century—found that many of the top organizations and institutions in the world were led by *humble* people.[1] These were people that Collins identified as "Level Five Leaders"—there are very few of them, and there is no higher level. They possess "humility and fierce resolve," because humility is multidimensional and includes self-understanding, awareness, openness, passion, and perspective. He continues, "the most powerfully transformative executives possess a paradoxical mixture of personal humility and professional will. They are timid and ferocious. Shy and fearless. They are rare—and unstoppable."[2]

Collins never set out to study humble leaders. His study was the usual business school fare: how a good company might become great. But what he found was that great companies were developed by modest and willful people, who had low ego needs and could often come across as shy, peaceable, and quiet. But they were also deeply resolved and highly resilient. They were not especially charismatic. They were more inclined to give praise to others and to be quite self-effacing. Such leaders might say, "It's not about me, but it is about we."

Their humility meant that they did not need much external validation. They tended to inspire with their concern for the small details of other people's lives. They tended to look only in the mirror for critical self-reflection, but otherwise looked out of windows. Leaders who were the opposite spent a lot of time in front of mirrors and rarely glanced through the proverbial window.

I used to remark to students training for ordained ministry that they had no job and no profession to look forward to when the bishop laid hands upon them. What they were preparing for was a life that was an occupation. Our priests are to be occupied with God. And then to be preoccupied with all the people, places, and

---

[1]   Cf. *Jim Collins, "Level 5 Leadership: The Triumph of Humility and Fierce Resolve," Harvard Business Review (2001): 66–76;* Rob Nielsen, Jennifer Marrone, and Holly Slay, "A New Look at Humility: Exploring the Humility Concept and its Role in Socialized Charismatic Leadership," *Journal of Leadership & Organizational Studies* 17 (2010): 33–43; J. Andrew Morris, Celeste M. Brotheridge, and John C. Urbanski "Bringing Humility to Leadership: Antecedents and Consequences of Leader Humility," *Human Relations* 58 (2005): 1323–50.

[2]   Collins, "The Triumph of Humility" (note 1), 67.

parishes that are given by God into our care: to dwell among, care for, and love those people and places as Christ would himself.[3]

But holding such an occupation can be done only when one is grounded in humility. Status has no value here. Moses led the Hebrews out of Egypt and into the Promised Land, and his humility was a sign of his godly strength and purpose, not weakness: "For Moses was a person of exceeding meekness above any that that dwelt upon the earth" (Numbers 12:3). It would seem, then, that Collins's findings in the *Harvard Business Review* reaffirm the sentiment expressed by Jesus in Matthew 23:12—"Those who exalt themselves will be humbled; but those who humble themselves will be exalted." We might also remember the words from the Letter of James (4:6): "God opposes the proud but gives grace to the humble."

Here I have a theory. Humility is strength, but pride can be weakness. And the key to living a humble life is grounded in grace and gratitude, not in grasping. As the exquisite hymn in Philippians puts it, Jesus did not "cling to" or "grasp at" equality with God "but emptied himself, taking the form of a servant . . . and being found in human form, humbled himself." From that place, it was a life of obedience, blessing, and gratitude—and of raising up those around him. Correspondingly, spirituality is essentially a lesson in love, but a difficult one to grade. If you wish to understand and excel at humility, think of love as something that is earthed in doing normal, simple, mundane things. It is not about the greatest kiss, or the most self-fulfilling intimate relationship. Because, as the aphorism attributed to Jesus in the Acts of the Apostles has it, "In everything I did, I showed you that by this kind of hard work we must help the weak, remembering the words the Lord Jesus himself said: 'It is more blessed to give than to receive,' which teaches that there is joy in the act of giving when it is done with pure motives" (Acts 20:35).

Love is rooted in humility: stooping to care for the small details of other people's lives. U.A. Fanthorpe expresses this sentiment in her poem **"Atlas"**:[4]

> There is a kind of love called maintenance
> Which stores the WD-40 and knows when to use it;
> Which checks the insurance, and doesn't forget
> The milkman; which remembers to plant bulbs;
> Which answers letters; which knows the way
> The money goes; which deals with dentists
> And Road Fund Tax and meeting trains,
> And postcards to the lonely; which upholds
> The permanently rickety elaborate
> Structures of living, which is Atlas.

---

3   Cf. Ian Tomlinson and Martyn Percy, eds., *Clergy, Culture and Ministry: The Dynamics of Roles and Relations in Church and Society* (London: SCM Press, 2017), vii–xvii and 165–75.

4   U.A. Fanthorpe, "Atlas," in *Safe as Houses* (Norwich: Peterloo Poets, 1995), 10.

And maintenance is the sensible side of love,
Which knows what time and weather are doing
To my brickwork; insulates my faulty wiring;
Laughs at my dry-rotten jokes; remembers
My need for gloss and grouting; which keeps
My suspect edifice upright in air,
As Atlas did the sky.

Wisdom consists of knowing our place before God. In humility, we are invited to occupy ourselves with God and, in turn, to let God occupy us with all the cares and concerns that Christ has for this world. We are to put others before ourselves. We are invited to clothe ourselves in humility. God gives grace to the humble. If we can humble ourselves, we may also be exalted.

The Crucible

Many people will associate humility with the excessive and posturing character of Uriah Heep in the novel *David Copperfield*, by Charles Dickens.[5] Heep stalks Dickens's novel with his cloying humility, obsequiousness, and insincerity, and he is often to be found making frequent references to his own "'umbleness." Yet the truth about humility is that when authentic, it is often so natural that it is unconscious. Moreover, humility is most tested—one might say refined in the fire—under persecution.

I think of the unassuming character John Proctor in Arthur Miller's *The Crucible*.[6] Miller's play is a partially fictionalized story of the Salem witch trials that took place in the Massachusetts Bay Colony during 1692-93. Miller wrote the play primarily as an allegory—as a critical censure of McCarthyism, when elements of the United States government, led by Senator Joseph McCarthy, were hounding and persecuting American citizens suspected of being communists. In the play, John Proctor is a man of steely integrity, with a degree of fierce resolve, and tempered with cool anger. But he is a person of humility and probity, and it is this that Miller focuses on. The play dwells on the pressure placed on John Proctor to compromise—in order to save his own life. But the saving of his own life would come only at the cost of his integrity and probity. He cannot negotiate this away. So he submits to an unjust trial and is destroyed by a social construction of reality that is mired in hysteria and hatred. Miller's play is based on the real John Proctor,

---

5   Published in installments by Bradbury & Evans (London), 1849-50; and as a book by the same publisher, 1850.

6   First performed in 1953; edition cited: Arthur Miller, *The Crucible* (Harmondsworth: The Viking Press, 1971).

an innkeeper and farmer in Massachusetts Bay who was executed when he was sixty years old. He was outspokenly opposed to the witch trials overrunning his community. Unlike the character in the play, the real John Proctor maintained his innocence throughout the ordeal and was hanged in August 1692.

I am no John Proctor. But I do know something of what it is to be tested in the crucible of false and pernicious accusations that attack one's probity and integrity. Such attacks can often be motivated by the desire to humiliate. I think of two examples here from my own life, where I have been threatened—menaced, really—with allegations that would have existential consequences for my vocation and identity.

In one case, I faced a vexatious litigant who was determined to prosecute the college over a range of issues. During the course of the grievance, I was accused of being a chronic alcoholic and incapable of fulfilling my role as the head of a theological college. I am a teetotaler and have been for a great many years, but such allegations can be ruinous for the individual and the institution. The litigant lost their case, and both the college and I were vindicated. Yet I still remember the sleepless nights, the loss of weight, the worry, the migraines, and the veritable "pit of despair" as I faced the ruin of both my reputation and the good name of the college.

In a very different context, I have stood accused of being "immoral, scandalous, and disgraceful" over a dispute with a college committee. In both of these cases, the accusers consciously calculated the damage such denunciations would do and assumed that their menacing would result in bargain and compromise—that somehow the very exercise of their threats would enable them to achieve their goals. Put simply, the end would justify the means.

In both cases, I resisted intimidating charges, albeit at considerable personal cost. Some compromise would have been the easy path—the broad way (Matt. 7:13). The narrow path is sometimes to take a principled and uncompromising stance. I claim no heroism here, only that firm, principled ethical resistance is also rooted and grounded in concern for the other, rather than one's (mere) self-preservation. In this case the other was the perpetrator of the threat. In other words, it would not have been good for the perpetrator if their will had prevailed. To some extent, the self-conscious kenosis of Christ anticipates this in the way of the cross. Golgotha is not for Christ; it is for us. Here, humility remains the ground of wisdom, and it confounds and further infuriates others. So we must know and remember that others may want to humiliate those with vocations to leadership. This is part of the costly path of leading and serving.

The human response to attacks on leaders (and by leaders) can often be one of anger and retaliation,[7] and while such reactions have a certain legitimacy, the on-

---

[7]   On theologies of legitimate anger, see Lytta Bassett, *Holy Anger: Jacob, Job, Jesus* (London: Continuum, 2007), 70 ff. On the place of aggression and anger in ecclesial life, see Bar-

ly response that we ever learn from the cross is, "Father, forgive them, for they know not what they do" (Luke 23:34), which finally breaks the cycle of violence. Moreover, the leader is required–charged, I think–with trying to understand the unconscious forces at work in such situations of stress.[8] Aggression in organizations and institutions can be expressed positively and negatively. In its positive form it is about drive, about the activity that moves things forward so that love and relationship might flourish. In its negative form, it reacts with violence to those things that appear to deny or destroy the self. But when directed toward the affirmation of life and well-being, aggression can have positive personal and collective dimensions.[9]

I am not alone in taking this journey. I have met other clergy, academics, and folk from other walks of life who have been subjected to abusive bullying, humiliation, and false accusation. In each case, the symptoms are the same: excessive weight loss or gain; stress and sleeplessness; anguish and anger; exhaustion and low energy. In all this, the accusations and the bullying cloud one's judgment and also isolate the victim, often reducing them to silence. It is also very rare for the institution that is supposed to care for and carry individuals through such nightmares to act with pastoral integrity.

It is no wonder, then, that some of these victims find their anger turning to bitterness and vengeance. But I note that many in leadership positions do not find this, and somehow summon up reservoirs of grace that refuse to do to others what is being done to them (Luke 6:31). How can this be? It can only be done, I think, if one's own humility is lodged in some kind of rich ecology of love and mercy, soaked through with grace, such that we genuinely do not count others less than ourselves. That we do not cling to equality, but somehow continue to serve. Moreover, that we also grasp that God's love and grace are poured out on the underserving, not on the self-righteous.

For those who are the victims of dysfunctional leadership, this is an especially hard truth to hold. Moreover, if abuse by the leader is vented from a pathological root, such as narcissism, this can be a highly demanding and lonely road to travel for the victim, as many companions will abrogate their responsibility and desert their calling to exercise moral courage. Here, practicing leadership, or resisting toxic

---

bara Harrison and Celia Robb, *Making the Connections: Essays in Feminist Social Ethics* (Boston: Beacon Press, 1985). These are discussed in Martyn Percy, *Shaping the Church: The Promise of Implicit Theology* (Farnham: Ashgate, 2014).

8   Anton Obholzer and Vega Zagier Roberts, *The Unconscious at Work: Individual and Organizational Stress in the Human Services* (London: Routledge, 1994).

9   Cf. Kathleen Greider, "Too Militant? Aggression, Gender, and the Construction of Justice," in *Through the Eyes of Women: Insights for Pastoral Care*, ed. Jeanne S. Moessner (Minneapolis: Fortress Press, 1996); cf. Celia Hahn, *Growing in Authority, Relinquishing Control: A New Approach to Faithful Leadership* (Bethesda, MD: Alban Institute, 1994).

forms of leadership, can be a solitary vocation and leave one in a place of (seemingly) lengthy desolation.[10] *It requires considerable introspection and inquiry to under-stand the nature of the individual and the institution under such circumstances.*[11]

So an ecology of grace (that is, deeply comprehending God's full and uncondi-tional love for the other), alloyed with an appropriate and natural humility, might be the only way to cope with the projections and detriments done to us. For this reason, I admire Harry Smart's poem "Praise":[12]

> Praise be to God who pities wankers
> and has mercy on miserable bastards.
> Praise be to God who pours his blessing
> on reactionary warheads and racists.
>
> For he knows what he is doing; the healthy
> have no need of a doctor, the sinless
> have no need of forgiveness. But, you say,
> They do not deserve it. That is the point;
>
> That is the point. When you try to wade
> across the estuary at low tide, but misjudge
> the distance, the currents, the soft ground
> and are caught by the flood in deep schtuck,
>
> then perhaps you will realise that God
> is to be praised for delivering dickheads
> from troubles they have made for themselves.
> Praise be to God, who forgives sinners.
>
> Let him who is without sin throw the first
> headline. Let him who is without sin
> build the gallows, prepare the noose,
> say farewell to the convict with a kiss.

To complement this poetry, I simply note the plea of Stanley Hauerwas:

---

[10]   See Paul Babiak, *Snakes in Suits: When Psychopaths Go to Work* (New York: HarperBusi-ness, 2006); John Fitzmaurice, *Virtue Ecclesiology: And Exploration of the Good Church* (Farnham: Ashgate, 2016).

[11]   On this, see Ronald Heifetz, Alexander Grashow, and Marty Linsky, *The Practice of Adap-tive Leadership* (Cambridge, MA: Harvard Business Review Press, 2000); Roysto Green-wood, et al., *The Sage Handbook of Organizational Institutionalism* (London: Sage, 2008); Nitin Nohria and Rakesh Khurana, *The Handbook of Leadership Theory and Practice* (Cam-bridge, MA: Harvard Business Review Press, 2010); Luk Bouckaert and Laszio Zsolnai, *The Palgrave Handbook of Spirituality and Business* (London: Palgrave, 2011).

[12]   Harry Smart, *Fool's Pardon* (London: Faber & Faber, 1995), 7.

It is not enough, in other words, that those called to the ministry refrain from or do certain things; it is necessary that they be the kind of persons, that they have the character, to sustain them in the ministry. . . . It is not enough that a person is not "immoral"; neither should they be vain, proud, intemperate, cowardly, ingratiating, and unloving. Moreover, it must be asked whether a person exhibits the patience and hope so necessary to the ministry. For without patience and hope there is little chance a person will have the constancy to sustain him or her through the disappointments and betrayals so often involved in the ministry.[13]

Kenosis, Power, and Leadership: Towards A Theology of Humility

In view of this, where might we locate a Christian theology of humble leadership? Here I turn to kenosis—a term that generally refers to the "self-emptying" of Christ and is an aspect of the doctrine of the Incarnation. It is expressed most succinctly in the so-called Christological Hymn found in Paul's letter to the Philippians (2:6–11):

> Christ Jesus, who, though he was in the form of God,
> did not count equality with God a thing to be grasped,
> but emptied himself, by taking the form of a servant,
> being born in human likeness.
> And being found in human form,
> he humbled himself by becoming obedient to the point of death,
> even death on a cross.
> Therefore, God has highly exalted him
> and bestowed on him the name that is above every name,
> so that at the name of Jesus every knee should bow,
> in heaven and on earth and under the earth,
> and every tongue confess that Jesus Christ is Lord,
> to the glory of God the Father.

The hymn follows on from a meditative soliloquy from Paul on the nature of character in Christian leadership (Phil. 2:1–5):

> So if there is any encouragement in Christ, any comfort from love, any participation in the Spirit, any affection and sympathy, complete my joy by being of the same mind, having the same love, being in full accord and of one mind. Do nothing from selfish

---

[13]   Stanley Hauerwas, *Christian Existence Today: Essays on Church, World, and Living In Between* (Durham, NC: The Labyrinth Press, 1998), 135, 143.

ambition or conceit, but in humility count others more significant than yourselves. Let each of you look not only to his own interests, but also to the interests of others. Have this mind among yourselves, which is yours in Christ Jesus.

Theological reflection of this kind would have resonance centuries later in the Rule of Benedict (instructing the abbot), Gregory's Pastoral Letter (instructing bishops), all the way through to Robert Greenleaf's more modern meditative discourse on servant leadership.[14]

Churches are, as Hauerwas notes, "communities of character."[15] In such communities, people are being *disciplined* by the grace of God into the new life that God, in Christ, has claimed them for. Such communities are not mere gatherings of groups with shared interests. Nor are they homogeneous units. Rather, they are a "thick gathering" of those being renewed by the salvific action of God in Christ. Such communities have to be called back, constantly, to the exposure of "all desires known," so that "the thoughts of our hearts might be cleansed by the inspiration"—the very breath—of the Holy Spirit. This has an ontological depth to it, as it is kenotic in character. It is only by following the one who "emptied himself" that one discovers the foundation for humility.

Donald MacKinnon, commenting on the theology of Donald Baillie, states that "in Christ God is revealed as submitting himself to the very substance of human life, in its inexorable finitude, in its precarious ambiguity, in its movement to despair."[16] Correspondingly, notions of omnipotence and omniscience are transformed by kenosis. Jesus becomes the obedient one—but the one who becomes obedient unto death, even when that death is totally unjust. The obedience must mean that the crucifixion is real; for in his humanity, Jesus must embody it all in its fullness—including despair. This, argues Mackinnon, leads the church to living "an exposed life; it is to be stripped of the kind of security that tradition, whether ecclesiological or institutional, easily bestows."[17] So, rather than attending to security and safety, underpinned by a fear or death, humiliation, and annihilation, the church is asked to "let go and let God." This means there is a potential unfaithfulness to the gospel when opposing any enemy or external threat that poses a risk to the church's very existence. As MacKinnon further noted, when the Christian God is endowed with the attributes of a human Caesar, the church takes on

---

14   Robert K. Greenleaf, *Servant Leadership: A Journey into the Nature of Legitimate Power and Greatness* (Mahwah, NJ: Paulist Press, 1977).

15   Stanley Hauerwas, *Communities of Character: Towards a Constructive Christian Social Ethic* (South Bend, IN: University of Notre Dame Press, 1991).

16   Donald MacKinnon, "Reflections on Donald Baillie's Treatment of the Atonement," in *Christ, Church and Society: Essays on John Baillie and Donald Baillie*, ed. David Fergusson (Edinburgh: T & T Clark, 1993), 115–21.

17   Donald MacKinnon, *The Stripping of the Altars* (London: Fontana, 1969), 34.

the image of a "transcendent Caesar" rather than the more fundamentally disruptive calling of embodying the "vulnerable Nazarene." For MacKinnon,

> From Christ there issues a continually repeated question, and his Church is his authentic servant only in so far as it allows that interrogation to continue. It is always easier to escape its remorseless probing: to take refuge in the security of a sharply defined orthodoxy, or to blur the riddling quality of its disturbing challenge by conformity to the standards of the age.[18]

What this means in practice will vary across individuals, congregations, and communities. But what can be said is that all Christians are incorporated into Christ's perpetual oblation. Our being part of the priesthood of all believers means that everything that comes to us, or comes upon us, we return to God in confession and intercession—offering it up for sanctification and blessing. Christians participate in the life of Christ, and in our own self-emptying, willful descent, and conscious path of humility, bound to an ecology of obedience rather than one of mere self-preserving resistance.

This, I should say, does not call the church, or individuals or groups within the church, to a life of passive acceptance. Rather, it commits us to a very different vocation, and one that is far more costly. It invites us to contemplate the formation and habitation of the character of community or individual that is being afflicted or persecuted. But here we are asked to model not weakness but *meekness*. We are invited to utter the words we hear from the cross: "Father, forgive them, for they know not what they do."

There is, then, a paradox at the heart of kenosis. It is not a kind of weary resignation in the face of the malign forces of fate. It is, rather, an act of determination and resolve, an exercise of deep power from within that chooses—in the example of God in Christ—to limit power and knowledge, but not to limit love. The path of obedience accepts that a conscious and deep form of humility will no longer privilege power and knowledge. Rather, these will be set aside in a continuous, willful, and generative life of humility that will place others above the self. The self-limiting of power and knowledge allows love to both cover and hold those who need it most. Indeed, I think many parents will understand something of this. What the child needs to experience is a parent with *some* power and *some* knowledge, but not too much, or else the child's growth and individuation will be stifled. But this self-limitation can only take place within a paradigm of unconditional love, which seeks to sustain and serve the ones we seek to set free. Only love can

---

[18]   Cf. John McDowell, ed., *Philosophy and the Burden of Theological Honesty: A Donald MacKinnon Reader* (Edinburgh: T & T Clark, 2011), 264.

do this. As it frees, it binds us. There can be something apophatic about Christ's way of leadership: humility preferred to privilege.[19]

Such kenosis is, as I say, something of a paradox. Because the love can be fierce, just as Christ's Passion is a willful act of determination, not resignation. Moreover, this love can contain anger, and even make space for disruptive acts of prophetic leadership. This poem from Piers Plowright contrasts the Christian God with some alternatives:[20]

Considering the other Gods
Would you really want them round your place?
Thor banging about in the hall
Kali destroying the kitchen
Aphrodite coming on strong
In the bedroom—then turning nasty.
All tricksy, changeable—to hell with right and wrong.
I think I'll stick with Jesus:
His half-smile, fierce love,
Amazing Grace.

Mind you, he too could send the plates flying,
Turn things upside down,
The maddened swine stampeding
Into the wine-dark sea,
The wrong pardoned,
And all that crying.
Still he's the one for me
As the world darkens
And drunk captains run the ship.

He's there, in the eye of the storm,
On the cruel tree, facing it down,
Throwing across time and space,
Beyond ambition, pride the dip of Fate,
A thin line of light
That we can grab before we drown.

Yes, "beyond ambition, pride . . . a thin line of light that we can grab before we drown."

God's power is rooted in relinquishing and transforming. It is not kept or traded: it is given away, free. Human power, typically, takes for its own ends, to maintain and grow itself. God's power, located on a foundation of sacrificial love, hospital-

19   Cf. Jane Williams, *Seeking the God Beyond: A Beginner's Guide to Christian Apophatic Spirituality* (London: SCM Press, 2018).

20   Piers Plowright, "Choosing," in *The Tablet: The International Catholic News Weekly* (January 17, 2019), https://www.thetablet.co.uk/features/2/15188/the-tablet-poem.

ity, and humility, builds up and is eternal. Human power, based on competition and dominance, is temporal and decays. As Moises Naim notes, "even as rival states, companies, political parties, social movements, and institutions or individual leaders fight for power as they have done throughout the ages, power itself—what they are fighting so desperately to get and keep is slipping away. Power is decaying."[21]

As I have remarked before on power in Christian leadership, the relationship between the formation of character of the individual and the community is often a negotiation between behavior (exemplary and otherwise) and (potentially problematic) divine-human conflation.[22] Mixed into this will be elements of projection, along with fantasy, narcissism, and the basic human fragility. Leaders should beware; leaders should be aware.

The formation of character is a subject receiving increased attention from theologians. John Barton draws our attention to how much of the Old Testament wisdom tradition emphasizes suffering and the apophatic as a key to development.[23] But so is, equally, the concept of *disciplined attention:* watchful patience, moral sagacity, emotional intelligence, vicarious virtue, honed perception—all can be found in Proverbs, Ecclesiastes, Ecclesiasticus, and the Psalms. Similarly, Joanna Collicutt's recent work on character formation[24] helps us to see that good leadership is often formed through adversities that are stayed from decaying into despair and vengeful self-protection. Kenosis is a form of being that does not allow negativity to germinate. To be sure, the true servant leader is often mocked.[25] Yet the self-emptying paradigm exemplified in Jesus leads to a humble kind of leadership that serves the other. The meekness is magisterial. The one who reigns does so from a tree, and the crown is made of thorns.

Conclusion

The homiletic tone of this essay is intended to do what all sermons and homilies aspire toward—namely, to prompt reflection, self-examination, and some soul-searching. At the same time, it seeks to induct us into imaginative ways of think-

21 Moises Naim, *The End of Power: From Boardrooms to Battlefields* (New York: Basic Books, 2013), 1f.
22 Cf. Martyn Percy, *Anglicanism: Confidence, Commitment, Communion* (London: Routledge, 2013); Id., *The Future Shapes of Anglicanism: Maps, Currents, Charts* (London: Routledge, 2016).
23 John Barton, "Character Formation in Biblical Wisdom," *Crucible* (January 2019): 18–28.
24 Joanna Collicutt, *The Psychology of Christian Character Formation* (London: SCM Press, 2015).
25 On this, see Michael Screech, *Laughter at the Foot of the Cross* (London: Penguin, 1997).

ing critically about the scriptures and our Christian tradition, alongside the challenges we face in our daily lives and complex social existences.[26] Leadership is just one such area. And here our concern has been to wrestle with some of the issues that leaders face in relation to humility, humiliation, and hope.

In closing, let me suggest that something flowing naturally from a person's leadership as a consequence of their humility might be kindness. Kindness is a rare quality, and it has been shown that in modeling kindness, and in creating a culture of kindness, leaders can have a positive energizing effect, creating improved interpersonal relations and increasing commitment. Moreover, kindness is infectious. Granted, kindness requires balance, because it cannot recuse leaders from making difficult and costly decisions. However, kindness does express appropriate concern for others, and it communicates value and empathy in contexts that some can experience as alienating and marginalizing. However, that "kindness" as a term has been absent from leadership vocabulary is both intriguing and concerning. It is a term that many in leadership want to explore—not least because many will perceive it to be a sign of weakness, or possibly manipulative when, in fact, flowing from an authentic humility it is energizing and enabling. Kindness is extremely important as a leadership behavior.[27]

I am mindful of Paul Johnson's biography of Winston Churchill, which recounts that great leader's call to heed the lessons of leadership: aim high and work hard, and eat your problems like elephants—one mouthful at a time.[28] But then Johnson goes on to remind us of lessons from Churchill's life: to be patient and not let mistakes and failure get you down. You'll have them; learn from them, and don't deny them. Equally, he counsels not spending emotional energy on recrimination or vindictiveness—because hatred is exhausting and draining. Leave room for joy and laughter. And be humble; because it isn't about you.[29] Scott Cairns has written this poem on perspective in roles, taking the Beatitudes and extending them into the terrain we often find ourselves journeying in as leaders:[30]

---

[26] Cf. Simon Western, *Leadership: A Critical Text* (London: Sage, 2007).

[27] See Gay Haskins, Lalit Johri, and Michael Thomas, *Kindness in Leadership and its Many Manifestations* (London: Routledge, 2016).

[28] Paul Johnson, *Churchill* (London: Penguin, 2009).

[29] Lucy Kellaway for the *Financial Times* (July 1, 2011) notes how essential humility is for good leadership, and warns of the dangers of bullying and narcissism: https://www.bbc. co.uk/news/business-13974474.

[30] See Scott Cairns, "Late Sayings," in *Slow Pilgrim: Collected Poems* (Orleans, MA: Paraclete Press, 2015); Mark Burrows, ed., *The Paraclete Poetry Anthology* (Orleans, MA: Paraclete Press, 2017).

Blessed as well are the wounded but nonetheless kind,
for they shall observe their own mending.
Blessed are those who shed their every anxious defense,
for they shall obtain consolation.
Blessed are those whose sympathy throbs as an ache,
for they shall see the end of suffering.
Blessed are those who do not presume,
for they shall be surprised at every turn.
Blessed are those who seek the God in secret,
for they shall hear His very voice rising as a pulse.
Blessed moreover are those who refuse to judge,
For they shall forget their most grave transgressions.
Blessed are those who watch and pray, who seek and plead,
for they shall see, and shall be heard.

In ending here, I simply invite all who lead to practice kindness, to be authentically humble, and to be charitable, even to those who seek to humiliate you. Do not be afraid. There will be humiliations, naturally. But if we dare to wait in hope (Rom. 8:18-39), there will be light. Indeed, it is often in the waiting and the kenosis that we are refined—formed to become the very people and leaders God has called us to be.

Part Three

Interdisciplinary and Ethical Perspectives on
Societal Impacts of Religion

The Impact of Religion on Shaping Values in Pluralistic Societies

A Case of Opposing Interpretations and Unintended Consequences?

Piet Naudé

In his classical work *Dimensions of the Sacred*,[1] Ninian Smart distinguishes seven dimensions shared by all religions, including the ethical and legal dimension.[2] This dimension refers to the "aspect of belief which incorporates moral and legal values,"[3] which in turn serve as guidelines for human behavior. The phenomenological observation is that commitment to a religion implies that human attitudes and action are shaped by moral values, reinforced by (moral) narratives/myths, and encapsulated in doctrinal teachings.

This essay focuses on the ethical dimension of the Christian faith and attempts to demonstrate that there is a complex interaction between religious values and the shaping of societal ethics beyond the institutional boundaries of this religion.[4] Christianity is not a homogeneous religion, and competing traditions developed over time, each with its distinctive emphases on how and which values shape public life.[5] Even within the same tradition, the founding scriptures are read from different angles, leading to deep divisions on social questions.[6] There is sometimes a significant values impact from religion on society.[7] Conversely,

---

[1]   Ninian Smart, *Dimensions of the Sacred: An Anatomy of the World's Beliefs* (Berkeley: University of California Press, 1999).

[2]   Ibid., 196–214. The other dimensions are ritual, narrative, experiential, institutional, doctrinal, and material.

[3]   Ibid., xvi.

[4]   The focus here is solely on how values shape social questions, and not on the formation of values or morals at a personal level.

[5]   Cf., for example, Catholic social doctrine with Reformed confessions and Pentecostal social action.

[6]   Cf. the opposing positions taken by Christians from the same tradition during National Socialism and apartheid, and the issue of gay marriage and gay ordination that still causes divisions in the Anglican tradition.

[7]   Cf. the process leading to the freedom of African Americans and black South Africans based on prophetic Christian leadership.

developments in secular society impact Christian convictions, which, over time, lead to a change in churches' stance on social matters.[8]

To claim that religious values shape public life is therefore a complex matter that may be approached from many different interpretative angles. For the sake of illustration, this essay presents two mini case studies. The first demonstrates the social impact of contrasting interpretations of an authoritative Christian theologian, Karl Barth, for the sociopolitical situation in South Africa during its transition from a (pre)modern to a pluralist society.[9] The second case outlines how the theological idea of "a preferential option for the poor" (Gutierrez) influenced values and decisions in political philosophy (Rawls) and economics (Stiglitz) on a global scale.[10]

Case Study One: The Contestation in Reading Karl Barth in South Africa

South Africa formally became an apartheid state in 1948, when the National Party won the elections in which only people classified as "white" were permitted to vote. It is not necessary to recount the well-researched economic, political, and, especially, the theological roots underlying white nationalism and providing support for South Africa's policies of racial and church segregation.[11] When continued moral legitimacy was sought for apartheid in the period between 1948 and 1960 in response to increasing internal and external critique of the system, the work of Karl Barth became known in Reformed circles at the influential Stellenbosch Theological Faculty. At stake was the value-formation of the Reformed tradition which had been—up to that point—predominantly used to justify apartheid based on a particular interpretation of scripture and the (neo)-Calvinist tradition.

---

[8]   Cf. the initial reluctance of churches to endorse the notion of human rights or to provide women equal access to leadership ordination in the church until after those rights were constitutionally endorsed.

[9]   This is a reinterpreted extract from Piet Naudé, "The Reception of Karl Barth in South Africa 1960–1990: Selected Perspectives," in *Reformed Churches in South Africa and the Struggle for Justice: Remembering 1960–1990*, ed. Mary-Anne Plaatjies-van Huffel and Robert Vosloo (Stellenbosch: SunMedia, 2013), 186–99.

[10]   The full version of this case study was published as Piet Naudé, "In Defense of Partisan Justice—An Ethical Reflection on 'the preferential option for the poor,'" *Verbum et Ecclesia* 28/1 (2007): 166–90.

[11]   See John W. DeGruchy, *The Church Struggle in South Africa* (Cape Town: David Philip, 1979); Piet Naudé, *Neither Calendar nor Clock: Perspectives on the Belhar Confession* (Grand Rapids, MI: Eerdmans, 2010), 23–48.

The Relegation of Barth to the Margins of Society

The first important reading of Barth was by F.J.M. Potgieter, professor of dogmatics at Stellenbosch and a staunch supporter of racial segregation on theological grounds.[12] How would Potgieter respond to Barth's critique of natural theology and religion, as well as Barth's call for the visible unity of the church? Potgieter first wrote a highly critical article on Barth's controversial notion of divine inspiration of the scriptures[13] and subsequently made a short but telling reference to Barth in relation to the question of the visible unity of the institutional church.[14] As demonstrated below, the combination of these two framings of Barth provided a highly effective strategy to inhibit the positive reception of Barth for the subsequent two decades.

In relation to the inspiration of scripture, Potgieter asks how we should interpret 2 Timothy 3:16, the well-known passage that asserts that all of scripture is inspired by God (*pasa graphe theopneustos*). He commences by rejecting a number of viewpoints.[15] Mechanical inspiration—as if God directly wrote through the authors as passive instruments—denies the human aspect of scripture writing, he argues. Dualistic inspiration—as if scripture is inspired with respect to matters of salvation but not in terms of history, chronology, and geography—does not take seriously enough that the whole of scripture is inspired. The personalistic theory—as if divine inspiration refers to the writers of the Bible in their own person, but not to their actual words and the content they provide—is once again a limitation of the full inspirational character of scripture.

Over and against these views, Potgieter argues for an organic-verbal inspiration of scripture.[16] He explains that verbal inspiration implies that each specific word in the Bible is inspired on condition that words are read in context and that intracanonical writers could freely use earlier words of scripture. This must be seen as complementary to organic inspiration, namely that the Holy Spirit inspired people via the use of their own talents and insights to actually write the scriptures.

---

[12] F.J.M. Potgieter, "Veelvormige ontwikkeling: Die wil van God," *Die Gereformeerde Vaandel*, March 1958, 5-15.

[13] F.J.M. Potgieter, "Die teopneustie van die Heilige Skrif met besondere verwysing na Karl Barth," *Nederduits Gereformeerde Teologiese Tydskrif* (June 1963): 131-49.

[14] F.J.M. Potgieter, "Die wese van die kerk van Christus," *Nederduits Gereformeerde Teologiese Tydskrif* (Dec. 1961): 271-77. The reference to Barth, Brunner, and Van der Leeuw (all without motivation) is accompanied by a critique of Prof. A.S. Geyser, who defended the visible unity of the church based on his analysis of New Testament texts and the Apostles' Creed (Ibid., 273).

[15] Cf. Potgieter, "Teopneustie" (note 13), 134-36.

[16] Ibid., 136-37.

Having set out his view, Potgieter then rejects Barth's view of *theopneustos* on a number of grounds.[17] Barth does not see scripture itself as the object of inspiration. Barth understands inspiration as the dynamic act of God's grace through the Spirit, who makes the human words of scripture into the actual Word of God as it pleases God. The Bible, therefore, is not the Word of God, it becomes the Word of God. Barth perceives the biblical texts as fallible products of ordinary sinful human beings, subject to the questions raised by higher criticism. These fallible words become God's Word via the miracle of the internal witness of the Holy Spirit.

Potgieter maintains that the texts are themselves the object of *theopneustos* and therefore constitute the infallible Word of God, including the historical information contained in them. If this view is not upheld, Potgieter sees the rise of full relativism vis-à-vis the authority of scripture. He employs the doctrine of the two natures of Christ as an analogy to reconcile the human and divine dimensions of scripture: "According to its essence, the Holy Scripture is the Word of God; according to its nature, it is a human word."[18]

This brings us to Potgieter's second encounter with Barth from this period. In an essay on the visible unity of the institutional church, published in 1961, Potgieter lists Barth as one of the authors who (in his view, wrongly) defends the visible unity of the church.[19] This essay demonstrates a specific reading of Abraham Kuyper, whom Potgieter cites on numerous occasions, and the essay should be read together with Potgieter's earlier article on pluriform development of different races as the will of God.[20] In short, Potgieter argues that visible unity belongs to the well-being (*wel-wese*) but not to the being/essence (*wese*) of the church.[21] This he argues from the perspective that the visible unity of the church is an eschatological and not a historical reality to be realized here and now. He defends race-based ethnic churches—separate in visible structures—on the basis of pluriformity as a creation principle.[22] The differentiation among peoples is indeed caused by sin, but then blessed under God's general grace as God's will in the course of human history. In a sentence that is difficult to translate, Potgieter writes that differentiated development is God's will for the intermezzo between creation and the second coming of Christ. This differentiation "finds its initial

---

[17] Ibid., 138–46.

[18] Ibid., 143. My translation of "*Na sy wese is die Heilige Skrif Woord van God; na sy natuur is dit mensewoord*"; emphasis in the original.

[19] Potgieter, "Wese van die kerk" (note 14), 273.

[20] Potgieter, "Veelvormige ontwikkeling" (note 12), 6. This is probably one of the most coherent and well-defined defenses of separate churches for different races and cultures.

[21] Potgieter, "Wese van die kerk," 274–75.

[22] Ibid., 276–77.

source in sin, but its subsequent origin in God's general grace."[23] This pluriform-ity was clearly confirmed after the Fall by God's general grace in history, notably in both the Babel and Pentecost narratives, where different nations and languages are channels of God's work. Potgieter goes further to state that an insistence on the visible unity of the institutional church is in fact a Roman Catholic idea,[24] as it grows from the conviction that the differentiated church is held together as one by the papal hierarchy, a view of church authority clearly rejected by the Reformers.

Based on this reading of some of Potgieter's essays, one can therefore detect a two-pronged rhetorical strategy in his reading of Barth: by demonstrating that Barth deviates from the orthodox position on the inspiration of scripture, and by arguing that seeking visible unity for institutional churches is not only against the Bible and Reformed tradition but actually Catholicism in disguise, Potgieter effectively relegated the critical and evangelical dimensions of Barth to the side-line of the mainstream Reformed tradition as it unfolded in South Africa from 1960 to 1985. What Jaap Durand observed about the period up to 1960 was re-confirmed for at least the next two decades: "One of the great tragedies in the de-velopment of Afrikaner Reformed theology in the three decisive decades of its evolvement (1930–1960) was that Barth's criticism of religion and natural theol-ogy was never really heard."[25]

By the mid-1980 s, the situation in South Africa was on a knife edge. There were frequent black uprisings within the country, attacks by military-trained ex-ternal forces on civilian targets, impactful international economic sanctions, ecu-menical isolation of the white Reformed churches by the World Council of Church-es (WCC),[26] and strong alternative theological voices. All these developments were met by increasing state violence and suppression, while the system of racial separation started to lose its moral legitimacy even among whites, and the tran-sition to a pluralist democracy became a possibility (fully realized by 1994).

Reading Barth as a Modern and Critical Social Voice

I turn now to the way Barth would be read by Potgieter's colleague and later suc-cessor, Willem Daniel (Willie) Jonker, who exerted a decisive influence on the dis-

---

23   Potgieter, "Veelvormige ontwikkeling," 13. My translation of: *"vind sy aanleidende oor-saak in die sonde, maar sy bewerkende oorsaak in sy (God se) algemene genade."*

24   Potgieter, "Wese van die kerk," 275.

25   Jaap Durand, "Afrikaner Piety and Dissent," in *Resistance and Hope*, ed. Charles Villa-Vicencio and John De Gruchy (Cape Town: David Philip, 1985), 40.

26   World Council of Churches (WCC), *Confessing the One Faith: An Ecumenical Explication of the Apostolic Faith as it Is Confessed in the Nicene-Constantinopolitan Creed (381)* (Geneva: WCC Publications, 1991).

mantling of the theological base for apartheid. What is represented here, is but a small part of Jonker's thinking about Barth developed in the mid-1980 s, and it focus on explicit reflections on Barth's influence on his generation.[27] This chapter does not take into account, for instance, Jonker's quite lengthy and important Christological discussions of Barth.[28]

Jonker is quick to point out the controversial aspects in Barth's thinking that would not be considered in line with positions generally held in the Reformed tradition. He refers to Barth's actualistic notion of revelation, his universalism, his somewhat reductionist reading of scripture from a Christological perspective, and his rejection of infant baptism.[29] These aspects, however, in no way detract from the huge significance and influence of Barth's theology on Jonker's own thinking.

Jonker sketches a broad appreciation for Barth: God and theology are sources of joy due to the radical grace of God and objectivity of salvation. There is the centrality of Christ in line with the Pauline vision of the New Testament. Barth further exudes an evangelical enthusiasm for the proclamation of Biblical truths and can —in a qualified and positive sense—be called an "orthodox"[30] theologian.

Less than a decade before South Africa would—in dramatic fashion—make a transition from a premodern and monist apartheid dispensation to a modern, pluralist society guided by a rights-based secular constitution based on Enlightenment values, Jonker makes use of Barth to prepare the church and society for this new era. For Jonker, the crucial contribution of Barth lies in the fundamentally different response he gives to the challenges of modernity. For him, Barth is a modern theologian in his own right, and his theology "can only be understood against the background of the Enlightenment."[31] Far from being a positivist or retreating into a premodern position that tries to escape the difficult questions of historicity and freedom, Barth exactly addresses those questions, but he does so from a radically different paradigm. He shifts the basis of theology from the transcendental subjectivity of religious humanity (as put forward by the Cartesi-

---

[27]   See W. D. Jonker, "Die relevansie van die kerk. Aktuele teologiese reaksies op die vraag na die betekenis van die kerk in die wêreld," 1987, unpublished HRSC report. The manuscript was published in 2008 as *Die relevansie van die kerk. Teologiese reaksies op die vraag na die betekenis van die kerk in die wêreld* (Wellington: Bybel-Media). It is to this latter publication that references are made. The second source is W. D. Jonker, "Some Remarks on the Interpretation of Karl Barth," *Nederduits Gereformeerde Teologiese Tydskrif*, Part 29, No. 1 (Jan. 1988): 29–40.

[28]   See for example, W. D. Jonker, *Christus, die Middelaar* (Pretoria: NG Kerkboekhandel, 1977), 118–25; 182–84.

[29]   Jonker, "Karl Barth," 30, 32.

[30]   Jonker, *Relevansie*, 44–49; Jonker, "Karl Barth," 31.

[31]   Ibid., 35.

an theologies of Schleiermacher, Bultmann, and Tillich) to the transcendental subjectivity of God. In the light of this starting point, Barth has no place for hermeneutical (prolegomena-type) questions and no room for apologetics: "It was not necessary to indulge in hermeneutics in order to help modern man, to understand the gospel. What he really needs to know, is that God loves him."[32]

In Jonker's assessment, Barth provides a "hidden accommodation" of the modern critical mind via a radical Christological reinterpretation of core concepts like freedom, autonomy, and change. Barth in fact confronts the issues of modernity head-on, but from a quite distinct evangelical position which Jonker—despite some criticism—judges to be the most appropriate response in the first part of the twentieth century.[33]

Jonker further expresses appreciation for the sociopolitical thrust of Barth's theology. Barth's "political" significance is derived from his Christological concentration where (for example) the bodily resurrection of Christ points to the fundamental material (not only spiritual) character of salvation, and prepares the ground for Barth's later emphasis on the humanity of God that in fact transforms social reality: "God's freedom in love also calls us to freedom in love, so that the humanity of God calls us to every form of action that will serve the humanization of society."[34]

Jonker specifically endorses the critical power of Barth's theology. This critical element "touched us in a special way"[35] and enabled a new generation of theologians to formulate their critique of the theology underlying the apartheid system. Jonker refers to the "self-satisfaction of some forms of neo-Calvinist theology with which we were acquainted," while neo-Calvinist theologians themselves "were all very critical about him (Barth)."[36] Barth also unmasked "the self-deception of the pietistic, Arminian and Methodist preoccupation with personal holiness and perfection which we were perpetually confronted within our circles," and assisted a new generation to be critical of "the religious familiarity with God which we knew all too well."[37] For Jonker, Pietism is a complex historical phenomenon that at times provided a positive alternative to an overt objectivism in theology; however, he judges the kind of pietism that mixed with neo-Calvinism in South Africa as too individualistic and too anthropocentric[38]—traits that stood diametrically opposed to the dialectical theology of Karl Barth.

---

32 Ibid., 34; Jonker, *Relevansie*, 45–46.
33 See the whole argument in Jonker, *Relevansie*, especially the conclusion on 52.
34 Jonker, "Karl Barth," 38.
35 Ibid., 30.
36 Ibid., 29. Potgieter would fit well into this description.
37 Ibid., 31.
38 Jonker, *Relevansie*, 35–37.

Despite questions about controversial aspects of Barth's theology, Jonker could fundamentally shift the value-forming nature of Reformed theology in a crucial transitional period: the engagement in South Africa with the emerging challenges of the first and second Enlightenment; the critique of a self-satisfied theology which was simultaneously blind to its social consequences while ideologically supporting racial segregation; and reading Barth's Christological theology as a basis for the humanization of society.

Placing Barth at the Center of the Quest for Social Justice

A third reading of Barth occurred in the early 1980 s and addressed the looming question of justice for the formerly oppressed people in a postapartheid and pluralist society in the making. Whereas Potgieter resisted Barth's social impact, and whereas Jonker read Barth from the perspective of a theological response to the Enlightenment, Dirk Smit (the successor to Jonker in dogmatics at Stellenbosch) approached Barth as a direct source for social justice.

With the acceptance of the Belhar Confession in draft form by the Dutch Reformed Mission Church in 1982, a collection of explanatory essays, edited by Daan Cloete and Dirk Smit, was published as A Moment of Truth.[39] In this volume, Smit made two invaluable contributions: he explained the dogma-historical origin and significance of a status confessionis (pages 7–32) and provided an exegetical rationale for the controversial claim in the Belhar Confession that God is in a special way the God of the destitute, the poor, and the wronged.[40]

The essay under discussion here[41] was published in 1988 as part of a volume edited by Charles Villa-Vicencio under the title On Reading Karl Barth in South Africa. One could argue that this later essay by Smit provides the theological mirror image of the exegetical work done a few years earlier in his essay on the God of the destitute and the poor. For this theological rationale, Smit turns to Barth's doctrine of reconciliation (Church Dogmatics/IV)[42] and specifically his exposition of Jesus as the royal man (Church Dogmatics IV/2) who performs miracles that are seen as paradigms of the kingdom of God. This kingdom is marked by God's radical grace, which liberates unconditionally from the destructive powers of evil.

---

39   G. Daan Cloete and Dirk J. Smit, eds., A Moment of Truth: The Confession of the Dutch Reformed Mission Church (Grand Rapids, MI: Wm. B. Eerdmans, 1984).

40   Dirk Smit, "In a Special Way the God of the Destitute, the Poor, and the Wronged," in Cloete and Smit, A Moment of Truth, 53–65.

41   Dirk Smit, "Paradigms of Radical Grace," in On Reading Karl Barth in South Africa, ed. Charles Villa-Vicencio (Grand Rapids, MI: Wm. B. Eerdmans, 1988), 17–44.

42   Karl Barth, Church Dogmatics (Edinburgh: T. & T. Clark).

Following Barth, Smit first states that Jesus, the royal man, exists analogously to the mode of God's existence.[43] The royal man—through his humiliation—shares fully in the destiny of humankind. Almost to the point of prejudice, the royal man shows remarkable affinity for the weak, the lowly, and those who are poor in moral, economic, spiritual, and social terms. This affinity is not based on any merit that might lie in the situation of the poor or in poor people themselves—love flows only because of God's infinite grace. The royal man thus affirms and reflects the divine YES to humanity, especially suffering humanity. The cross can therefore be viewed as the triumph and coronation of the royal man.[44]

The miracles of Jesus, the royal man, are done toward those "with whom things are going badly"; for whom human life is "like a great hospital."[45] Their suffering is mostly physical, and the focus of the miracles is not primarily salvation from sin but release from suffering, irrespective of sin. This is a powerful demonstration of God's interest in humankind itself—in humans as cosmic beings, created by God. In the miracles, God is placed on the side of humanity and against hostile powers, nothingness, evil, and destruction that cause suffering and death.[46]

An interesting question now arises: why did Protestantism miss this point? Barth's answer—affirmed by Smit[47]—is that the message of the Gospels was understood from the side of humanity, where sin and need for forgiveness were seen as almost "meritorious" grounds for God's action. In contrast to this, the message must be understood from the view of the kingdom, that is, from God's unconditional free grace toward humanity, understood not only as sinners but as God's creatures in need of total redemption.

The option for the poor is therefore not a simple ethical matter or socioeconomic description of a specific class of people—it is a deeply theological matter, steeped in the doctrine of reconciliation, because in this option we see "the astonishing light" of God's radical, free grace. "We can now conclude," writes Smit, in line with his 1984 exegetical view, "that Reformed Protestantism finds in Karl Barth an important witness to testify that the God of Jesus Christ is indeed in a special way the God of the poor."[48]

---

[43]   Ibid., 23.

[44]   Ibid., 25–27.

[45]   Ibid., 29.

[46]   Ibid., 31–32.

[47]   Ibid., 33.

[48]   Ibid., 42.

Conclusion on First Case Study

The reading/interpretation of an authoritative figure has a significant impact on the value-forming potential of religion. The case study above illustrates how Barth was first sidelined to exert almost no influence on social developments in South Africa (Potgieter), whereas later interpretations opened the door to provide a theological response to modernity (Jonker) and to address the question of inequality and social justice in a pluralist democracy (Smit). Let no one render reading of theological texts as a mere innocuous exercise of limited academic significance!

Case Study Two: The Notion of Preferential Justice

This minicase study attempts to establish a trajectory of thought beginning with Gustavo Gutierrez's treatment of a preferential option for the poor,[49] proceeding through John Rawls's criterion of justice as fairness for the least advantaged representative person, and ending with the differential international trade regime proposed by Joseph Stiglitz.

Gustavo Gutierrez and Preferential Justice from a Theological Perspective

The advent of a cluster of liberation theologies—Latin American, black, African, feminist/womanist, gay/lesbian, and ecological—was accompanied by a specific understanding that what is at stake is not just new theological themes of liberation but the very way of constructing theology as such. Despite the inner complexities of, and differences among, this pluralistic array of liberation theologies,there is a specific methodological convergence: each liberation theology generally takes as its methodological point of departure the oppressive experience of those who fall within its focus. These focal points explain in each case who would be seen as poor, marginalized, and oppressed.

For the purpose of this case study, I take only one example—the Latin American liberation theology of Gustavo Gutierrez.[50] There is a twofold motivation of this particular choice. First, the historical origin of the specific term "the preferential option for the poor" lies in Latin American Catholicism. What later became Latin American liberation theology has the closest ties to these historical roots.

---

49   Gustavo Gutierrez, "Option for the Poor," in *Mysterium Liberationis: Fundamental Concepts of Liberation Theology*, ed. Ignacio Ellacuria and Jon Sobrino (New York: Orbis, 1993), 235–50.

50   Gustavo Gutierrez, *A Theology of Liberation* (London: SCM, 1973).

The first indications of the term are already present in *Gaudium et Spes,* emanating from Vatican II (1965). The term found its way more directly into the second general conference of Latin American bishops at Medellin (1968), and was taken up explicitly as a chapter titled "The Preferential Option for the Poor" in the final document of the third bishops' conference in Puebla, Mexico (1979).[51] Secondly, although "the option for the poor" has been adopted by other liberation theologies, and later by the ecumenical movement, Latin American liberation theology is, in my view, the best example of a theology constructed specifically around this option as a lens through which to view all theological loci.

In a short, illuminating passage, Gutierrez[52] explains the preferential option for the poor: "The very term *preference* obviously precludes any exclusivity; it simply points to who ought to be the first—not the only—objects of our solidarity." He points out that liberation theology "has insisted on the importance of maintaining both the universality of God's love and the divine predilection for 'history's last.'"[53] What the word *option* seeks to emphasize "is the free commitment of a decision. The option for the poor is not optional in the sense that a Christian need not necessarily make it, any more than the love we owe every human being, without exception, is not optional. It is a matter of a deep, on-going solidarity, a voluntary daily involvement with the world of the poor."[54] The reference to *the poor* denotes at least three forms of poverty: material (being physically poor), social (being marginalized as a result of racial, cultural, or gender oppression), and spiritual (lacking openness to God's will and solidarity with the poor).[55]

The methodological renewal brought by liberation theology was formulated by Gustavo Gutierrez in a classic exposition in 1971. According to him, liberation theology "offers us not so much a new theme for reflection as a *new way* to do theology."[56] He thus states: "Theology is a critical reflection on Christian praxis in the light of the Word."[57] The starting point of theological reflection is not revelation or tradition but "purely and simply, the daily experience of the unjust poverty in which millions of our fellow Latin Americans are obliged to live."[58] What

---

[51]   See the discussion of original documents by Gutierrez, "Option for the Poor", 239–40, and the more detailed overview and analysis by Heinrich Bedford-Strohm, *Vorrang für die Armen. Auf dem Weg zu einer theologischen Theorie der Gerechtigkeit* (Gütersloh: Chr. Kaiser Verlag, 1993), 151–66.

[52]   Gutierrez, "Option for the Poor".

[53]   Ibid., 239.

[54]   Ibid., 240.

[55]   Ibid., 235–37.

[56]   Ibid., 15.

[57]   Ibid., 13.

[58]   Roberto Oliveros, "History of the Theology of Liberation," in Ellacuria and Sobrino, *Mysterium Liberationis*, 4.

informs theological reflection at the beginning are the facts and questions derived from the world. And this world is the world of the poor and the marginalized, a reality of social misery. It is the experience of these poor and marginalized people from "the underside of history" that informs theology as liberating process.

It is important to note that "the preferential option for the poor" was highly controversial at the time of its first formulation, but in the meantime it has found its way into mainstream theology, as is evident, for example, from Catholic social doctrine and the ecumenical interpretation of the Nicene Creed. [59]

John Rawls and Preferential Justice from a Philosophical Perspective

In his well-known *A Theory of Justice*,[60] John Rawls develops a difference principle[61] in which redistributive policies allow for social and economic inequalities, but only if they result in compensating benefits for everyone, "and in particular for the least advantaged members of society."[62] The protection or improvement of the least advantaged therefore receives absolute priority in determining justice.

Rawls's defense of this priority is philosophically based on his opposition to utilitarianism and his preference for the contract tradition stemming from Hobbes, Locke, Rousseau, and Kant. His methodological defense is based on his strategy to show that the difference principle (or maximum criterion) would be the rational choice for members of a future society who find themselves behind a veil of ignorance[63] in an original contract position.[64] The (re)distribution of primary goods, identified by Rawls as "rights and liberties, opportunities and powers, income and wealth,"[65] must always satisfy the criterion of improving the worst-off person's situation.

---

[59]   This theological view is, for example, echoed by the ecumenical church in an exposition of the Nicene Creed: "In the particular case of human oppression, the victim is assured that God is never on the side of the oppressor, the bringer of death, but will, in justice, protect the rights and lives of the victims": WCC, *Confessing the One Faith* (note 26), 63.

[60]   John Rawls, *A Theory of Justice* (Cambridge, MA: The Belknap Press of Harvard University Press, 1971).

[61]   Ibid., 60–90.

[62]   Ibid., 14–15.

[63]   Ibid., 136–42.

[64]   Ibid., 17–22.

[65]   Ibid., 62, 92.

The measurement of this "worst-off" person, or what Rawls calls the identification of "the least advantaged representative man,"[66] may be determined by economists in terms of the Gini index coupled to social welfare functions, or by the Lorenz curve, which depicts the percentage of the total amount of income possessed by any given percentage of the poorest among the population (e.g., the poorest 20 percent of people sharing 4 percent of total income). Harry G. Frankfurt argues that this priority of those worst off should be given only to those below a certain threshold.[67] One could apply his view to the current distinction between people living in poverty and those living in absolute poverty.

In his later book, *The Law of Peoples*,[68] Rawls extends his notion of justice as fairness to an international society composed of different peoples who have "distinctive institutions and languages, religions and cultures, as well as different histories."[69] In an initial compact (the second original position), where representatives of the peoples meet behind a thick veil of ignorance,[70] eight principles of the "Law of Peoples" would hypothetically be agreed to.[71] This is not an agreement among free and equal individuals, as in Rawls's "domestic version," but an agreement reached by distinct peoples via their rationally inclined representatives.

In what way could Rawls's "international" version of justice as fairness be interpreted as prioritarian, as described above? Rawls proposes eight principles of justice among free and democratic peoples.[72] Whereas the first seven principles all presume equality and nonpartisanship, the addition of the last principle is significant: "8. Peoples have a duty to assist other peoples living under unfavorable conditions that prevent their having a just or decent political and social regime."[73] This is the law that moves Rawls's egalitarianism toward its special version of prioritarianism, namely "a duty" toward those "living under unfavorable conditions." Rawls refers to these as "burdened societies"[74] because they "lack the political and cultural traditions, the human capital and know-how, and often, the material and technological resources needed to be well-ordered."[75] The

---

[66] Ibid., 91.

[67] Harry G. Frankfurt, "Equality as a Moral Ideal," *Ethic* 98/1 (Oct. 1987): 21–43.

[68] John Rawls, *The Law of Peoples* (Cambridge, MA: Harvard University Press, 1999).

[69] Ibid., 54–55.

[70] Ibid., 32–33.

[71] Ibid., 37.

[72] Ibid.

[73] Rawls himself remarks, "This principle is especially controversial" (*The Law of Peoples*, 37).

[74] A well-ordered and even rich society may become a burdened society through a natural disaster. Irrespective of the cause, Rawls argues that a rational view of reciprocity would agree to the principle that peoples have a duty to assist burdened societies.

[75] Rawls, *The Law of Peoples*, 106.

duty to assist in the context of relations among peoples therefore carries—despite qualifications and restrictions—the same egalitarian consequences as the difference principle in domestic societies.[76]

The principle, if applied to asymmetrical power relations, has a number of implications. Where, for example, indigenous people sharing membership in a domestic society with better-off persons also happen to be in the worst-off position (which is mostly the case), the difference principle would require that the indigenous people receive absolute priority in any redistributive policy decision. And in situations of global distributive decision-making, Rawls's principle of assistance would require that, whatever the outcome of such a decision, it should not diminish the fulfillment of basic needs of the poorest people on the margin, where citizens are unable to build just institutions or take advantage of available rights and opportunities. The rational and just thing to do in the (second) original position is to maximize the minimum, where the latter is linked to the potential to build a well-ordered "Society of Peoples," because the people represented in the second original position might find themselves to be a burdened society.

Joseph Stiglitz and Preferential Justice from an Economic Perspective

Stiglitz's critique of economic globalization, eloquently detailed in his bestseller *Globalization and its Discontents*,[77] is fierce, but his ultimate aim is "to make it work." He commences his subsequent book, *Making Globalization Work*,[78] with his interpretation of the slogan "Another world is possible," which is the motto of the World Social Forum, a gathering of a hundred thousand people in Mumbai in January 2004. He argues for a differential trade system and challenges a number of traditional, conservative economic views on market fundamentalism.

Stiglitz first of all rejects the separation of efficiency and equity considerations in the context of a market economy. The belief that markets and the pursuit of self-interest would—through an invisible hand—lead to economic efficiency is only partially true, he says. If markets by themselves lead to socially unacceptable income distributions, questions around equity arise. And to address equity, economic policy has to include appropriate government intervention and regulation.[79] Stiglitz argues that economic efficiency should not be isolated as the sole criterion of economic performance, but that so-called noneconomic values,

[76] Rawls remarks that among various interpretations of liberalism, "justice as fairness is the most egalitarian": *The Law of Peoples*, 14.
[77] Joseph E. Stiglitz, *Globalization and its Discontents* (New York: W.W. Norton, 2002).
[78] Joseph E. Stiglitz, *Making Globalization Work* (New York: W.W. Norton, 2006).
[79] See his reference to Keynes on page xvii.

such as "social justice, the environment, cultural diversity, universal access to health care, and consumer protection," should be codeterminants of economic success.[80]

Stiglitz further rejects two long-standing premises of trade liberalization. The first is that liberalization of trade automatically leads to more trade and higher economic growth, and the second is that such growth inevitably leads to a "trickle-down" benefit for all.[81] Apart from his own research in information economics, he argues that neither economic history nor current economic theory supports these two premises. There are consequently no grounds to believe that the best way to help the poor is simply to strive for more liberalization of trade and higher growth. Opening up the markets *alone* will not solve the problem of poverty but may even make it worse.[82]

In a reference to Rawls,[83] Stiglitz does intimate that a fairer and more equitable trade system would "entail putting ourselves in others' shoes: what would we think is fair or right if we were in their position?"[84] What type of international trade regime would we, in Rawlsian terms, choose behind the veil of ignorance? It is in this context that Stiglitz argues for his *differential option for the poor* and—reminiscent of Rawls—suggests that trade regimes be judged by whether they make the poorest countries actually worse or better off.[85]

When trade agreements were established among advanced industrial nations under GATT (the General Agreement on Tariffs and Trade, signed in 1947), the principles of nondiscrimination, equality, and reciprocity were upheld. Signatory countries would not discriminate against other members of GATT, and each country would treat all others the same—all were considered to be "the most favored." This system of multinational trade was founded on strict reciprocity. Each country agreed to lower tariffs and to open up markets if the others reciprocated.[86] Coupled to these arrangements was the principle of national treatment: foreign producers were subject to the same regulations as domestic ones.

When GATT was replaced by the World Trade Organization (WTO) in 1995, these principles were carried over into the new, much more expanded trade regime. There is much hard empirical evidence (listed by Stiglitz[87]) to show that an asymmetrical system, with grossly uneven playing fields and uneven implemen-

---

[80] Stiglitz, *Making Globalization Work*, xvii, xiv, 17, 22.
[81] Ibid., 23, 99.
[82] Ibid., 14.
[83] See Stiglitz's reference to Rawls at ibid., 296, footnote 15.
[84] Ibid., 22.
[85] Ibid., 58.
[86] Ibid., 75.
[87] Ibid., 77–78, 85–97.

tation, subsequently evolved and actually made developing countries worse off.[88] What is needed is a global trade regime "that promotes the well-being of the poorest countries and that is, at the same time, good for advanced industrial countries as a whole," although current special corporate interest groups might suffer and lose some of their unfair advantages.[89]

In what he calls "fair trade for the poor," Stiglitz suggests a reform of international trade. This reform would entail that the principle of "reciprocity for and among all countries—regardless of circumstances"—be replaced by the principle of *"reciprocity among equals, but differentiation between those in markedly different circumstances"* (my emphasis).[90]

On what grounds would this proposal be accepted? Stiglitz consistently argues for two grounds: conscience/morality and self-interest. Concerning self-interest, he notes that greater stability and security in poor and developing nations will contribute toward stability and security in the developed world.[91] The flood of immigrants from poor to rich countries might be slowed down if the circumstances compelling people to leave were improved. Obviously, there are also responsibilities on poor countries with regard to governance.[92] A fairer trade regime would in the long run diminish the need for development aid and debt write-offs—mainly sponsored by developed countries. In fact, rich countries have cost poor countries three times more in trade restrictions than what they give in total development aid.[93] The growth attained under a differential system has a far greater chance of actually benefiting everyone (excluding special-interest groups).

The emphasis on morality must be seen in the context of Stiglitz's introduction of noneconomic values as well as the retention of equity with efficiency. He does not argue his case at length, but simply states that to create a trade regime with differential and special treatment is a moral issue and a matter of conscience.[94] The empirical and social realities of poverty among and within countries are socially unacceptable and constitute moral appeals in themselves. "It appears that it is better to be a cow in Europe than a poor person in a developing country," he writes,[95] referring to agricultural subsidies for cows in the European Union that are equivalent to the poverty line of two dollars a day per person in poor countries.

---

88   Ibid., 58.
89   See his notes on "special interests"; see also 13, 24.
90   Ibid., 83.
91   Ibid., 59.
92   Ibid., 58.
93   Ibid., 78.
94   Ibid., 100–01, 59.
95   Ibid., 85.

Following some of Bedford-Strohm's insights,[96] an important implication of preferential justice is that it does represent a broad consensus despite differences of interpretation, content, and motivation among the three positions outlined above. It is possible to see a synergy among a global ecumenical consensus, one of the most plausible political philosophies of the twentieth century, and the work of a leading, Noble Prize–winning economist. This (constructed) consensus gives social and political credence to the notion of a preferential option for the poor. This synergy is no small achievement, as it bears witness to the influence of theological ethics (broadly speaking) on political theory, but in turn it provides evidence of secular arguments for and confirmation of a primary theological notion.

Conclusion on Case Study Two

On the assumption that a credible thought trajectory has been chartered from liberation (ecumenical) theology to social theory and global economics, there might be adequate grounds to state that the impact of religion on value formation may transcend its initial understanding and find unintended complementary interpretations and fruitful policy implementation in secular contexts.

Final Note

The two cases presented in twhis chapter illustrate the complexity of the claim that religion has an impact on value-formation in society, but at the same time they confirm that religion indeed matters and can—in surprising ways—shape social formation and create moral meaning within and beyond the confines of its own institutionalization.

---

[96]   Bedford-Strohm, *Vorrang für die Armen* (note 50), 306–13.

Optimal Environments for the Formation of Character
Challenges and Prospects for Religion

Stephen Pickard

Introduction

To the extent that the major religions of the world embed powerful ethical and moral systems of thought and practice, it is axiomatic that they provide important foundations and conditions for the formation of character, moral vision, and values. This is certainly the case in modern Western pluralistic societies. However, the rise of religious fundamentalism and violence, and the widespread evidence of abuse of children in religious institutional life, particularly in Christianity, raises serious questions about the capabilities of religious life to engender traditions of moral vision and virtuous practices. The very character of religion is deemed suspect by many.

This chapter takes the foregoing as a starting point and inquires about the persistence of religion in secular and emerging postsecular societies, and the impact of corrosive host cultures on religion as a power for good. In the latter sections of the chapter, the focus shifts to the church and a concern for the conditions necessary for the emergence and nurture of character and moral vision. These aspects of Christianity have been and are foundational for the development of modern Western pluralistic societies. A question is posed: is there an optimal ecclesial environment for the formation of character and moral vision as a counterpoint to the corrosion of character and moral virtue in modern Western societies?

Predicting Religion

The fate of religion in the West—its definition, possibilities, even its legitimacy—remains highly contested and controversial, raising a question about the possibility of predicting the future of religion.[1] In terms of the focus of this book of essays,

---

[1]   Grace Davie, Paul Heelas, and Linda Woodhead, eds., *Predicting Religion: Christian, Secular and Alternative Futures* (Aldershot, UK: Ashgate, 2003).

a question arises regarding the capacity of religion to remain a source and power for the shaping of character, moral vision, and values both for individuals and societies. This question is made even more urgent and difficult to assess in light of the numerous discussions and arguments about the course of modernization, globalization, secularization, and the fate of religion in the West.[2] The prospects for religion to contribute in a real and meaningful way to the shaping of the moral vision of peoples requires more careful interrogation and research.

Perhaps we have to begin again in the concrete realities of our existence, where religion is evidently not going away but is simply undergoing significant and somewhat unpredictable transformations within the increasing pluralism of the West.[3] The matter is significantly complicated when we take account of developments in religion beyond the West, within very different cultures, customs, and institutional settings. Instructive at this point is the assessment of the future of religion in the world by the American sociologist of religion Christian Smith, who predicts that (a) some, if not many, humans will continue to want to practice religion; (b) humans will continue to generate new religions; (c) all living religions will be internally, qualitatively transformed over time; and (d) some religions will grow in size, strength, and significance, while others will decline.[4]

The Secular Fate of Religion

The Enlightenment inheritance with regard to religion requires reassessment. From the late seventeenth century, Europe could tolerate religion only once it had withdrawn from the public square, allowing it to be safely privatized and consigned to the status of cognitive deviancy before a prevailing scientific rationality. Until that point, religious beliefs and institutions had substantively shaped societies, provided a vision of the ideal moral community, and underpinned the character and aspirations of society. Henceforth the religious canopy was effectively supplanted by new, functionally sacred realities—the nation-state and the market. The domains of the state and market increasingly shaped the values and purposes of human life in society within the framework of a materialist utilitarian ethic shorn of any transcendent telos. In a climate of enlightened skepticism and a growing Western hunger for freedom from religious constraint, secular society has insisted that religion keep its place. Such sidelining, however, has also invited militantly secular agendas—be they communist, fascist, or radically free market—to define re-

---

2   Ibid, Part 1.

3   Ibid. See also Bryan Turner, *Religion and Modern Society: Citizenship, Secularisation and the State* (Cambridge: Cambridge University Press, 2011).

4   Christian Smith, *Religion: What It Is, How It Works, and Why It Matters* (Princeton: Princeton University Press, 2017), 234–38.

ality. Accordingly, antireligious sentiment now underwrites a new form of social cohesion in the West, ironically inheriting the mantle of bygone religious sacrifices. But religion cannot evidently be so easily partitioned off from mainstream public life in the West. It may be a more deeply encoded feature of human beings and, as such, susceptible to multiple transpositions or migrations.[5]

The Naturalness of Religion

Notwithstanding popular sentiment as evidenced in media and general society, religion is no longer so easily regarded by serious scholarship as the unnatural, abnormal, and irrational threat to stable, secular peace and good order that early modern Europe began to imagine. Christian Smith, mindful of the various negative assessments of the reasons for religion in much Western social thought, surveys the growing body of scholarship among theorists of religion and argues for the "naturalness of religion."[6] His focus is on the concrete reality of religions rather than debates about the concept of religion as such (that is, definition, complexity, usefulness, and reality).[7] Smith turns his attention to the habituated practices of religions and proposes the following definition:

> Religion is a complex of culturally prescribed practices, based on premises about the existence and nature of superhuman powers, whether personal or impersonal, which seek to help practitioners gain access to and communicate or align themselves with these powers, in hopes of realizing human goods and avoiding bad things.[8]

---

[5]   On the migration of the sacred see Richard Roberts, *Religion, Theology and the Human Sciences* (Cambridge: Cambridge University Press, 2001), chap. 1.

[6]   Cf. Smith, *Religion.*

[7]   At least from the last decades of the twentieth century, the contested nature of religion as a category for inquiry into its definition and function has been a matter of serious debate in Western scholarship. See, for example, Russell T McCutcheon, *Manufacturing Religion: The Discourse on Sui Generis Religion and the Politics of Nostalgia* (New York: Oxford university Press, 1997), chap. 5: "The Category of Religion in Recent Scholarship." In light of the upsurge of radical religious movements in the globe and their associated violence, the debate has focused more intently on the relationship between religion and violence, and to this extent has drawn upon much earlier seventeenth-century discussions about the relationship between religion and the body politic. See, for example, William Cavanagh, *The Myth of Religious Violence* (New York: Oxford University Press, 2009); and Jonathan Sacks, *Not in God's Name: Confronting Religious Violence* (London: Hodder & Stoughton, 2015). Both authors are indebted to the work of René Girard on the scapegoat mechanism and accordingly consider religion to have traditionally provided the means for the management rather than the catalyst for violence. The debate continues.

[8]   Smith, *Religion,* 22.

Smith is persuaded by evolutionary cultural approaches to religion, and from these he develops an account of human agents as endowed with "astoundingly powerful capacities and strikingly severe limitations." Within this context,

> Religion is . . . grounded in human persons pursuing their natural goods amid challenging circumstances, exercising their amazing personal capacities to address their weaknesses, and responding creatively to try to overcome objective limitations and threats. Religion, in this sense, is natural to, in being grounded in, the human constitution and condition.[9]

The methodological agnosticism of Smith's naturalism leaves open the possibility of the existence "superhuman powers."[10] Moreover his naturalism provides a positive basis for recognizing religion per se as an important and arguably powerful source for the emergence of societies whose values, virtues, and aspirations are orientated toward what is deemed good and wholesome for human flourishing.

What is the basis for this view? The naturalist position, at least according to Smith, begins with actual concrete phenomena. Of course, this comes with its own filters, but it begins with what is to be discovered, analyzed, assessed, and reflected upon. Theologically, this critical realist position resonates with a doctrine of creation imbued with the presence and work of God.

This is not a working hypothesis of naturalism per se, but it does nevertheless provide an important point of interdisciplinary conversation and learning. Minimally, what it offers, on the basis of Smith's depiction, is the presumption that religion ought to provide a domain for the development of the moral imagination

---

[9] Ibid., 210. Moreover, religion is unique to humans because "only they possess the set of capacities required to be religious." Smith articulates ten such requirements to be religious (208–09) and concludes that humans are uniquely religious "because only human beings possess the capacities for abstract reasoning, creative imagination, and symbolization (and arguably certain other capacities) at levels of sophistication sufficient to generate and sustain the practice of religion" (Ibid., 209).

[10] Smith's naturalist explanation presumes to leave open the reality or not of the existence of "superhuman powers." On this particular matter, the British philosopher Stephen L Clark comments: "If it were established that theistic (or Buddhistic) claims are false, 'religion' would not vanish from the world. But the 'great religions,' in their greatness—a class that may once have included Isis worship and Olympian religion—would." See Stephen L. Clark, *God, Religion and Reality* [1998], reprint with intro. by David Bentley Hart (Peterborough: Angelico Press, 2017), 10. Clark's point is that those religions that are located in a particular place and time and focus on "local deities" exist only "in the hearts and minds of [their] people" (Ibid., 10). As such, they "cannot look beyond the glass—and therefore only see themselves." Clark's concern is with "the real Outside: the truth professed in theism" (Ibid., 11).

and a vision for a flourishing life directed to the common good. I say *ought*, but we must be wary of baptizing religion in whatever form and shape it may take. Not everything appertaining to religions and their practices might contribute to a positive social good. Assessments about this will increasingly have to be made on the basis of local, enculturated forms and practices. For example, Christianity is incorrigibly localized with universal intent. One consequence is that Christianity is necessarily susceptible to all the dangers as well as the positive possibilities that necessarily arise from its local historical forms and interwovenness with host cultures. Accordingly, we might say that while religion per se may be "natural," not everything natural of a religious kind might make for a flourishing society within the purposes of God. Naturalism may be a useful phenomenological starting point at best.

Corrosive Powers of Host Cultures

One of the problems with social cohesion underpinned by pragmatic utilitarianism is that it offers a truncated vision (at best) of the good—of a society informed and directed by the virtues. Indeed, the emergence of predatory behavior of markets and nation-states during the modern era can seriously distort the way social cohesion operates, such that the vision of a flourishing society simply evaporates. This can lead to the corrosion and corruption of the character of people and eventually of the institutions and entities that have dominated the arenas of public life and work.[11]

This social corrosiveness has been linked to the internal disintegration of those institutions that have hitherto been foundational to societal functioning (banks, government, media, police, and, more recently, the church).[12] The foundational paradigm of the new capitalism has been economic growth shorn of any criteria to assess whether such growth contributed to the common good. This view entailed the "abandonment of any teleological vision for society and individuals."[13] The growth mantra of the market economy has spread into other domains, including the service sector in education, health, and the processes of government and religion, and it and deeply infects patterns and aspirations for human life.

---

[11]   See, for example, Richard Sennett, *The Corrosion of Character: The Personal Consequences of Work in the New Capitalism* (London/New York: W. W. Norton & Company, 1998).

[12]   For example, John Fitzmaurice, *Virtue Ecclesiology: An Exploration of the Good Church* (Farnham, UK: Ashgate, 2016).

[13]   Ibid., 23.

These developments were examined and critiqued by Alasdair MacIntyre almost four decades ago.[14] The fragmentation and incoherence of modernity is itself a corrosive influence on society's capacity to develop and sustain coherent accounts of those virtues necessary to generate the moral vision and communal character for a good and just society. Importantly for MacIntyre, fragmentation is not the same as pluralism. The latter implies "multiple traditions and communities with coherent and integral histories."[15] For MacIntyre, the problem we face in the West is the shift in focus from internal goods—that is, "those intrinsic to the action involved, for example the performance of a beautiful piece of music for the music's sake"—to external goods—that is, "those which are coincidental, in the case of musical performance—fame, more concert bookings, adoring fans."[16] The shift in focus from internal to external goods "leads to the soullessness of society and a breakdown of character."[17] This results from the failure of the Enlightenment project associated with the rejection of the virtue ethics of Aristotelianism and the emergence of "the foundationalism of an individualised morality," in which "all moral pronouncements are considered merely statements of personal preference." The end of this is the loss of "any sense of the common good of teleological endeavour."[18] The recovery of character and moral vision will necessarily involve the "formation of an internal conscience through habituated virtuous practice."[19]

MacIntyre's focus on practices and the nurture of good conduct and right action—virtue ethics—requires a major societal reorientation. But there are no quick fixes—no clear strategic directions, no generalist notions of religion per se that might provide a new foundation to craft something new for human life on the planet. However, it is also the case that religious traditions have well-developed, tried-and-tested practices to ground and orient human life together toward God. These traditions might have a great deal to offer the emerging polymorphic communities and polities of the West, whose narratives are grounded in and guided by self-interest and increasingly driven by authoritarian and top-down institutional leadership.

---

14   Alasdair MacIntyre, *After Virtue: A Study in Moral Theory* (London: Duckworth, 1981).

15   Fitzmaurice, *Virtue Ecclesiology*, 32, following J. R. Wilson, *Living Faithfully in a Fragmented World: Lessons for the Church from MacIntyre's "After Virtue"* (Harrisburg, PA: Trinity Press, 2010).

16   Fitzmaurice, *Virtue Ecclesiology*, 33.

17   Ibid.

18   Ibid.

19   Ibid.

A Postsecular Church?

Today's dawning, postsecular insight is that religious beliefs and faith communities are not going away and still have much to contribute from their own perspectives to the flourishing of civil society. Noncombative dialogue and open engagement furnish significant opportunities for postsecular societies to harness the good will of their religious citizens and subgroups to the common good, with such engagement providing a model for wider positive engagement across other social, political, and ideological divides. To undertake such engagements requires a mature embeddedness within the cultures and institutions of society. It eschews the simpler and appealing security associated with separation from society. Nor does it presume a smooth and untroubled alignment with the values and aspirations of society.

In some sense, such an engagement has to be carved out from within and crafted over against a more suspicious secularism. For example, the reality of religions and their faith communities in the West, with their public agencies, runs plainly counter to the religious privatization thesis. Nonetheless, the way in which secular authorities regularly view such public agencies (regarding their rights as employers, for instance) suggests that the incorrigibly public profile of religious traditions is not considered to be a legitimate dimension of religious freedom. Hence, modernity's self-defining suspicions about religion are stubbornly maintained. But the emerging postsecular reality is more complex, challenging the privatization of religion. Consequently, religious expression, freedoms, and public engagements will no longer be able to be managed within the established secular modern mindset.

None of this is about unduly favoring religion. We simply recognize and acknowledge that certain key conversations and commitments have shaped Western civilization. One of these is the conversation between Christianity and the classical culture of Greco-Roman antiquity, which continues in those many contests where faith and reason find a productive synergy. One such contest is the conversation between faith and science, which is by no means purely a matter of contestation. Another example concerns the relationship between autonomy and authority, in which the church has played a pioneering role in its dealings with other religions and with modern nation-states, providing a model for what today's societies seek to do. Consequently, we can regard the rising postsecular tide as an invitation to recover things that matter critically to us all from these conversations that have defined our identity, without fear that our modern Western society is being called on to betray its defining commitments. Pluralism rightly understood offers an opening of the aperture for an expanded vision of the common good and the way religion might play its part, albeit from a chastened and decentered location.

Ecclesial Deficits

The expectation and hope that religion might provide an alternative to the corrosive effects of secular utilitarian pragmatism needs to be checked with a strong dose of realism concerning the actual situation of religion. In the first place, we have to reckon with the fact that the corrosion of character and the undermining of the virtues tradition is intense, widespread, and substantive. Religious traditions—in particular, Christianity in the West—are not immune from its impact. This is implicit in MacIntyre's final remarks regarding the barbarians within the gates, when the only hope for a vital and sustaining Christian culture will be one that begins from the ground up, St. Benedict–style.

It is hard to underestimate the thrall within which the churches of the West are caught. For example, the important theological understanding of humans in the image of God (*imago Dei*) is now infused with a conception of the human agent as "a self, orientated to the short term, focussed on potential ability, willing to abandon past experience."[20] This may sound unproblematic, almost attractive. It is certainly in keeping with a materialist capitalist culture. However, as Sennett comments, "Most people are not like this; they need a sustaining life narrative, they take pride in being good at something specific, and they value the experiences they've lived through."[21] The corporate ethos and implicit underpinning anthropology of new capitalism is part of the everyday life of the churches and generates an ecclesial economy focused on growth, the arrest of decline, operation on a scarcity model, rationalization of resources, and promotion of forms of leadership and management that model a corporatist understanding of human beings (and their expendability), all externally driven by the anxieties of the age. This situation leads one ecclesiologist to state that for the Church of England, "much of its policy making and discourse has become based on a utilitarian foundationalism of growth."[22] He continues: "This use of growth as foundational I would suggest is the overarching paradigm in the contemporary church and with it has come the corrosion of character that we have witnessed within secular world's failed obsession with growth as its prevailing paradigm."[23]

[20]   Richard Sennett, *The Culture of New Capitalism* (New Haven/London: Yale University Press, 2006), 5.
[21]   Ibid.
[22]   Fitzmaurice, *Virtue Ecclesiology* (note 12), 36.
[23]   Ibid.

A Case in Point—the Anglican Church in Australia

The Anglican Church in Australia exhibits many of the trends and problems of society and religion discussed above.[24] Historically in Australia, the Church of England has been the dominant denomination (41 percent in 1921) functioning as a quasi-established church, though it now represents less than 14 percent of the population. The 2016 national census indicates that approximately 60 percent of Australia's 22 million population claim a religious affiliation; 50 percent of Australians claim Christian affiliation (88 percent in 1960); those declaring "no religion" have become the most numerous group (30.1 percent), while Catholics comprise 22.6 percent, Anglicans 13.3 percent, Buddhists 2.4 percent, Muslims 2.6 percent, Hindus 1.9 percent, Pentecostals 1.1 percent, and Lutherans 0.7 percent.

The Anglican Church of Australia has a long track record of being deeply involved in matters of welfare, social justice, and education, to name but a few key areas. This same church has also been historically quite fragmented and captive to a party spirit. This only serves to point to the fact that the Anglican Church of Australia is very much a derivative of the Church of England. It has inherited that church's tensions and conflicts and creatively adapted them to Australia's own situation. Despite some gallant and important efforts to the contrary, the church has found it exceedingly difficult to grow a genuinely enculturated form of Christianity on Australian soil. Moreover, the Anglican Church of Australia, like the church of the West more generally, is deeply influenced by the modern competitive market economy, with an emphasis on material and corporate success and growth. This underlying materialist and acquisitive spirit has an insatiable appetite. It requires continual sacrifices deemed necessary to maintain the status quo.

The impact of this environment on the Anglican Church of Australia is complex. At times the church appears blind to the precariousness of its situation and apparently content to remain on the well-worn paths of yesterday. Permanence, fixity, and stable identity are prized above all else. Relevance is easily sacrificed. One response to this not-untypical situation is to react in the opposite direction, leaving the familiar paths and striking out on new ones. The church and, especially, its leaders furtively begin the search for the program or action plan that will arrest decline, turn the ship around, and rebuild the church. This can result in an overfunctioning church that exhausts everyone. The focus here is not permanence but innovation, change, and relevance. Identity then can become shallow. On balance, when we consider current developments in church life, it's a

---

[24]   Bruce Kaye, ed., *Anglicanism in Australia: A History* (Melbourne: Melbourne University Press, 2002). The change of name from the Church of England to the Anglican Church of Australia occurred in 1981.

mixed bag with an overriding sense that the church is in transition without a clear picture of what the church will become.

Perhaps we might best depict the church's present challenge as one of reseeding—of planting and growing the gospel in the church and society for the sake of the coming kingdom. In the church garden, some parts look healthy and are thriving, while other sections are overgrown and require pruning back or weeding, while elsewhere new exotic varieties seem to appear from nowhere. In this context, a major challenge is to till the ground, refertilize, and continue the patient task of reseeding and tending the new shoots.

An Optimal Ecclesial Environment for Character Formation

Alas, there are no simple pathways for the churches of the West in a period of significant transition. But a question does arise. Is it possible for the church to recover a pace, rhythm, and presence in step with Christ?[25] Is there a coming church that can truly begin to manifest the riches of God's wisdom for the world (Ephesians 3:10)? The coming church will belong to the new thing God is doing. The visionary of the Book of Revelation captures it well: "Behold, I am making everything new" (21:5). The sense here is something new from something old rather than something new, entirely distinct from what is already present. So, rather than making "a new thing," the reality will be, as the text indicates, "everything new." Where the creative energy of God is transforming the world, new structuring emerges from within the old where the wound is.

This process takes time, for good things take time. It requires an imaginative moral vision, generosity of heart, and great patience. It is first and foremost a matter of building ethically resilient institutions and leadership that embody the character of Christ. Fundamentally "making everything new" is a work of God, lest we fall captive to the illusion that we are the manufacturers of our destiny. In this way, reform of the church is essentially "the risen Christ's self-discipline in the Spirit."[26] The pace of reform is Christian in character to the extent that it is patterned after the way God works in the world. Such reform requires spiritual discernment and is a deeply humbling activity for the church. It is also the place from which fresh energy arises. It points to the fact that mission begins deep within the folds of the brokenness of the church. This transformation of brokenness in turn generates a sympathetic resonance with the brokenness of the world.

---

[25]   I have discussed this in Stephen K. Pickard, *Seeking the Church: An Introduction to Ecclesiology* (London: SCM, 2012), chap. 9.

[26]   Robert Jensen, *Systematic Theology*, vol. 2 (Oxford: Oxford University Press, 1999), 77.

The coming church will be one that moves at a pace that is not easily missed in the busyness of life. Other attractive substitutes for true community with God flood the market today. A major task for the churches of the West is to find a pace and rhythm conducive to God's presence on the journey of faith. Long-distance runners know how critical it is to pace themselves so that they will have sufficient energy and stamina to finish and can respond to unforeseen contingencies on the way (Hebrews 12:1–2). Learning again to travel at the pace of the Spirit following the footsteps of Christ is key here. Through word, sacrament, Spirit, and entanglement in the world, this ancient pilgrimage is ever new.

Importantly, the pace of this journey is one step at a time with the broken, needy, and foolish. Furthermore, the pathway of the Spirit will lead the church up a hill called Calvary and into a tomb (unless a grain of wheat falls to the ground . . .). From this place, the church has to learn again to confess its sins and pray for the rejuvenating work of the Holy Spirit. It is only as the pilgrim church travels at the pace of the Spirit that God can be truly present.

Pace and presence are co-related. For when the church seeks to be in step with the Spirit, then God can be truly up close and personal—close to the wound. The healing and repair of the Body of Christ always begins just underneath the wound. This is where God's love is to be found, slowly and patiently doing its work, for nothing can be loved at speed. And from this place, energy flows for new life and witness in the world.

This may sound somewhat abstract and fanciful, but in fact it is really about identifying the kind of environment in which the debilitating effects of corrosive cultures, both within and without the church, can be addressed. The formation of character and the nurture of a moral vision requires the patient and prophetic attention to building alternative environments within the dysfunctionalities of our present sites of discourse and public life. The ecclesial body, notwithstanding internal and external challenges, is well placed to make a significant contribution to the repair and renewal of environments for human flourishing.

"With Religion, not *from* Religion"

Christian Antimoralist Moralism and its Impact on Moral Formation

Bernd Oberdorfer

This essay has a historic part and a systematic part. Historically, it sketches the processes of differentiation between religion and ethics in eighteenth- and nineteenth-century philosophy and (Protestant) theology, which changed the understanding of the impact of religion on moral formation. Systematically, it aims at rationalizing the intuition that it is exactly an "antimoralist" impulse which models a specific Christian contribution to moral formation.

Outsourcing Religion, Outsourcing Ethics: Kant and Schleiermacher on Religion and Ethics

Since the eighteenth century, Christian morality has been under pressure, from "outside," as it were, as well as from "inside." From outside, the need for a Christian justification of moral arguments has been doubted, if not contested. Morality, according to Kant, must be justified in itself, that is, by reason. Religious motives spoil morality, making it heteronomous. This critique is directed even against Enlightenment philosophy and theology, which interpreted Jesus as the "new Socrates" (J.A. Eberhard)[1]—as a teacher of morality—and, thus, thought to have given religion a proper place in a rational system of orientation in life.

Kant himself, however, did not cut every link between morality and religion. First, he attributed to religion the function of a "vehicle" of morality: religion can give individuals additional strength to materialize or put into effect the moral intentions they have developed in a process of autonomy, by means of pure reason

---

[1]   Cf. Johann August Eberhard, *Neue Apologie des Sokrates, oder Untersuchung von der Lehre der Seligkeit der Heiden*, vol. 2 (Berlin/Stettin: Nicolai, 1772–78; reprint, Hildesheim: Olms, 2010).

Bernd Oberdorfer

without religion.[2] Second, he implemented the idea of God as a necessary background assumption ("postulate") of autonomous morality: God warrants the justice of the universal moral order by safeguarding a just correlation between virtue (*Glückswürdigkeit*) and happiness (*Glückseligkeit*, eudaemonia) in the eternal lives of souls.[3]

From "inside" religion, Schleiermacher accepted the separation of religion from morality and even radicalized it, defending the intrinsic dignity of religion. In his 1799 speeches *On Religion*,[4] he distinguished religion, metaphysics, and morality as three different basic ways of dealing with reality. They cannot be derived from each other, nor can one of them be regarded as a dependent epiphenomenon of any other. Thus, religion is neither a form of world theory nor a doctrine of how to act in the world. This does not mean, however, that religion has nothing to do with metaphysics and ethics. Religion, according to Schleiermacher, is not supposed to orient but rather is to accompany human acting. "Everything with religion, nothing from religion."[5] Religion—to paraphrase that statement—means and constitutes an attitude of being in the world; it forms the fundaments of understanding oneself and the world, and exactly this is ethically relevant. If religion is a way of feeling oneself as an interwoven moment of the universe and prevents one from egocentrically distancing oneself from the world, it constitutes an ethos of "forming oneself" (*Selbstbildung*) in the horizon of the world.[6] Forming themselves is, thus, the way individuals participate in the realization of the "highest good" (*höchstes Gut*), which—according to Schleiermacher's *Lectures on Philosophical Ethics*—is the substance and aim of human history, understood as the process of shaping nature by reason.[7]

---

[2]   Cf. Immanuel Kant, *Die Religion innerhalb der Grenzen der bloßen Vernunft* (Königsberg, 1793), in *Kants Werke in zehn Bänden*, vol. 7, ed. Wilhelm Weischedel (Darmstadt: Wissenschaftliche Buchgesellschaft, 1983), 647–879.

[3]   Cf. Immanuel Kant, *Kritik der praktischen Vernunft* (Riga 1788), in Weischedel, *Kants Werke in zehn Bänden*, vol. 6, 103–302.

[4]   Friedrich Schleiermacher, *Über die Religion. Reden an die Gebildeten unter ihren Verächtern* [1799], in Idem, *Kritische Gesamtausgabe*, vol. I/2, ed. Günter Meckenstock (Berlin/New York; DeGruyter, 1984), 185–326; in English, *On Religion: Speeches to Its Cultured Despisers*, trans. John Oman (New York: Harper & Row, 1958).

[5]   "alles mit Religion . . . , nichts aus Religion" (KGA I/2, 219).

[6]   Cf. Friedrich Schleiermacher, *Monologen. Eine Neujahrsgabe* [1800], in Meckenstock, *Kritische Gesamtausgabe*, vol. I/3, 1–61.

[7]   Cf. Friedrich Schleiermacher, *Ethik. mit späteren Fassungen der Einleitung, Güterlehre und Pflichtenlehre* [1812/13], ed. Hans-Joachim Birkner (Hamburg: F. Meiner, 1981); in English, *Lectures on Philosophical Ethics*, ed. Robert B. Louden (Cambridge: Cambridge University Press, 2002).

In this process, religion is part of one of four substantial functions of social life, the function of *individual symbolizing.* Religion, in other words, is a form of individual expression of the process of "humanizing nature." It is *individual* (not general, as science is), and it is *expression* (not production [*Herstellung*], as politics and economy are). Thus, religion in itself is a specific form of human acting—this is further developed in Schleiermacher's *Christliche Sitte*[8]—but, as such, it also has (indirect) impact on the other forms of human acting (like in politics, economy, law, and sociability [*freie Geselligkeit*]). In his *Glaubenslehre* [doctrine of faith], therefore, Schleiermacher characterizes Christianity as a teleological form of religion, which means that Christian religion gives the believers impulses to act.[9] More exactly: the "Christian pious self-consciousness" (*christlich frommes Selbstbewusstsein*) experiences itself as a consciousness of God which has been liberated from its weakness by Christ to be a full confidence in God, enabling the individual to realize acts of finite freedom.

To summarize my point: religion, according to Schleiermacher, is something nonmoral which has moral implications or consequences.

In the later nineteenth century, Albrecht Ritschl, most influentially, affirmed Schleiermacher's basic idea of religion as an independent source of dealing with reality, but with reference to Kant he put emphasis on the moral implications. Thus, Ritschl polemicized against any form of religious life that was of no practical use—for instance, in his view, Pietism and mysticism—and he identified religion in itself as a means of realizing the kingdom of God as the perfection of human society.[10] In this concept, religion maintained its independence from science but lost its independence from morality. In the current essay, however, I refer principally to Schleiermacher's intuition of a difference between religion and morality, including religion's interferences with and impacts on morality, rather than to Ritschl's idea of religion as a form of ethical impulse.

Christianity and Moralism

The second part of this essay analyzes the relations between religion and morality from a different angle, highlighting a Christian perspective on moralism. I begin

---

[8]   Cf. Friedrich Schleiermacher, *Die christliche Sitte*, ed. Ludwig Jonas, 2nd ed. (Berlin, 1884).

[9]   Cf. Friedrich Schleiermacher, *Der christliche Glaube*, 2nd edition [1830/31], ed. Rolf Schäfer (Berlin: DeGruyter, 2003) (= KGA I/13,1 and I/13,2), esp. §11; in English, *The Christian Faith* (New York: Harper & Row, 1963).

[10] Cf. Bernd Oberdorfer, "Albrecht Ritschl. Die Wirklichkeit des Gottesreiches," in *Theologen des 19. Jahrhunderts. Eine Einführung*, ed. Peter Neuner and Gunther Wenz (Darmstadt: Wissenschaftliche Buchgesellschaft, 2002), 183–203.

with an observation: secular criticism often associates Christianity with a restrictive moralism, of which historic examples are easily found: the Puritan ban on dancing, smoking, and alcohol; Calvinist paternalistic control; Catholic discrimination of sexuality and general disdain of corporality; and on and on. Christianity seems to stand for a big "NO!" that overshadows any life-affirming impulses. To be Christian, in this view, means to follow rigid rules. The Christian impact on moral formation, then, would seem to be the implementation of these rules in social life, legal systems, and education. And, of course, the adequate secular reaction could only be to limit the influence of Christian churches in the name of freedom and autonomy.

Not incidentally, this critique is often complemented by an allegation of hypocrisy. Christians, from this viewpoint, enforce rules for others that they are unable or unwilling to comply with themselves. They preach water and drink wine. Or, even worse, they pretend to act altruistically while they actually follow a hidden agenda of egoism. In other words, they claim to observe spiritual norms while actually pursuing very earthly goals.[11] In our time, the disastrous consequences of the diagnosis of hypocrisy drastically became apparent in the context of the (especially Catholic) church's scandal of sexual abuse. The obvious contradiction between rigid moral norms (and, more, the rigid enforcement of these norms with reference to divorce and remarriage) and the violation of these norms by church leaders—even violating more fundamental norms of human dignity and sexual integrity (or tolerating it in church officials) caused a general loss of credibility of the church's moral teaching.[12]

This example, however, deserves further examination. To diagnose an institution's hypocrisy implies the accusation of not complying with norms that the institution itself has declared to be morally binding. Thus, the critique of hypocrisy does not deny but rather presupposes that the institution formulates moral expectations and commitments, because this critique reminds the institution of those commitments by stating that it has not complied with them. The critique thus can have at least a threefold form. First, it can *affirm* the norms and simply challenge the institution to observe them more seriously in the future. This happened, for example, when the Catholic Church in the sixteenth century, at the Council of Trent, decided to maintain the norm of celibacy for priests but to implement the norm more strictly. Second, the charge of hypocrisy can *challenge* the norms themselves, asking whether they are still plausible or should be modified or abolished. This happened, for example, when the sixteenth-century Reformers

---

[11]   This, e. g., was the focus of anti-Pietist criticism in Luise Adelgunde Viktorie Gottsched's famous Enlightenment comedy *Die Pietisterey im Fischbein-rocke* (1736).

[12]   A striking example is the results of referenda in Ireland, where a huge majority voted in favor of same-sex marriage (2015) and less-restrictive abortion legislation (2018), both against the declared will of the Catholic Church.

introduced marriage for priests. Third, the charge of hypocrisy can challenge the *forms* of making and implementing norms. This happened, for instance, when, as noted above, Catholics in Ireland (and elsewhere) started to doubt the unqualified (and unqualifiable) binding character of the Catholic Church's moral teaching and changed their attitude toward it.[13]

It is important to see that this analysis does not mean to contest the moral relevance of the Christian faith but rather reveals the intuition that a legalist misunderstanding of that moral relevance must be overcome. In this essay, I would like to follow this train of thought by showing that there actually is something like a Christian ethos, and that this ethos does actually *include* moral norms but goes far beyond them, because it develops sensitivity to the potentially destructive consequences of blindly enforcing norms (or, in other words, of moralism) and moreover entails specific forms of dealing with deviance. This complex structure, then, constitutes a Christian impact on moral formation.

It is obvious, first, that a faith-based ethos which derives from the biblical traditions includes moral norms. In the Old Testament, the Torah is understood as a gift: God dignifies God's people by giving them rules for a "good life." The wonderful Psalm 19 draws a parallel between cosmic and social order. Just as God protects the cosmos from chaos by stabilizing the regular processes of nature, so God preserves the social order by providing the rules of Torah. This understanding of the God-given law, however, does not apply only to the Old Testament. In Jesus's Sermon on the Mount, for example, the law is not only confirmed but rather intensified. Thus, the anti-Jewish cliché of Judaism as a religion of (only) law and Christianity as a religion of (only) love is wrong in both directions. Law is a form of love. And the long and successful career of the Decalogue in Christian (at least Lutheran) religious education indicates that Christianity itself has not followed this antinomian cliché.

But it takes only a superficial survey of the biblical traditions to confirm the intuition that they do not support a rigid moralism so much as give a broader picture of moral orientation. Let me highlight only a few aspects. First, the Torah itself not only entails norms and commandments but also introduces cultic institutions to deal with failure and trespasses by symbolic actions of reestablishing order. Moreover, it presents narratives which display, to say the least, moral ambiguity, even in the lives of the ancestral heroes. And it tells the history of the Israelites as a history of confidence and doubts, altruism and hate, human failure and God's new beginning. It is not a "heroic" narrative, and this has moral implications. Second, there has always been a strong consciousness of the crucial rele-

---

[13]   In Protestant churches, this change of authorization processes has already taken place. The Evangelische Kirche in Deutschland (EKD) e. g. does not publish binding moral teaching but rather *Denkschriften* (memoranda), which are deliberately intended to be (only) contributions to the public discourse rather than final and binding solutions.

vance of mercy and forgiveness for a Christian ethos. If God again and again starts anew with God's people, even though they do not "deserve" it, Christians are called to start anew with their neighbors "seven times seventy times" (Matt. 18:22). Third, Jesus did not limit himself to the "perfect" but rather turned toward people who were excluded economically, ethnically, culturally, religiously, and morally (Zacchaeus, for instance, in Luke 19:1–10).

These narratives, which qualify rigid moralism, are deeply embedded in Christian cultures. To care for the excluded has always been a characteristic of Christian *diakonia*. The churches in our current day, therefore, do not practice an *opus alienum*, or a work that is foreign to their mission, when they raise their voice for refugees. Moreover, to engage in reconciliation (among individuals, peoples, and nations) is an important element of the Christian ethos.

Antimoralism, therefore, is not amoralism. Rather, antimoralism has a moral function. It is even a (more reflected, more elaborated, more realistic) form of moralism itself. It raises sensitivity to the possible disastrous consequences of a rigid moralism. Moreover, it conveys the deep conviction that forgiveness does not indicate weakness but rather is a basic requirement of social life. It is rooted in the idea of a God who does not stay in splendid isolation but incarnates himself in order to liberate and renew his lost people.

What does this mean for moral formation?

Schleiermacher was right to accuse Enlightenment theology of functionalizing religion for morality. Religion is not simply an instrument or medium to generate, implement, and enforce "values" or norms. It is a way of dealing with reality in its own right. As such, however, it introduces, as it were, "second-order values"—that is, values to deal with values and, moreover, to critically deal even with values or norms that religion itself has introduced.[14] A classic example of this self-critical religious discourse is Jesus's discussion on the function of the Sabbath (Mark 2:23–28). Here, religion reflects upon itself. Jesus does not contest the legitimacy of the Torah rules, but he emphasizes their God-given function as a tool for a good life which enables persons to qualify the application of the rules in a concrete situation (as, in this case, hunger). Of course, this happens within an ethical horizon and has ethical implications—but is far from simple moral indoctrination.

Forgiveness and reconciliation are also second-order values. They show ways of continuing life in and after situations of distortion, violation, and humiliation, when the rules and routines of common, first-order morality have lost applicability because they no longer can warrant peace and stable order in society (when,

---

[14] This is, by the way, the function of the theological doctrine of "Law and Gospel."

for example, the enforcement of laws cannot interrupt the sequence of violence and revenge violence[15]).

It is important to see that forgiveness and reconciliation cannot be enforced. Nobody can be forced to forgive. Thus, forgiveness and reconciliation are not moral norms in the sense of a simple order-obedience scheme. People can be encouraged but not commanded to forgive. Therefore, I would argue that religion can help to establish a supportive environment to encourage an ethos of forgiveness and reconciliation by providing respective narratives and authentic examples. This can have an enormous impact on moral formation.

How, then, can Christian individuals, communities, and churches contribute to the implementation of such a culture of second-order values?

First, their liturgical life communicates narratives and semantics and gives symbolic representations of God's ethos of reconciliation. Thus, simply by doing properly their core business—preaching the gospel, celebrating the sacraments—churches help to provide semantics of moral reflexivity and sensitivity.

Second, the lives of Christians and Christian communities can display encouraging examples of a culture of reconciliation. Not incidentally, critics of Christianity are very sensitive to the contradictions between doctrine and practice in the lives of Christians because these discrepancies endanger the authenticity and credibility of the gospel itself. Conversely, authentic experiences of reconciliation can have inspiring and encouraging effects on others.

Third, the work of *diakonia* is not a *donum superadditum* but an essential element of the Christian witness, because it realizes the inclusion of the excluded, which is the core message of the Gospel.

Fourth, churches can contribute to moral formation by committing themselves to public engagement and advocacy, to public theology.

One final remark: a culture of forgiveness is at risk of becoming (or at least appearing to be) an easy excuse for and even justification of injustice. The religious impulse to forgive, then, seems to make any action to take earthly responsibility redundant. In this spirit, for instance, Catholic officials after World War II helped some Nazi criminals escape to South America. But this is, to say the least, a misunderstanding. What I have called a culture of second-order values is not a way of eliminating first-order values but a way of analyzing, understanding, and implementing them. Thus, it was out of deep wisdom that South Africa, after the end of apartheid, started a process of justice *and* reconciliation which aimed at avoiding reconciliation at the expense of justice. Nevertheless, the history of that

---

[15]   It should be noted, nevertheless, that establishing a law system itself was a crucial step in the history of overcoming the fatal automatism of (private) revenge and antirevenge. The revenge cycle is classically displayed in a basic narrative of Western culture, Aeschylus's *Oresteia*.

process shows how difficult it can be to balance values, yet how necessary it is to try.

Formation as Figuration
The Impact of Religion Framed by Media Anthropology

Philipp Stoellger

Some Preconditions on Perspective and Method

Religion certainly has an impact on the social and individual formation of character, ethical education, and communication of values. But *which* religion, *where*, and *how*—that is the question under consideration here. A relevant problem, then, is how to evaluate religion analytically and descriptively.

One could propose a widespread theological interest as the *normative claim*, thus justifying the question how religion can influence the public sphere (through public theology or its normative claims). But the normative interest of theology can appear as an outdated model, as if theology could explain what church believers and the public should acknowledge, accept, and follow in their lives. I would hesitate to accept this framework as a model for orientation. It appears more as a will to power than a scientific exploration. One may be pleased about normative statements, but their effects are not as strong as their claims—that is, they are highly questionable. Thus, the effects of normative claims cannot be predicted if the effects are precisely the question of research. The question is not about the effects of claims but about the alleged effects of religions.

Between *history* (what may have been the case) and *normative* claims (what may be the case in the future), the difficult question arises as to which methods can be used for a contemporary assessment of the effects of religion. The dominant and usual answer would be *empirical* research. One could ask, for example, what is taught at the university and in churches and schools, and what is the living orientation of private, public, or political life. The Bertelsman Stiftung Religion Monitor[1] and similar surveys would show that what is taught has almost no effect on real life. But to conclude that *religion* has no impact would be a misunderstanding. It would require empirical evaluations to be able to fully assess the impact, but it is always the interpretation of data that matters—always, so to speak, the researcher who judges and draws consequences. And if one follows

---

[1] See https://www.bertelsmann-stiftung.de/en/our-projects/religion-monitor/.

the incorrect but dominant secularization model, the prejudgment is obvious. If one does *not* follow that dominant model, the consequences can be different—that is, the normative effect of the secularization model leads to a normative rejection of the effect of religion and preconditions the production and interpretation of data. When the interpretative power of the model diminishes or is questioned, the floor is open again (without celebrating a no less problematic return of religion). A relevant prerequisite for the research question is thus obviously an assumed model of orientation.

Although it *may* be true that empirical evidence of the impact of religion is weak, empirical methods can overlook basic facts or even more basic orientations that are not or are no longer *explicitly* religious—for instance, Christian conceptions of dignity, gift (vs. exchange), the other (as neighbor), love, recognition, and so on. The driving forces, dominant frameworks, living passions, and ruling dispositions are not only empirical data but frames of perception and interpretative patterns. That means that these data *frame* research and interpretations, but they are not simply given data.

Therefore, I would prefer methods of phenomenology (for description) and hermeneutics (for interpretation and understanding) to meet the challenge of the research question. The latent backgrounds (such as a tacit dimension of culture) and the manifest claims (such as the normative interventions of religion) are less an empirical than a hermeneutical and structural topic.

Religion as Normative Order—or Prenormative Root of Order?

From the normative point of view, the question is, how can the impact of religion be *reinforced* (if one wishes)? This reinforcement can be the main interest of churches, congregations, and theology. But the question presupposes that they have fruitful contributions to offer. The Jubilee of the Reformation in 2017 was a celebration of the impact of religion on history. In the fields of education, music, art, literature, law, science, economy, and more, the historical impact has been documented. But the present and future impacts are a different field of research, not accessible by historical methods.

Globally and generally—as the topic of "religious impact" under discussion here is phrased within that scope—the impact of religion and its desirability is not as obvious as it may be with regard to the Reformation. Moreover, the search for public theology as reinforcement of the effect of the Protestant religion in Berlin is comparatively a quite provincial problem: an empowerment of Protestantism in times of loss and lack of public recognition. One example, in northern Germany, is the (re)establishment of October 31, Reformation Day, as a public holiday, a manifestation of religion's impact on the public sphere. But does it have *any* impact in the formation of character and ethical education? Are the "values" of the Reformation communicated by such a holiday?

Thus, a general consideration or hesitation appears: are different varieties of Protestantism on the right track if they search for "formation of character" and "ethical education"? Is it not a little self-contradictory to look for *ethics*, while soteriology is unlinked from "works"? And are Protestantisms well-advised to look for their sociopolitical impact in the line of Böckenförde, if his thesis was not only wrong but developed in a Roman Catholic orientation?[2]

Not a definitive answer, but pointing in the right direction, would be to ask more about *metaethical* implications of religion if the Protestant perspective is the guiding principle. What can we hope, what is human, where from can "salvation" be expected, what is the impotence of law (or the gospel, or love, etc.), and how should the institution of the church *order* things in the name of the extraordinary? If one were to follow this direction of metaethics, the *prenormative roots of normativity* may come to mind: the decisive conditions and roots of normativity. These may include the recognition of the other, the recognition of *coram Deo* (living in the presence of God), or the Hegelian logic of recognition, the Kantian subjectivity, or "public" recognition, if recognition is decisive at all.

From a Lutheran perspective, the *passions and fruitful passivities* become more relevant than ethics of recognition, because all ethics and education are rooted in *pre*normative grounds or conditions, by which they are oriented, grounded, and directed. That is a reason for *phenomenological* perspectives, not as eidetic reduction to an essence of religion, but as *pathic reduction* to the basic passions and passivities by which a religion (or culture) is driven. What others may call dispositives are dispositions of and by passions. The decisive differences are not just the ones of logos (thought, rationality) or ethos (morality or ethics), but of pathos, the passions by which we are driven with regard to strangers, to our nation, to Europe, and so on. Not merely the (construction) of values but the passionate *construals* (or perceptions) make the difference. The vivid challenge for a legal culture is driven by the passion for justice, perhaps even for *another* justice (Christ's justice, what we call *communicative* justice: making just the unjust) or for the *others of justice* (grace, love).

Christ then is not a value, not even a messenger of values, but first and last a *figure of passions* by which morality is driven and ruled. The basic impact of religion consists in this figure—as *figuration* of a way of life (of passions, thoughts, habits, desires). Thereby all values in a Christian form of life are explications of Christ and are to be justified *coram Christo* (or *are* justified by him). God is the

---

[2] The Böckenförde dilemma, named for German constitutional judge Ernst-Wolfgang Böckenförde, asserts that the freedoms guaranteed by a liberal secular state depend to some degree on an ethos that the state cannot generate by its own authority but must come from the shared virtues, customs, and culture of the people.

epitome of prenormativity. And Christ is the embodiment of a singular passion for the neighbor, not just a value-maker. The gift of justification is not an exchange by moral evaluation but the frame and condition for all values.

A consequence for the impact of Protestantisms is the imperative to make use of the decisive difference of prenormativity and normativity, so as not to reduce religion to its normative impact. The wider horizon is to cultivate the awareness of *the others* of normativity, like gift, gospel, and grace. The formation of character and moral education would be reduced and misjudged if they were not grounded in the prenormative roots offered by religion's tradition and innovation, given by the basic figure of this religion and the figuration of a new perspective and horizon. Insofar as religion is always in danger of being reduced to a moral order, milieu, or culture, the potentialities of the singular contribution of religion would be lost.

To claim religion as a prenormative root of order and culture is ambiguous. It may sound like Tillich's idea of religion as ground of culture, or like the Schleiermacher tradition of subjectivity as the ground of culture. One may follow these traditions, but there are two risks: reducing religion to culture; and reducing God and faith to religion. The theological difference is that first and last, *God* is the prenormative root of religion, morality, and culture. Concretely, that means that Christ as the embodiment of God's essence is the appearance (or revelation) of this ground-breaking prenormativity. An impact of *religion* should preserve this theological difference. Otherwise religion would be superfluous.

That is why the impact of "religion" has (at least) two different meanings: religion as social system, or as symbolic form, or as part of culture has impact on its "environment" (system/*Umwelt*). But then the intriguing problem is how a systemic communication can have impact on its environment. Isn't the internal communication a mere rush to other systems? The Luhmann question for "structural coupling" of systems is quite open.

The second meaning would be that religion—if it is speaking "in the name of God" or in distinctively *Christian* ways, for example—claims to manifest the impact of God in religion, and *by* religion in the other systems or public spheres. The latter question is far more intriguing, and also the theologically decisive one. Then one must claim that religion is "God's medium" for "immanent" interaction and impact—*without* mixing religion and God (or Christ's body) and *without* mixing religion and its salvific media (word and sacrament and others).

Religion as Medium—and Religious Patterns as Frames of Perception

Religion can have an impact only *in and by communication*, insofar as religion *is* communication. A "tacit" religion would have no impact; only a "speaking" and "showing" religion can have impact (cf. Wittgenstein's distinction between saying and showing, like verbal and visual communication). Religion is not just *communication*, but—what I propose—*religion is a medium by, in, and through which we perceive, communicate, think, speak, feel, and believe in a distinct mode.* That is what I suggest calling its *Deutungsmacht:* symbolic, deictic, and medial power in *framing* communication.[3]

The question of impact then shifts: how do the ways of communicating within religion have impact on other forms of communication? Insofar as religious communication frames modes of perception and thought, the broader impact would necessarily frame not only communication within the realm of religion but also communication in other fields (systems, symbolic forms). It is not necessary that religious communication frame the explicit and manifest communication in spheres of, for example, politics, law, and science but (more important) that it frames the implicit and latent dimensions of communication.[4]

One example may be the "church-friendly" disposition of the Bundesverfassungsgericht (the German Federal Constitutional Court) or the (possibly) "neighbor-friendly" disposition of the German border opening to refugees in 2015. But—as the comparison with Hungary and its "Christian rhetoric" even in the political (and scientific?) elite shows—neither religion nor even "Christianity" but a certain Christian tradition and perspective has this impact; another perspective could have another impact. There is no strict conclusive ratio between Christianity and a distinct disposition—even if from one's perspective the ratio seems obvious.

If religion is thus a medium—and a vivid religion is a medium even for extra-religious spheres—the theological claim goes further: not only is religion a medium but first and foremost God is the main medium of religion, forming religion. Or, said otherwise, God is the medium of world-making, world-saving, and world-completion.[5] *Christian* theology should thus claim: the medium of God as medium

---

3   Cf. Philipp Stoellger, *Deutungsmachtkonflikten. religion und belief systems in Deutungsmachtkonflikten* (Tübingen: Mohr Siebeck, 2014); Philipp Stoellger and Martina Kumlehn, eds., *Wortmacht - Machtwort. Deutungsmachtkonflikte in und um Religion* (Würzburg: Königshausen and Neumann, 2017); Philipp Stoellger and Martina Kumlehn, eds., *Bildmacht - Machtbild. Deutungsmacht des Bildes: Wie Bilder glauben machen* (Würzburg: Königshausen and Neumann, 2018).

4   Cf. Philipp Stoellger, "Max Weber und das Recht des Protestantismus. Spuren des Protestantismus in Webers Rechtssoziologie, oder: Einverständnis als Geltungsgrund einer verstehenden Soziologie?" in *Recht als Kultur? Beiträge zu Max Webers Soziologie des Rechts*, ed. Werner Gephart and Daniel Witte (Frankfurt am Main: Klostermann, 2017), 279–311.

5   Cf. Philipp Stoellger, "Gott als Medium und der Traum der Gottunmittelbarkeit" in *Das Letzte-der Erste. Gott denken. Festschrift für Ingolf U. Dalferth zum 70. Geburtstag*, ed.

is *Christ.* Therefore, Christ is the principal "given" medium, guiding and forming religion—and thereby governing the impact religion may have.

The actual and future *presence* of Christ is the spirit (that is, *Christ's* spirit, not just any spirit that blows wherever it wants, but the spirit of Christ that blows wherever *he* wants). And the spirit is the formative medium of the media of religion: word and sacrament and forms of life.[6]

We might live in, by, and through media, in a *labyrinth* of mediality, yet there is an orientation within the labyrinth: the "rule" of religion as medium *is* the trinitarian God *as* medium, forming religion, which may form our ways of life.[7] The impact on culture claimed by religions becomes manifest "in the name of God." That phrase, however, is highly liable to misunderstanding and misuse. The misuses are evident and well known (in all their ambiguous plurality in history). The root of ambivalence is that religions can take over God's claim in their own interests. And religion can be taken over by other communications in their own interests.

But the challenge for and by religion is nevertheless to claim to be *a medium of God's presence:* by word, sacrament—and images, rituals, education, diaconia, and other forms of the church's life and work. Not to take over God, but to be taken over by him, as God's medium, religion may carefully claim to articulate "God's voice." The risks and dangers are obvious; nevertheless, without such an impossible claim, religion would lose its backing and challenge—its *impact.* If one would no longer try the impossible, to speak in the name of God, but just in the name of a religion or a spirituality, the decisive difference would be lost—and religion would become more or less irrelevant. That may be the case for theology as well.

"Impact," like "influence," is a word in the semantic field of power. That is why religion's impact means *religion's power* over or about formation of character and education. The mode of power is then decisive: *what power* do we mean? (*Whose* power is already identified: *God's* in Christ by the Spirit—yet the "who" remains abusable.) I suggest that *Deutungsmacht*, the power of interpretation, is a symbolic power, framing our way of life, speech, and action. That is *not* just power from above and top-down (as from kings, popes, or institutions), but rather power from below, bottom-up, by recognition. In late modern societies, of course,

---

Hans-Peter Großhans, Michael Moxter, and Philipp Stoellger (Tübingen: Mohr Siebeck, 2018), 351–93.

[6]   Cf. Philipp Stoellger, "Die Medialität des Geistes oder: Pneumatologie als Medientheorie des Christentums. Zum Medium zwischen Gottes- und Menschenwerk," in *Risiko und Vertrauen. Risk and Trust: Festschrift für Michael Welker zum 70. Geburtstag,* ed. Heike Springhart and Günter Thomas (Leipzig: Evangelische Verlagsanstalt, 2017), 139–74.

[7]   I differ from Luhmann in that the decisive distinction through all media practices is, in my view, *not* transcendence and immanence but the eschatological difference of old and new.

the stratification model of society (top-down/bottom-up) is misguiding. We do not live in a world dominated by the hierarchy of kings and subordinates. But we live in a world framed and formed by media of communication. That is why the modes of power are media powers (not only "symbolic powers" from above, as Pierre Bourdieu pointed out with a little hermeneutics of suspicion).

There is a "figure of the third": in order to "de-dualize" the old alternative of God's word and human words, or God's work and human works, it is worth looking for the in-between: the words and works and passions, like the parables, which allow and make us to see in a new way.

The media *in between* God and humanity are figures of the third, through which we perceive and communicate Christ. Thereby the powers of media are relevant: *through and by* which media religion becomes manifest and articulated. That is a third mode of power (and therefore impact): not just from above (kings, bishops, presidents: *potestas*, power), not just from below (recognition and reception: *auctoritas*, authority), but from in between (media: *potentia*). The *potentialities* are the *potentiae* of religion, the realm of (im)possibilities. Media of religion can make possible what otherwise would remain impossible. A strange responsivity and responsibility in regard to strangers is neither Greek nor Roman, neither German nor American, but distinctively Christian—if and only if the response to the stranger is given in the spirit of Christ, but the spirit may be present without visible unity and semantic markers: it is not the explicit rhetoric or semantic that is decisive, but the implicit passion and disposition.

Media of Religion: Word and Image (Verbal and Visual Communication)

So far I have shown that researching the question before us requires (1) a *method* which can perceive and make explicit the implicit and latent dimensions of the impact of religion; (2) a *concept* of God as medium, religion as medium, and therefore the media of religion as cultural forms of religion; (3) a concept of impact as *power*, and a concept of power as *Deutungsmacht*, which is a "soft" power in all communication; (4) the de-dualizing interest in *mediality* as cultural power in between stratification hierarchies.[8]

Religion *as medium* is the decisive presupposition for *formation* (of character, education, sociality), because media are *forms of perception* (speech, thoughts, feelings) *forming* the perceived and the perceivers. Thus, *media* form perception—and religion *as* medium is integral to religious media practice. In this case, the media practice of religion is the potential impact in question.

---

[8]   Cf. Philipp Stoellger, "After Pluralism: Transcultural Responsivity in Respect to Religious Diversity" (in print).

How, then, may religion contribute (in competitive constellations among other communications) to personal and social formations? That depends of course on the religion and its traditions. If one looks at various forms of Protestantism, the main media of communication are (1) *speech*, words (together: *saying*); (2) *living images*, persons, gestures, rituals, scenes (together: *showing*); (3) specific modes of *institutionalizing*, that is, *orders*, like the extraordinary forms of order on the horizon of the origin of Christianity, and *interventions* like "reformations" as critique and ruptures of the old order. "Institutionalizing" is what I would call the *embodiments* of religion.

A fitting hypothesis for research may be that religious communication is framed by certain patterns, which also *may* frame other communication in public spheres. To elaborate the media-specific potentialities of religion would constitute a "media phenomenology of religion" as a distinct methodology. But three hints may be given, nevertheless.

With Regard to Patterns of Speech

One basic medium of speech is narrative, like the parables. Therefore, one may claim that the culture of narrative has a strong impact in forming character and moral education (remember the parable of the good Samaritan). This is why, in preaching and teaching, narratives are not only objects but also "subjects": they are "presence-makers" of Christian values. Even more, they are the main media of Christ's spirit. And thereby they become patterns of actions and even relevant for constitutions and laws (like those against the failure to render assistance). That narratives are subjects of teaching and preaching implies that they can become the main media of educational practice and public interactions.

But this idea can be a little too reassuring. There is a latent ambivalence: are narratives like the parables media for Christian values, or do the parables become media for quite different traditional values and prejudices? What is mediating what? Is the teacher using the narrative for mediating his or her values? Is the audience using the narrative to recognize their own values? Or is the narrative so strong that it contradicts the a priori moral orientations of teacher and audience?

Because narratives are capable of interpretation (they always need interpretation again and again), they can be "entered" in a kind of friendly takeover by a teacher, preacher, or audience. Therefore, the *impact* of the narratives has to be carefully analyzed and interpreted. *Moralizing* the parables is customary and traditional, but in danger of losing the *salvific* impact. To take care for the narrative's impact is a challenge for professional interpretation and hermeneutics. Otherwise the impact weighs more on the side of the users and their interests.

The case of narratives points toward a distinction between *formation and figuration*. *Formation* of character sounds like *biopolitics*, with will to power over the body and life (*zoe* and *bios*). To avoid this hermeneutics of suspicion, Paul Ricoeur's response was to understand narratives not as narrative formations forming our lives but as *configurations* with the potential for *refigurations* of the reader's/hearer's life. That is why I would prefer to speak not of formation but of *figuration*. The main medium, Christ, is the figurative figure (*figura figurans*) for the narrative figurations. And the narratives communicate (hopefully) Christ's spirit–for a *trans*figuration of those addressed. The further impact can then be described as follows: narrative figures can (and should) become cultural *patterns*–up to the spirit of law and language. In education the narrative figurations can become traditional patterns.

But is this a story of "success"? The successful transformation of a culture by religion? I am not quite sure when it comes to writing the patterns of the history of Christianity. Ricoeur invented the idea of living and dead metaphors. Even if the distinction is a little misguiding, one can apply it to narratives (which Ricoeur left out): *as cultural pattern* the narrative figure like the Samaritan is a *dead* narrative if it becomes traditional. Would the impact of religion be fulfilled in that way: becoming an accepted and widespread pattern of interaction–and thereby losing its extraordinary challenge? Neoprotestants (like Hegelians) may claim this as the "elevation" of religion in culture. But then the difference between religion and culture would be lost.

To dare to speak "in the name of God" maintains that difference if (and only if) in the actual use of narratives the *prenormative spirit* of Christ becomes present. The vivacity of media like narratives is their potential to become media of the real presence of *his* spirit. Could education, for example, be capable of this? Or would it violate the distinction of public school and religion?

With Regard to Patterns of Visual Communication

Images appear not to be relevant media for many forms of Protestantism. But that is a deception, primarily a self-deception of church and theology. Although the Reformation was a media event, it was not in the end a conflict in visual communication. To become visible is perhaps the fundamental desire and passion–not only in theology but in churches, communities, and public life. Visibility has become the highest value in academia, just as in politics and in churches. Remember the strange idea of "visible unity" as the final fulfilment of ecumenism; or remember the will to visibility in public theology. Whenever visibility is desired and recognized as the highest value or success, visual communication becomes a field that religion never can resist. But, the *how* of playing in this game makes the difference.

For Protestantism the problem is that the religion of the *word* in *visual* cultures appears to be a little helpless and lost in old media. The paradoxical challenge for Protestantism is how to make the word *visible*. Otherwise, Protestantism would not be able to have an impact in public spheres, which are ruled by visual media. The desire to become manifest and visible may contradict the self-understanding of Protestantism. But the dream of global visibility and powerful images can also produce megachurches with their will to powerful visibility.

Christ was quite reserved in this regard; Luther a little less so. But at any rate, contemporary Protestantisms have a problem with their impact in visually oriented cultures. In the focus on modes of visual communication, the *use of images* becomes interesting. If Protestantisms desire a sociocultural impact, their *image* and their iconic media are in question. Remember the quincentenary celebration of the Reformation and its "image-politics."

I pass over that, however, to focus on the central challenge: instead of public image-making and image-politics, the Protestant concept of *image* may be inspired by the distinction of *dead* and *living* images or even more, vitalizing images. We do not believe in the salvific power of old images on a wall. The images of saints are not quite relevant for Protestant service. They appear as old as the dead: dead images of dead saints. We do not pray to them and do not ask them for help.

Instead of dead images on the wall, we hope for *living images*. Imagine the communion as a living image of God's kingdom, celebrating the coming community of Christ. Imagine the community as the living image of Christian life. And imagine the presence of Christ by vivid interaction of churches in the public sphere: giving signs and examples of a life in the name of Christ.

The narrative figures profess not to be mere history but to transfigure actual and future life. The media of *showing* (in iconic difference to media of saying) in the media practice of religion are analogous: not as demonstration of dead images or wishful image politics, but as the embodiment of living images.

What may sound strange becomes concrete in the Eucharist as *figura vera* of the coming community. In the ritual, a distinct community is embodied in visual communication. The ritual is the figuration of community in the hope for the real presence of the figurative figure (Christ). But what for? For a distinct impact: not for the transubstantiation of things, but for the transfiguration of the participants —into the body of Christ. The living image of the Eucharist is a medium for an end: that the participants are transfigured into living images, the embodiment in life of the spirit of Christ.

Given this model of living image as transfiguration of the participants of Christian rituals, some relevant impacts may be named. For example, the concept of "image" seems often to be influenced by this central image practice of Christianity. What is desired from an image is life, new life, transfiguration of life. Another impact is that the *immersive power* of images (their transfigurative potential) becomes a model for "making present" or "real presence" in film and games. Even the image politics of bishops like the bishop of Rome or the federal bishops in German Protestantism are not without the desire to become present in, by, and as image.

The crucial question remains: should we hope for a social or even global impact of living images? In regard to communion we hope for a world-completion by the embodiment of Christ's spirit indeed. But as a model for image politics or for the image culture in our visual cultures, I would prefer not to burden the images with salvific desires. Therefore, the concept of the one living image may be a prenormative root for image critique.[9]

With Regard to Patterns of Institutionalization

"Order of the extraordinary" is the paradoxical impact of Christ as the basic figure for the institutionalization of Christian religion. If he is the central and singular figure as the visual embodiment of God, he is also the critique of traditional orders of state and religion. The problem then is how to build a new order—not just as repetition of old orders, not just as another order, but as *another* order *in the name of the extraordinary.* The analogous problem reappeared in the "second" Reformation, when Luther had to suggest new ways of order for Protestantism.

The theological problem is how to understand and construct a *Christian* normative order in the name of Christ. Is it just *another* order? Hopefully a *better* one, more just, more open to the stranger? Or is it *no* order, because the extraordinary rejects all order, as charismatic forms of Protestantism would claim? Or is the solution somewhere in between, perhaps *an order in the name of the extraordinary?* Then the form and function of order changes radically.

For the *normative* order of Protestantism, I insist on the crucial difference of salvation and morality. Decisive is the *prenormative root* of normativity in salvation: the prenormative and salvific passivity as root of Christian forms of life, as in the "mere passive" of justification. To remember and actualize *this* crucial difference will be the central contribution to the "normative impact of religion."

---

[9]   Cf. https://www.eikones.ch.

Learning to Care for the Whole Person

The Significance of Body and Soul for Diaconal Work

Johannes Eurich

Introduction

Diaconia[1] addresses the whole person. Even as supportive or helping action has become more varied, and professional standards have been applied in the respective fields of social services, the claim for human attention in the name of loving one's neighbor is more than just a demand for professional help: it is about the human being as God's image, about the individual in his or her dignity, about help for body and soul.

Sometimes it is not clear what the "more than" refers, to as professional standards also perceive people in a wider sense, even despite the division of social-service delivery into small-scale cost formats. The social services still address different life situations, as, for example, when fighting against poverty or trying to integrate assistance from different cost bearers in a comprehensive concept by means of case management approaches. If the "more" is related to the religious dimension of human life, there would be access to spiritual aspects of helping. This approach is particularly obvious when it comes to the topic of corporeality, because empathy for other people and their individual purposes in life—their needs, joys, and suffering—is constitutive of a helping and supporting attention to fellow human beings. The understanding for life impairments and distressful living conditions derives—diaconically—from the underlying image of the human being, which includes an imperfect body that is obliged to die.

Neither flawlessness nor youthful beauty is an ideal image to guide one through life, which also entails frailty, fracture, and finitude. Vulnerability is a basic condition of human life, opening access to the religious dimension of life: "A crucial key to understanding life-affecting conditions lies in human corporeal-

---

[1] Diaconia is the term for the Christian social engagement and assistance to the poor and needy and has a long history of charity and advocacy.

ity as a religious dimension of life."[2] Nevertheless, two things must be considered here.

First, diaconal organizations must continue to work on developing a spiritual or religious profile that goes beyond the formulations of mission statements and is formulated in terms of specific religious elements of care that are applicable and can be experienced. Examples of this kind of care include the approach to spiritual care in hospitals (often in the realm of palliative treatment) or in hospices.[3] For this purpose, trained personnel must be available who can take up existential questions and offer interpretations to life's meaning from a religious perspective. One education that tries to ensure this is the training to become a deacon or a deaconess in social work in many European Protestant churches, with dual qualification in social work and theology; nevertheless, only a minority of employees in diaconal organizations are approachable for explicitly religious questions.[4]

Second, even within religious traditions, an open approach toward the different dimensions of human life is by no means guaranteed. For a long time, Christian traditions cultivated hostility toward the human body, or at least a derogatory or instrumental attitude toward it. The human body was regarded as transient, the

---

[2]   Silke Leonhard, "In der Mitte und an den Grenzen. Leiblich lernen," in *Diakonisch Menschen bilden. Motivationen–Grundierungen–Impulse*, Diakonie 13, ed. Klaus Kießling and Heinz Schmidt (Stuttgart: Kohlhammer, 2014), 33–48, at 33; see Phillip A. Mellor and Chris Shilling, *Re-Forming the Body: Religion, Community, and Body* (London/Thousand Oaks, CA: Sage, 1997), 11.

[3]   Cf. as well Johannes Stockmeier, Astrid Giebel, and Heike Lubatsch, eds., *Geistesgegenwärtig pflegen. Existenzielle Kommunikation und spirituelle Ressourcen im Pflegeberuf*, Vol. 1: Grundlagen *und Werkstattberichte* (Neukirchen-Vluyn: Vandenhoeck & Ruprecht, 2012); cf. Stockmeier, Giebel, and Lubatsch, eds., *Geistesgegenwärtig pflegen. Existenzielle Kommunikation und spirituelle Ressourcen im Pflegeberuf*, Vol. 2: *Studien und Projektergebnisse* (Neukirchen-Vluyn: Vandenhoeck & Ruprecht, 2013); cf. Jürgen Armbruster, Nicole Frommann, and Astrid Giebel, eds., *Geistesgegenwärtig begleiten. Existenzielle Kommunikation, Spiritualität und Selbstsorge in der Psychiatrie und Behindertenhilfe* (Neukirchen-Vluyn: Vandenhoeck & Ruprecht, 2014); cf. Astrid Giebel, et.al. eds., *Geistesgegenwärtig beraten. Existenzielle Kommunikation, Spiritualität und Selbstsorge in der Beratung, Seelsorge und Suchthilfe* (Neukirchen-Vluyn: Vandenhoeck & Ruprecht, 2015); cf. Samon Peng-Keller, et. al. eds., *Studies in Spiritual Care*, vol. 1 (Berlin/Boston: De Gruyter, 2017); Wim Smeets, *Spiritual Care in a Hospital Setting: An Empirical-Theological Exploration* (Leiden/Boston: Brill, 2006).

[4]   Cf. the study about religious attitude of nurses in Protestant hospitals in Lower-Saxony: Heike Lubatsch, *Führung macht den Unterschied. Arbeitsbedingungen diakonischer Pflege im Krankenhaus*, SI konkret 5 (Münster: Evangelische Verlagsanstalt, 2012); cf. Linda Ross, "Spiritual Care in Nursing: An Overview of the Research to Date," *Journal of Clinical Nursing* 15 (2006): 852–62, doi: https://doi.org/10.1111/j.1365-2702.2006.01617.x.

soul as immortal. Moreover, the body was associated with sin. Even if sin arose just as much from mental impulses, such as envy, greed, and lust, the body had to be chastened in order to avoid the seduction of sin. As is well known, the body-soul (or body-spirit) dualism was not originally a concept in Jewish or Christian thinking. Especially in the Hebrew Bible, body and soul form an inseparable body-soul unity.

On the basis of these observations, it is advisable not to simply speak of diaconal action as a holistic approach toward people, or even to praise the diaconal approach unthinkingly as "surplus" to other aid providers, unless diaconal aid is convincingly presented at the same time in terms of how the whole person is addressed and how far this can play a role in providing aid. The current chapter seeks to explain and justify, on the basis of the Protestant tradition, diaconal bodily care for people and to discuss it within today's challenges. For this purpose, the first section outlines two historical developments that provide exemplary models of how the focus is placed above all on appreciative approaches to physicality. Building on these references to the diaconal tradition, the second section asks for theological reasons for diaconal bodily care. Here physicality and examples of dementia and disability will be the focus of theological and ethical reflection. In the third section, these considerations are related to challenges of diaconal bodily practice today.

Two Historical Examples for Diaconal Bodily Help

The manifold beginnings of grass-root diaconal groups in the nineteenth century in Germany and other countries, which contributed decisively to the development and expansion of diaconal organizations, had diverse connections to the revivalist movement and to Pietistic communities. August Hermann Francke, on the basis of the orphanage and school complex he founded, is regarded as one of the forerunners, if not one of the great role models, of the founding of diaconal organizations in Germany and beyond in the nineteenth century. Soon after the founding of his orphanage in Glaucha, near Halle, Germany, Francke thought about including medical care and hired his own resident physician to provide medical care for the sick children and adolescents.[5] When the new orphanage was built in 1701,

---

5   Cf. Werner Piechocki, "Gesundheitsfürsorge und Krankenpflege in den Franckeschen Stiftungen in Halle/Saale," in *Beiträge zur Geschichte des Gesundheitswesens der Stadt Halle und der Medizinischen Fakultät der Universität Halle*, Acta Historica Leopoldina 2 (Leipzig: Barth, 1965), 29–66; cf. Idem, "Die Krankenpflege und das Klinikum der Franckeschen Stiftungen," in *August Hermann Francke. Das humanistische Erbe des großen Erziehers*, ed. Franz Hofmann, et al. (Halle: Francke-Komitee, 1965), 52–59; cf. Heinrich Ernst Ferdinand Guericke, *Life of Augustus Herman Franke: Professor of Divinity and*

separate rooms for sick persons were set up, and later a separate building for nursing care was prepared, while a matron to look after the sick was hired along with nurses. In addition, medical students and theology students were appointed to supervise the rooms for the sick persons. Francke opened the nursing care of the orphanage for sick people who did not live in the orphanage.[6] The destitute sick were to be treated as well as poor students.

Little is known about how patients were treated in the orphanage. However, connections can be made between the theological interpretation of illness at that time and physical therapy in dealing with the sick. In keeping with the thought of the day, Francke regarded physical illness as the result of calculated divine action. A person did not become ill by chance, but it was God who determined when "natural causes" of diseases would occur and whether there would be a recovery.[7] For in Francke's eyes, the actual cause of illness was the "sin of man," understood not as a single moral transgression but as a life in disbelief, turned away from God.[8] This transgressive life orientation represents the actual "fundamental sin" that could be overcome only through knowledge of sin and conversion to God by the experience of divine grace. From this perspective, illness played an important role, as it was understood as God's instrument to persuade the unbeliever to repent and to turn back to God: "God the Lord uses the bodily need just as a means / by which he wants to draw men to himself and to repentance / so that they may be relieved inwardly."[9] Illnesses also have a purifying function for the true believer: they represent "fatherly visitations of God" (checkups), which the believer should bear joyfully and patiently, for they serve to recognize his inner condition and to continue the daily battle of repentance. "For both the unbeliever (sic) and the converted Christian, the physical illnesses must always lead to a serious examination of one's own state of the soul."[10]

Founder of the Orphan-House in Halle, available online at https://archive.org/details/augustushe00guer/page/n6.

[6] Cf. Jürgen Helm, "Der Umgang mit dem kranken Menschen im Halleschen Pietismus des frühen 18. Jahrhunderts," in *Medizinhistorisches Journal* 31 (1996): 67–87, at 68; cf. Guericke, *Life of Augustus Hermann Franke.*

[7] Cf. August Hermann Francke, "Die geistliche Seelen-Cur," in Idem, *Sonn-, Fest- und Apostel-Tags-Predigten / darinnen die zum wahren Christenthum gehörige nöthigste und vornehmste Materien abgehandelt sind* (Halle: Waysenhaus, 1704), vol. 2, 652–96.

[8] Cf. Petra Kurten, *Umkehr zum lebendigen Gott. Die Bekehrungstheologie August Hermann Franckes als Beitrag zur Erneuerung des Glaubens* (Paderborn: Schöningh, 1985), 55; cf. Wolfgang Splitter, "The Fact and Fiction of Cotton Mather's Correspondence with German Pietist August Hermann Francke," *The New England Quarterly* 83 (2010): 102–22, at 105.

[9] Francke, *Seelen-Cur* (note 7), 672.

[10] Helm, "Umgang" (note 6), 72.

This theological interpretation of illness was also important to Francke's resident physician, Christian Friedrich Richter (1676–1711), who, beginning in 1697, was responsible for the treatment of the sick people in Francke's orphanage and later took over the management of the orphanage pharmacy. Richter helped to further promote the expansion of the link between Georg Ernst Stahl's medical theory and Francke's Pietism by publishing his book *Kurtzer und deutlicher Unterricht von dem Leibe und natürlichen Leben des Menschen* (Short and clear instructions on the body and the natural life of man, 1705)[11]

At the same time, the link between physical illness and spiritual mindset made pastoral care an essential aspect of the care for sick people. The two most important books on pastoral care for the sick from the beginning of the eighteenth century were written by theologians who were part of Francke's circle of friends.[12] The "soul cleansing" in turn focuses on the examination of conscience, through which the sick are to recognize and accept their illness as part of the divine order. For unbelievers, it is an occasion for repentance and conversion, while for the faithful it is for uncovering possible hidden sins and for strengthening of faith. It is therefore striking that the connection between illness and divine order and the resulting view of illness as a means of awakening the conscience did not result in a devaluation of the body or in the alleviation of physical needs. Rather, the physical healing of illnesses appeared as a path to the inner healing of the soul, just as physical illness was interpreted as an indication of the sick soul. This view resulted in a corresponding appreciation of physical therapy and its conscious connection to pastoral care: "Physical therapy almost appears as a prerequisite for a successful 'soul cure': Nothing, however, can make people more willing to let their souls be cured by external means than when they are first relieved from their bodily complaints."[13]

---

[11] Christian Friedrich Richter, *Kurtzer und deutlicher Unterricht von dem Leibe und natürlichen Leben des Menschen. Woraus ein jeglicher / auch Ungelehrter erkennen kan / Was die Gesundheit ist / und wie sie zu erhalten: auch welches die menschlichen Kranckheiten / deren Ursachen und Kennzeichen sind / Und wie sie Von einem jeden zu verhüten / oder auch bey Ermangelung eines Medici, ohne Gefahr und mit gutem Success zu curiren: Nebst einem Selectu Medicamentorum, [...]* (Halle, 1705), new print ed. by Hans-Joachim Poeckern (Leipzig: Schweitzer Verlagshaus, 1984). After Richter dropped out of his theology studies, he started to study medicine at Georg Ernst Stahl. He spread his teachings through his books. His studies were published as "the most important knowledge for humanity" until the end of the eighteenth century; cf. Eckhard Altmann, *Christian Friedrich Richter (1676–1711). Arzt, Apotheker und Liederdichter des Halleschen Pietismus* (Witten: Luther-Verlag, 1972), 216f.

[12] Cf. Helm, "Umgang" (note 6), 74.

[13] Ibid., 77. He quotes the important essay "Programmschrift des Halleschen Pietismus."

A further aspect of the connections among disease treatment, pastoral care, and everyday life is presented by Richter in his book. In Richter's view, the body serves the soul as "an instrument . . . to practice the will of God in the visible world."[14] The focus is not only on the treatment of illnesses but also on the preservation of health. In summary, the people related to Pietism in Halle aimed at a comprehensive treatment of the human being and encouraged people to maintain their health or, in the case of illness, to include pastoral care in their medical treatment—all this with the Pietistism-supported goal that the body should be used for the glory of God.[15]

With good reason, one may criticize the link between illnesses and religious ideas of salvation (conversion or purification) from today's point of view.[16] Nevertheless, the openness of the Halle Pietists toward medical therapy, including appreciation for the medical faculty at the University of Halle, is remarkable.[17] Together with the focus on the salvation of the soul, which is important for Pietism, the work of the Halle Pietists led not only to an appreciative view of the body but also to organizational measures for treating physical and mental aspects of illness together.[18]

A similar orientation toward comprehensive help for body and soul can be observed almost 150 years later among deaconesses, though now under changed social conditions and with a different objective. Here reasons for the introduction of the office of deaconess can be revealing. In the 1830 s, Theodor Fliedner established the first nursing, or deaconess, institution in Kaiserswerth, near Düsseldorf, Germany. He included in his instructions for the deaconesses the following examination questions, on the basis of which each deaconess was to give account to herself at least once a week within the framework of the evening faith examination. In some of the questions quoted below, the connection between practical nursing activities and spiritual attitude becomes clear.

---

[14] Richter, *Kurtzen und deutlichen Unterricht*, "Vorrede" (note 11) page 3r, quoted after Helm, "Umgang," 77.

[15] Ibid., 8r (unpag.).

[16] Cf. the speech by Richter, who said that the doctor could try to do something against the barriers, "which are against the soul's movement. But he is not able to dispose a 'new chaotic nature.' Therefore, he needs God's spiritual succor." Richter quoted by Helm, "Umgang," 79. Nature and soul are synonyms for Richter.

[17] Cf. Helm, "Umgang" (note 6), 78 about honoring the university medical science.

[18] Cf. Helm, "'Kinder- und Lehrkrankenhaus' im frühen 18. Jahrhundert? Die Einrichtungen zur Krankenfürsorge in den Franckeschen Stiftungen," *Medizinhistorisches Journal* 33 (1998): 107–41.

About my physical care and work:

8. Was I as attentive as possible during the visitation of the doctor while I had to take care of the sick? Have I carefully memorized his prescriptions and followed them conscientiously? Have I always cared for the sick with gentleness, patience, kindness and holy earnestness?

9. Have I always taken care that my patients receive good and sufficient food and drink according to the recommendations? Was I further not too afraid to report when this was not the case?

10. Have I also done my best to prevent the patients from enjoying too much food which they were not allowed to consume? Did I moreover prevent them being spoilt and pampered in any other way?

11. Did I care for the physical needs of the sick, poor, children, and asylum seekers etc.? Have I encouraged them to fend for themselves concerning their needs and cleanliness as well as to do suitable and useful work?

12. Did I myself make enough effort to learn such useful jobs with diligence? E. g., the female handicrafts, the garden work, etc., and also small surgical tasks? ...

About my spiritual fostering and teaching:

15. Have I diligently used my best endeavors to provide my patients—especially the poor— with sufficient spiritual food, e. g., with appropriate edifying writings, especially the Bible, and instructed them to enjoy them for their salutarily effects?

16. Did I seek to please and amuse the sick, children, or other patients enough, e. g., by walking, singing, telling stories, playing, etc., so that they may learn to be joyful and content in the Lord by all means? (Phil. 4:4)

17. Have I instructed the patients to sanctify Sundays and the feasts and to use them as beneficially as possible for their souls, both during the public service and before and after it, namely the poor, sick, children, and other patients, according to their particular circumstances?[19]

In this examination of conduct and spiritual life, care-related and faith-related questions were connected. In this way Fliedner aimed at promoting inner motivation to a qualitatively good care for faith reasons. The basic conditions were established through the creation of the office of deaconesses. The quality of the care for the sick and needy depended decisively on the effects of the intrinsic motivation, because professional standards in medical care were only slowly devel-

---

[19]   Theodor Fliedner, "Selbstprüfungs-Fragen für Diakonissen und Probeschwestern," *Der Armen- und Krankenfreund* (Sept.-Oct. 1855): 10–18, at 11 f.; cf. Catherine Winkworth, ed., *Life of Pastor Fliedner* (Oxford, 1867), 59–60, available at https://archive.org/details/lifepastorflied00fliegoog/page/n98.

oping at that time. Thus, the exhortation to act mercifully was repeatedly and strongly imposed, as, for example, in the request to the deaconesses of Neudettelsau, Germany:

> Be merciful, which means, fifth, dedicate yourself as much as you can to the service of the poor. Without personal service for the miserable, you will not achieve much in any demonstration of mercy. This holds true for every Christian, but for a deaconess it is a sacred and indispensable official duty. On top of that, personal service against misery must not provide relief in the sense of recklessness, nor must it be done in despair, but in indestructible respect and love for the sick person, who is obliged to die. This person is to be seen as the subject of God's redeeming love. Whoever draws away from the sick and poor earlier than God and his angels leaves too soon and moreover damages his/her soul.[20]

Wilhelm Löhe, from whom this quote comes, had founded a home for deaconesses in Neudettelsau, in Franconia, in 1854, about twenty years after Fliedner. He emphasized in particular the education of deaconesses. Already Fliedner had counted education among the core components of the office of deaconesses, extending the classical monastic ideal of celibacy, possessionlessness, and obedience. For Löhe, education seems to have been a fundamental consideration for founding a diaconal institution:

> When we pastors come out to our villages to visit the sick, we find female persons everywhere who take care of the sick and miserable more than others, because they are incited to do so by an inward gift. They follow their natural urge. What they lack is the possibility to form their gift. Many of these women would be biblical deaconesses, if one would administer to them and offer education. The education of these gifted women in order to enable them to serve suffering humanity is a *pium desiderium*, and the longer it lasts, the more it becomes a demand to the church.[21]

It becomes clear how much gender-stereotypical views were guiding Löhe. Diaconal help takes up the "natural" dispositions identified as typically feminine and transforms them into a diaconal ideal of service. Thereby also another aspect appears which may also have contributed to the acceptance of the diaconal ministry: to become a deaconess meant the chance for unmarried women to receive a better

---

20   Wilhelm Löhe, "Die innere Entwicklung der Diakonissenanstalt. Idee des Diakonissentums und Diakonissenideal nach Löhes Anschauung," in Johannes Deinzer, *Wilhelm Löhe's Leben. Aus seinem schriftlichen Nachlaß zusammengestellt*, vol. 3 (Gütersloh, 1892), 175–97, at 182; cf. Erika Geiger, *The Life, Work, and Influence of Wilhelm Loehe, 1808–1872*, trans. Wolf Dietrich Knappe (St. Louis, MO: Concordia, 2010).
21   Löhe, quoted by Krimm II, 375.

education than otherwise possible and to be able to exercise a profession outside the family home and the supremacy of the father or husband. Löhe consciously addressed these educational aspirations when he encouraged the assumption of a profession otherwise reserved for men: deaconesses were to enter the male domain of school teaching.[22] The emancipatory potential inherent in open access to education was at least partly prevented and limited by the integration of deaconesses into the hierarchical community of the deaconesses' mother house. At the head of the institution was the female superior, but above that woman again was a man, who was in charge of the diaconal institution as a whole.

The deaconesses' schools shaped the image of the developing profession of nurses. Florence Nightingale had already received decisive impulses for her work in nursing care during her stay with Fliedner in 1850.[23] While Nightingale turned more strongly to the reform of the British medical system and addressed structural questions, especially after the Crimean War (1853–56), the ideal of nursing in the spirit of religiously motivated charity dominated the deaconess model in Germany for a long time to come. It was not until the 1890 s that emancipatory Protestant women's movements emerged, although they initially played a subordinate role.

Among the Halle Pietists as well as among many other deacon communities, one can find different motives of pietistic faith interlinked. The concentration on spiritual life in their way of living and the resulting intrinsic motivation for service to one's neighbor occurred with specific objectives, which did not include withdrawing from the reality of life or being hostile to one's body. On the contrary, in Halle, medicine was integrated as an essential part of care in order to strengthen the body as an image of the soul and to use it as a tool for the glory of God. In the deaconess communities, spiritual exercises (self-examinations) to practice an attitude of service in favor of the sick and needy were aimed at restoring physical health or alleviating illness. This soon led to the development of standards of care and nursing and the training of deaconesses. Thus diligence, obedience, humility, and compassion formed important virtues.

This of course did not show the extent to which one cared for or mistreated one's own body while practicing strenuous ministries. Hence, two aspects seem to have played a significant role in the view of diaconia and the body. First, the prac-

---

[22]   Cf. Ute Gause, "'Aufbruch der Frauen'. Das vermeintlich 'Weibliche' der Weiblichen Diakonie," in *Dienerinnen des Herrn. Beiträge zur weiblichen Diakonie im 19. und 20. Jahrhundert*, Historisch-theologische Genderforschung 5, ed. Jochen-Christoph Kaiser and Rajah Schepers (Leipzig: Evangelische Verlagsanstalt, 2010), 57–71, at 65.

[23]   Cf. Florence Nightingale, *The Institution of Kaiserswerth on the Rhine: For the Practical Training of Deaconesses, under the Direction of the Rev. Pastor Fliedner, Embracing the Support and Care of a Hospital, Infant and Industrial Schools, and a Female Penitentiary* (London, 1851).

tical proof of faith in everyday life, which Pietism emphasized in particular, included an appreciation of the body as a tool that should be used for the glory of God. Therefore the body should also be nurtured through physical exercise, which at the same time meant that no physical exercise and games should be practiced which did not correspond to this goal.[24] Second, the care and attention given to the sick in the spirit of charity led to the beginning of a profession that promoted professional care in the sense of appropriate physical care. The general educational contents conveyed in the training as well as theological and social subjects also contributed to taking into account not only the physical condition of sick people but also their spiritual and living conditions.

Corporeality as a Point of Reference for Diaconal Action

Created Life is Bodily Life

Corporeality means the human being in all his or her existence as an "inspired" or living body. It is more than just the mere body of a human being. Corporeality is a mode of existence which the individual shares with other human beings, and which enables her or him to perceive others. "The body is our general medium of world participation. Here the body stands in a double relation: in a relation to the world and to the ego, which has the world for himself. The ego is not the ego without the world."[25]

It is also true from a Christian perspective that the created being is constitutively bound to corporeality. The body represents the "social and communicative anchoring of the body in the intersubjective world"[26] and forms the "interface"[27]

---

[24] Cf. Erich Geldbach, *Sport und Protestantismus. Geschichte einer Begegnung* (Wuppertal: Theologischer Verlag R. Brockhaus, 1975), 62 f. Francke frowned on free play, unused time, and idleness as well; cf. Patricia Vertinsky, "God, Science and the Market Place: The Bases for Exercise Prescriptions for Females in Nineteenth Century North America," *Human Kinetics Journal* 17 (1989): 38–45, at 38, doi: doi.org/10.1123/cjhs.17.1.38..

[25] Bernhard Waldenfels, "Das Problem der Leiblichkeit bei Merleau-Ponty," *in Leiblichkeit. Philosophische, gesellschaftliche und theoretische Perspektiven*, ed. Hilarion G. Petzold (Paderborn: Junfermann, 1985, 149–72, at 157.

[26] Peter Dabrock, "Bedingungen des Unbedingten. Zum problematischen, aber notwendigen Gebrauch der Menschenwürde-Konzeption in der Bioethik," in *Menschenwürde und Lebensschutz. Herausforderungen theologischer Bioethik*, ed. Peter Dabrock, Stefanie Schardien, and Lars Klinnert (Gütersloh: Gütersloher Verlagshaus, 2004), 147–72, at 167 f. (highlighted in original text); cf. Bernhard Waldenfels, *Das leibliche Selbst. Vorlesungen zur Phänomenologie des Leibes* (Frankfurt am Main: Suhrkamp, 2000); cf. Dennis

between the outside world and the inside world, between recognition as a person by others and self-perception as a person in one's own consciousness. "Accordingly, the body is shaped by *social signatures*, because the conditions of life and the experiences each individual person made are imprinted in the body and thus are of great significance for how a person experiences himself and the world he or she is part of."[28] Corporeality is therefore the physical reference to the reality of the subject: the body can be grasped objectively, whereas this is not possible for the subjective experience of the body. Plessner's pointedly formulated distinction between the *body one has* and the *body one is*, is not uncontroversial due to the made difference between consciousness and body.[29] Nevertheless, the body can be understood as the form of expression of a human being in his or her unique identity in relation to others: "Corporeality is the field of events of the biographical uniqueness."[30]

Even though the body, because of its sensual nature, is first and foremost a perceptive medium, it also has a memorative and an expressive dimension.[31] In its memorative dimension, the body stores traces of memory of a life story inscribed in the body. The body derives its expressivity from its mobility: through movements, postures, gestures, facial expressions, looks, and so on, it expresses itself. Physical movements can be understood as an essential aspect of social behavior,

---

Waskul and Phillip Vannini, "The Body in Symbolic Interaction," available at https://www.researchgate.net/publication/267210235_The_Body_in_Symbolic_Interaction.

[27] Michael Oelker, "Person, Menschenwürde und Gottebenbildlichkeit," in *Menschenwürde*, JBTh 15, ed. Igor Baldermann, et. al., (Neukirchen-Vluyn: Neukirchener Verlag, 2001), 247–62, at 252; cf. Linda Woodhead, "Apophatic Anthropology," in *God and Human Dignity*, ed. R. Kendall Soulen and Linda Woodhead (Grand Rapids, MI: William B. Eerdman, 2006), 233–46, at 236.

[28] Markus Dederich, *Behinderung, Medizin, Ethik. Behindertenpädagogische Reflexionen zu Grenzsituationen am Anfang und Ende des Lebens* (Bad Heilbrunn: Klinkhardt, 2000), 150; Cf. Woodhead, "Apophatic Anthropology," (note 27), 328–29.

[29] Cf. Helmuth Plessner, *Die Stufen des Organischen und der Mensch. Einleitung in die philosophische Anthropologie* (Tübingen: De Gruyter, 1928); Cf. Robert W. Wenson, "Anima Ecclesiastica," in Soulen and Woodhead, *God and Human Dignity* (note 27), 59–72, at 65.

[30] Andreas Lob-Hüdepohl, "Leib," in *Diakonielexikon* (2016), 264–66, at 264; cf. the definition by Helmuth Schmitz, *Kurze Einführung in die Neue Phänomenologie* (München: Verlag Karl Alber, 2009), 35, who describes the body as "that which one can feel of oneself, as belonging to oneself, in the region (not always within the limits) of one's body, without using the five senses, namely seeing and touching, and the perceptive body schema (the habitual idea of one's own body) gained from their experience."

[31] Cf. Hilarion G. Petzold, *Integrative Therapie. Modelle, Theorien und Methoden für eine schulenübergreifende Psychotherapie*, Vol. 1: *Klinische Philosophie* (Paderborn: Junfermann Verlag, 1993); cf. Edward S. Casey, *Rememebering: A Phenomenological Study*, 2nd ed. (Bloomington/Indianapolis: Indiana University Press, 2000), 246.

"since this behavior becomes visible only through its embodiment and thus comprehensible to others."[32] In a body-phenomenological perspective, one characteristic of the body therefore is the relation of human life to others as well as to its sociality.[33]

Already the two historical developments outlined above in Halle Pietism and among the deaconesses of the nineteenth century have shown that diaconal action is about more than a pure physical treatment: in each case, the combination of physical and spiritual aspects played an important role. Even if this came from a certain tradition of piety with corresponding moral ideals, one can generalize that diaconal action aims at the well-being of persons in their holistic nature, "which is present in [their] corporeality to [themselves] and to all others."[34] Diaconia is therefore given the task of taking care of the comprehensive well-being of the body, which, on one hand, includes the care for the soul "as an *immaterial place* of subjective meaning positing," and, on the other hand, "embodies itself in the way of life of a human being in lived joy and confidence."[35] Soul and body must therefore not be separated from each other or played off against one another.

Especially in the Gospels, it becomes clear that the incarnation of God in Christ means an appreciation of corporeality within Christianity. This is in contrast to a body-hostile dualism, which exposes the mind and the soul as the essential core of the human being and devalues the body as an external, material shell. In the Incarnation (literally, in German, *Einfleischun*) God takes the shape of the Son and literally operates in person among men and women. It is striking, "how much the Nazarene . . . documents God's salvation for humankind in his care for the physical well-being of the sick, weak, and marginalized: 'Blind people can see again, and lame people walk. The lepers become clean, and the deaf can hear again' (Matt. 11:5)."[36] The healing presence of God manifests itself in the physical realm; it is experienced within the sensual-physical level, that is, in the body. This becomes particularly visible in healing narratives in the Gospels, because the mo-

---

[32] Dederich, *Behinderung* (note 28), 146.

[33] Cf. Bernhard Waldenfels, *Antwortregister* (Frankfurt am Main: Suhrkamp, 1994), 477, where he describes the complex process of interaction between two persons on the basis of their physical dimensions as a prereflexive interphysical interphysosity that represents an area in which "the own and the foreign interweave, entangle, intermesh, without thus coinciding, but also without completely separating from each other. This creates the possibility of an incarnated conversation in which gesture responds to gesture."; cf. Thomas Fuchs, "The Phenomenology and Development of Social Perspectives," 2012, doi: 10.1007/s11097-012-9267-x. 25–26.

[34] Lob-Hüdepohl, "Leib" (note 30), 265; cf. Fuchs, "Phenomenology" (note 33), 9.

[35] Lob-Hüdepohl, "Leib," 265.

[36] Ibid.

ment of physical contact is given a prominent meaning.[37] In the healing touch, "there is a tangible and concrete contact between the two persons, a mutual physical confirmation of the physicality of being a person."[38]

In this respect, the sick body is not simply an object for healing but a starting point for human subjectivity and the ability to build relationships; consequently, the body is perceived as *body in relation*. The healing stories are therefore primarily to be understood as relationship stories. They reach beyond the relationship between Jesus and the healed person to the social relationships, and in this they also thematize the relationship of humanity to God. "Thus it is understandable that the dimensions of the tactile—the *bodily touching* and the *letting oneself be touched*—are fundamental privileged spaces of experience in which the salutary presence of God at all times (thus also today and tomorrow) takes place within interpersonal relationships on a sensual, physical level."[39] Diaconal care therefore always has to apply to the whole person and aims at the well-being of the person in his or her wholeness as well as uniqueness: "Diaconal action therefore acts fundamentally *in person:* it seeks the encounter with the people in need 'face to face.' It seeks personal dialogue, which can only be replaced by intermediation in emergency situations. It touches and can be touched."[40] The pastoral dimension must therefore not be separated from physical attention and therapy.

Because physicality includes the vulnerability of the human being, he or she is exposed to suffering and pain and can experience existential hardship and despair of life. A diaconia that would focus purely on physical treatment would therefore miss its mission, just as much as a treatment of a sick person that aims only at conversion or purification of the soul.

> This is why diaconal action basically unites both perspectives: diaconal care for the soul and a soul-comforting diaconia. Diaconal action that is exclusively limited to the physical well-being of the person would promote the fatal dualism between body and soul just as much as pastoral care that misunderstands the concern for the physical well-being merely as unavoidable preliminary work for its actual field of activity— namely the individual relationship to God as a mere mental-spiritual, 'unworldly' event."[41]

---

[37] Cf. ibid.; cf. Charles Kingsley Barrett, *The Holy Spirit and the Gospel Tradition* (Eugene, OR/London: Wipf and Stock, 1958), 75, who refers to Mark 1:40–45.

[38] Regina Ammicht Quinn, *Körper-Religion-Sexualität* (Mainz: Matthias Grünewald, 1999), 134; Cf. Suzanne M. Peloquin, "Helping Through Touch: The Embodiment of Caring," *Journal of Religion and Health* 28 (1989): 299–322.

[39] Lob-Hüdepohl "Leib" (note 30), 265; cf. Zach Thomas, *Healing Touch: The Church's Forgotten Language* (Louisville, KY: Westminster John Knox Press, 1994), 30.

[40] Lob-Hüdepohl, "Leib," 266.

[41] Ibid., 265 f.

In this holistic perspective, diaconal attention corresponds to what is already indicated in the healing stories about the kingdom of God: salvation applies to the human being in all of existence. Diaconal action may thus be part of God's salvation even today.

The understanding of human life as vulnerable life sketched in the healing stories of the Bible can be seen as one access to a bodily dimension. It is indeed part of the bodily existence that is vulnerable, can be inflicted with pain, and ultimately suffers death. Accident, illness, and other forms of bodily harm can affect human life up to the body's decomposition in death. In the Christian faith, however, the body is not simply abandoned to transience. In all its fragility and decrepitness, the body is included in the salvation of humanity through Christ, as already indicated in the healing narratives.[42] The overcoming of death takes place in faith in the word of God that has become flesh. The hope for the resurrection of the body is concentrated in the risen Jesus[43] and thus allows a wider view of human corporeality and mortality: "The last appreciation for human corporeality can be found in the Christian resurrection. This resurrection stands for confidence that every experience of a person throughout his or her life, what he or she has 'incarnated' as an unmistakable and unique form of life, will forever be accommodated into the completion of the world promised by God."[44]

Corporeality as an Invitation for Diaconal Action

The corporeality of the human being includes the vulnerability and fragility of the body. Thus, whenever a person perceives the other as needy, defenseless, frail, or sick, there comes an appeal or claim to help the other. "In this respect, the cor-

---

[42]   Cf. Quinn, *Körper* (note 38), 132: "Healing is the concrete and physical part of the promised salvation."; cf. Howard A. Snyder and Joel Scandrett, *Salvation Means Creation Healed: The Ecology of Sin and Grace. Overcoming the Divorce between Heaven and Earth* (Eugene, OR: Cascade Books, 2011), 65: "gospel is about healing the disease of sin—and the healing of all creation through Jesus Christ by the Holy Spirit. Sin is the disease; salvation is the cure. New creation is the final fruit—something greater and more glorious than healing sins."

[43]   Cf. Günter Thomas, *Neue Schöpfung. Systematisch-theologische Untersuchungen zur Hoffnung auf das "Leben in der zukünftigen Welt"* (Neukirchen-Vluyn: Vandenhoeck & Ruprecht, 2009), 409 ff., for information about the similarity and difference between the risen and fleshly body; cf. Robert M. Grant, "The Resurrection of the Body," *The Journal of Religion* 28 (1948): 120–30, at 120.

[44]   Auer quoted by Lob-Hüdepohl, "Leib" (note 30), 265.

poreality raises (in its neediness, dependence, and infirmity) a 'claim'"[45] which can be accepted and answered or rejected by the other person. The relevance of this "ethics from below"[46] is based on the nonreciprocity of bodily needs and actions, which is given because action always responds to the claim that emanates from corporeality.[47] Because the claim irrefutably addresses the other human being, it makes him or her accountable for responding to it. This claim is exemplified in one of the foundation stories for diaconal action in the New Testament, the story of the Good Samaritan (Luke 10:25–37). From the injured man who fell among robbers and was injured, the same appeal is made to every person passing by:[48] the demand for help. Those who pass by the needy man and who do not help come under pressure to justify their behavior, especially in the eyes of the readers.

They form a counterfoil to the actions of the merciful Samaritan, who is deeply moved in his heart by the misery of the injured man.[49] In the Samaritan's re-

---

[45] Karl Mertens, "Verletzlichkeit des Leibes und Ansprüche der Natur," in *Der Anspruch des Anderen. Perspektiven phänomenologischer Ethik*, Übergänge 32, ed. Bernhard Waldenfels and Iris därmann (Munich: Wilhelm Fink Verlag, 1998), 239–57, at 246 (higlighted in original text); cf. Jean-Pierre Wils, "Person und Leib," in *Wann ist der Mensch tot? Organverpflanzung und "Hirntod"-Kriterium*, ed. Johannes *Hoff* and Jürgen in der *Schmitten* (Reinbek next to Hamburg: Rowohlt, 1994), 119–49, at 143: "The body is the visible personality. . . . Without its perishable corporeality man would live in a universe irrelevant to him: Precisely his bodily finiteness at the mercy of death makes his relationship to himself, to others and to the world morally significant first and foremost."

[46] Bernhard Waldenfels, "Einführung. Ethik vom Anderen her," in Waldenfels and Därmann, *Anspruch* (note 45), 7–14, at 13.

[47] Cf. Dederich, *Behinderung* (note 28), 154; cf. Leonhard, "Mitte" (note 2), 41f. "This leads to asymmetrical situations and relationships–asymmetrical, because we are called to help and the opportunity of helping that determines this call creates unbalanced possibilities, behaviour and roles." Cf. Moore Sidgwick and Anthony Skelton, "Late Utilitarian Moral Theory and Its Development: A Companion to Nineteenth-Century Philosophy," in *A Companion to Nineteenth-Century Philosophy*, ed. John Shand (Hoboken, NJ: Wiley, 2019), 281–310, at 281, doi: 10.1002/9781119210054.ch11.

[48] Cf. Arne Manzeschke, "'Ressourcen der Nächstenliebe'. Eine fundamentalethische Besinnung auf die Erfahrung des Nächsten," in *Nächstenliebe und Organisation. Zur Zukunft einer polyhybriden Diakonie in zivilgesellschaftlicher Perspektive*, VWGTh 37, ed. Heinz Schmidt and Klaus D. Hildemann (Leipzig: Evangelische Verlagsanstalt, 2012), 169–89, at 180: "It is not about acting for someone. But it is about welcoming someone as naked, defenseless, and needy as he is." Cf. Ruben Zimmermann, "The Etho-Poietic of the Parable of the Good Samaritan (Lk 10: 25–37): The Ethics of Seeing in a Culture of Looking the Other Way," *Verbum et Ecclesia* 29 (2008): 269–92, at 279.

[49] Cf. Manzeschke, "Ressourcen" (note 48), 169–89, at 180: "The physical other's presence provokes a reaction in the Samaritan. Physical corporeality describes the place and the modus of the encounter. The Samaritan has a deep sense for the appearance of the rob-

sponse, he not only helps the injured man by dressing his wounds but also ensures further treatment in a guesthouse and spends his own money on it. This response to the plight of an injured person clearly shows the nonreciprocity of bodily demands, which becomes particularly visible in the (diaconal) help and support for socially disadvantaged, needy, and sick people.

> It is characteristic of the diaconal response that longing and fragmentarity as well as a lack of physical autonomy of persons in need can be addressed and partly overcome by encounters and voluntary actions—in responding to the claim for help, however, in the knowledge that this claim can never be fully met. Also in diaconal action, and especially in interbody attention, the strangeness and closeness, the relatedness and aloofness of the attention, comes through.[50]

In the case of theological hope for a life beyond death, its aloofness cannot be denied but must be recognized and committed.[51]

Death, like other human experiences, represents a situation in which the religious dimension of physical life appears and can be taken up. Pain, suffering, and being sick as well as loneliness, fear, and being forgotten "are fragile characteristics of corporeality," which belong to the understanding of "vulnerable life and which can refer to the other, whole and healed dimension of life."[52] This other, whole and healed dimension can be guessed, sensed, and felt and refers to the transcendence of human life, for which religion offers interpretations. "It is precisely at these borders, which represent suffering and death, loneliness and other existentialities, that one becomes aware of what Schleiermacher has addressed with 'absolute dependence'; at the border, the limited life can be not only accepted but perceived as part of the greater whole."[53]

Taking these considerations into account, one can state that the dimension of corporeality can provide orientation for diaconal action. Above all, at the beginning and end of life—not least due to new technical possibilities—the status of human life and consequently the way of dealing with it at these borders is negotiated in society. Two questions currently under discussion relate to changes in the human gene pool and to self-determination at the end of life in connection with assisted suicide. The ethical dilemmas associated with this cannot be discussed in

---

bed."; Cf. Zimmerman, "The Etho-Poietic," 278: "What is decisive, rather, is the act of being touched, an internal empathy."

[50] Leonhard, "Mitte" (note 2), 42.

[51] Cf. ibid; cf. Wolfhart Pannenberg, "A Theology of the Cross," *Word & World* 8 (1988): 162–72.

[52] Leonhard, "Mitte" (note 2), 40; cf. Miroslav Volf and Dorothy C. Bass, eds., *Practicing Theology: Beliefs and Practices in Christian Life* (Grand Rapids, MI: Eerdmans, 2001), 105.

[53] Leonhard, "Mitte," 40 f.

detail here, but the fundamental orientation should be pointed out, which opens up a view onto these questions from a body-phenomenological perspective.

As life is vulnerable, the dimension of corporeality encloses both the genesis and the passing away of a person. If being a person means being constitutively bound to the human body, "its physical life must be considered in its entirety: there is no time at which it is not yet or no longer the life of a person."[54] Thus the foundation of personality, which is rooted in the creation of human beings in the image of God, does not presuppose any specific qualities of a person such as self-reflection, but applies to every form of human life. "The dignity of the creation of humanity in the image of God, which is accorded to all human beings in the same way, means at the same time that every single human person, even in its incompleteness and deficiency, deserves protection."[55] Even an impaired life thus falls under the unconditional protection of personal dignity because of its very existence. Accordingly, in the absence of the ability to self-reflect mentally—for instance, because of dementia—the dignity of the person must still be recognized, because "in expectation toward other persons as well as in memory, the life story of a person begins before the development of these abilities and does not end with their loss."[56] The presence of the body therefore indicates that the necessary prerequisites for being a person are present. In the body, the biological-physical component and the social are inseparably linked together, so that the body functions as the foundation to attribute dignity to every human life.[57] Ultimately it is true that "Even if humans are not in a position to express themselves as persons, they remain present for other persons as a person with all their rights and claims due to their manifold relations to others and their physical presence."[58]

---

[54] Lars Klinnert, "'Menschenwürde' als Leitprinzip medizinrechtlicher Normenbildung. Eine theologische Positionsbestimmung im Streit um die europäische Bioethik-Konvention," in Klinnert, Dabrock, and Schardien, *Menschenwürde und Lebensschutz* (note 26), 235–87, at 264; Robert N. Butler, "The Life Review: An Interpretation of Reminiscence in the Aged," *Psychiatry* 26 (1963): 65–76, at 65.

[55] Cf. Hartmut Kreß, "Verantwortungsethik als Ethik der Person," *Verantwortungsethik heute. Grundlagen und Konkretionen einer Ethik der Person*, ed. in Hartmut Kreß and Wolfgang Erich Müller (Stuttgart/Berlin/Cologne: Kohlhammer, 1997), 115–238, at 161.

[56] Klinnert, "Menschenwürde" (note 54), 264.

[57] Cf. Peter Dabrock, "Verbrauchende Embryonenforschung. Kommt allen Embryonen Menschenwürde zu?," in Klinnert, Dabrock, and Schardien, *Menschenwürde und Lebensschutz* (note 26), 173–210, at 184; cf. Nancy Krieger, "A Glossary for Social Epidemiology," *Journal of Epidemiology & Community Health* 55 (2001): 693–700.

[58] Robert Spaemann, *Personen. Versuche über den Unterschied zwischen "etwas" und "jemand"*, 2nd ed. (Stuttgart: Klett-Cotta, 1998), 79; cf. Jane Haddock, "Towards Further Clarification of the Concept 'Dignity,'" *Journal of Advanced Nursing* 24 (1996): 924–31, at 926.

On this basis, diaconal action turns to people whose cognitive abilities are diminished by mental impairment or disease: "Even in the extreme helplessness of dementia, the dignity of the human being can be perceived by others."[59] Turning to persons suffering from dementia and accepting them in their changed state of being, one perceives them in their dignity. "Encounter with people who have dementia always embodies an act of recognition, in which the relative, the caretaker, or the physician expresses the ability to build and maintain relationships."[60] This holds especially true in situations where verbal communication reaches its limits, as when people suffer from dementia or are in a vegetative state. Just as memory is not limited to brain activity alone, but there is also body memory, so human memories and personal life stories are not limited to cognitive processes but are inscribed in the whole human body.[61]

The face of a coma patient or of an old and perhaps demented person who is lined with many wrinkles can tell something about the person because it bears witness to the life difficulties that have been overcome. Haggard facial characteristics tell us about experienced disappointments, losses, and bitterness. Like the face, the rest of the body is inscribed with the life story and suffering of a person.[62]

For diaconal action, the perception of the body language of another person is indispensable, because where words are lacking, an open perception and new answers to the other person are required.[63]

---

59   Verena Wetzstein, "Alzheimer-Demenz. Perspektiven einer integrativen Demenz-Ethik," *Zeitschrift für medizinische Ethik* 51 (2005): 27–41; cf. Maura McIntyre, "Dignity in Dementia: Person-Centered Care in Community," *Journal of Aging Studies* 17 (2003): 480–81.

60   Wetzstein, "Alzheimer," 27–41, 35; cf. McIntyre, "Dignity," 481.

61   Cf. Andreas Kruse, "Die Lebensqualität demenzkranker Menschen erfassen und positiv beeinflussen. Eine fachliche und ethische Herausforderung," *Demenz. Ende der Selbstbestimmung? Vorträge der Tagung des Deutschen Ethikrates 2010* (Berlin: Deutscher Ethikrat, 2012), 27–50, at 35 and 41; cf. McIntyre, "Dignity" (note 59), 482.

62   Ulrich h. J. Körtner, *Diakonie und Öffentliche Theologie. Diakoniewissenschaftliche Studien* (Göttingen: Vandenhoeck & Ruprecht, 2017), 189; cf. Wils, *Person*, 144: "The body carries suspended and past history of a person as a whole. . . . As a whole body he carries the current story of a person: he is *subject* of an individual, social, political and medical-therapeutic existence" (emphasis in original version); cf. John Bond, Lynne Corner, and Ruth Graham, "Social Science Theory on Dementia Research: Normal Ageing, Cultural Representation and Social Exclusion," in *Dementia and Social Inclusion: Marginalised Groups and Marginalised Areas of Dementia Research, Care and Practice*, ed. Anthea Innes. Carole Archibald, and Charlie Murphy (London/Philadelphia: John Wiley & Sons, 2004), 220–36, at 228.

63   Cf. Leonhard, "Mitte" (note 2), 41.

Challenges of Diaconal Bodily Care for People Today

The task of diaconia is the care for the body and soul of human beings in need. This refers to those people who need support and help as well as to those providing the care. Nevertheless, diaconal approaches to corporeality have often fallen behind, perhaps also as a result of the ambivalent attitude towards the human body in the history of theology.[64] In the following, two challenges for diaconal bodily care today are outlined.

Body Cult and Body Oblivion

One's relationship to the body provides information about one's concept of life. On one hand, the physical rhythm of life is given to the human being;

> [E]lementary characteristics of physicality are connecting beyond cultural borders, namely birth and death, growth, prosperity and decay, lust and pain. On the other hand, corporeality as a cultural mirror of life reflects currents, insecurities, consolidations of the respective culture: As a medium and gate to the world, the body absorbs what is in itself and energetically implements it, in all brokenness.[65]

Current social trends dealing with the body reflect an ambivalent relationship to it. In everyday life, the functioning of the body is simply assumed, and one's own body is only actually thematized during few occurrences or activities: illness, old age, sexuality, and sport. Direct physical contact is reduced to a minimum (except when dealing with children). Only when the body "strikes," when it no longer functions as we naturally assume it should, does the body break into everyday consciousness. The doctor must then restore the functioning of the body.

Next to this forgetfulness of the body is a body cult which is mutating into a lifestyle due to increasing digital applications. Normative ideas about a beautiful body lead to diets and extensive fitness hypes; the body becomes the primary medium of self-presentation (note cosmetic surgery). The body must be kept fit and is always subjected to new fashions (body styling, fit-trim machines, movement

---

[64] For example, it is conspicuous that one of the few volumes that talk about bodyness in Protestant perspective—the festschrift for Dietrich Stollberg: Michael Klessmann and Irmhild Liebau, eds., *Leiblichkeit ist das Ende der Werke Gottes. Körper-Leib-Praktische Theologie* (Göttingen: Vandenhoeck & Ruprecht)—does not say anything about diakonia as a practical-theological sphere of activity; cf. Eberhard Winkler's review in *ThLZ* 123 (1998): 568-70.

[65] Silke Leonhard, "Zur Leibräumlichkeit religiösen Lernens und Lehrens," *Theo-Web. Zeitschrift für Religionspädagogik* 5 (2006): 29-43, at 31.

apps, etc.). The marketing of the body and its degradation to a commodity is progressing.

One can interpret the body cult as a compensatory movement against body oblivion, but both follow the same access to the body: the body becomes available body mass—either by being subjected and exploited in everyday life as a forgotten basis for the pursuit of life goals, or by taking on a special significance and now having to serve specific ideas and being determined by others via the body cult.

Against this background, the conscious perception and handling of one's own body offers opportunities for diaconal learning, for example in school (in diaconal internships) or in leisure time. In diaconal action, needs and impairments of the body are pointed out, and thereby the possibility is opened up to experience encounter and relationship through the body.[66] One student reports: "And then I simply joined in with the handicapped people and moved to the music. To experience this sense of community was simply moving."[67]

Physicality means something different than staging the body. You are not always fully present with your body, soul, and mind. Attentiveness is normally focused. This is why physical learning paths are important in order to be able to feel and respond; to feel the connection with the environment, not only through direct sensations (hunger, fear, anger, joy) but also through resonances to external influences (the senses).[68] "Whoever learns, changes his attitude towards the world and takes into account the incidents of the world, does not educate himself alone with the heart or the mind. Sensing and feeling are as much a part of being human as thinking and acting; the physical interaction plays an important role."[69] It is also a central aspect of diaconal action; diaconal action itself is often bodily action:

> A nurse experiences this in a diaconal care center: she washes and applies lotions to the body of the patients and dresses their wounds, so they can feel more comfortable in their skin afterwards. The geriatric nurse, who combs the hair of a resident and cuts her fingernails and compliments her in front of the mirror. The occupational therapist, who plays music from earlier times and rehearses a dance with the help of a rollator with a senior woman, so that she can enjoy. This importance of body contact and body movement is also experienced by students of the sixth grade, who learn how to gently

---

[66] Cf. Michael Fricke and Martin Dorner, *Werkbuch Diakonisches Lernen* (Göttingen: Vandenhoeck & Ruprecht, 2015), 28.

[67] Oscar, eighteen years old, diakonia P-seminar, Paul-Pfinzing-grammar school Hersbruck, cited by Fricke and Dorner, *Werkbuch*, 28.

[68] Cf. Leonhard, "Leibräumlichkeit" (note 65), at 31; cf. Line S. Löken and Håkan Olausson, "The Skin as a Social Organ," *Experimental Brain Research* 204 (2010): 305–14, at 312.

[69] Leonhard, "Leibräumlichkeit," 31, referring to Pestalozzi.

massage the back of the hand of the elderly during their visit in a senior citizens' home. They soon experienced for themselves how their massages made the elderly people feel valued and good.[70]

The body as a "gate" to the world can open the space between the self and the environment and enable a conscious shaping of relationships to others and to one's own body. Diaconal action can be beneficial as it creates an opportunity to perceive and shape corporeality (one's own as well as that of the other person). Therefore, body contact, appreciative attention, and bodily pleasures should be given a high priority within diaconal work.

Considering this, the challenge for diaconia lies in making the importance of the physical dimension for diaconal work and social action obvious and to incorporate it. It is the task of diaconia to show "that and how the attention of God's spirit for human beings includes attention for the body."[71] The physical dimension of spirituality must be rediscovered, and its appropriate forms of expression further developed. For instance, through a blessing with the laying on of hands, through anointings or prayers in connection with physical gestures, spiritual support can be expressed bodily. In this way the devotion of God can be felt (cf. Psalm 23:5: "You anoint my head with oil; my cup overlfows"). Therefore, touches and gifts, bodily pleasures, and celebrations should have a high value in diaconal encounters and should be consciously shaped. This point is further elaborated in the following section.

The Rediscovery of the Spiritual Dimension of the Physical

In spite of all the technical devices, medicine, care, and therapy, diaconia depends on the ability to be in direct contact with the patient and "on the ability to perceive how a patient's aura, smell, body temperature, and voice change."[72] The more technical methods are included in the care of patients in diaconia, the more important it is for diaconal staff to be able to pay attention to and respond to aspects of physicality. "How do I read people's pain, and how do I let them touch me? How do I deal with the things of everyday life? Am I capable of honoring them as gifts or

---

[70]   Fricke and Dorner, *Werkbuch*, 28.

[71]   Ibid.; cf. David Hay, *Something There: The Biology of the Human Spirit* (London: Darton Longman and Todd, 2006).

[72]   Cornelia Coenen-Marx, "Dem Geist Gottes Raum geben. Spiritualität als diakonische praxis pietatis," in, *Spiritualität in der Diakonie. Anstöße zur Erneuerung christlicher Kernkompetenz*, ed. Beate Hofmann and Michael Schibilsky (Stuttgart/Berlin/Cologne: Kohlhammer, 2001), 47–61, at 54; cf. Bessel van der Kolk, *The Body Keeps the Score: Brain, Mind, and Body in the Healing of Trauma* (New York: Penguin, 2015).

am I exclusively the user and disposer of the world?"[73] Ultimately, this attitude of mindfulness opens avenues to the spiritual dimension of diaconal action. It is necessary to rediscover the spiritual dimension of the physical, which can be expressed and shaped in the physical dimension of spirituality.[74] "Where a person of flesh and blood becomes transparent to God, diaconal work becomes a challenge that also changes the helpers."[75]

This can happen in two ways. On one hand, being touched by another person can lead to thinking about one's own life, to a more conscious perception of the elementary things in life and perhaps to a new discovery of how one lives.

> This enables a new approach to faith, a new understanding of biblical texts, experience-oriented and not dogmatic. This diaconal *praxis pietatis* changes the perspective on our everyday life: a good meal with friends, a trip to a foreign country, buying a nice sweater, getting well after an illness is a gift. Accepting it is part of the mercy towards oneself.[76]

On the other hand, being touched by the other can lead to a stronger isolation. "Every genuine contact with a human being of flesh and blood makes us vulnerable."[77] A natural reaction to this is to build up protective mechanisms like walls around one's own vulnerability, because—especially in the profession of helping—one cannot allow every need to move one's self. Internal exhaustion and burnout would otherwise be the inevitable consequence. However, isolation and inner insensitivity bear the danger of missing successful encounters and of no longer noticing the traces of God in everyday life. Especially in the diaconal actions driven by organizational efficiency pressure, the moment of pausing and perceiving the need of another person is more difficult to consider. Therefore—as the example of the diaconal institutions by Francke in Halle exemplifies—it is important to create institutional conditions to enable the staff to work with a holistic (including body and soul) diaconal approach.

This goes beyond the corresponding conceptual foundation of personal care. The Halle Pietists set up their own hospital rooms and later hospital buildings,

---

[73] Coenen-Marx, "Geist Gottes," 54.

[74] Cf. Peter F. Schmidt, "Seel-Sorge und Körper-Sorge. Eine kleine Kairologie der Leiblichkeit," *Diakonia* 33 (2002): 229–34, at 233. Schmidt demands a bodyness for believing; cf. a. Elizabeth Rippentrop, et al., "The Relationship between Religion/Spirituality and Physical Health, Mental Health, and Pain in a Chronic Pain Population," *Pain* 116 (2005): 311–21, at 314–15.

[75] Coenen-Marx, "Geist Gottes," 55; cf. Gerhard Wegner, "Christian Love in the Community: Theological Perspectives," *Diaconia* 5 (2014): 113–31, at 122.

[76] Ibid., 58 (emphasis in original).

[77] Sam Keen, quoted by Coenen-Marx, "Geist Gottes," 58.

organized nurses, and commissioned a matron, or "mother," for the sick. They further tried to implement a treatment of the sick that also included spiritual aspects with reference to the university faculty of medicine of the time. Even if today one may criticize their one-sided theological interpretation of illness and the moral charge associated with it, it becomes clear that efforts for appropriate institutional framework conditions were made,[78] which should benefit the recovery of the sick.

Since then, the institutional care for sick people has been differentiated and professionalized into different types of medical treatment. Today, the challenge is to resist succumbing to the temptation to functionalize one's life under the given framework conditions—in nursing, for example, the high pace of the daily routine can be exhausting. "We know that,"[79] writes Cornelia Coenen-Marx. "But who has the time to hear the questions behind the questions? The nurses? Rarely. The breathing-therapist, the movement therapists? Perhaps. The hospital chaplains? Many interlocutors—but who really builds up a relationship?"[80] The open space for interruptions must be fought for again and again under a lack of time and against exploitation pressure or at least it must consciously be produced.

This challenge, however, must not simply be shifted to the individual level and burdened onto the nurse, especially when there is no corresponding (temporal) possibility for her or him to spend more time with the patient. Rather, the problem must also be seen as a structural one and defined as a management responsibility—for instance, by adapting organizational structures in such a way that carers are given time for the actual nursing care and thus the meaningfulness of professional work is strengthened with striking results in terms of the satisfaction of patients and staff;[81] or, for example, by shaping the organizational culture spiritually, creating appropriate space for interruptions and offering opportunities for reflection.[82]

In the meantime, there are different approaches, tried and tested in practice, to form a "Christian-spiritual corporate culture"[83] by means of a culture of intermission, a culture of reflection, a culture of existential communication, a culture

---

[78] Cf. Helm, "Kinder- und Lehrkrankenhaus" (note 18).

[79] Coenen-Marx, "Geist Gottes" (note 72), 53.

[80] Ibid.

[81] Cf. for the new approach by Buurtzorg Ute Burtke, "Idee für häusliche Pflege: buurtzorg," *Heilberufe* 70 (2018), 52–53, doi: https://doi.org/10.1007/s00058-018-3223-2; cf. Simone Kirpal, "Work Identities of Nurses: Between Caring and Efficiency Demands," *Career Development International* 9 (2004): 274–304.

[82] Cf. Beate Hofmann, *Diakonische Unternehmenskultur. Handbuch für Führungskräfte*, Diakonie 2, 2nd ed. (Stuttgart: Kohlhammer, 2010).

[83] Cf. Joachim Reber, *Christlich-spirituelle Unternehmenskultur* (Stuttgart: Kohlhammer, 2013).

of prayer, which opens up spaces for individual caregivers to deepen their spiritual diaconal activities. In addition, there are already corresponding approaches that combine body and soul within medical therapy for psychosomatic illnesses or in palliative care.

Outlook

The body is not simply a "given thing; it must be experienced and grasped.... The body is given to us in a way that we need to shape it just like our life. We *are* alive and live."[84] The body and one's references to the body have become a social topic again today and are also dealt with in human sciences in the sense of "embodiment." Here, theology can relate to a rich incarnational tradition which assigns to the body a central position within faith. "The body is neither only to be endured nor merely to be tolerated and finally to be overcome; it is an inseparable component of being human, which is taken into the resurrection and thus into the relation to God and everlasting life with God."[85] It is the task of the church (the "body of Christ") and its diaconia to take up the subject again and again on all levels of faith, both theoretical and practical, if it wants to do justice to human beings.[86] Diaconia is called to do this even under the prevailing marketized and technical conditions of care and support of people in need of help today, by responding with head, heart, hand, and mouth to bodily appeals, adopting a responsive attitude, and following paths of learning in bodily diaconal education, in which the religious dimension of corporeality can be referred to. Thus, not only do the ability to adapt and the life-affirming attitude of the Christian faith become apparent, "but beyond that the promise of living together between familiarity and strangeness appears."[87]

---

[84] Schmid, *Seel-Sorge* (note 74), 232.
[85] Ibid., 233.
[86] Ibid.
[87] Leonhard, "Mitte" (s. note 2), 48.

The Uses of Law for the Formation of Character

A Classic Protestant Doctrine for Late Modern Liberal Societies?

John Witte Jr.[1]

Introduction

This volume, like the others in this series, explores the role of sundry social systems, separately and together, in shaping individual character and collective values in late modern pluralistic societies. Here we focus on the shaping influences of religious systems, particularly Christian churches of various denominations. Until the nineteenth century, churches led Western society in establishing values and forming character–through their worship, sacraments, and education; creeds, catechisms, and canons; sanctuaries, charities, and monasteries; and their communion, embodiment, and celebration of the cardinal commandments of love of God, neighbor, and self.

Today, by contrast, churches have more marginal influence in Western liberal societies. While some new or newly arrived religious communities are thriving, many churches in North America, Europe, Australia, and beyond have emptier pews, dwindling coffers, crumbling denominations, and waning cultural power.[2] The growing popular narrative is that churches and other organized religions are outmoded, abusive, dangerous, and discriminatory. The growing academic narrative is that religious freedom, once taken for granted as a cornerstone of Western constitutional order, is now very much up for grabs, particularly when religious freedom collides with claims of sexual freedom, self-determination, and personal

---

[1]   This chapter is part of ongoing work on a volume tentatively titled *The Religious Vindication of Law*. It draws, in part, on an earlier chapter in my *God's Joust, God's Justice: Law and Religion in the Western Tradition* (Grand Rapids, MI: Wm. B. Eerdmans, 2006), 263–94.

[2]   See, e. g., Robert P. Jones, *The End of White Christian America* (New York: Simon & Schuster, 2016); and ongoing statistical analysis by the Pew Research Center–Religion & Public Life, https://www.pewforum.org/data/.

autonomy.[3] "Why tolerate religion?" reads the title of a recent influential text, given that religion is so irrational, unscientific, categorical, abstract, and impervious to empirical evidence or common sense.[4]

Social scientists call this the process of secularization, and some scholars predict that religion will gradually wither away altogether in Western liberal lands.[5] But this process is not so inevitable, unilinear, or irreversible as is often assumed. Leading sociologist José Casanova has shown that modern secularization theory describes three distinct movements, which need not necessarily coincide: (1) the separation of the economic, scientific, and governmental spheres from the religious sphere of the church; (2) the privatization, spiritualization, and deinstitutionalization of religion within the religious sphere; and (3) the decline of religious belief and practice in society, often accompanied by the rise of science, technology, and markets as a more reliable standard of value and validation in our modern secular age. Casanova warns, however, against confusing "the historical processes of *secularization proper* with the alleged and anticipated consequences which those processes were supposed to have upon religion." The differentiation and specialization of institutional spheres of religion and nonreligion do not necessarily coincide with or require the decline or privatization of religion.[6]

A number of other social scientists concur in this view. They have shown how even modern purportedly secularized Western societies retain and rely on religious resources.[7] Religion is not only contained within the realms of conscience or worship settings. Religion is also present in all kinds of spaces and specialties that would seem to be hermetically and hermeneutically closed to religion—in state schools, hospitals, and prisons, in state legislatures, courts, and tribunals, and in the discourses of human rights, public policy, and public health.[8] Indeed,

---

3   See John Witte Jr., *Church, State, and Freedom: Protestant Teachings for a Post-Modern Society* (Cambridge: Cambridge University Press, forthcoming), quoting Paul Horwitz, "The Hobby Lobby Moment," *Harvard Law Review* 128 (2014): 154,155.

4   Brian Leiter, *Why Tolerate Religion?* (Princeton, NJ: Princeton University Press, 2013).

5   See, e.g., Bryan S. Turner, et al., eds., *Secularization*, Vol. 4 (London: Sage Publishers, 2010).

6   José Casanova, *Public Religions in the Modern World* (Chicago: University of Chicago Press, 1994), 19. See also Charles Taylor, *A Secular Age* (Cambridge, MA: Harvard University Press, 2007), 423.

7   See, e. g., Rosemarie van den Breemer, et al., eds., *Secular and Sacred? The Scandinavian Case of Religion in Human Rights, Law and Public Space* (Göttingen/Bristol, CT: Vandenhoeck & Ruprecht, 2013); Roger Trigg, *Religion in Public Life: Must Faith be Privatized?* (Oxford: Oxford University Press, 2008); Christian Smith, *The Secular Revolution: Power, Interests, and Conflict in the Secularization of American Life* (Berkeley: University of California Press, 2003).

8   See, e. g., Kim Knott, *The Location of Religion: A Spatial Analysis* (London: Equinox, 2005).

our public life, legal discourse, and policy debates on many matters are suffused with religious metaphors, values, beliefs, and frameworks—sometimes hidden, sometimes syncretized, sometimes masquerading under other labels, but all vitally important to communal identity, integrity, and function.[9]

Moreover, the institutionalized social sphere of churches and other organized religions might now be a weakened cultural force in the West, but it remains an important source of character formation, moral education, and the communication of values in late modern pluralistic societies. America's leading religious historian, Martin E. Marty, has documented some of the private and public goods that these overt and hidden forms and norms of religion still contribute. Religions, he shows, deal uniquely with the deepest elements of individual and social life. Religions catalyze social, intellectual, and material exchanges by triggering charitable, educational, and economic impulses in citizens. They provide valuable checks and counterpoints to social and individual excess. They help diffuse social and political crises and absolutisms by relativizing everyday life and its institutions. Religions provide criticism and exemplars for society, forcing persons to examine their presuppositions. They are distinct repositories of tradition, wisdom, perspective, and counseling against apathy. They often represent practiced and durable sources and forms of community, providing leadership and hope, especially in times of individual and social crisis. They contribute to the theory and practice of the common good, representing the unrepresented, teaching stewardship and preservation, providing fresh starts for the desperate, and exalting the dignity and freedom of the individual.[10] No religion lives up to all these claims all the time. Some religions never do, and a few even work hard to destroy these goods. But these private and public goods offered by most organized religions argue strongly for the continued recognition of the sphere of religion in shaping character, values, and morality in late modern differentiated societies.

Other chapters in this volume document the shaping influences of Christianity on Western values and practices of freedom, communication, education, social organization, moral formation, political activism, land use, and cultivation of leadership. This chapter explores Christianity's historical and enduring influence on law and morality in the Western legal tradition. The topic is vast, and another volume on law and character formation in the same series addresses it more fully. Here, I focus on a distinct Protestant doctrine on the uses of the law for creating

---

9   John Witte Jr., "Law, Religion, and Metaphor," in *Risiko und Vertrauen / Risk and Trust: Festschrift für Michael Welker zum 70. Geburtstag*, ed. Günter Thomas and Heike Springhart (Leipzig: Evangelische Verlagsanstalt, 2017), 177–95.

10 See Martin E. Marty and Jonathan Moore, *Politics, Religion, and the Common Good: Advancing a Distinctly American Conversation About Religion's Role in Our Shared Life* (San Francisco: Jossey-Bass, 2000).

both a basic civil morality for all members of society and a higher spiritual morality that becomes the Christian life.

Protestant theologians developed this framework of uses initially to describe the place and function of the law of God in Christian life. While the law of God is not a pathway to salvation—justification comes by faith in God's grace, not by works—it still has uses in this life. The law of God has (1) a civil use that restrains persons from sinful conduct by threat of divine punishment; (2) a theological use that condemns sinful persons in their consciences and drives them to repentance; and (3) an educational use that teaches those who have already been saved the good works that please God and induce others to come to God. Hence the need for the church to preach on the Old Testament law, to catechize the young in the Ten Commandments, and to encourage Christians to meditate on the law of God as the Bible instructs. "Not one jot or one tittle" (Matt. 5:18) of the moral law of God should thus be ignored, even if the ceremonial laws of the Old Testament are no longer binding, and the juridical laws of the Bible are more illustrative than prescriptive of Christian morality.

Already in the Reformation era, Protestant theologians began to apply this same three-uses framework to explain the purposes of other types of human law as well—particularly the internal laws of the church, which in their view had comparable civil, theological, and educational uses.[11] Protestant jurists, in turn, adopted this uses framework in their theories of state law, which in their early view built in part on the law of God.[12] They used this framework most directly to define and integrate the three purposes of the state's criminal law. A society needs criminal law and punishment for: (1) deterrence of individuals and groups through the threat of criminal punishment—much like the civil use of the moral law; (2) retribution, the necessary punishment needed to restore a convicted criminal to the community—akin to the theological use of the moral law; and (3) rehabilitation, teaching a person the good works that exemplify state citizenship—analogous to the educational use of the moral law. Just as the three-uses framework provided Protestant theologians with an integrated theory of the moral law of God, the same

---

[11] See examples in the volumes in this series on law, economics, family, and the academy.

[12] See, e. g., recent overviews in Mathias Schmoeckel, *Das Recht der Reformation* (Tübingen: Mohr Siebeck, 2014), esp. 207–45; Wim DeKock, et al., eds., *Law and Religion: The Legal Teachings of the Protestant and Catholic Reformations* (Göttingen: Vandenhoeck & Ruprecht, 2014); Martin Heckel, *Martin Luthers Reformation und das Recht* (Tübingen: Mohr Siebeck, 2016). For recent studies of particular areas of law, see, e. g., Paolo Astorri, *Lutheran Theology and Contract Law in Early Modern Germany* (Leiden: Verlag Ferdinand Schöningh, 2019); Markus M. Totzek, *Die politischen Gesetze des Mose: Enstehung und Einflüsse der politia-judaica-Literatur in der frühen Neuzeit* (Göttingen: Vandenhoeck & Ruprecht, 2019).

framework helped Protestant jurists develop an integrated theory of the criminal law of the state.

The Theological Doctrine of the Uses of Moral Law

The theological doctrine of the uses of law, while rooted in patristic and scholastic teachings, emerged clearly in the sixteenth-century Protestant Reformation.[13] It was a popular doctrine, particularly among the earliest Lutheran and Reformed Protestants. Martin Luther (1483–1546), Philip Melanchthon (1497–1560), Heinrich Bullinger (1504–75), and John Calvin (1509–64) expounded the doctrine, but so did many later Protestants of various denominations.[14] It was also a pivotal doctrine, for it provided the reformers with a middle way between radical Catholic legalism, on one hand, and radical Anabaptist antinomianism on the other. It allowed the reformers to reject the claims of certain Catholics that salvation can be achieved by works of the law as well as the claims of certain Anabaptists that those who are saved have no further need of the law.

The reformers focused their uses doctrine primarily on the moral law—that compendium of moral commands, duties, and rights that transcend the positive laws of the state. God, they believed, has written a moral law on the hearts of all persons, rewritten it in the pages of scripture, and summarized it in the Ten Commandments. A person comes to know the meaning and measure of this moral law both through the counsel of conscience and reason and, more completely, through the commandments of scripture and the Holy Spirit.[15] Though persons can be

---

[13] For discussion of pre-Reformation texts on point, see Edward A. Engelbrecht, *Friends of the Law: Luther's Use of the Law for the Christian Life* (St. Louis, MO: Concordia Publishing House, 2001), 1–70. Luther was the first to give prominence to what he called "uses of the law." In his 1513–15 Lectures on the Psalms, he first used the term *usus legis* (WA 3:144). In his 1522 Commentary on Galatians 3, he spoke of "threefold use of the law" (*drey wysse am brauch des gesetz*), though in this tract as well as his 1531 Commentary on Galatians, he focused only on the civil and theological uses of the law (WA 10/1:457). Martin Bucer, in his 1525 Latin translation of Luther's sermon, rendered Luther's German phrase as *triplex usus legis*, a Latin phrase which other reformers adopted (WA 10/1:457, note 2). Philip Melanchthon, in his 1535 *Loci communes* and Calvin, writing independently in his 1536 *Institutes*, were the first to expound systematically all three uses of the moral law (CR 21:405–06; *Institutes* [1536], 48–50).

[14] Philip Melanchthon, *Catechesis puerilis* (1558), in CR 23:176–77; John Calvin, "The Geneva Catechism," in CO 6:80; "Formula of Concord (1577), part 6," in TC, 805.

[15] See numerous examples in John Witte Jr., *Law and Protestantism: The Legal Teachings of the Lutheran Reformation* (Cambridge: Cambridge University Press, 2002); John Witte Jr.,

saved if they obey the moral law perfectly, their inherently sinful nature renders them incapable of such perfect obedience. This human incapacity does not render the moral law useless, however. It retains three important uses or functions.

First, the moral law has a *civil* use to restrain persons from sinful conduct by threat of divine punishment. "[T]he law is like a halter," Calvin wrote, "to check the raging and otherwise limitlessly ranging lusts of the flesh. . . . Hindered by fright or shame, [persons] dare neither execute what they have conceived in their minds, nor openly breathe forth the rage of their lust."[16] The law thus imposes upon saints and sinners alike what Calvin called a "constrained and forced right-eousness," or what Melanchthon called "an external or public morality."[17] Threat-ened by divine sanctions, persons obey the basic commandments of the moral law —to obey authorities, to respect their neighbor's person and property, to remain sexually continent, to speak truthfully of themselves and their neighbors.

Although "such public morality does not merit forgiveness of sin,"[18] it bene-fits sinners and saints alike. On one hand, it allows for a modicum of peace and stability in this sin-ridden world. "Unless there is some restraint," Calvin wrote, "the condition of wild beasts would be better and more desirable than ours. [Nat-ural] liberty would always bring ruin with it if it were not bridled by the moder-ation" born of the moral law.[19] On the other hand, such public morality enables persons who later become Christians to know at least the rudiments of Christian morality and to fulfill the vocations to which God has called them. "Even the chil-dren of God before they are called and while they are destitute of the spirit of sanc-tification become partly broken in by bearing the yoke of coerced righteousness. Thus, when they are later called, they are not entirely untutored and uninitiated in discipline as if it were something foreign."[20]

Second, the moral law has a *theological* use to condemn sinful persons for their violations of the law. Such condemnation ensures both the integrity of the law and the humility of the sinner. On one hand, the violation of the law is avenged, and the integrity, the balance of the law is restored by the condemnation of those who violate it. On the other hand, the violator of the law is appropriately chastened and driven to God's grace. In Luther's hard words, the law serves as a mirror "to reveal to man his sin, blindness, misery, wickedness, ignorance, hate, contempt of God. . . . When the law is being used correctly, it does nothing but reveal sin, work wrath, accuse, terrify, and reduce consciences to the point of

---

The Reformation of Rights: Law, Religion, and Human Rights in Early Modern Calvinism (Cambridge: Cambridge University Press, 2007).

[16] *Institutes* (1559), 2.7.10.

[17] Ibid., 4.20.3.; CO 52:255; CR 1:706–08.

[18] CR 22:151, 250.

[19] CO 39:66.

[20] *Institutes* (1559), 2.7.10.

despair."[21] "In short," Calvin writes more mildly, "it is as if someone's face were all marked up so that everybody who saw him might laugh at him. Yet he himself is completely unaware of his condition. But if they bring him a mirror, he will be ashamed of himself, and will hide and wash himself when he sees how filthy he is."[22] Such despair, the reformers believed, was a necessary precondition for the sinner both to seek God's help and to have faith in God's grace. "For man, blinded and drunk with self-love, must be compelled to know and confess his own feebleness and iniquity. . . . [A]fter he is compelled to weigh his life in the scales of the law, he is compelled to seek God's grace."[23]

Third, the moral law has an *educational* use of enhancing the spiritual development of believers, of teaching those who have already been justified "the works that please God."[24] Even the most devout saints, Calvin wrote, still need the law "to learn more thoroughly . . . the Lord's will [and] to be aroused to obedience."[25] The law teaches them not only the public or external morality that is common to all persons but also the private or internal morality that is becoming only of Christians. As a teacher, the law not only coerces them against violence and violation but also cultivates in them charity and love. It not only punishes harmful acts of murder, theft, and fornication but also prohibits evil thoughts of hatred, covetousness, and lust.[26] Through the exercise of this private morality, the saints glorify God, exemplify God's law, and impel other sinners to seek God's grace.

The early reformers rooted this uses doctrine in part in their theology of salvation. Following St. Paul, they recognized various steps of the Christian walk before God—from predestination to justification to sanctification—and the relevance of the moral law of God for all three steps.[27] The moral law coerces sinners to obey through (threat of) force so that they can be preserved. It condemns them in their sin so that they can be justified. It counsels them in their works so that they can be sanctified. The doctrine was also rooted in the Protestant theology of the person. The reformers emphasized that even the most devout person is, in Luther's signature phrase, *simul iustus et peccator*—at once saint and sinner, spirit

---

21 WA 40:481–86.

22 CO 50:535.

23 *Institutes* (1559), 2.7.6.

24 CR 21:406.

25 *Institutes* (1559), 2.7.12

26 Ibid., 2.8.6; CR 1:706–08; Martin Bucer, *Deutsche Schriften*, ed. Robert Stupperich (Gütersloh: Gütersloher Verlagshaus C. Mohn, 1960), 1:36 ff.

27 Romans 8:28–30 and Galatians 3:21–29 and the reformers' commentaries thereon in CR vol. 15:654–78; LW 25:371–78; 26:327–58. Calvin also follows this sequencing from predestination to justification to sanctification in the arrangement of Books 2 and 3 of his *Institutes* (1559).

268 John Witte Jr.

and flesh.[28] The moral law caters to both the spiritual and the carnal dimensions of his or her character. The person of the flesh is coerced to develop at least a minimal public or external morality; the person of the spirit is counseled to develop a more holistic private or internal morality.[29]

Later Elaborations

The theological doctrine of the three uses of the moral law was not merely a concept of the early Reformation that died with the magisterial reformers.[30] The doctrine remained a staple of Protestant dogma after the early Reformation. The classic texts of Luther, Melanchthon, Calvin, and others, which expounded the uses doctrine, were constantly reprinted and translated and circulated widely in Protestant circles. Some Protestant editions of the Bible set out the uses doctrine in their marginal glosses on the relevant texts of Moses and St. Paul. A steady stream of references to the doctrine can be found in Protestant monographs, sermons, catechisms, and confessional writings from the seventeenth century onward. A number of distinguished Protestant theologians in the twentieth century–Dietrich Bonhoeffer, Emil Brunner, and Alec Vidler, among others–included the doctrine in their theological systems.[31] One could multiply examples to demonstrate the continuity of this doctrine in the Protestant tradition–a worthy exercise, given the paucity of studies available.[32] But a few texts will serve to illustrate the wide

---

[28]   WA 7:50.

[29]   A good modern summary is provided by Dietrich Bonhoeffer, *Ethics*, ed. Eberhard Bethge, trans. Neville H. Smith (New York: Macmillan, 1955), 303–19.

[30]   This has been argued most forcefully by Karl Barth and his student Hermann Diem. See Hermann Diem, *Dogmatik: ihr Weg zwischen Historismus und Existentialismus* (Munich: Chr. Kaiser Verlag, 1955), arguing that the three-uses doctrine died after the Reformation because it gives the law priority over the Gospel, suggests stages of justification, and is a sort of Trojan horse for smuggling natural law into theology. See further discussion in Coslett Quin, *The Ten Commandments: A Theological Exposition* (London: Lutterworth Press, 1951), 32. Even sympathetic accounts of the uses doctrine generally focus only on the early Reformation era.

[31]   See, e. g., Bonhoeffer, *Ethics*, 303 ff.; Emil Brunner, *Dogmatik*, Vol. 3 (Zürich: Zwingli-Verlag, 1960), 2:131 ff; 3:306 ff; Emil Brunner, *The Mediator: A Study of the Central Doctrine of the Christian Faith*, trans. O. Wyon (London: Lutterworth Press, 1934), 441 ff.; Alec R. Vidler, *Christ's Strange Work: An Exposition of the Three Uses of God's Law* (London: SCM Press, 1963); Quin, *Ten Commandments*, 31ff.

[32]   For a list of books on "the modern debate on the use of the law," see Engelbrecht, *Friends of the Law*, Appendix E, 275–77.

acceptance of the uses doctrine among Anglican, Reformed, and Methodist groups on both sides of the Atlantic.

Leading Anglican divines of the later Tudor Reformation embraced the uses doctrine. John Hooper (d. 1555), for example, offered a brisk rendition of the doctrine before launching into his exposition on the Decalogue:

> Seeing that the works of the law cannot deserve remission of sin, nor save man, and yet God requireth our diligence and obedience unto the law, it is necessary to know the use of the law, and why it is given us. The first use is civil and external, forbidding and punishing the trangression of politic and civil ordinance. . . . The second use of the law is to inform and instruct man aright, what sin is, to accuse us, to fear us, and damn us. . . . These two uses of the law appertain as well unto infideles, as to the fideles. . . . The third use of the law is to shew unto the Christians what works God requireth of them.[33]

Heinrich Bullinger (1504–75), who bridged the Anglican and Reformed worlds, described the theological use as "the chief and proper office of the law"—"a certain looking-glass, wherein we behold our own corruption, frailness, imbecility, imperfection"—and he waxed eloquently on the doctrine for several pages. He also insisted, however, that the moral law has a vital civil use to teach the unregenerate "the first principles and rudiments of righteousness" and an educational use to teach the redeemed "the very and absolute righteousness" and morality that becomes true sanctified Christians.[34] By the end of the sixteenth century, Bullinger's printed sermon on the topic became a standard classroom text for budding Anglican clergy.[35] Comparable sentiments on the uses doctrine are peppered throughout the classic eight-volume *Laws of Ecclesiastical Polity* by Richard Hooker (ca. 1553–1600).[36]

An early Anglican liturgical handbook from Waldegrave put a crisp distillation of the doctrine into the hands of parishioners. The "godly order and discipline" born of adherence to the moral law, the handbook reads,

---

[33] *Early Writings of John Hooper, D.D* (Cambridge: University Press, 1843), 281–82.

[34] *The Decades of Henry Bullinger*, 4 vols. (Cambridge: University Press, 1849–52), 2:235–45.

[35] See H.A. Wilson, *Episcopacy and Unity* (London: Longmans, Green, 1912), 39; Vidler, *Christ's Strange Work*, 34.

[36] For a suggestive tabular summary of the three types and offices of law set out by Hooker, see Francis Paget, *An Introduction to the Fifth Book of Hooker's Treatise on the Laws of Ecclesiastical Polity* (Oxford: Clarendon Press, 1899), 99. See further Norman Doe, "Richard Hooker," in *Great Christian Jurists in English History*, ed. Mark Hill and R.H. Helmholz (Cambridge: Cambridge University Press, 2017), 115–37.

is, as it were, sinews in the body, which knit and join the members together with decent order and comeliness. It is a bridle to stay the wicked from their mischiefs; it is a spur to prick forward such as be slow and negligent: yea, and for all men it is the Father's rod, ever in a readiness to chastise gently the faults committed, and to cause them afterward to live in more godly fear and reverence.[37]

The prayers of Thomas Becon (chaplain to Thomas Cranmer), which enjoyed broad circulation in the English and American Anglican churches, plead with God to allow each of the Ten Commandments to work their three uses in the lives of individuals and the church.[38] Anglican sermons and catechisms of the seventeenth and eighteenth centuries, in England and America, also propounded the uses doctrine, both in their exegesis of Moses and St. Paul and in their elaborations of the cryptic statements on law in the Thirty-Nine Articles.[39]

Reformed groups in England and America embraced the uses doctrine, both in its classic Reformation form and with a distinctive covenantal cast. The short catechism of the Scottish lawyer and theologian Samuel Rutherford (ca. 1600–61), for example, has classical language on the theological and educational uses of the moral law:

Q. What is the use of the law if we can not obteane salvatione by it?

A. It encloseth us under condemnation as a citie beseiged with a garrisone of souldiers that we may seek to Christ for mercie.

Q. What is the use of the law after we are com to Christ?

A. After Christ has made agreement betwixt us and the law, we delight to walk in it for the love of Christ.[40]

---

37   Quoted by Horton Davies, *The Worship of the English Puritans* (Oxford: Oxford University Press, 1948), 232–33.

38   See, e. g., *Prayers and other Pieces of Thomas Becon, S.T.P.*, repr. ed. (New York: Johnson Reprint, 1968), a series of prayers against idolatry, swearing, pride, whoredom, covetousness, gluttony, idleness, slandering, and other general offenses arising out of the Decalogue.

39   See, e. g., John Smalley, *The Perfection of the Divine Law; and its Usefulness for the Conversion of Souls: A Sermon Delivered in the College Chapel in New-Haven . . . in 1787* (New Haven, CT: Josiah Meigs, 1787), 16–28; C.E. De Coetlogon, *The Harmony Between Religion and Policy, or Divine and Human Legislation* (London: J.F. Riverton, 1790), 24 ff.; Ezekial Hopkins, *An Exposition of the Ten Commandments* (London: G. Whitfield, 1799).

40   "Ane Catachisme Conteining The Soume of Christian Religion by Mr. Samuell Rutherfurd (c. 1644)," chap. 33, in Alexander F. Mitchell, *Catechisms of the Second Reformation* (London: James Nesbit, 1886), 226 (citations and question numbers omitted).

An American Reformed catechism, prepared a century later, has a similar entry on the use of law:

> Q. Of what use, then, is the law unto men, since righteousness and life cannot be attained by it?
>
> A. It is of manifold use. . . . [T]o unregenerate sinners, it is of use to discover to them their utter impotence and inability to attain justification and salvation by the works thereof. . . . [T]o believers, it is of use to excite them to express their gratitude and thankfulness to Christ.[41]

Both catechisms also devoted several pages to exegesis of the Decalogue, which included ample discussion of the civil and spiritual uses and of the letter and spirit of the moral law.

Puritans and Presbyterian Calvinists cast the uses doctrine in covenantal terms.[42] The Westminster Confession of Faith (1647) provided a classic early statement, which was often glossed in sermons and commentaries:

> Although true believers be not under the [moral] law as a covenant of works, to be thereby justified or condemned; yet is it of great use to them, as well as to others; in that, as a rule of life, informing them of the will of God and their duty, it directs them and binds them to walk accordingly; discovering also the sinful pollution of their nature, hearts, and lives; so as, examining themselves thereby, they may come to further conviction of, humiliation for, and hatred against sin; together with a clearer insight of the need they have of Christ and the perfection of his obedience. It is likewise of use to the regenerate, to restrain their corruptions, in that it forbids sin; and the threatenings of it serve to show what even their sins deserve, and what afflictions in this life they may expect for them.[43]

---

[41] James Fisher and Ebenezer Erskine, *The Westminster Assembly's Shorter Catechism Explained, By Way of Question and Answer*, Part 2 (Philadelphia: J. Towar and D.M. Hogan, 1831), Q. 40.25, 28 (citations and question numbers omitted).

[42] See, e. g., Thomas Hooker, *The Faithful Covenanter* (London: Christopher Meredith, 1644); Peter Bulkeley, *The Gospel-Covenant; Or the Covenant of Grace Opened* (London: Matthew Simmons, 1651); John Cotton, *The Covenant of God's Free Grace* (London: Matthew Simmons, 1645).

[43] "Westminster Confession of Faith (1647)," art. 19, in Philip Schaff, *The Creeds of Christendom With a History and Critical Notes*, Vol. 3 (New York: Harper and Brothers, 1882), 3:640–42 (citations and subpart designations omitted). See also "The Savoy Declaration of 1658," a classic Congregational confession which tracks the Westminster formulations closely, in *The Creeds and Platforms of Congregationalism*, ed. Williston Walker (Boston: Pilgrim Press, 1960), 387.

Half a century later, Samuel Willard (1604-1707), the great New England system-
atizer of Puritan theology, linked explicitly the three states of covenantal existence and the three uses of the moral law. Effectively, both the covenant and the
moral law which it embraces have distinctive uses, which Willard spelled out in
some detail:

> As for natural men that are without the Gospel, the [moral] law is serviceable to them
> on such accounts as these. (1) to keep them in awe and prompt them to duty . . . (2) for
> the maintenance and preservation of civil societies from ruin . . . (3) to direct in the
> ordering of the civil government of mankind . . . [and] (4) to dispose them to entertain
> the Gospel, when it should be offered to them.

> With respect to natural men that are under the Gospel dispensations, [b]esides what
> they have in common with others in the forecited benefits, . . . it serves, (1) to convince
> men of sin, which is the first step to conversion . . . (2) to discover in them their woeful
> misery by sin . . . (3) to slay them as to any expectation of help by any righteousness or
> strength of their own . . . (4) to awaken in them, an apprehension of their absolute need
> of help from abroad . . . (5) to make the glad tidings of Christ and salvation by him
> welcome.

> As to those that are under grace, the law is no more a covenant of works to them . . .
> [nor] a covenant of life to them, having life secured to their personal obedience, yet it is
> a rule according to which God expect that they should order their life and conversa-
> tion. This is denied by some, practically abused by others, and not rightly understood
> by many. And may therefore be made clear and evident in the following conclusions,
> (1) that God's people have a life and conversation to lead in this world . . . (2) that it is
> not at the liberty of God's people to live as they list, nor ought they to live as other men .
> . . (3) there must therefore be a rule for their direction in leading such a [redeemed] life
> . . . (4) the children of God and therefore sanctified, that they may be fitted for com-
> pliance with this rule . . . (6) this rule is not made known to everyone, by immediate
> inspiration, but is laid down in the Gospel. . . . (7) [I]t is the moral law which is rein-
> forced in the Gospel, as a rule for the children of God to order their lives by.[44]

---

[44]   Samuel Willard, "Sermon 149, Question 40 (January 14, 1700)," in Samuel Willard, *A
Compleat Body of Divinity [of 1726]* (New York: Johnson Reprint Company, 1968),
568-72 (spelling modernized and citations and numbering omitted). Similar sentiments
on Question 40 appear in Thomas Watson's weighty seventeenth-century volume *A Body
of Divinity*, reprinted several times in England and in America. See, for example, a later
American edition published in Philadelphia, Thomas Watson, *A Body of Practical Divinity*
(Philadelphia: T. Wardle, 1833), and a London version, Thomas Watson, *A Body of Divinity
Contained in Sermons upon the Assembly's Catechism* (London: Passmore, 1881).

Willard's formulations were repeated by American Calvinists until well into the nineteenth century.[45]

Free churches of various sorts occasionally included the uses doctrine in their literature and sermons as well. Early on, Dutch Anabaptist Menno Simons (1496-1561) touched on the civil and theological uses of the law: "This is the real function and end of law: To reveal unto us the will of God, to discover sin unto us, to threaten with the wrath and punishment of the Lord, to announce death and to point us from it to Christ, so that we, crushed in spirit, may before the eyes of God die unto sin, and seek and find the only eternal medicine, and remedy for our souls, Jesus Christ."[46] John Wesley (1703-91), the father of Methodism, devoted ample attention to the uses doctrine, both in his writings on law and in his sermons on salvation and sanctification.[47] For example, in his sermon *The Original, Nature, Property, and Use of the Law* (ca. 1749), Wesley declared:

> The first use of the law [is] to slay the sinner, . . . to destroy the life and strength wherein he trusts, and convince him that he is dead while he liveth; not only under the sentence of death, but actually dead unto God, void of all spiritual life, "dead in trespasses and sins." The second use of it is, to bring him unto life, unto Christ, that he may live. . . . The third use of the law is, to keep us alive. It is the grand means whereby the blessed spirit prepares the believer for larger communications of the life of God.[48]

Similar statements appear occasionally in Methodist sermons and handbooks of the nineteenth and twentieth centuries.[49]

There are plenty of other examples, but these are enough to demonstrate that the doctrine of uses of the law remained a staple of the Protestant tradition over the centuries. To be sure, this doctrine was no centerpiece of Protestant dogma on the order of the doctrines of God and humanity, or sin and salvation. Nor did this doctrine win universal assent or uniform articulation. To this day, Protestants still argue about the order of the uses of the law—some preferring to call the theological use (of inducing a person to salvation) to be the first or primary use of the law, and

---

[45]   See, for example, Thomas Ridgeley, *A Body of Divinity: Wherein the Doctrines of Christian Religion are Explained and Defended*, Vol. 2, ed., John M. Wilson (New York: R. Carter, 1855), 300-07.

[46]   *The Complete Writings of Menno Simons* (Scottdale, PA: Herald Press, 1956), 718.

[47]   See discussion in Harold Lindström, *Wesley and Sanctification* (Grand Rapids, MI: Francis Asbury Press, 1980), 75-83.

[48]   Reprinted in Edward H. Sugden, ed., *Wesley's Standard Sermons*, Vol. 2 (London: Epworth Press, 1964), 2:52-53.

[49]   See, e. g., Adam Clarke, "Life, the Gift of the Gospel; Law, the Ministration of Death [Sermon on Galatians 3]," in Adam Clarke, *Discourses on Various Subjects Relative to the Being and Attributes of God*, Vol. 2 (New York: M'Elrath and Bangs, 1830, 1:156-72).

treating the other uses as secondary, even incidental.[50] Some recognize a civil and theological use of the law, in whatever order, but not a pedagogical use; after all, Galatians 3:24–25 says that "the law was our teacher to bring us unto Christ, that we might be justified by faith. But after that faith is come, we are no longer under a schoolmaster."[51] Some focus on the twofold morality that the law produces—a basic civil morality of duty that even the state can coerce, and a more spiritual morality of aspiration that only conscience and the church can encourage. These differences are serious and require deeper theological exposition than space permits here. But it is enough to show that the doctrine of uses of law had ample enough coherence and adherence to provide a common theological touchstone for fiercely competing Protestant sects.

The Legal Doctrine of the Purposes of Criminal Law and Punishment

The theological doctrine of the three uses of God's law that emerged out of the Reformation had a conceptual cousin in the legal doctrine of the three purposes of criminal law and punishment that emerged in early modern Protestant lands. Protestant jurists on both sides of the Atlantic argued that the criminal law serves three purposes in the lives of the criminal and the community: (1) deterrence, (2) retribution, and (3) rehabilitation. The precise definition and priority of these three purposes of criminal law and punishment were and are subjects of endless debate, but all three are still prominent in criminal law theory today. The deterrent, retributive, and rehabilitative purposes of the criminal law bear a striking resemblance to the civil, theological, and educational uses of the moral law.

First, the jurists believed that criminal law has a *deterrent* function. The criminal law prohibits a variety of harmful and immoral acts—homicide, rape and sex crimes, battery, assault, kidnapping, defamation, and other violations of the person; arson, theft, burglary, trespass, embezzlement, fraud, and other violations of property; riot, tumult, treason, racketeering, terrorism, and other violations of public peace and order. A person who violates these prohibitions must be punished, but the ideal is to deter them from committing these offenses in the first place.

Criminal punishment and its threat are designed to deter both the individual defendant and other members of the community from committing such violations. The punishment threatened must be sufficiently onerous and automatic to deter the individual defendant from committing or repeating the violation, with harsher punishments for recidivists or those crimes or criminals harder to detect.

---

[50] See Bonhoeffer, *Ethics*, 303–19.
[51] Engelbrecht, *Friends of the Law*.

The punishment must also be sufficiently grave and public so that others will see the defendant's plight and be deterred from similar conduct, however tempting.[52]

This thinking accounts for the traditional publicity of the criminal justice system, with its public trials, public confessions, public pillories, public brandings, public executions, and public records. Samuel Johnson (1709–84) once quipped that criminal punishments, particularly executions, "are intended to draw spectators; if they do not, they don't answer their purpose."[53] Contrary to Kant's categorical imperative that no one should be used "as a means to the end of another," the criminal justice system uses the punishment of one individual to serve the ends of both the criminal and the community.[54] "When a man has been proved to have committed a crime," Sydney Smith (1771–1845) put it, "it is expedient that society should make use of that man for the diminution of crime; he belongs to them for that purpose."[55]

Through these prohibitions and punishments, jurists believed, the criminal law coerces all persons to adopt a basic civil or public morality. This, to be sure, is only what Justice Joseph Story (1779–1845) called a "coerced minimal morality," and what Lon Fuller later called "a morality of duty," rather than a "morality of aspiration."[56] It defines only the outer boundaries of propriety and civility. It provides only the barest modicum of civil order and stability. Yet the jurists believed that, given the proclivities of human nature, such a deterrent function of criminal law and punishment is indispensable to minimal social order.

This deterrent function of criminal law runs closely parallel to the civil use of the moral law. A number of moral laws of God are echoed in the state's criminal law—homicide, theft, rape, battery, defamation, fraud, treason, and other offenses

---

[52] See, for example, Samuel von Pufendorf, *The Law of Nature and Nations* (1688), ed., W.A. Oldfather (New York: Oceana, 1964), bk. 8, chap. 3.9, 11, 12; Hugo Grotius, *On the Law of War and Peace* (1625), trans., Francis W. Kelsey (Indianapolis, IN: Bobbs-Merrill, 1962), bk. 2, chap. 20.7–9.

[53] Quoted in James Boswell, *Boswell's Life of Samuel Johnson*, Vol. 2 (New York/Chicago: A.S. Barnes, 1916), 447. See also Pufendorf, *The Law of Nature and Nations*, bk. 8, chap. 3.11.

[54] Immanuel Kant, *The Metaphysical Elements of Justice* (1785), trans., John Ladd (Indianapolis, IN: Bobbs-Merrill, 1965), 100: "Judicial punishment (poenis forensis) is entirely distinct from natural punishment (poenis naturalis). In natural punishment, vice punishes itself, and this fact is not taken into account by the legislator. Judicial punishment can never be administered merely as a means to promote some other good for the criminal himself or for civil society, but instead it must in all cases be imposed on him only on the ground that he has committed a crime; for a human being can never be manipulated merely as a means to the purposes of someone else."

[55] Sydney Smith, *Elementary Sketches of Moral Philosophy* (New York, Harper and Bros., 1856), 252.

[56] Lon L. Fuller, *The Morality of Law* (New Haven, CT: Yale University Press, 1964), 3–9.

are expressly prohibited in the Bible, and a good number of other crimes punished by the state today have long been prohibited by church law and punished through church discipline. Moreover, the purposes served by the (threat of) enforcement of these laws are also parallel. Theologians stressed the "wrath of God against all unrighteousness" to coerce persons to resist sinful temptation, and they adduced ample biblical examples of the ill plight of the sinner, not least the threat of hell fire, to drive home their point.[57] Jurists stressed the severity of the magistrate against all criminal conduct and used examples of the law's harsh public sanctions of convicted criminals, most powerfully the threat of long imprisonment, even execution, to deter all persons from criminal conduct.[58]

Both theologians and jurists understood that such coercion produces only a minimal morality. It allows people to live with their neighbors, not necessarily to love them; to coexist in a society, not to bond together in covenant union. But this minimal morality born of the law is indispensable for any human society. Aristotle noted this already at the beginning of his *Politics:* "Just as man is the best of the animals when completed, when separated from law and adjudication he is the worst of all."[59] American founder James Madison (1751-1836) had the same insight: "If men were angels, no government would be necessary. If angels were to govern men, neither external nor internal controls . . . would be necessary . . . but experience has taught mankind the necessity of auxiliary precautions," not least a fully functioning criminal law system.[60]

Second, many Western criminal jurists believed that criminal law has a *retributive* function. Retribution, too, has both a communal and an individual dimension. On one hand, it recognizes that crime is not just a civil harm to a victim, whose person, property, or reputation has been harmed by the defendant and requires compensation. Crime is also a harm to the community, to society's basic standards of moral conduct that it expects all citizens to abide by. Criminal punishment provides a formal procedure for the community to avenge a defendant's violation of its standards rather than relying on private vengeance or on the blood feud. As Henry Fielding (1707-54) once put it, criminal conduct "tears the moral fabric of the community; criminal punishment serves to mend that tear."[61] It al-

---

[57]　See J.A. Sharpe, "'Last Dying Speeches': Religion, Ideology, and Public Execution in England," *Past and Present* 107 (1985):144-67; Ronald A. Bosco, "Lectures at the Pillory: The Early American Execution Sermon," *American Quarterly* 30 (1978):156-76; David Edwards, *Sermons to the Condemned* (London: R. Hawes, 1775).

[58]　Cotton Mather, *The Call of the Gospel Applied Unto all Men in General, and Unto a Condemned Malefactor in Particular* (Boston: Richard Pierce, 1687), 58.

[59]　Aristotle, *Politics*, bk. 1, ch. 2.

[60]　*Federalist Papers*, No. 51.

[61]　Henry Fielding, quoted by Adolf Bodenheimer, *Recht und Rechtfertigung* (Tübingen: Mohr, 1907), 177. See also J. Welland, *Difficulties Connected With Punishment as Part of*

lows the community to right the wrong, to restore the imbalance that the criminal has caused, to reset the moral order, to renew the terms of the social contract.

This is a second reason for the publicity of the prosecution and punishment of criminals—not only so that others may be deterred from crime, but also so that the community can avenge the violation of itself and its law. In the words of James Fitzjames Stephen (1829-84):

> [T]he sentence of the law is to the moral sentiment of the public in relation to any offence what a seal is to hot wax. It converts into a permanent final judgment what might otherwise be a transient sentiment. . . . [T]he infliction of punishment by law gives definite expression and a solemn ratification and justification of the hatred which is excited by the commission of the offence, and which constitutes the moral or popular as distinguished from the conscientious sanction of that part of morality which is also sanctioned by the criminal law.[62]

A century later, Henry Hart put it similarly: "What distinguishes a criminal from a civil sanction . . . is the judgment of community condemnation, which accompanies and justifies its imposition. . . . 'It is the expression of the community's hatred, fear, or contempt for the convict' [by] . . . a formal and solemn pronouncement."[63]

Beyond its communal effect, retribution further works to confirm the defendant's moral agency, to impose on the defendant his moral desert, and drive him to repent and seek reconciliation. Though the state itself cannot forgive the sinner—that is for God to do—it can, through punishment, induce the criminal to repent from his evil, to confess his wrong, and to seek forgiveness—at least from the community, and sometimes from the victim or victim's family as well. This is one of the principal rationales for that fateful step in a common law trial when the judge gives the convicted criminal, before sentencing, a chance to express remorse and

---

the Divine System of Government (Calcutta: R.C. LePage and Co., 1864), 12: "[P]unishment may be inflicted for some benefit [of] pointing out that sin is not to be regarded as a solitary act, beginning and ending in ourselves, but as an offence and injury to the supreme Law, and so to all, for the law is the life of the community."

[62]   James Fitzjames Stephen, *A History of the Criminal Law of England*, 3 vols. (London: Macmillan, 1883), 2:81. See also A.L. Goodhart, *English Law and the Moral Law* (London: Stevens, 1953), 93: "[I]f this retribution is not given recognition, then the disapproval may also disappear. A community which is too ready to forgive the wrongdoer may end up condoning the crime."

[63]   Henry M. Hart, Jr., "The Aims of the Criminal Law," *Law and Contemporary Problems* 23 (1958): 402-06, quoting in part George K. Gardner, "Bailey v. Richardson and the Constitution of the United States," *Boston University Law Review* 33 (1953): 176, 193.

to seek forgiveness.[64] This was one of the early rationales for the establishment of criminal penitentiaries, or *Zuchthäuser*, in the early modern West: to give prisoners the solitude and serenity needed to be penitent, to reflect on their crime and seek forgiveness for it, aided by prison chaplains.[65] This was one of the principal rationales in earlier days for inflicting hard labor on criminals in workhouses and on labor gangs—"to soften the hardened soul the way fire softens hardened steel."[66] This is also one of the principal rationales for delaying the execution of a capital felon for a time after conviction, and furnishing chaplain services and (in earlier days) execution sermons—to give the defendant the opportunity to seek reconciliation with God before meeting his end.[67] And this is why, to this day, those who are comatose or too mentally damaged or handicapped to understand their punishment will not face the ultimate punishment of death by execution.

The retributive function of criminal law runs parallel to the theological use of the moral law, though the emphases are different. Both theologians and jurists emphasize the role of law in setting moral standards, in exposing human weakness and wrongdoing, and in inducing offenders to confront and confess their guilt for their offense. Both emphasize that the law convicts persons in an effort to stop them from continuing their bad behavior and setting them on a path of restoration and reconciliation. The theologians, however, present a more benign picture of the moral law as a mirror in which a person discovers his own depravity and weakness and, in despair, is induced to accept the gracious gift of salvation made available by Jesus's sacrificial death, the substitutionary punishment for humanity's grave violations of God's moral law. The jurists present a much harsher picture of the criminal law, as a spotlight shining on a person's crime and wrongdoing and compelling the criminal to accept the merited punishment—mitigated, perhaps, by a confession of guilt but usually not waived; a contrite criminal still goes to prison. In the end, the sinner who accepts God's grace and the

---

[64] See Jeffrie G. Murphy, *Punishment and the Moral Emotions: Essays in Law, Morality, and Religion* (Oxford: Oxford University Press, 2012).

[65] See Basil Montagu, *The Opinions of Different Authors Upon the Punishment of Death*, 3 vols. (London: Longman, Hurst, Rees, Orme, and Brown, 1816). On the history of the penitentiary and its connections to religion, see Schmoeckel, *Das Recht der Reformation*, 207-45; Leon Radzinowicz, *A History of English Criminal Law and its Administration from 1750*, repr. ed. (Oxford: Clarendon Press, 1990), Vol. 5; Michael Ignatieff, *A Just Measure of Pain: The Penitentiary in the Industrial Revolution* (New York: Pantheon Books, 1978); W.J. Forsythe, *The Reform of Prisoners 1830-1900* (London: Croom Helm, 1987).

[66] Lance Falconer, quoted in Walter Moberly, *The Ethics of Punishment* (Hamden, CT: Archon, 1968), 124. See also the discussion of the penitentiary as "moral hospital" in Isaac Kramnick, "Eighteenth-Century Science and Radical Social Theory: The Case of Joseph Priestly's Scientific Liberalism," *Journal of British Studies* 25 (1986):1-30.

[67] See Sharpe, *Last Dying Speeches*; Bosco, "Lectures at the Pillory."

criminal who serves time both get a fresh start and a chance to be newly reconciled to the community. But the criminal's road is much harder, since he must bear the punishment alone, rather than having Christ bear it.

Third, criminal law has a *rehabilitative* function. It serves to reform and reeducate criminals, to instruct them on the path of virtue. Before the twentieth century, this was the second principal rationale for the penitentiary and the workhouse, as Mathias Schmoeckel has shown.[68] Those punishments served, as one early statute on penitentiaries put it, "by sobriety . . . solitary confinement, . . . labour, [and] due religious instruction . . . to accustom [prisoners] to serious reflection and to teach them both the principles and practices of every Christian and moral duty."[69] In modern formulations, rehabilitation comes in the form of therapy and education aimed to "make offenders less antisocial by altering their basic character, improving their skills, or teaching them how to control their crime-producing urges." It aims to make them welcome and productive citizens, sometimes offsetting the effects of deficient education, bad role-modeling, broken households, drug addiction, peer pressure, and other trauma they may have experienced in an abusive or misspent youth. It gives them work experience and vocational training so they can regard "legitimate employment a more attractive alternative to criminal endeavors."[70] Sometimes rehabilitative punishment comes in the form of community service—say, serving in a soup kitchen or emergency room to see the hard plight of others, working in a ward for neonates whose mothers were prey to drug kingpins, or helping to clean up a waste dump or build a new playground in a blighted neighborhood that a privileged white-collar criminal has never seen.

Advocates of rehabilitation have always recognized that even in the best rehabilitative circumstances, the criminal law can do only so much to educate civilly and rehabilitate morally the recalcitrant criminal. Alexis de Tocqueville's (1805–59) noted this soberly two centuries ago in reflecting on penitentiaries:

> The moral reformation of . . . a depraved person is only an accidental instead of being a natural consequence of the penitentiary system[;] it is nevertheless true that there is another kind of reformation, less thorough than the former, but yet useful for society, and which the system we treat of seems to produce in a natural way. We have no doubt, but that the habits of order to which the prisoner is subjected for several years, influence very considerably his moral conduct after his return to society. The necessity of labor which overcomes his disposition to idleness; the obligation of silence which

---

[68]   Schmoeckel, *Das Recht der Reformation*, 242–43.

[69]   18 Geo 3, c. 17. See other examples in Montagu, *The Opinions of Different Authors*, 3:284–85.

[70]   Kent Greenawalt, "Punishment," in *Encyclopedia of Crime and Justice*, ed. Joshua Dressler, 2d ed. (New York: Macmillan Reference, 2002), 1286–87.

makes him reflect; the isolation which places him alone in presence of his crime and suffering; the religious instruction which enlightens and comforts him. . . . Without loving virtue, he may detest the crime of which he has suffered the cruel consequences; and if he is not more virtuous he has become at least more judicious; his morality is not honour, but interest. His religious faith is perhaps neither lively nor deep; but even supposing that religion has not touched his heart, his mind has contracted habits of order, and he possesses rules for his conduct in life; without having a powerful religious conviction, he has acquired a taste for moral principles which religion affords.[71]

There are striking analogies between this rehabilitative function of the criminal law and the educational use of the moral law, though here, too, the emphases differ. The theologians emphasize the moral reeducation of justified sinners alone—those who convert to the Christian faith and who now seek to live by the letter and spirit of the law of God more fully to glorify God, to grow in spiritual sanctity, and to encourage others to follow them in the faith. The jurists' emphasis on rehabilitation flies lower. They are happy to have a criminal convert to the faith and live fully by the whole moral law of God. But that is not a necessary condition or expectation for the rehabilitation born of criminal punishment. Rehabilitation is designed to educate each criminal to live more fully by the letter of the criminal law alone, to abide more fully by the basic civil morality of the social order. It is a happy byproduct of criminal punishment if the rehabilitated defendant goes further and now pursues spiritual morality as well—not only stops killing others but actively loves them, not only stops stealing others' property but now gives charity to those in need.

It would be too strong to say that the Protestant theological doctrine of the three uses of moral law was *the* source of the modern legal doctrine of the purposes of criminal law and punishment. Western writers since Plato have reflected on the purposes of criminal law,[72] and Protestant jurists had at their disposal a long tradition of reflections on this subject from patristic and scholastic theologians as well as from scholars of civil and canon law. Yet the Protestant doctrine of three uses seems to have provided an important source of integration and instruction for Protestant jurists. The doctrine was a commonplace of Protestant theology and ethics from the sixteenth century on—taught in Protestant seminaries, preached in Protestant churches, and catechized in each new generation. Several sixteenth-century Protestant writers—notably Philip Melanchthon and John Calvin—explicitly linked the theological and legal discourses on the uses of

---

[71]   Gustave de Beaumont and Alexis de Tocqueville, *On the Penitentiary System in the United States and its Application in France* (1833), trans., Francis Lieber (New York: Augustus M. Kelley Publishers, 1970), 58–59.

[72]   M. McKenzie, *Plato on Punishment* (Berkeley: University of California Press, 1981).

the law, and their writings were constantly reprinted and studied by later Protestants.[73] Protestant jurists and Protestant theologians thereafter regularly collaborated in formulating criminal doctrines, hearing criminal cases, and inflicting criminal punishment. The close analogies between the structure and content of these theological and legal doctrines suggest ample doctrinal cross-fertilization.

The Uses Doctrine in Contemporary Law

The foregoing brief case study illustrates how religion has helped shape and integrate one type of law that still governs all late modern societies—the state's laws of crime and punishment. Contrary to modern secularization theory that teaches that religion is dying, religion lives on in late modern societies, both in its own institutional forms and through its embeddedness in other institutions, including law. Many of the Bible's basic laws on crime are still at the heart of state criminal law today. "Thou shalt not kill" remains at the foundation of our laws of homicide. "Thou shalt not commit adultery" is at the heart of many modern family crimes. "Thou shalt not steal" grounds our laws of theft, embezzlement, and tax fraud. "Thou shalt not bear false witness" remains the anchor of our criminal laws of perjury and defamation. The ancient laws of sanctuary still operate for fleeing felons and asylum seekers. The ancient principles of jubilee have inspired modern laws of bankruptcy and debt relief to replace debtors' prisons. Other Mosaic laws and New Testament injunctions condemning assault, battery, mayhem, kidnapping, treason, incest, bestiality, and similar crimes all remain part of our modern penal codes. To be sure, some biblical crimes like sacrilege, blasphemy, idolatry, and Sabbath-breaking have fallen aside, or are now enforced only by the church and its internal religious laws and tribunals. And to be sure, many modern criminal laws have developed additional rationales and justifications that go well beyond their initial biblical inspiration. But basic biblical morality is at the heart of modern criminal law, whether we like it or not.

Moreover, basic Protestant teachings on the moral responsibilities of the state to balance coercion, discipline, and education in the enforcement of these laws are also embedded in modern criminal law. Emulating the theological doctrine of the civil, theological, and pedagogical uses of God's moral law, Western criminal law today still includes deterrence, retribution, and rehabilitation among the principal purposes of punishment. Late nineteenth- and early twentieth-century experiments at reducing the purposes of criminal punishment to deterrence or rehabilitation alone have proved to be unpersuasive in theory and unworkable in

---

[73]   See sources in notes 13–46 above.

practice.[74] The United States Federal Sentencing Act, for example, now reaffirms that criminal punishments must be imposed on criminals "(A) to reflect the seriousness of the offense, to promote respect for the law, and to provide just punishment for the offense; (B) to afford adequate deterrence to criminal conduct; (C) to protect the public from further crimes of the defendant; and (D) to provide the defendant with needed educational or vocational training, medical care, or other correctional treatment in the most effective manner."[75] Various modern jurists still argue that criminal law and punishment must induce respect for formal law and social norms, confirm moral inhibitions and habits of citizens, and "shape the framework of moral education" for the duly convicted.[76]

This case study further illustrates how the criminal law of the state is directly involved in character formation, moral education, and the communication of values in late modern societies. Modern criminal law enforces, by (threat of) coercion, a baseline civil morality that every citizen must abide by. Through published penal codes, publicized criminal cases, and the publicity of punishments, state criminal law teaches and communicates some of the basic values of this civil morality—the dignity and rights of each person, even criminals, that deserves respect; the moral agency of each rational person, and their duties and rights of moral desert; the essential duty of all, on pain of punishment, to respect the body, property, interests, and reputation of their neighbors; the command for all to honor the legitimate authorities of the state in their administration and enforcement of the law, so long as they, too, respect the basic rights and liberties of each defendant. State criminal law further helps form and reform the character and morality of duly convicted criminals—forcing them to confront and confess their guilt, making them pay for their violations of the community's norms, rehabilitating them through teaching or reteaching the basic norms of sociability and good citizenship that they will need for reconciliation and reentrance into society.

Beyond the hard "thou shalt" and "thou shalt not" commands of the criminal law, the modern liberal state uses many other tools that nudge and channel citizens toward better behavior. Nudging is now a common legal strategy, alongside criminal law, for promoting desirable public and private goods in many areas of life. The modern liberal state facilitates, licenses, encourages, and sometimes

---

[74]   See critical analysis in Jerome Hall, *Studies in Jurisprudence and Criminal Theory* (New York: Oceana Publications, 1958), 242 ff.; George Fletcher, *Rethinking Criminal Law* (Boston: Little, Brown, 1978), 416 ff.; Herbert Packer, *The Limits of the Criminal Sanction* (Stanford, CA: Stanford University Press, 1968), 38 ff.

[75]   18 USCA § 3553(a) (2) (1988).

[76]   See, e.g., Johannes Andenaes, *Punishment and Deterrence* (Ann Arbor: University of Michigan Press, 1974), 110 ff.; Fuller, *The Morality of Law*; Joel Feinberg, "The Expressive Function of Punishment," *The Monist* 49 (1965): 397–423; Walter Moberly, *Legal Responsibility and Moral Responsibility* (Philadelphia: Fortress Press, 1965).

even pays for or rewards all kinds of desirable behavior: think of voting in a state election, getting a free vaccine, or going to college on a state scholarship. The state imposes taxes or fines or withholds state benefits or opportunities for those who indulge in undesirable behavior: think of smoking, not wearing seat belts, or dropping out of high school. The theory of nudging or legal channelling stipulates that, over time, desirable behavior encouraged by the state will become more customary, even natural or reflexive among citizens, and undesirable behavior will be viewed as aberrant and perhaps even stigmatized, if not criminalized.[77]

But the state and its laws, whether hard or soft, can do only so much in the moral field. Late modern societies also need broader communities and narratives to stabilize, deepen, and exemplify the natural inclinations and rational norms of responsibility, sociability, and morality that all human beings have written on their hearts if not embedded in their genes. Even the most progressive liberal societies need models and exemplars of love and fidelity, trust and sacrifice, commitment and community to give these natural teachings further content and coherence. They need the help of stable institutions beyond the state—families, neighborhoods, churches, schools, charities, hospitals, and recreational, athletic, artistic, and creative associations—to form the rich moral characters and refined ethical outlooks of their citizens, to teach not only the minimal morality of duty that keeps the sinners within all of us at bay but also the morality of aspiration that brings out the angels in all of us who are called to love God, neighbor, and self.

---

[77]   Richard H. Thaler and Cass R. Sunstein, *Nudge: Improving Decisions about Health, Wealth, and Happiness* (New York: Penguin Books, 2008); Eric A. Posner, ed., *Social Norms, Nonlegal Sanctions, and the Law* (Cheltenham: Edward Elgar, 2007); Carl E. Schneider, "The Channeling Function in Family Law," *Hofstra Law Review* 20 (1992): 495–532.

Forthcoming

John Witte | Michael Welker | Stephen Pickard (Eds.)
The Impact of the Law
on Character Formation, Ethical Education, and the Communication
of Values in Late Modern Pluralistic Societies
approx. February 2021

William Schwelker | Michael Welker | John Witte | Stephen Pickard (Eds.)
The Impact of Academic Research
on Character Formation, Ethical Education, and the Communication
of Values in Late Modern Pluralistic Societies
approx. February 2021

John Witte | Michael Welker | Stephen Pickard (Eds.)
The Impact of the Family
on Character Formation, Ethical Education, and the Communication
of Values in Late Modern Pluralistic Societies
approx. 2021

Stephen Pickard | Michael Welker | John Witte (Eds.)
The Impact of Education
on Character Formation, Ethics, and the Communication
of Values in Late Modern Pluralistic Societies
approx. 2021

The Impact of Military/Defense
on Character Formation, Ethical Education, and the Communication
of Values in Late Modern Pluralistic Societies
approx. 2022

The Impact of Media
on Character Formation, Ethical Education, and the Communication
of Values in Late Modern Pluralistic Societies
approx. 2022

The Impact of Healthcare
on Character Formation, Ethical Education, and the Communication
of Values in Late Modern Pluralistic Societies
approx. 2023

The Impact of Politics
on Character Formation, Ethical Education, and the Communicatio
of Values in Late Modern Pluralistic Societies
approx. 2023

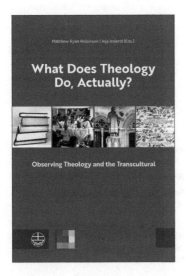

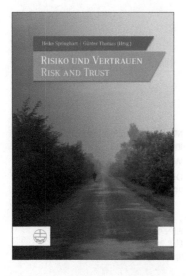